"As a woman saying Kaddish for my father daily this year, I have felt stymied by the lack of feminine voice and room for personal prayer in the siddur. Yet Professor Zierler begins to fill that lacuna, expanding prayer to include modern Hebrew poetry, and women's voices in particular. For this, I am deeply grateful. I only wish I had had this beautiful memoir earlier to sustain me through these trying times."

—RACHEL ADELMAN, associate professor of Hebrew Bible, Hebrew College

"My suggestion: savor small installments. Allow yourself to absorb the fine nuances in the discussion of each poem. When Zierler masterfully weaves together her extensive knowledge of modern Hebrew culture and traditional Jewish texts, there are multitudes of gems along the way."

—NAOMI SOKOLOFF, coeditor of *Since 1948: Israeli Literature in the Making*

Going Out with Knots

University of Nebraska Press Lincoln

Going Out with Knots

My Two Kaddish Years with Hebrew Poetry

WENDY I. ZIERLER

The Jewish Publication Society Philadelphia

Acknowledgments for the use of copyrighted material appear on pages 251–55, which constitute an extension of the copyright page.

 Published by the University of Nebraska Press as a Jewish Publication Society book.

∞

For customers in the EU with safety/GPSR concerns, contact:
gpsr@mare-nostrum.co.uk
Mare Nostrum Group BV
Mauritskade 21D
1091 GC Amsterdam
The Netherlands

Library of Congress Cataloging-in-Publication Data
Names: Zierler, Wendy, author.
Title: Going out with knots: my two Kaddish years with Hebrew poetry / Wendy I. Zierler.
Description: Lincoln: University of Nebraska Press; Philadelphia: The Jewish Publication Society, [2025] | Includes bibliographical references and index.
Identifiers: LCCN 2025010524
ISBN 9780827615700 (paperback)
ISBN 9780827619340 (epub)
ISBN 9780827619357 (pdf)
Subjects: LCSH: Zierler, Wendy—Tragedies. | Parents—Death—Poetry. | Grief—Poetry. | Bereavement—Poetry. | BISAC: BIOGRAPHY & AUTOBIOGRAPHY / Jewish | RELIGION / Judaism / Rituals & Practice
Classification: LCC PJ5055.51.I32 G65 2025 | DDC 892.41/609—dc23/eng/20250626
LC record available at https://lccn.loc.gov/2025010524

Designed and set in Adobe Text Pro by L. Welch.

Dedicated to my parents,
David and Marion Zierler

דוד שלמה בן אברהם ולאה

1928–2019

מרים אסתר בת זאב ושרה

1934–2020

שִׁמְעִי בִּתִּי מוּסַר אָבִיךְ וְאַל תִּטְּשִׁי תּוֹרַת אִמֵּךְ.

My daughter, heed the lessons of your father,
And do not forsake the instruction of your mother.

ADAPTED FROM PROVERBS 1:8

CONTENTS

List of Illustrations . . . xiii
Acknowledgments . . . xv
Introduction . . . xix

Part 1. So Much Has Been Severed

1. Learning to Mourn: Going Out with Knots . . . 3
Things Fall Apart . . . 8
The End of Stories . . . 9
Loose Thread . . . 13
Going Out with Knots . . . 19
Settling In . . . 22
Mourning and Metaphor . . . 24
Sewing a Seam . . . 30
A Kaddish/COVID Journal with Poems . . . 33

Part 2. Transitions and Translations

2. Picturing God in Grief and Prayer: Beginning to Mourn with Lea Goldberg . . . 39
"To Mother's Portrait" . . . 46
"By Three Things" . . . 50
"In My Prayer Book" . . . 54
"Let Winter Be Blessed" . . . 57

"Blessing" ... 59
From "One Spring" ... 61
From "My Silences" ... 64
"Night Psalm" ... 68
"He Passed Over Our Door and There Was Light" ... 71
From "Ending" ... 74

3. Facing an Absent God: Grief and God Struggle in the Poetry of Avraham Ḥalfi ... 77
"Dream of Your Footsteps" ... 81
"I Know Not the Words" ... 84
"Crowned Is Your Forehead with Black Gold" ... 88
"Here a Person Believed" ... 91
"And Songs Are the Dust of Antiquities" ... 94
From "Heretic's Prayers" ... 97
"At Night Birds Fell" ... 100
"Jewish Fall" ... 103

4. Living with a Lesser, Closer God: Yehuda Amichai's Secular Theology of Everyday Life ... 105
"And That Is Your Glory" ... 107
"In the Morning I Stand by Your Bed" ... 112
"Half the People in the World" ... 114
"God's Hand in the World" ... 117
"A Sort of End of Days" ... 120
"My Mother Baked Me the Whole World" ... 123
"Whoever Wrapped in a Tallit" ... 127
"Men, Women, and Children" ... 133
"God Has Mercy on Kindergarten Children" ... 138
"I Filtered from the Book of Esther" ... 142
"My Father on Passover Eve" ... 144

5. Searching for Female Liturgical Voices: Mourning and Studying with Rachel Morpurgo 147
"Behold the Letter" 150
"And Thus Sang Rachel about Her Wedding" 155
"See, This Is New" 158
"On Those Fleeing the Cholera Epidemic" 166
"A Voice Is Heard in the Heights" 169
"This One Shall Be Called 'My Delight Is with Her'" 172
"I, Leah, Was So Very Tired" 176
"Fount of Wisdom from a Flowing Stream" 178
"Buried Here Is the Lady" 182
"The Monument Is a Witness" 182
"This Is the Burial Monument that Rachel Morpurgo Prepared for Herself in Her Youth" 183

6. Retying the Knots: Learning and Relearning with Ruhama Weiss 189
"I Throw Down My Supplication" 191
"Lament for Rashi's Daughters" 195
"I Am Still Praying" 199
"And Once Again, I'll Sin and Return" 202
"Chapters of the Mothers" 206

7. Penning Pandemic Torah: Rachel Bluwstein's Feminist/Illness Poetry 213
"Soul Walking" 216
"Barren Woman" 219
From "In the Hospital" 224
"Or Maybe" 227
"Ḥoni the Circle Maker" 231
"Day of Tidings" 234
"Sorrow Song" 238

8. Final Thoughts: Still in Knots . . . 243
"Behold I'll Craft a Ball from the Pain" . . . 247

Source Acknowledgments . . . 251
Appendix: Four Poems by the Author . . . 257
Notes . . . 263
Bibliography . . . 281
Subject Index . . . 289
Scriptural Index . . . 303

ILLUSTRATIONS

1. My mother and father's engagement announcement in the *Sarnia Observer*, May 3, 1952 . . . 5
2. My father David Zierler's green card . . . 7
3. My Kaddish journal . . . 18
4. *Windsor Star* article reporting on the death of my paternal grandmother, Lea Zierler, March 29, 1960 . . . 29
5. Ex libris of Lea Goldberg . . . 41
6. Portrait of Marion Zierler as a young girl . . . 47
7. Glowing refrigerator . . . 111
8. "Lonely Woman of Faith": a portrait of the author praying . . . 132
9. Headstone of my parents, Marion and David Zierler . . . 187
10. Headstone of my grandmother, Shirley Goldfarb . . . 187
11. *Ha-Makom Yenaḥem* consolation card by the recycling bin . . . 239

ACKNOWLEDGMENTS

Traditional Jewish morning prayers begin with the words *modeh/ah ani*—with personal gratitude. Here, too, I begin with expressions of appreciation.

Many thanks to the 6:45 *tefillah* attendees at the Hebrew Institute of Riverdale, the Bayit, for providing a weekly forum for the *Shir Ḥadash shel Yom* and for teaching me so much. Special thanks to Dr. Steven Bayme, Dr. Pinny Bulman (poet in his own right), Dr. Ira Epstein, Rabbi Steven Exler, Rabbi Jeffrey Fox, David Freudenstein (all the way from Toronto—thanks for all the audio-recordings!), Bernie Horowitz, Rabba Sara Hurwitz, Hillel Jaffe, Rabbi Dov Linzer, Rabbi Dina Najman, Mia Diamond Padwa, Rabbi David Schwartz, Rabbi Ezra Seligsohn, and Rabbanit Devorah Zlochower, who listened attentively and shared wonderful insights along the way; to all the members of the *Shir Ḥadash* e-list for their responses to my weekly posts; and to Shuli Boxer Rieser for weekly photocopying. Thanks to my Maharat *ḥevruta*, Rabba Dr. Lindsey Guthartz, for hours of laughter and wisdom; and to my other Maharat study buddy, Rabbi Dr. Sarit Kattan Gribetz, for sharing her magnificent scholarship. Extra special thanks go to Dr. Lisa Hirsch for planting that feminist flag with me on our minyan moon and circling it with me day after day. May that flag wave ever more securely and boldly in the years to come.

I deeply thank many individuals connected with my work home, Hebrew Union College–Jewish Institute of Religion: Dr. Andrew Rehfeld, HUC-JIR president, and Rabbi Dr. Andrea Weiss, former provost and longtime colleague, for moral and financial support; as well as librarians Abigail Bacon, Yoram Bitton (now at the Library of

Congress), Dr. Jordan Finkin, Eli Lieberman, and Tina Weiss (now at Yeshiva University) for invaluable research assistance. I am grateful to my HUC-JIR students for their insightful participation in my "Hebrew Poetry and Prayer" courses, which helped plant the earliest seeds for this book, and for organizing a Zoom *Minḥah-Ma'ariv* minyan for my colleague Dr. Sharon Koren and me when we were both saying Kaddish for our parents. Special gratitude is owed to my former student and thesis advisee, Rabbi Juliana Karol, for the supremely thoughtful gift of the leather-bound, ribbon-tied, multicolored-paged journal that I used to write down my Kaddish experiences (see the photo on page 18), and also many early ideas for the *Shir Ḥadash* and for this book. Thanks also to inimitable Israeli writer Etgar Keret for the conversation and the anecdote that furnished the beginning of this book.

Appreciation goes out to fellow scholars Professors Maya Barzilai, Tova Cohen, Miki Gluzman, Adriana X. Jacobs, Chana Kronfeld, Dana Olmert, Haim O. Rechnitzer, and Gidon Ticotsky for information regarding various poets and for opportunities to share thoughts about translation and feminist scholarship; and to Professor Maeera Shreiber of the University of Utah for enlisting me in an ongoing discussion and collaboration about Hebrew poetry and prayer.

Huge thanks to editor extraordinaire Elisheva Urbas for slogging through two massive early drafts of this book and helping me shape it into something that could be felt as well as read. Equally massive appreciations go to Dr. Elias Sacks, former director of The Jewish Publication Society (JPS), for welcoming this project and shepherding the first stage of editing; and to the indefatigable Joy Weinberg, JPS managing editor, for her patient, helpful, and painstaking corrections and for numerous suggestions as to how to tie the literary and emotional content of this book in a tight knot that could hold for my readers. Thanks to Michelle Kwitkin for meticulous and thoughtful copyediting, as well as to Kayla Moslander of the University of Nebraska Press for guiding the volume through the final stages of production. Note that all translations of biblical texts are taken from *THE JPS TANAKH: Gender Sensitive Edition* (RJPS), unless otherwise noted.

To Leif Milliken of UNP, Hana Amichai, Racheli Edelman, Ofra Friesel, Dr. Yael Hadass, Deborah Harris, Liat Karat, Yehuda Landau, Elena Novikova of Postmedia, Rabbi Jeffrey Saks, Ksenia Tserkovskaya, Sharon Yannay, and Ziv Roisman Adan: thank you for your help with permissions. Much appreciation to Meagan Sinclair of the Lambton County Library for help tracking down citation information and images related to my parents and Zierler family history. Many thanks to Marc Sherman for his fastidious indexing—and in the midst of the Iranian bombardment, no less. And I thank JPS's copublisher, the University of Nebraska Press, for helping to send this book out into the world.

Thanks to my beloved siblings, nieces, nephews, great-nieces, and great-nephews for the gift of family, care, and support. Thanks until the end of time to my children—Shara, Yona, and Amichai—for accompanying me through this journey of care, grief, and learning; and to my husband, Daniel Feit, for being my partner, reader, and listener in all things.

Daily, I thank my precious parents, Marion and David Zierler, of blessed memory, for bringing me into the world and teaching me how to inhabit it with integrity, kindness, humor, and Jewish devotion.

Above all, I thank God, Compassionate Mother and Father of Life, my most sought-after and elusive conversation partner in this writing, with whom I aspire, every day, to go out with knots.

INTRODUCTION

July 2024, Shakespeare & Co., Lenox, Massachusetts. I was onstage, interviewing Israeli short story writer Etgar Keret about the origin of his story "Kavanah" ("Intention"), written after Hamas's attack on Israel, when Keret recounted a post–October 7 conversation he'd had with his sister. At the time Keret and his filmmaker wife, Shira Geffen, were scurrying to do whatever they could to help victims of the violence: displaced Israelis, wounded soldiers, friends with missing or dead family members. His sister, an ultra-Orthodox adherent of Breslover Hasidism, told him what she had been doing since the attack: praying more intensely and frequently, by going to the *Kotel* (Western Wall) twice rather than once a day, for example, and reciting ever more psalms.

Listening to her, Keret grew increasingly annoyed. He never got angry at his sister—she was too good, too nice, too much of a *tzadeket* (righteous woman) to provoke a negative reaction from him—but he just couldn't take all that talk about prayer. Eager not to say anything he'd regret, he told his sister he needed to get off the phone. And then he did what he always does when he finds himself getting annoyed or angry at someone: write a story from their perspective, as a way of understanding them better. In this case, the result was "Intention."[1]

In the story, a character named Yeḥiel (Let God Live) Naḥman (Merciful One), an amalgam of Keret's sister and his nephew (whose middle name is Naḥman), as well as a nod to Rebbe Naḥman of Breslov, the founder of the Ḥasidic sect to which his sister belongs, hears about the tragedies and hostage-taking of October 7 and responds by praying with unprecedented fervor and *kavanah* (intention). He prays and prays, but nothing happens: the war rages on, and the hostages remain captive in Gaza. He becomes despondent, on the verge of apostasy, in fact, but his rebbe convinces him he needs to pray even more intensely and attentively. Eventually, his prayers deepen and broaden, encompassing not just personal and Jewish communal hopes and yearnings, but even those of his enemies. And wouldn't you know: the next morning he wakes up to the news that two of the hostages have been released. (The story includes some ironic, Keretesque twists that I won't divulge here.)

The point Keret made to our audience, though, was that in the course of writing the story, he realized that Yeḥiel Naḥman stood not only for his ultra-Orthodox sister and nephew, but *also for himself*. He, Etgar Keret, was giving vent to the same hopes and yearnings, and undertaking the same quest for meaning, as his protagonist. And in writing stories, he was, in his own way, praying.

In writing this book, I too was praying. I too was giving vent to my hopes and yearnings and seeking meaning in the aftermath of unremitting personal loss: first, the sudden, shocking death of my father and then, within less than a year, the loss of my mother. It was a dogged, sometimes paradoxical effort as a professor of Hebrew literature at a Reform rabbinical seminary, as a woman devoted to living in a Modern Orthodox community, and, later, as a newly ordained Orthodox rabbi, to find my place in the male-centered liturgy and prayer rituals that Jewish tradition has prescribed for such loss. I had to wrestle with challenges to faith and hope arising in the wake of successive bereavements and a liturgy that often did not seem to speak in my voice. And I had to come to terms simultaneously with a worldwide pandemic isolating us all, a trauma necessitating a renewed sense of communal wholeness, as the Old English *hāl*, meaning, "whole," the origin of the expression "to heal," implies.[2]

I did find healing, solace, and hope through a project I came to call *Shir Ḥadash shel Yom* (New Poem of the Day), a self-created regimen of reading, translating, writing, and teaching modern Hebrew poems written by poets who, like me, come to their writing deeply connected to Jewish tradition, and yet also at odds with it. I began to share my insights about these Hebrew poems in the context of communal prayer in my Modern Orthodox congregation. And I came to understand from the inside out poet and feminist scholar Alicia Ostriker's fitting teaching that "any poem one loves is a healing poem."[3] In selecting, assembling, and tying together through my personal story and fifty-two (plus one) teachings of poems I loved, one for every week of the year, I endeavored to illustrate, poem by poem, the theological and recuperative power of modern Hebrew poetry.

Integrating Modern and Classical Jewish Literature

I have long believed that the integration of modern Jewish literature and classical sources offers a rich vision of Torah and Jewish theology: one that honors the messy, provisional, creative, joyous, and, in some instances, traumatic aspects of our Jewish lives. As a professor of modern Jewish literature and feminist studies, and a scholar, teacher, and writer for nearly three decades, it is my pedagogical mission to expose students both in classrooms and community settings to the spiritual and cultural resources of modern Hebrew literature as an additional, vital layer of commentary to classical Jewish texts and liturgy. And as a specialist in modern Hebrew women's writing, I see it as my calling to illustrate how women's entry into the Hebraic tradition has enhanced Jewish culture and religiosity, while also challenging age-old gender biases.

Recent liturgical ferment has fueled these spiritual and pedagogical passions, inspiring both my writing and teaching on modern Hebrew poetry and prayer.[4] In particular the rabbis and prayer book editors in the liberal or progressive movements have made meaningful space for modern Hebrew poetry both in studies of Jewish liturgy and in new Reform, Conservative, and Reconstructionist prayer books.[5] As early as 1981, the late Hebrew poet and HUC-JIR Jerusalem professor T. Carmi began offering guidance on postbiblical poetry that could be incorporated into Reform liturgy. Elyse D. Frischman and the other editors of *Mishkan Tefilah*, the Reform movement's weekday and Shabbat prayer book (2007); and Edwin Goldberg, Janet Marder, Sheldon Marder, and Leon Morris, editors of *Mishkan Hanefesh*, the movement's two-volume High Holy Day maḥzor (2015), introduced modern Hebrew poetry in bilingual form and in meaningful juxtaposition with traditional prayers. Esteban Gottfried of Beit Tefilah Israeli, an Israeli Reform community in Tel Aviv, has been an inspiring force behind this kind of creative liturgizing; his continually evolving *Siddur 'Erev Shabbat U-Mo'ed* (*Sabbath and Holiday Prayer Book*) boasts more than one hundred modern Hebrew poems and songs, making it one of the most significant extant contemporary Israeli poetry anthologies, shaped around and in dialogue with prayer.[6] The innovative and progressive Israeli Reform siddur, *T'filat Ha-Adam* (2021), edited by Dalia Marx and Alona Lisitsa, further develops this project in ways that match my own appetite for creative traditionalism, by reintroducing "prayers that were edited out of previous Reform prayerbooks (such as the various *Musaf* prayers traditionally recited on Shabbat and Festivals, *Kiddush Levanah* recited at the first sighting of the new moon, the weekday *Taḥanun* supplications, and the Psalm of the Day) . . . [and] many prayers and *piyyutim* [liturgical poems] that reflect the zeitgeist [spirit of the age]."[7] All of these creative liturgies assert the significance of modern Hebrew poetry and model how this material can offer deep inspiration, solace, an escape-valve for self-expression, and space for doubt and skepticism at a time of crucial personal, spiritual crisis.

At the same time, feminist literary scholars and anthologists have helped bring attention to forgotten or underacknowledged women's poems and prayers in Hebrew. Works such as *The Defiant Muse: Hebrew Feminist Poems from Antiquity to Present*, *Tefilat Nashim*, and *A Jewish Woman's Prayer Book* help recover and spotlight an alternative canon of women's Hebrew poetry and prayers, works of learning, creativity, and spiritual genius that deserve their place in the record of our communal efforts to address God and formulate our core values through prayer.[8] And yet very little, if any, of this kind of liturgical innovation has made its way into the Modern Orthodox prayer context where I grew up and that I continue to call home.

And so it was, in the wake of my own personal trauma and grief, that I found myself turning to Hebrew poetry as an alternative liturgy, theology, and Torah, in a new, urgent, deeply necessary way—as if my religious life and that of my daily minyan community, depended on it.

Grief precipitated the teaching that led to the writing of this book. And so it is that grief, and its attendant need for poetic healing, forms the through line for what follows.

Writer and professor Donald M. Murray, who published "in many forms—poetry, fiction, academic article, essay, newspaper column, newsletter, textbook, juvenile nonfiction," famously contended that all of his work, and indeed "all writing is autobiographical." He insisted that "[w]e are autobiographical in the way we write; my autography exists in the examples of writing I use in this piece and in the text I weave around them. I have my own peculiar way of looking at the world and my own way of using language to communicate what I see."[9] In a similar vein, Jewish feminist theologian Mara Benjamin observes that "[f]rom Ludwig Feuerbach to Sigmund Freud, modern theorists of religion have insisted that theology arises from human experience."[10]

In marrying autobiographical reflection on varied experiences of saying Kaddish as a woman and scholar with close readings of thematically relevant modern Hebrew poems, this book takes shape from these same convictions.

Scope of the Volume

Going Out with Knots is at once theological and liturgical reflection, literary close readings of poetry, and feminist interpretations of personal and collective experience. Central strands include personal and persistent response to shock, tragedy, and bereavement; prayer; modern Hebrew literature; and faith, doubt, and hope.

To be sure, this is not a conventional anthology of modern Hebrew poetry or a scholarly study thereof, though I do draw significantly from extant works of scholarship on modern Hebrew poetry, including my own work on the first modern Hebrew women poets.[11] By translating and explicating great Hebrew poems relevant to my Kaddish/COVID experience, I hope to draw more people closer to the rich cultural resource of modern Hebrew verse, to whet the appetite for more such reading, study, and spiritual reflection. Readers of this volume who would like to widen their exposure beyond these selections are encouraged to consider T. Carmi's *The Penguin Book of Hebrew Verse* (1981), a bilingual English-Hebrew selection of Hebrew poetry from the Bible to the twentieth century, or Ruth Finer Mintz's earlier collection, *Modern Hebrew Poetry* (1966). Stanley Burnshaw et al.'s *The Modern Hebrew Poem Itself* (updated, 2003) offers a rich selection of poems in both Hebrew (including transliteration) and English translation, together with close readings of each of the poems. As of this writing, the most recent English-Hebrew anthology is poet and translator Robert Friend's posthumously published *Found in Translation* (2006). There are also English-only anthologies of Hebrew poetry.[12] For a scholarly but accessible discussion of the nexus of Hebrew poetry and prayer, see David Jacobson's *Creator, Are You Listening?* (2007), which includes, among other poets, a discussion of the God-centered poetry of Yehuda Amichai, one of the poets featured in this book.

Likewise, *Going Out with Knots* is not a Jewish bereavement manual. For that, the go-to-book, from an Orthodox perspective, is Maurice Lamm's *The Jewish Way in Death and Mourning*; for a more liberal and egalitarian Jewish perspective, Anita Diamant's *Saying Kaddish: How to Comfort the Dying, Bury the Dead, and Mourn as a Jew* fits the bill. My HUC-JIR colleague Lisa Grant's *The Year of Mourning: A Jewish Journey* supplements these works by supplying a set of resources—prayers, poems, intentions, and discussions, largely in English—to accompany people on their mourning journey "during this period of disequilibrium."[13]

This book also does not attempt to offer an in-depth study of the meaning and history of the Kaddish prayer and related Jewish writings on death and mourning. Leon Wieseltier's magisterial *Kaddish* accomplishes that task masterfully, all the while combining devotion and doubt, and in-depth text analysis with memoiristic reflection, as I myself do. Indeed, rereading that tome—with its trove of sources and poignant reflections on the origins, meaning, and laws of Kaddish, and its reflections on the effect of the living on the souls of the departed and vice versa—I was reminded that death remains the central conundrum of human life and Jewish theology, and thus there can never be enough meditating on its meaning and relevance to our lives.

For a more recent collection of essays that explore the meaning and history of Kaddish, see also *Kaddish*, edited by David Birnbaum and Martin S. Cohen.

Yet Wieseltier writes as a man counted in the minyan, who dares to be rebellious and then come back; who dons his tefillin (phylacteries) as an act of return; and who (respectfully) describes from the outside two women who appear in shul "looking like tourists. But they were not tourists, they were mourners. They rose to say Kaddish with the rest of us."[14] By contrast, I write as a female minyan regular whose tallit and tefillin wearing is still viewed as an act of rebellion in certain traditional circles outside my own home congregation, a woman who lives in a strange middle zone between Orthodoxy and Reform, between liturgy and literature.

On Women and Kaddish

To be expected, a number of men have written memorable Kaddish memoirs. Ari L. Goldman's *Living a Year of Kaddish: A Memoir*, for example, is engagingly told from a Modern Orthodox male mourner's perspective, though I will confess that in reading this book in particular I felt most keenly the need for a woman's perspective on this experience (see my chapter 1 below). Samuel C. Heilman's *When a Jew Dies: The Ethnography of a Bereaved Son* offers my same mix of memoir and academic discipline, in his case, specific analysis "reflecting [his] role as a social scientist as well as [his] role as a bereaved son and observant Jew."[15] But this book, too, offers a decidedly male-centered depiction of bereavement and mourning.

In her 1990 essay "Women and Kaddish," which details some of the halakhic impediments to women reciting Kaddish in traditional congregations, scholar Rochelle Millen closes with a call for more women's participation in this ritual in traditional congregations. If women themselves make Kaddish "a *sine qua non* aspect of observance of mourning," she writes, then "its recitation will become accepted—and expected practice."[16] Stepping resolutely into the breach to answer Millen's call, Michal Smart and Barbara Ashkenas's pioneering anthology, *Kaddish:*

Women's Voices (2013), assembled more than fifty short essays or poetic reflections by women on the Kaddish experience—a veritable literary congregation of female Kaddish reciters—most, if not all, of them Orthodox. Notably, though, in 2013 Yeshivat Maharat (where I myself would be trained) ordained its first class of Orthodox women rabbis—and yet the idea of the Orthodox woman rabbi or rabbinical student is nowhere to be seen in the anthology. This absence of women's rabbinic voices seems all the more pronounced given the inclusion of three essays by male Orthodox rabbis, two of whom assume the authoritative tone of halakhah (Jewish law), in contrast to the more impressionistic tone of the female-authored pieces.[17]

Sarah Birnbach's *A Daughter's Kaddish: My Year of Grief, Devotion, and Healing* (2022), a kind of Conservative female rejoinder to Goldman's *Living a Year of Kaddish*, closes by acknowledging (among other things) the founding of Yeshivat Maharat.[18] Occasionally, she describes joining Chabad or another Orthodox minyan to say Kaddish.[19] Her larger theme, though, is her experience as a Kaddish reciter within a Conservative community, including traveling to faraway places where members of the local Conservative Jewish community go to great lengths to assemble a minyan for her so she can say Kaddish for her father.

Thus, this volume's account of my Kaddish journey interspersed with my Maharat rabbinic training and ordination offers a hitherto unrepresented perspective on Kaddish originating in but not circumscribed by Orthodox Jewish community life.

Refracting Loss through Another Prism

Even as the connective tissue of *Going Out with Knots* is memoir, its core is Hebrew poetry analysis, an approach informed by the notion that a picture of loss often becomes clearest not when you stare at it directly, but when it is refracted through some other prism. In this, the volume might be compared to writer and bird-of-prey enthusiast Helen Macdonald's idiosyncratic decision, as depicted in her stunning literary memoir *H is for Hawk*, to process her grief over the sudden death of her beloved father, the photographer Alisdair Macdonald, by training a goshawk, immersing herself in literary representations of such training, and then writing about it. Macdonald's book includes a stunning realization about loss after Helen's dog snaps her leash and is temporarily missing in the wind and rain:

> There is a time in life when you expect the world to be always full of new things. And then comes a day when you realise that is not how it will be at all. You see that life will become a thing made of holes. Absences. Losses. Things that were there and are no longer. And you realise, too, that you have to grow around and between the gaps, though you can put your hand out to where things were and feel that tense, shining dullness of the space where the memories are.[20]

This volume is my own account of discovering these absences, losses, and holes, but also of seeking through the *Shir Ḥadash shel Yom*—to my knowledge the only weekly synagogue-based class of its kind in the world—to fill them in some way, and reconnect torn or loose threads.[21]

"Translation" in This Book

In a *Paris Review* interview, Hebrew translator Peter Cole locates his attraction to Hebrew translation in an effort to pass from the left side (the English) of the bilingual Bible or siddur to the right (the Hebrew): "I felt it in prayer as well, especially in the disconcerting back and forth across the facing pages of the Hebrew-English prayer book. Opaque but luscious Hebrew on the right-facing page and the inert English on the left. It's as though the English side were blank, and that's what I've been writing into all my life."[22]

When asked "when did you pass from one page to the other?" Cole recounts the tragic death of his younger brother and his subsequent travel to Jerusalem to study and recover the Hebrew of his youth as "a coming into a new life."[23] His moving through present grief by way of the Hebrew words of his past resonated powerfully in me. That's translation: being moved, from one place or state or mode or time or language to another. It offers its own form of healing.

In all, this book demonstrates "translation" in several ways and directions:

- from the personal to the dialogical and the communal
- from Hebrew to English, with accompanying annotation of classical source material
- from fixed liturgy to "open siddur" (calling attention to the fluidity inherent even in "fixed" liturgy)
- from secular to sacred
- from literary to liturgical
- from words to feelings
- from static ritual to transformation
- and from mourning to consolation.

Some of these translation processes work in both directions simultaneously. Much of modern Hebrew poetry, for instance, is said to be the result of a process of political-theological translation of foundational religious notions and texts into secular Zionist terms.[24] Many of the first modern Hebrew poets, some of them showcased in this book, were former yeshiva students. Fully conversant in Bible, Talmud, midrash, Hasidism, and more, they went on to incorporate these and other traditional sources into their poetry in radical, secularized, defamiliarized forms, resulting in what poet and scholar Haim O. Rechnitzer refers to as "untapped theological treasure."[25] These poets left the sphere of traditional observance, but translating and then teaching their work at the end of a morning *Shaḥarit* prayer service, before the final Rabbis' Kaddish, in a sense brings them back. Inviting them into my Modern Orthodox prayer world, and into my HUC-JIR classroom too, and hence bridging a secular–sacred as well as a denominational divide, feels to me like redressing a multilayered sense of loss.[26]

What, When, How

The poems, interpretations, and reflections presented here appear in the sequence of personal chronology—not in the order in which the poems themselves were published, but when I taught them, throughout the stages of my mourning, first for my dad, then for my mom. Each poet and poem was selected to wrest meaning from personal and current events—daily praying and Kaddish recitation, moving both living and deceased family members across national borders, navigating my mother-in-law's worsening dementia, adjusting to the pandemic and increasing political upheaval, learning at a women's Orthodox rabbinical seminary, teaching students at a Reform rabbinical seminary, preparing for my own forthcoming rabbinic ordination, and more.

I chose poets based on personal affinity, and what seemed, at the time, necessity (see below as well as at the beginning of each chapter). Some of the poets, such as Goldberg, Amichai, and Ḥalfi, are featured in recent Reform and liberal prayerbooks, though not all my choices match with those prior liturgical decisions. Due to considerations of space, only about half of the poems I taught made their way into this book. I lived with each poet for four, five, even six months, and then shifted to a new figure. The selection and analyses of the poems, as presented here, reflect those passing days, and the connections drawn in the process.

The volume is divided into two parts. Part 1, "So Much Has Been Severed," consists of chapter 1, "Learning to Mourn," the story of my bereavement as it unfolded first for my father and then for my mother, along with the onset of the COVID pandemic and the consequent formal writing of my teachings for the *Shir Ḥadash*.

Part 2, "Transitions and Translations," encompassing six chapters, is my intimate working through of grief, loss, and continuing life challenges through fifty-two poem teachings (with one more in the "Final Thoughts" section to total fifty-three) healing Hebrew poems.

Chapter 2 is dedicated to the poetry of Lea Goldberg, one of the first modern Hebrew woman poets to achieve both canonical and popular status in modern Hebrew culture. My choice to begin with Goldberg reflected my desire—as a professor of feminist studies, as one of the few female participants in the Bayit's 6:45 a.m. weekday service, and as a new caregiver for my recently widowed mother—to immerse myself in the work of a truly great woman poet and share it with my community. The poems included here were chosen for their sustaining, maternal images of God or for their reimagining of core values of work, art, interconnection, and shared humanity at a time of heightened personal and communal crisis. As winter turned to spring and COVID was disrupting our organic connection to the natural order, these works also suggested a vital way to connect to nature and to identify resources of hope. And since several of Goldberg's poems had been set to music, the intersection between Israeli poetry and Israeli popular song became a feature of the *Shir Ḥadash*, a way to experience these texts as we often did with liturgy: in song.

Chapter 3 features the iconoclastic poetry of Avraham Ḥalfi, who claimed to be staunchly atheist and yet never stopped seeking God. His poetry felt like the perfect vehicle to channel the psychic and spiritual challenge of mourning from late spring to early fall of 2020, when America had moved from lockdown to socially distanced outdoor gatherings, when the George Floyd protests had erupted and people were out in the streets, but many of us still felt deeply unsafe and unsure about our way forward in God's (yet unvaccinated) world. The unconventionality and seeming heresy of some of Ḥalfi's poems allowed me to consider personal and communal trauma anew: to weigh the benefit of expanding Judaism's sacred or canonical corpus to include alternative voices, specifically those expressing theological doubt, protest, and disappointment.

Yehuda Amichai's poetry, the subject of chapter 4, takes Ḥalfi's secular theologizing in a more immanent direction. Whereas Ḥalfi's poems (often paradoxically) address an absent, transcendent deity, Amichai brings God into the center of everyday life: the car repair shop, the guts of a chicken prepared on the Sabbath eve, a kindergarten, a mother's baking for her child. In the second half of my year of mourning for my mom, against the backdrop of the pandemic High Holy Days of 2020 and the fraught 2020 U.S. presidential election, through the first yahrzeit for my dad in late February 2020 and the end of nearly two years of Kaddish recitation in December 2021, teaching these poems that drew God close in ironic, funny, and mundane ways felt like a necessary tonic and a form of spiritual homecoming.

The devotional poems of Rachel Morpurgo, the first modern Hebrew woman poet and the focus of chapter 5, are deeply learned, liturgically resonant, and also subtly subversive. In the lead-up to my rabbinical ordination in June 2021, after more than two years of attending thrice-daily public prayer using a fixed liturgy that included not a single prayer written by a woman, her poetry filled a massive gap in my soul and reassured me: My own seeking of learned belongingness in the traditional world of rabbinic letters had ample and impressive precedent in Morpurgo's own life and career. The stark awareness of mortality in many of the poems, including several poems composed as gravestone epitaphs, also fit my chronic-mourner mindset at that time, as I planned my parents' unveiling and the global toll of COVID reached four million.[27]

Chapter 6 delves into poems by my former HUC colleague, contemporary Israeli talmudist, bibliotherapist, poet, and author Ruhama Weiss. As part of my rabbinical training, I had taken an independent study course with her, entitled *Sugyot Ḥayyim* (meaning "Talmudic Units of Life" or "Life Issues"), in which we probed talmudic passages for their personal, emotional, and spiritual content. Personal responses to talmudic and liturgical sources felt so crucial in the months following the conclusion of both my formal mourning and my rabbinical training: They gave me ways to integrate what I was experiencing emotionally and intellectually, and to address some of my feminist discomfort with the masculine rabbinic tradition to which I was apprenticing myself.

Finally, chapter 7 gleans from the poetry of Rachel Bluwstein, often referred to as the Poetess (*Meshoreret*) Rachel. She wrote most of her poetry while she battled terminal tuberculosis, the leading pandemic of her generation, and now, in the context of the *Shir Ḥadash*, her poems were helping our community process our own ongoing COVID experiences—a living modern Torah. Her writing on isolation-induced trauma in the wake of her illness also helped me gain perspective on the worsening dementia of my mother-in-law, Dvora.

In my view, the four modern Hebrew women poets in this book—Lea Goldberg, Rachel Morpurgo, Ruhama Weiss, and Rachel Bluwstein—form a feminist liturgical through line and response to the sense of exclusion experienced by many women in the traditional Kaddish setting. My readings and translations of their works alongside those of male poets Avraham Ḥalfi and Yehuda Amichai tie together elements of skepticism, play, subversion, humor, and hope that are rarely connected in the classical Hebrew liturgical tradition. Together this body of poetry constitutes an alternative liturgical canon, one that includes both women and men's voices of faith, doubt, and hope, supplementing the traditional *Pirkei 'Avot* (Chapters of the Fathers) with *Pirkei 'Imahot* (Chapters of the Mothers), the title of one of Ruhama Weiss's poems included here.

Returning to where this introduction begins, chapter 8's "Final Thoughts" chronicles my early attempt to wrest meaning from poetry with the *Shir Ḥadash* community after the shock of October 7, 2023. This fifty-third and final poem-teaching focuses on "Kadur Min ha-Tza'ar" ("Ball out of the Pain") by Amir Gilboa, a secular Hebrew poet versed in classical Jewish sources and modern Hebrew poetry and well acquainted with hardship and war. The poem plays on the multiple meanings of the Hebrew word *kadur* as ball, bullet, and (medicinal) pill—a fitting acknowledgment of our war-torn reality, but also a reminder of Alicia Ostriker's teaching about the healing properties of poetry.

The appendix includes a few of the poems I wrote over the course of this praying/learning journey, as I apprenticed myself to the poets I was reading, and sought to articulate my singular grief in my own words.

Finally, the bibliography gives you a sense of where I sought my learning, should you wish to supplement the experience of this book by undertaking learning on your own.

Deepening Your Experience

To deepen your involvement with this material, I have provided an extensive complementary study and discussion guide aimed at mourners, prayers, and college or seminary students, as well as all adults who want to know more about the resources of poetry and prayer in general, and about these poets in particular—including some poems that didn't make their way into this book. You'll find questions on how to look at the poems and what to find in them; information on the biblical, liturgical, and other classical sources they allude to; guidance on how to explore and contemplate the relevance of these poems to your life and prayer experiences; and recommendations on how to continue your learning. Download the guide at JPS's "Study Guides to JPS Books" page (https://jps.org/study-guides/).

In essence, the book you are reading is an invitation:

- to join me in my journey for solace after the deaths of my parents by wresting meaning from modern Hebrew poetry;
- to connect with a growing effort to raise up feminist religious and literary voices in the Jewish liturgical and literary canon;
- and, finally, to discover your own meanings from my quest to tie together various threads of an academic, literary, personal, devotional, and interdenominational life in a knot that can be grasped by others, and won't easily come undone.

Going Out with Knots

PART 1 So Much Has Been Severed

1 Learning to Mourn

Going Out with Knots

March 2019. I was finally nearing the completion of a fiction collection informed by my father's experiences growing up in a small Jewish community in the U.S.–Canada border town of Sarnia, Ontario. I'd just finished the third-to-last story based on my paternal grandmother's death in a car accident and was struggling with the next story on the aftermath of her death, when I received word from my sister that Dad himself had been hit by a truck and killed.

For a number of years, while I'd been writing these stories, Dad and I had developed a special writing *ḥavruta* (study partnership). I'd call him up once or twice a day, ask him about what he had been writing for his creative writing class at the Betel Senior Centre in North Toronto, pepper him with questions about his life in Sarnia, his furniture store, his childhood, whatever related to the current story on my laptop screen, and write it all down in my journal. That February and March he'd told me about a police officer knocking on the family door with the news of his mother Lea's death just a block away from our home, how the car that hit her had dragged her body several feet down the block. He recalled his tortured ruminations on how best to break the news to his Pa. Should he do it on his own? With the rabbi? In the end, he walked over to his father's house with our family doctor and friend, known to all simply as Doc Mann. "I want to see her," was all his father said upon hearing the news. At the hospital, they met a night nurse named Mrs. Jefferson, who took them to see the body. My father mentioned that his mother's face had been cleaned off, that she still looked "like herself." She hadn't yet "turned white." A sheet was draped over her lower body so they wouldn't have to see her mangled legs.

My father had faced major challenges in assembling a minyan (the necessary prayer quorum of ten men) to say the Kaddish memorial prayer for his mother in our small Jewish community of Sarnia. He had a list of the names of all the men and boys over the age of thirteen in the community whom he called every night in hopes of assembling a morning minyan. On Sunday mornings he'd bring the teenage boys to our house for breakfast as a reward for joining in the minyan effort. Once, he went out to a construction site where one of the community members worked to try to cajole him into occasionally attending morning services. A man named Ben Sherwood, whom my father phoned on Friday afternoons to help make the minyan, thanked my father for calling, "because that's how I know that it's *Shabbes*."

After thirty days of chasing a minyan for Kaddish, Dad told Mom, "I just can't take it anymore." She encouraged him not to give up. Somehow he persevered and made it through the eleven customary months of Kaddish recitation after the death of a parent, but not without cost.

After the conclusion of his year-of-mourning period for his mother, on one of the intermediate days of Passover in 1961, Dad woke up with a rubbery feeling in his legs. His arms were heavy, too. He joined his father at their furniture store, but felt too unwell to work a full day. The next morning, he awoke to the sound of my sister struggling with a cough—both of my older sisters had come down with the measles. When he tried to get out of bed to bring one of my sisters a glass of water, he fell to the floor. The paramedics came, lifting him down the stairs and into an ambulance.

In describing that moment, Dad recalled an observation his own father had made right before his older brother Isaac (nicknamed Bucky) shipped off to England in 1944 to serve in the Royal Canadian Air Force. "Isaac is surveying the room," my grandfather had said. A few months later, in April 1945, Bucky was declared missing in action, having been shot down over Lepizig, Germany. That last bit of surveying comprised Bucky's last view of home before he was killed. As my now paralyzed father was carried down the hall and out of the house, he too looked around the house, wondering whether his would be a similar fate. Would he ever see his home and family again?

FIG. 1. My mother and father's wedding announcement in the *Sarnia Observer*, May 3, 1952. Courtesy of Wendy Zierler.

The doctors in Sarnia couldn't figure out what was wrong with Dad. At first they diagnosed him with hysterical paralysis, owing to the traumatic year he had just endured, but the resident psychiatrist dismissed that theory. Another ambulance transported Dad 180 miles to Toronto, where he was seen by a variety of neurologists and diagnosed with Guillain Barré syndrome, a rare autoimmune-related neurological disorder that affects the peripheral nervous system, causing full-body paralysis, in many cases temporary. Eventually, after a six-week hospitalization in Toronto, Dad regained the use of his arms and legs and was brought home. From then on, though, he would be a slow, stiff walker.

It was during a final slow, stiff walk that he met his end.

The next page in my journal, dated March 12, 2019, shifts—abruptly, crushingly—to notes for a eulogy. Dad had just gotten out of his car in a parking lot. He was slowly making his way to the entrance of the McDonald's on Bathurst near Steeles, where every Tuesday morning he'd meet his friend Manny for coffee and conversation.

Yes, a McDonald's, even though he kept kosher and couldn't eat at such a restaurant. Stopping in at McDonald's was a remnant of Dad's many years of driving all over Toronto as a furniture salesman, and picking up a needed cup of take-out coffee wherever he could find it along the way. Years earlier, when Manny had been caring for his terminally ill wife, he would stop in at the Bathurst McDonald's now and again to take a needed break. On one such occasion, Dad had popped in too, and struck up a conversation with this man who seemed to Dad to have a lot on his mind. They had been meeting there weekly to give each other moral support ever since.

Mid-walk from the car to meet Manny that Tuesday, Dad was struck backward by a distracted truck driver and instantly killed.

Unbeknownst to me, all those discussions with Dad had prepared me for something beyond writing a work of prose fiction. After spending so much time talking to Dad about his Kaddish odyssey and its aftermath, my own was about to begin—a journey I would take not in prose but in poetry.

Ten days earlier I had sent my sister a triumphant email. It was an achievement four years in the making. In 2015, my mother experienced kidney failure and began thrice-weekly dialysis treatments in Toronto. Given her health challenges and the fact that all of us Zierler kids lived in New York State, we'd been encouraging Dad to get a green card. Should Mom succumb to her illness, we needed to make sure Dad, a Canadian citizen, could move closer to us. We hired an immigration lawyer, and completed and submitted numerous rounds of forms. I flew to Toronto to take Dad by train to the U.S. consulate in Montreal for his green card interview, after which there were other letters and forms to submit, and more weeks of waiting. Dad flew into to New York for

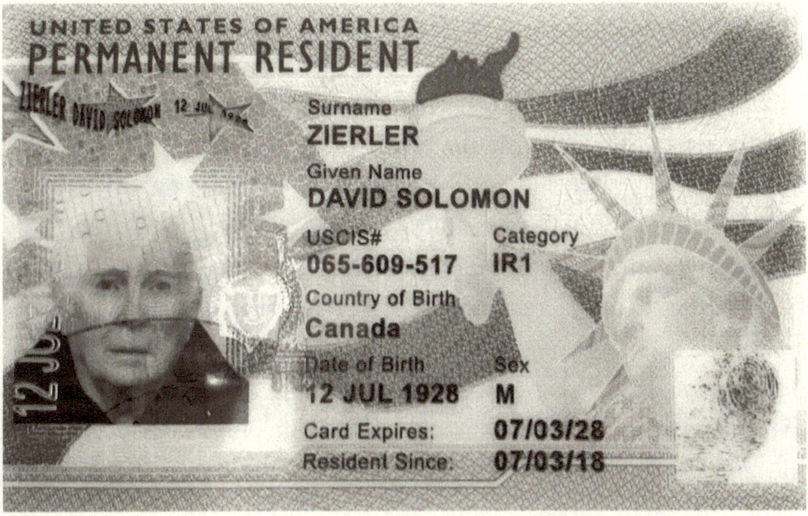

FIG. 2. My father David Zierler's green card. Photo by Wendy Zierler.

a second set of fingerprints taken at a Homeland Security Office in the Bronx—and then, finally, in March 2019: success!

The photo on the green card, which isn't even green, didn't do Dad justice. The consulate staff didn't let him smile; there was no inkling of Dad's sparklingly handsome face, his twinkly blue eyes. Looking at the picture now, I can see traces of dread, of eerie fear. At the time, though, his green card only meant unadulterated accomplishment. I had bested the American immigration system—in the Trump era, no less! In the face of obstacles, I'd set out to do something good and gotten it done.

Immediately I booked a plane ticket to Toronto for the end of March to hand-deliver the green card to Dad. He'd be able to use it soon thereafter, when he and Mom came to visit us on Passover. Following that I received confirmation of a dialysis slot for my mother at a nearby clinic for the duration of their Passover stay—another major achievement, since that year extra visitor slots had become especially scarce.

The next step would be arranging my parents' move to New York. The planning would begin when Mom and Dad came for that holiday visit. Everything was falling into place.

That is, until it all fell apart.

Things Fall Apart

My sister Randi, the same sister who'd been sick with the measles as a baby, whom my father had gotten out of bed to help only to collapse to the floor, had the grim task of relaying the news to me: "Dad is gone." Earlier that morning, she'd called my mother, as was her habit, to make sure Mom had gotten home safely from dialysis, only to be greeted by a police officer at the other end of the line. How many patterns of my father's past would be recapitulated in our captive present?

We were always so concerned about my mother's health, it never dawned on Randi to consider that something could happen to Dad. "Where's my mother?" she anxiously asked the policeman. Only when the officer transferred the phone to our distraught mother did the awful reality take shape.

When Randi reached me, my eldest daughter Shara and I were at the bank. Shara was about to deposit the redemption of a bond she'd been gifted at birth that had finally matured. The two of us were waiting in line when my cell phone rang and I heard those words—*Dad is gone*. I let out a loud, long shriek and ran out of the bank. Outside, I slid down against the bank's storefront window, all the way to the ground, where I sat and wailed, a picture of primitive pain. The image that comes to mind now is of an open bottle turned upside down. "Daddy, Daddy, Daddy," I cried. Shara slumped down and convulsed in tears next to me. How did we manage to lift ourselves up from the pavement? How did I drive home without crashing? How did I pull myself out of the car and climb the steps of the house, the same steps where two rabbis from the Hebrew Institute of Riverdale were already sitting, awaiting our arrival? And then I made that first phone call to Mom to hear her wail: *"Can you believe it, Wendy? Can you believe something this terrible has happened?"*

And so it was that instead of the leisurely, triumphant visit to Toronto I'd planned for the end of the month, I found myself early the next morning in the Air Canada terminal at LaGuardia Airport with my husband, Daniel, and our three adult children, en route to Dad's funeral.

Just thinking about the ironies of his death makes me stop to catch my breath. I'd often felt powerless in the face of the genetic illness that landed my mother in dialysis, a lifesaving but extremely difficult regimen of ongoing treatment that more often than not left her nauseous, exhausted, itchy, unable to sleep through the night, and, consequently, depressed. None of us could alleviate her torment, other than suggest that she take the antihistamines or sleeping pills or blood pressure medication her doctor had prescribed, which most often she had already taken and hadn't helped.

And, otherwise, to validate her frustration. I will admit I am notoriously bad at validation; I much prefer to solve the problem. My father's immigration status was a problem I had solved. And now death had foiled the solution.

Over the next few days, I would be forced to develop and practice new skills and habits: to eulogize and then memorialize, every day, three times a day. I was about to enter and stake a claim in the communal, masculine world of Orthodox Jewish prayer and mourning. I would need to find some way of making it my world, too.

As a professor of modern Jewish literature and feminist studies, and a specialist in modern Hebrew women's writing, in particular, it was poetry—Hebrew poetry, to be precise—that would help me find that way.

The End of Stories

When first I saw the love-light in your eyes,
I dreamed the world held not but joy for me.
And even though we drifted far apart,
I never dream but what I dream of thee.

—James Thornton, "When You Were Sweet Sixteen" (1898)

This was the song my romantic, loving father loved to sing to my mother, and, by extension, to all of us kids. One of my earliest memories of Dad is seeing the love-light sparkle in his marble-blue eyes as he looked at Mom and us kids, all of whom he adored.

My mother wasn't always easy on him, not by a long shot. She could be brooding, dark, and unsatisfied. His optimism often galled her; it seemed too simple-minded in her acute view. But to me his contentment was no simple affair. It was a lifelong endeavor to salvage goodness and joy in the face of recurrent, familial tragedy.

Who else was as stubbornly content with his lot, as upbeat and friendly, as Dad? Who else knew so well how to spend his time, how to set his own agenda, and make himself happy? Who else could strike up a conversation with anyone, anywhere—at a truck stop, at a McDonald's, on a train, with people sitting next to him in synagogue, in a foreign country, with all of my friends, their parents, their kids?

My father gave my friends and me pet-names. My friend Debbie was Smitty. I was Popsicle, Popsie, or Pea*nuts*, the accent on the second syllable, Italian style, one of the many accents he'd perfected for telling stories about the customers in his Sarnia furniture store. He loved to tell jokes—sometimes corny, sometimes off-color. He had a distinct, hokey way with words: When someone told him a dirty joke, he'd say, "I'm commencing to blush." My friends used to make fun of me when I was a kid, because I liked to read the dictionary. But my love of lexicography came from Dad, who adored words, languages, and accents, and despite little formal education had developed a wonderfully rich vocabulary.

Rich was a keyword in Dad's experiential lexicon. He often reflected on how rich he was: not in dollars and cents, but in family and Jewishness. He treasured spending—not money but time: with his kids, his family, his friends. His favorite activity in Sarnia was to take us kids and our cousins for root beer and rides in the furniture delivery truck. After we moved to Toronto, he traded truck rides for bike rides down Yonge Street to the Dairy Queen—me on my blue bike and Dad riding his old brown childhood bicycle, neither of which had gears. We spent hours in the park behind our house as Dad and my brother Larry taught me how to catch and throw a ball. When my children were born, our family spent weeks in Toronto over the summer so the kids could go to Camp Robin Hood, my own childhood day camp—and so Dad could give his grandkids rides on the go-cart he'd proudly built, as well as in the red wagon of his childhood, which he lovingly repainted and restored to make it sturdy and safe.

When I was a little girl, the highlight of my year was when Mom and Dad let me take off school and go with Dad to work. In Sarnia Dad owned two furniture stores, but he gave them up when we moved to Toronto so he could stop working on the Sabbath and send us to Jewish schools. My parents made a costly, countercultural sacrifice for the sake of Judaism and our place in it.

In Toronto, Dad became a *Manufacturer's Representative*, as his business card boasted—a tag that, I later learned, simply meant "salesman." Being a salesman was a comedown for Dad, and Mom, too, after all those years of owning their own business, with all the pride and creativity that went with it. Now Dad lived at the mercy of not just one but several bosses. I confess: Later, when I entered my teens and realized all of my friends' fathers were doctors or lawyers or accountants, with fancy diplomas on the walls, and my dad was a salesman with no education, I was envious and ashamed.

But as a young child, Dad's being a *Manufacturer's Representative* was a portal to great adventure. He and I would get in the car and head to downtown Toronto, Dad showing off his amazing parallel parking skills; really, he could park in absolutely any spot. We'd go from store to store, Dad taking orders from the retailers in his "territory," as he called it, while introducing me and bragging about me; and then—treat of treats—we'd go for potato latkes and cheese kreplach at United Bakers on Spadina Avenue. Dad would also get the soup of the day. And rye bread—as many slices as he wanted. He knew I wouldn't tell my mother, who always nagged him not to eat too much bread.

One time, as we walked from the car to United, as we called it, somehow Dad tripped and fell on the sidewalk, ripping his pants and scraping his knees. There he was, my strong, sweet father, bleeding on the ground. Today, thinking of how he was so rudely snatched from this world, I can't get that image out of my head.

That morning near United Bakers, though, he got up, brushed himself off, walked back to the car, took the first aid kit out of the trunk, and bandaged his knees. We went for lunch as planned, and sang "Two for Tea," as we always did when we walked together—to and from synagogue, and to and from the car. Dad, who had suffered so many losses and challenges in his life, always knew how to get back up. He always believed that things would be good, even when, in my mother's view, that sanguinity seemed misguided or obtuse.

He loved so many things, both large and small: soup, salami, peanuts in the shell, potato chips, barbecuing, jokes, history, old movies, cantorial music, leading prayers, singing Jewish songs, the braised lamb shanks we'd make every year for Passover, going to the grocery store for treats, going to the variety store to treats, going to the drug store for treats, licorice—red and black. He loved his Underwood typewriter—how much effort he and my sister Randi expended one summer to find him a new ribbon for that old, heavy typewriter. He loved writing and his writing class at the Betel Center in Toronto, taught by Toronto writer Sylvia Warsh. He loved it especially when the other students in his class would ask him if what he had written was true, and with that glint in his eye, he'd tell him that he'd made it all up. He loved listening to "Down Memory Lane" with Ray Saunen on CFRB, or watching Lawrence Welk. Can I admit that I groaned, more than once, having to watch Lawrence Welk on our one TV? He loved all of his synagogue friends, including angelic Steve and David, who in those last years patiently accompanied him to shul (synagogue), at his snail's pace or pushed him in the wheelchair, all the while listening to his unending, oft-repeating stream of stories. He loved his children, grandchildren, great-grandchildren, and of course my mom: Marion, that young woman in a red corduroy dress, who appeared one Ḥanukkah night in 1951 in the basement of Ahavas Isaac Synagogue in Sarnia, and walked across the room and into his life; he was immediately smitten.

I adored what Dad was like when he was with the family: the way he'd look around the Shabbat or holiday table before reciting *Kiddush*, his face suddenly reddening, his nose crinkling, his belly shaking, the tears running down his cheeks—tears of perfect joy.

He had many simple pleasures. He loved cleaning things—ovens, floors, countertops. He loved designing and making things—go-carts, dollhouses, puppet theaters, matchbox car garages, and Barbie swimming pools. Perhaps most of all, he loved fixing things. He was a fixer at his core: a rare breed, a Jew with tools. All the tools in my house—the twine, wood glue, levels, screws, screwdrivers, nuts and bolts—come from him. Everything I know about house maintenance and repair emanates from his storehouse of smarts and know-how. He believed that great things, like loosening a zipper or a stuck drawer, could be accomplished with a graphite pencil and a bar of soap. The last time he was in my house, he fixed a chair and glued down a piece of wood that was peeling off our piano. He was never at a loss for something to repair and restore: a project, an idea, a story. And there we all were, utterly broken by his death, a sudden shattering that no measure of know-how and ingenuity could fix.

The ancient rabbis offer a taxonomy of different kinds of human loss. In the last chapter of Mishnah Sotah (9:11–15), they enumerate the things that ceased in the world because of the passing of certain rabbis or institutions: When the Sanhedrin dissolved, song was discontinued in the places of feasting; when Rabbi Meir died, the composers of parables ceased. When my father Davey Zierler was tragically taken, stories halted in the houses—at least that's how it felt. How would I ever finish that book in his absence? How would I write another sentence?

With his loss came the responsibility to fill in his cruelly vacated space, to perform the rituals and model for the next generation what it meant to pay respects and carry on.

Loose Thread

The first few months following my father's death were a blur: a funeral, then shivah, first in Toronto and then back in Riverdale, New York; a seemingly unending cycle of administrative, bureaucratic tasks on the one hand, and prayer services and Kaddishes on the other; a series of New York–Toronto roundtrips to visit my mother and shore up her broken spirits; other visits to help clean out and sell her house in order to move her to New York—prolonged visits when she suddenly took sick, was hospitalized with pneumonia, and failed to recuperate as quickly as we'd hoped.

While in Toronto I attended thrice-daily prayers to say Kaddish at the synagogue where my parents belonged and where I grew up, and where a women's gallery sits atop several flights of stairs—a very different place from the open Orthodox synagogue we attend in Riverdale, which employs women rabbis and where the women and men occupy equal-size spaces on either side of a transparent glass partition. Over the years my parents' synagogue community had dwindled in size; few women attended services, and on Friday nights the women's gallery was locked. And so, on the Friday night after the funeral and the subsequent Friday nights when I was back in Toronto, I found myself relegated to a one-row compartment carved into the back of the main (men's) sanctuary, framed by two wooden two-by-fours hanging directly in front of my eyes—a structure that male and female synagogue members alike dubbed "the penalty box." Better, but still not ideal, was the location of early Saturday and daily morning services: in the downstairs *beis medrash* (study hall), where the larger women's section was framed by wooden barriers topped with smoky brown glass. Both upstairs and downstairs, though, I was boxed out. Day after day, I was the only woman in the room. I knew a number of the men who comprised the minyan; a few were devoted friends to my parents. Still, I was largely irrelevant in practice and definition to this prayer assemblage. Two silver tzedakah boxes (for collecting charity) sat near the podium on the men's side of the partition; throughout the service, the men approached the boxes to bank coins or bills, in some cases taking change for larger notes. But I had no access to the boxes, no means of approaching or participating in this good deed. In our own synagogue, the tzedakah boxes are always stationed in a middle zone that both men and women can reach. I was used to a different kind of sensitivity, and the lack of it in my childhood community, in my parents' own synagogue, and in the aftermath of my father's appalling death smarted at the heart. Daily, I was reminded that in joining this group to say Kaddish, a practice generally not encouraged for Orthodox women, who remain uncounted in the minyan, I was not so much sustaining a tradition as disrupting it. I was a loose thread, attempting to tie myself to a place and a practice that didn't entirely want or know how to complete the knot.

In his memoir about his year of saying Kaddish for his father, journalist Ari L. Goldman offers observations about the constitution of the Kaddish community that brings my woman's mourning experience into high relief. Goldman lists off the names of the regulars at his morning minyan at Congregation Ramath Orah and then notes an exception to the rule:

> There was even the occasional woman worshipper, although, as Ramath Orah is an Orthodox shul, women cannot be counted as part of the minyan. We came for prayer, and we prayed, but we also talked, joked, laughed, and gossiped. We shared each other's stories and helped dissolve each other's pains. We became a community in the very best sense of the word. We knew that as individuals, we were bound to the earth, but as a minyan we could reach the very gates of heaven.[1]

In Goldman's account the women attending morning minyan at Ramath Orah were a curious counterintuitive presence.

Later in the book, he says more about this lone female attendee, a devout Barnard student: "She told me she had 'tremendous reverence' for halacha [Jewish law], and found no reason to question its wisdom in relieving women of the responsibility of participating in a minyan. At this stage in her life, as a college student, voluntarily going to daily minyan made sense . . . but she hoped one day to marry and have children, Then, her first obligation will be not to the synagogue but to her family."[2]

Reading about this student's acceptance of her uncounted status brought back the whole complex of feelings and reactions I'd experienced in the early days of my Kaddish experience and beyond. Unlike her, I had reason to question the wisdom of a system super-stuffed with legal detail and nuance—of the sort I had committed myself to studying as a rabbinical student at Yeshivat Maharat—that did not account for the differing stages of a woman's life. As an unmarried young adult, Goldman's lone female minyan attendee was unencumbered by child-rearing duties, and thus was fully capable of committing to public prayer attendance, even if she planned one day to be a mother. Why couldn't she be counted, then, as a full member of the community to which she was so devoted?

As for me, by the time Dad was killed and I was catapulted into my Kaddish commitments, I had already raised my children. My youngest child was in his first year of college. Aside from my professorial job, my most urgent obligation in the aftermath of my father's tragic death was caring for my mother and saying Kaddish for my father. But in my parents' community, my Kaddish experience was often alienating. On occasion I got a much-appreciated lift to synagogue with one of my father's friends, and we chatted along the way. In the synagogue proper, however, sitting there at a distinct remove, behind dark glass, I could no longer talk, gossip, joke, or commiserate with any of the members of the minyan. Nor, I found, could I "reach the very gates of heaven." If the Kaddish prayer aims to counter the devastations of death by offering blessings and praise for the Eternal God that reach "ever higher, beyond all blessing"—in this, my childhood shul, my own Kaddish, already weighed down by the tragic circumstances of father's death, was struggling to lift itself off the ground.

The struggle had begun, in fact, on the very first morning of post-funeral shivah in Toronto. Assembled at 7:00 a.m. that morning in my parents' family room were nine men and me, who according to Orthodox Jewish law, didn't count, resulting in the need to call for male reinforcements. And this problem was not unique to my parents' dwindling Toronto community. On Purim day, back in our bustling, otherwise women-friendly open Orthodox community in Riverdale, I rushed over to our shul after our family Purim feast for afternoon and evening services, only to confront, once again, a group of nine men, plus me, provoking a call, yet again, for men to complete the quorum. This pattern repeated on several occasions over the course of my Kaddish experience, regardless of which Orthodox synagogue I attended. I was there, but uncounted—as if I were merely practicing or feigning a role, laying down a marker for someone else to fill.

And then, on top of that, came a different sort of slight. I was in Toronto, some two weeks after my father's death, at the end of March—the very same weekend I'd originally planned to bring Dad his green card. I'd elected to attend the early service on Shabbat morning so I could be back home for Mom as soon as she rose from bed. One of my mother's friends had warned me that none of that service's regular (male) attendees were in a mourning period, and so the prayer leader might simply skip over the Mourner's Kaddish. To fend off that possibility, I contacted the rabbi, who happily agreed to alert the gabbai (the man in charge of running he service and giving out honors, such as *'aliyot*) of my desire to say Kaddish. All well and good.

When it came time to recite the prayer, however, I saw a man saying Kaddish along with me. It seemed my mother's friend was wrong; there was a mourner in the men's section after all. At the end of the service, I approached that man, the father of a childhood friend, and asked him if he was observing a yahrzeit, and if so, for whom? The man looked at me quizzically and shook his head. "No yahrzeit," he said. Naively, I pressed him further: "So why were you saying Kaddish?" "You know," the man replied, unflinchingly. "We can't allow a woman to say Kaddish, here, on her own."

From then on, I noticed that whenever the time came to say Kaddish with this group, the prayer leader or some other member of the community, often himself not a mourner, layered his voice over mine, like a blanket over a fire. Daily, my Kaddish, my unique experience of memorialization and grief, was being quelled. Daily, my voice, my experience, my personal connection to my parents and God, was being co-opted by otherwise well-meaning men who viewed their voices as more legally valid and acceptable to God than my own.

I considered abandoning this minyan and going to the nearby Conservative shul. Somehow, though, I couldn't bring myself, in the midst of heartbreak, to pray with strangers. I couldn't cut the cord of my parents' shul and its ways, as if doing so would mean abandoning *them*.

I resolved, then, to burrow inward, to join the community without expectations for communion. For as long as I'd be in Toronto, I would sit there by myself and pray. If I found it hard to concentrate on prayer, I would learn the tractate of Mishnah I'd committed to studying, so that at the end of the first thirty days of mourning for Dad our family could make a *siyyum ha-mishnah*, a traditional ceremony marking the

FIG. 3. My Kaddish journal. Photo by Wendy Zierler.

completion of studying the six orders of the Mishnah in memory of the deceased. I was also bringing my journal along with me, and when the spirit moved or when anger welled up, I would write.

The journal I had chosen for this purpose was a thing of unique beauty: leatherbound, handmade, comprised of a variety of textured and colored papers, tied up with blue ribbons, and embossed with my name. A gift from a rabbinical student whose senior thesis I'd advised, the multicolored paged journal reminded me that I had much to learn, write, and teach about this complex grieving experience.

So much had been severed. I redoubled my efforts to remain connected and committed to what I could.

Going Out with Knots

The reason most commonly given for the practice of studying Mishnah in memory of a departed loved one is that the Hebrew word *mishnah* (משנה), a unit of talmudic study, shares the same Hebrew letters as the word *neshama* (נשמה), meaning "soul." Together with the recitation of Kaddish, daily Mishnah study is traditionally seen as a way of elevating the soul of the departed. With this in mind, and with a desire to connect to the memory and soul of Dad, for whom Sabbath observance was such a hard-won privilege, I set out to study Tractate Shabbat.

I didn't expect that the study itself would deal its own emotional blow.

There I was again, attending morning services in the basement *beis medrash* of my parents' shul. I have long worn a tallit, a prayer shawl, when praying, but that particular morning, for the very first time, I was wearing Dad's tallit, with its lovely flowered neckband, adorned with silver and gold threads. During the repetition of the silent *'Amidah* (the central prayers of all services), I opened up my volume of Mishnah Shabbat to where I had last left off: the ninth *mishnah* in the sixth chapter, which discusses the various kinds of clothing and accessories one can wear outside on Shabbat without transgressing the Sabbath prohibition against carrying from a private to a public domain.

The *mishnah* opens with the words *ha-banim yotz'im biksharim*, "sons go out [of their homes into the public domain] with knots." What are these knots? The Gemara's commentary on this *mishnah* first suggests they are garlands of madder worn for their healing properties, but then rejects this interpretation, since daughters too can benefit from this medicine, yet the *mishnah* specifically refers to sons.

The Gemara then offers another explanation, which classical commentators on the Mishnah—Rabbeinu Ḥananel (Ḥananel ben Ḥushiel, eleventh century), Maimonides (1138–1204), and the Bartenura (Ovadiah Bertinoro, 1445–1515), all quote.[3] That morning, the Bartenura commentary met my eye: "In the case of a son who misses his father, the father takes a lace from his right shoe and knots it onto his son's shoe or arm. And so long as this knot is with him, the son's longings quell, as if talismanically." The Bartenura went on to clarify why the *mishnah* refers to sons and not daughters going out with knots: "The *mishnah* teaches this in relation to sons because daughters don't have the same longings for their fathers as do sons."

I let out a gasp. It was as if those words had formed fists and punched me in the gut. There I was, literally wrapped in my father's tallit with its ritual knots, still very much in the throes of early grief, and the *mishnah* I was learning in his memory was telling me that daughters don't "go out" with their father's knots, because daughters simply don't long for their fathers as do sons.

If this weren't bad enough, Rabbeinu Ḥananel's commentary on the related Gemara, which I read soon thereafter, specifically situated the wearing of these knots in the context of a son's mourning his father's death: "There are those who say that when a son's grief over the death of his father increases, the grieving son takes a lace from his father's right shoe and ties it to his left, and they say this quiets the heart."[4]

My heart failed to quiet. Quite the contrary: These three words—*habanim yotz'im biksharim* (sons go out with knots)—reverberated in my head throughout the first thirty days of mourning, compounding my grief and unraveling my ties to the spiritual world of my Jewish fathers.

In her exegesis of this same *mishnah*, as part of her ongoing effort to bring images of daily maternal care into our experience and conception of God, scholar Mara Benjamin suggests that "to be a parent is to gain insight into what it means to be the God of the Hebrew Bible and the rabbinic imagination."[5] I would add to this the message of the *mishnah*: To be a child, one who suffers the loss of a parent, is to gain insight into the ongoing challenges of faith and religious devotion. Given the commonplace, traditional usage of images of God as parent, the death of a parent deals a major blow to one's God concept. Finding a way to maintain one's ties to one's departed parents is thus as much a theological religious challenge as it is a form of psychological recuperation. And how much more so when one bumps up against traditional sources that efface one's primary attachment to a parent and deny one's very participation in this psycho-theological process!

Over the next few weeks I shared this *mishnah* and these commentaries with various rabbis and colleagues, seeking other ways to read the text. Rabbi Jeffrey Fox of Yeshivat Maharat, where I had been studying toward ordination since September 2018, suggested that I consider the words "sons go out with knots" in light of what immediately follows in the *mishnah*: "and princes go out with bells." In the same way that sons are given a special dispensation to go out into public spaces with the healing knots that remind them of their fathers, princes may go out wearing bells signifying their aristocratic station. The *mishnah* then rejects the unique status of princes, insisting that everyone may go out with bells, *'ella' she-dibberu ḥakhamim be-hoveh*—rather, that in referring to their distinct status and garb, the sages were speaking in the parlance and to the customs of their day. Rabbi Fox suggested that instead of reading the conclusion of the *mishnah* about the sages speaking in the parlance of their day as pertaining only to princes and bells, I should read it as relating to the first part as well: that everyone, sons and daughters alike, are permitted to go out wearing the knots that remind them of their parents and thus console them over their loss. The initial reference to sons merely mimics the gender-segregated conventions of the time; just as with the princes' special status, the sages were speaking to the customs of their day. It was no matter that none of the classical commentaries read the *mishnah* this way. It was no matter that the rabbis "on the page" were far more eager to imagine away the distinction between nobles and commoners than between men and women. The historicizing notion that the sages spoke in the language of their own day provided a crucial mechanism through which to view the text differently for our own times, and for me to tie myself spiritually to prior generations.

I was grateful for this alternative reading. I needed this affirmation of my ties to Dad. And I wanted this Kaddish period to fortify, not fray, my connections to a tradition my parents had sacrificed so much to pass on to my siblings and me. To do so, however, I would have to "lean into" the idea of sages speaking, in every generation, for their own times. And not just male sages, but female sages, and creative writers, too. The experience of learning Mishnah exposed the need for new interpretations and voices. It would not be enough to apply the old texts, rinse, and repeat.

Saying Kaddish for a parent in the context of a traditional Jewish service is, on the most basic level, an exercise in hyper-repetition: five Kaddishes (two Rabbis', three Mourner's) at every morning service; three more (one Rabbis', and two Mourner's) at afternoon and evening prayers. Other prayers, too—Psalm 145 (*'Ashrei*), the *Shema'*, *'Amidah*, and *'Aleinu*—are repeated, almost verbatim, mornings, afternoons, and evenings. I would have to add in some contemporary variation to sustain me through the over-and-over-again of it all. New texts that spoke in the present would have to mixed in to allow me to go out with knots (instead of naysaying "nots") and keep coming back.

Settling In

September 2019. After months of work with my siblings cleaning out, packing up, and selling our parents' house, securing a health insurance policy for Mom and a coveted dialysis placement, and finding her a rental apartment, I was finally helping Mom close up her house in Toronto in preparation for her move to Riverdale. Over the weekend of her departure, friends streamed into the house, sobbing to see Mom go. They were still shattered by my father's untimely passing. And my mother had been an exceptional friend, the kind who regularly checked in, who made meals for you when you got sick, who shared your joys and sadnesses sincerely and generously. Over the years I'd been awed by how Mom stayed in touch with all of her friends, by how much time she spent with each one of them on the phone even though she often felt unwell. Women of my generation—always busy, always moving between work and family and other obligations—just don't pick up the phone like that anymore, at least not regularly. Even with social media, we're not nearly as connected as Mom was with her friends.

When she moved to New York, however, the phone didn't ring nearly as much. It was a tough acclimation. Mom ached over Dad's sudden passing, over harsh words exchanged shortly before his death that she never got to take back. She missed her friends, her home, her neighborhood, even her old dialysis clinic at Humber Hospital in Toronto. The people at Humber knew her and her specific challenges: her chronic itchiness, her difficulty sleeping, the tendency of her blood pressure to dip perilously low during dialysis. They were accustomed to pausing and restarting the machine to get her dialyzed safely. Here in Riverdale, despite having grown up in the Bronx, she was a stranger, anomalous, alone.

Gradually, however, she began to settle in. She joined a bereavement group at the Riverdale Senior Center, conveniently located in her building. She joined a Mahjong group at the Riverdale Y, and even though she tussled with one of its more cantankerous members, she began to find her place in the group. She made friends at a weekly Bible class given by our rabbi and garnered a few invitations for lunch, too. I was a member of the gym in her building, and so I visited all the time. Daily I shuttled between my house, the Hebrew Institute of Riverdale, the HUC-JIR building at One West Fourth Street where I teach, my mother's apartment, and back again to the Hebrew Institute for afternoon and evening services. Sometimes, if the weather was unfavorable, if I seemed tired, or if Mom simply felt I was doing too much, she tried to dissuade me from going to minyan to say Kaddish. "Dad would understand," she said. "He wouldn't want you to kill yourself doing this." Whenever she said this, my husband chuckled. "Doesn't she know you already?" he asked. "Doesn't she know the more she tries to dissuade you from doing something, the more you'll insist on doing it?"

Daniel knows me well. But my motives weren't merely oppositional. Now that I was no longer running back and forth to Toronto, I had settled into my Kaddish routine and had begun to appreciate some of what Ari Goldman meant when he wrote of the comforts of the Kaddish community, feminist critique notwithstanding. Every morning I rose early, often when it was still dark outside, made myself coffee, grabbed the prepacked tallit bag replete with journal and extra reading material, and walked the seven-tenths of a mile to the Hebrew Institute, otherwise known as the Bayit (the Home), to join the 6:45 a.m. *tefillah* (prayer). The regulars included Hillel, the longtime synagogue gabbai; Bernie, the longtime Torah reader; Elli, the shul's celebrated lay cantor, who was saying Kaddish for his mother; my friend Steve, a minyan stalwart; and other mourners whom I had slowly gotten to know. At the beginning of my Kaddish journey, I was the only woman in the room. Now three or four other women were there in the morning—all of them women like me, who had recently lost their fathers.

A male mourner is traditionally called a *ḥiyyuv*, a personification of obligation, and customarily tapped to lead the prayers. Since losing my father, I had negotiated with the rabbis of the shul to allow us female mourners our own parts in the service, too. As a result, it became standard practice at our minyan for the women mourners in the group to lead all the *Mi Sheberakh* blessings after the Torah reading (including blessings for the sick and for the soldiers of the Israeli Defense Forces), as well as the lovely *Yehi Ratzon* (Let It Be Your Will) blessings after the lifting of the Torah on Mondays and Thursdays—a wish list of good, salutary things, from Torah learning to health and freedom from plague (a detail that took on special salience during the pandemic), safety, freedom from captivity, and good news for us all. We had also negotiated for one of the women to recite, before the final Rabbis' Kaddish of the morning, the customary mishnaic statement: "Rabbi Ḥananyah ben Akashyah said: The Blessed Holy One wished to bring merit to the people of Israel and therefore abounded their Torah and mitzvot, as it is said, 'For the sake of righteousness, God desired to make the Torah great and glorious.'"[6]

This was no egalitarian arrangement, to be sure. For the women who were there, though, it was *something*: evidence of a readiness, however partial and tokenistic, to acknowledge us as mourners and committed members of the community, to keep us connected and included.

Mourning and Metaphor

In early September 2019, after settling my mother in her new apartment, I began giving a weekly Tuesday morning talk at the end of minyan, before the final Rabbis' Kaddish, devoted to reading and interpreting modern Hebrew poems and their relation to mourning, prayer, or other matters of the day. I dubbed this practice *Shir Ḥadash shel Yom* (New Song/Poem of the Day), a play on the *Shir shel Yom*, the psalm of the day recited every morning at the end of prayers, and it became a spiritual/pedagogical practice that continues to this day—a way of broadening the theological and liturgical bookshelf, seeking healing and defamiliarizing my prayer experience, bringing new awareness and content into what I was saying and doing, injecting poetry, women's voices, protest, and skepticism, too.[7]

This strategy of translating and interpretating modern Hebrew poetry as a response to grief was rooted in my transformative experience of being introduced to the history and marvel of Hebrew poetry during a two-day seminar on Hebrew poetry taught by Yehuda Amichai in the fall of 1986, when I was a college sophomore. One of Israel's most beloved and translated Hebrew poets, Amichai had earned international recognition unprecedented for a modern Hebrew poet for his colloquial everyday language, honest humor, inventive wordplays, and wry metaphors. At the time I had admirable Hebrew skills (my childhood Jewish day school had always prided itself on the excellence of its Hebrew education), but no sense of wonder about the resurrection of Hebrew as a spoken and modern literary language and the remarkable cultural accomplishment that is modern Hebrew literature. Amichai changed that.

For two days this remarkable poet and teacher led us on a textual expedition through the history of Hebrew poetry and some of the writings of his favorite poets, from Yehuda Halevi and Shelomo Ibn Gabirol to Avraham Shlonsky, Lea Goldberg, and Natan Zach. He sketched for us the development not only of modern Hebrew verse, but of his own poetic idiom too. Never before had a writer and teacher spoken so closely to my own literary heart: that part of me that deeply loved but occasionally felt alienated from my tradition; that adored the Hebrew language, but recognized the essential strangeness of trying to write about modern, everyday, even sordid reality in the language of the Bible, the rabbis, and the prayerbook.

Everything written about Judaism, Amichai explained, was obsessively time-stamped. In appearing to Abraham, God said: "I am God who brought you out of Ur of the Chaldeans" (Gen. 15:7). Again at Mount Sinai, God self-identified not as the Creator of the universe, but in more historically immediate terms: as the God who liberated the Israelites from bondage in Egypt. To the Jew, the past loomed ever-present, a dark shadow but also a source of hope for future redemption. Amichai identified this duality as fundamental to Hebrew poetry through the ages: the nostalgic yearning for past glories with the simultaneous hope for an entirely new song and Zion. A Jew didn't live in an isolated present, but endeavored to imagine past experience as if it were one's own. "As if," "as though," "like": these were the threads and knots of metaphor, simile, and poetry. All of Judaism, Amichai dared us to consider—its literature, liturgy, and commandments—was textured with this metaphorical weave.

From Amichai I got the first inkling and inspiration as to my future literary-academic path—one that would later propel me to undertake doctoral studies in comparative literature and to write a dissertation about immigrant Jewish women writers to the United States and Israel, including the first modern Hebrew women poets and prose writers. That path also led to my weekly Hebrew poem teachings at the Bayit, and eventually to this book.

In Amichai's trove of verse (see chapter 4 below) I saw a life and corpus shaped by a paradoxical yoking of idealized, nostalgic Judaism and familial connection with the darker or more comical realities of things as they really are. I saw childhood reminiscences about parents and their religious ways that were still lovingly remembered, even though by now the child had departed from those ways. I beheld images of God brought down to the very ground levels of everyday human life. I experienced the tension and the potential of living between past and present, hope and fulfillment, crisis and resolution, exultation and loss that is so characteristic of modern Israeli culture, writ large, and of the experience of mourning a loved one, writ small. In the stubborn individuality and idiosyncrasies of his perspective, I recognized the challenges of endeavoring to go out into the world authentically bound to others and to the past, and appreciated how Amichai's honest depiction of estrangement also disclosed an earnest desire to reconnect. Amichai showed me a remarkable array of alternative, modern pictures of grief and prayer, none of which were available in a traditional siddur and many of which became crucial resources for my Kaddish journey.

The (frequently) autobiographical character of Amichai's poetry, as well that of the other poets I chose in my weekly synagogue teachings, also seemed to mesh with the unique culture of my Bayit community, which offered all members who were commemorating yahrzeits, men and women alike, a platform to share their family memories after one of the services that day, before the final Rabbis' Kaddish. In this way, for example, I learned about the death of Hillel's father in a plane crash; about Ken's mother's experience escaping Vienna during the Shoah and her later efforts to speak to student audiences about her experiences; about the secrecy shrouding Joanie's father's illness and death, when she was only seven years old; and about Artie's mother's exhausted travails taking care of his sick father, ultimately leading to her own passing.

In this I was reminded of Leslie Jamison's description of AA meetings in her memoir, *The Recovering: Intoxication and Its Aftermath*. "What is a meeting?" she repeatedly asks and answers, trying to distill its particular and yet, in some sense, very generic magic. "It's just one life after another, an anthology held together by earnestness. . . . What's a meeting? It takes you from one life to another—easy as that, with a raised hand, no segue or apology necessary."[8]

One might easily offer a similar answer to the question "What is a prayer community?" In our traditional *tefillah* we prayed the standard liturgy, but were also making time at the end to listen to each other's unique stories. Strung together, these Kaddishes and stories, as well as the poems I came to teach in the form of the *Shir Ḥadash Shel Yom*, were also an "anthology held together by earnestness" that our community worked together daily to compile.

"Good morning," I would say at the beginning of each *Shir Ḥadash* talk. "It's Tuesday, and this week's poem is . . ." If someone had a Tuesday yahrzeit, the *Shir Ḥadash* would move to a Wednesday or Friday, prompting the preface: "This week we're turning Wednesday [or Friday] into Tuesday, and this week's poem is . . ." It mattered to me, even with rescheduling, to keep Tuesday in mind. Dad was suddenly killed on a Tuesday morning. His beloved older brother Isaac "Buck" Zierler, after whom I am named, was shot down over Germany on Tuesday, April 10, 1945, an event that forever changed my father's life trajectory. His mother, Lea Zierler, was killed by a car also on a Tuesday, an event that shattered a 550-day-string of no car fatalities in my father's hometown.[9] September 11 was also a Tuesday; I'd just moved back to New York from Hong Kong and had been commuting downtown to teach one of my first classes at HUC-JIR in New York when the first plane hit the World Trade Center.

There is something so utterly and terribly distinctive about the way Dad, his mother, his older brother, and the 9/11 victims each died—and yet, in the sweep of human history, something so tragically common and generic, too. In saying Kaddish, I did what Jews have done for generations in response to the death of close relatives: I recited several times a day a rhymed, rhythmic, ancient Aramaic poem that heaps praise upon God and makes no mention whatsoever of the faith-crushing fact of death. Kaddish is a stubborn, mantra-like, countercultural and anti-empirical assertion of an ideal world where God is blessed beyond measure and where abundant peace reigns. It is an ego-effacing, anonymous exercise of merging with a multigenerational chorus of praise.

The *Shir Ḥadash*, however, was allowing me to do something else, too—to add different, modern, largely unfamiliar voices to the chorus. It was giving me a chance to lament in my own eccentric register: to the specific, idiosyncratic tune of poetry.

Poetry's distinctive feature is metaphor: the consideration of one thing in relation to another, and the fashioning of new connections between them—what poet and psychologist Keith J. Hollyoak refers to as "a mysterious human capability that links thought and emotion with language."[10] The *Shir Ḥadash* was forging these links between Jewish thought and liturgy, between the language of poetry and the raw, evolving emotion of grief. And not just any language, but that of modern Hebrew verse. As it turned out, the *Shir Ḥadash*, with Amichai's poetry a major part thereof, also became the vehicle for recording and

550-Day Record Ends With Fatality

SARNIA—This city's 550-day traffic fatality free record ended early today when an elderly woman pedestrian was instantly killed when struck by a car on Davis St.

Police identified the victim as Mrs. Abraham Zierler, 70, of 233 Davis St.

The victim was crossing Davis St. at College at 1:30 a.m. when she was involved in an accident with a car driven by Michael George, also of Davis St. Police said the George vehicle was proceeding east at the time of the mishap.

It is believed Mrs. Zierler suffered head and internal injuries, and she was pronounced dead at the scene. Police are contiuing their investigation into the accident.

The fatal accident was the first in Sarnia in 550 days. Only last week the Canadian Safety Council said this was a record for a city the size of Sarnia. The last fatal accident was in September of 1958.

FIG. 4. *Windsor Star* article reporting on the death of my paternal grandmother, Lea Zierler, March 29, 1960. Material republished with the express permission of *Windsor Star*, a division of Postmedia Network Inc.

memorializing yet another personal loss, and thereafter, a seemingly unprecedented worldwide trauma.

Sewing a Seam

Kaddish mornings, afternoons, and evenings passed, one after the next. Autumn slid slowly, unremarkably, into winter. And then, on a Saturday morning in early December, on the way out to synagogue, my mother tripped on the stairs outside our house and broke her wrist, the first of a series of increasingly concerning events. She complained of pain and nausea. She developed a cough and more serious nausea, and then one Thursday afternoon began to vomit what looked like coffee grounds, which my physician friend Laura explained was a sign of internal bleeding. An ambulance rushed us to the hospital, where Mom was diagnosed with a bleeding ulcer. Almost as soon as that was resolved, she suddenly couldn't find her breath. For ten days she was on and off bi-pap oxygen in the ICU. Speaking became increasingly difficult. Doctors struggled to keep her oxygen and her blood pressure high enough to complete her dialysis treatments and remove fluid from her lungs. A specialized dialysis machine filtered her blood slowly, all day long, but even so, the doctors couldn't keep her blood pressure high enough to remove the excess fluid.

And then, finally, a breakthrough! The doctors managed to dialyze her as needed. During that successful Saturday night dialysis session, my minyan buddy, the incomparable Bayit prayer leader Dr. Elli Kranzler, led a *Havdalah* service (marking the end of Sabbath and the beginning of the week) at Allen Hospital and sang her through dialysis. Three days later, on the next Tuesday, I marked her resurrection by teaching Lea Goldberg's "*Nisayon*" ("Test"), with its giddy note of celebration: "*How can I bear and not break in the face of blessing like this, joy like this*?"[11]

Mom was moved later that day to a "step-down" room, and there was talk of moving her to a rehabilitation facility in preparation for her coming home. But then, the next morning, on my way out to morning minyan, I got a call from the hospital that Mom had experienced another breathing emergency, this time even more severe. Instead of continuing on to synagogue, I ran to the hospital, where a stark picture emerged, with a stubbornly leaky heart valve in the foreground. Most likely, if Mom ever left the hospital, she would be constantly dependent on bi-pap oxygen, an option she simply refused to entertain.

Everyone in our family can attest to Mom's lifelong difficulty making decisions. She agonized over whether to buy a dress or skirt or pair of shoes. "Do they look good? Will they match enough things?" Many times she would buy something only to return it the next day. Having grown up in a family that struggled financially, she didn't take any purchase or any decision lightly.

Three major decisions in her life, however, came surprisingly easily: (1) to marry Dad, at the absurdly young age of eighteen, (2) to move from Sarnia to Toronto to build a richer Jewish life, and (3) in the face of respiratory problems that stood in the way of her returning to anything resembling her normal life, to terminate dialysis and prepare to die.

As soon as my mother made the decision to transition to palliative care, my sister Randi and I moved into the hospital. For the next number of days, as long as it took, my mother—who often thought I was wearing myself out running back and forth to shul to say Kaddish—would get her way: for that week, someone else would say Kaddish in my stead.

Throughout that week, New York Presbyterian–Allen Hospital, Field West, Room 41, the nurses' station across from the room, and the couches down the hall defined the limits of our world. The first night we slept upright in chairs next to Mom's bed. The second night we transitioned to yoga mats on the floor, only to be awakened at midnight by a nurse, who'd located a cot the two of us could share and proceeded to set it up to the right of Mom's bed. Like little girls on a sleepover, Randi and I made ourselves small and tucked into the cot next to each other and next to Mom.

On daily visits, our spouses and kids brought us towels, toiletries, food, and other needed supplies. Every morning we washed and showered in the hospital bathroom. We ate meals and snacks and drank coffee and tea in Room 41. Our sister Sharon and brother Larry and other family members streamed in and out. Mom dispensed words of wisdom, including dating advice, to my kids and my niece. She made phone calls to each of her friends, telling them she loved and appreciated them. Some of her friends insisted on wishing her a complete and speedy healing, but patiently, insistently, she explained that there would be no such recovery. She spoke individually to each one of her children, our spouses, our kids. Often, she would drift off to sleep, but then suddenly, unexpectedly, as if not wanting to miss out, her eyes would pop open and she would ask "Where's Randi?" or say "Hi Mammaleh" (a pet name for both of us) or reflect, "So this is what it's like, to die." In the middle of the night she suddenly moaned, but when we rushed to her side she said, "It's okay, it's okay, don't worry, it's okay."

On Friday afternoon, three rabbis from the Bayit came to the hospital to sing Mom into Shabbat. She smiled, she sang, she floated in and out of consciousness.

On Sunday my childhood best friend Carol, a doctor who'd helped us many times with Mom's health emergencies, who spent hours with us at North York and Humber Hospitals, flew in from Toronto. All that day, the family gathered round. Lunch was delivered, then dinner. Mom had been sleeping quietly throughout, but her vital signs suggested she was still very much alive.

Come evening everyone left, except Randi and me. We made tea and we settled in for yet another night, but Mom's breathing began to rattle and rasp. We called the nurse to make sure she was comfortable. We settled back into our spots. And then, suddenly, another rasp: the color drained from Mom's face, and she was gone.

The phone calls began. Carol hurried back to the hospital. Joel Simon, the righteous funeral director from Riverside Memorial Chapel, led us as we accompanied Mom's body out of the hospital and into the vehicle that would transport her to the funeral home.

There could not be two more different deaths, those of Dad and Mom. Dad died in a violent instant, and alone. Mom died slowly, over the course of a month, and in the loving company of family and friends. And yet, both died too soon: Dad, while perfectly healthy, and Mom, a scant five months after settling into the new home my siblings and I had worked so hard to make for her.

Both of these deaths occurred in under eleven months. Mom's funeral the next morning was just five days before the conclusion of my eleven-month period of reciting Kaddish for Dad.

The five-day overlap between my two Kaddish periods felt like two pieces of fabric pressed together, enabling the sewing of a seam. Or like the baton pass in a relay race, where the next runner runs alongside the previous one to gain momentum and simultaneously receive the baton. But instead of a team relay, I was passing the baton to myself. And instead of a sprint, my event in high school track and field, this Kaddish run was a marathon, with several unexpected turns along the way.

A Kaddish/COVID Journal with Poems

March 2020. On the first day of the month we observed the first yahrzeit for Dad. By mid-month the novel coronavirus had engulfed New York, subsuming personal mourning in a communal crisis, and making hospital deaths like Mom's, surrounded by loved ones until the very end, entirely impossible.

In the wake of all this, my Kaddish observance and the weekly *Shir Ḥadash* became something else again.

Like so many others, Daniel and I began working from home. At the Bayit, morning services moved from the smaller *beit midrash* in the basement to the main sanctuary, allowing attendees to spread out widely. That particular week, a string of unexpected yahrzeits in the minyan led to deferring the *Shir Ḥadash*, first to Wednesday, then Thursday, then Friday. When Friday finally came, and it was my turn to teach that week's poem, I was reluctant to distribute the printed sheets with the text as usual, for fear of viral transmission. Instead, I posted the text to our new weekday *tefillah* WhatsApp group, one of many new features of our emerging COVID reality, and people followed along on their phones.

The text I had chosen to teach that morning, a departure from a few weeks of study of the poet Lea Goldberg, was "Hakhnisini Taḥat Kenafeikh" ("Take Me Under"), a 1905 poem by the early twentieth-century national poet laureate of Israel, Ḥayyim Naḥman Bialik (1873–1934):

Take me under your wing,
Be my mother and sister.
Let your bosom be a haven for my head,
A nest for my far-flung prayers.

And at that merciful twilight hour,
Bow down and I'll share my secret distress.
They say in the world there's youth—
Where's my youth?

And another secret I confess:
My soul has been seared by a flame.
They say there is love in the world—
What is love?

The stars deceived me.
There was a dream; it too has passed.
Now I have nothing at all in the world,
Nothing at all.

Take me under your wing,
Be my mother and a sister.
Let your bosom be a haven for my head
A nest for my far-flung prayers.[12]

A then thirty-two-year-old, disillusioned Bialik wrote this poem after the horrific 1903 Kishinev pogrom, which he covered as a journalist-poet. Now, in March 2020, the poet's yearning for familial and emotional shelter uncannily matched not only my experiences of familial loss, but also our community's collective fears and trepidation about the pandemic. The speaker asks to be taken in under a sheltering wing, like that of the *Shekhinah* (Divine Presence). He imagines this Presence as a refuge for his far-flung or abandoned prayers. He laments his departed youth ("Where's my youth?")—a line that brought to mind elderly people's vulnerability to COVID. Many nursing home residents had succumbed to this deadly disease.

Immediately after I taught the poem, the rabbi stood up and announced that our Bayit would be closing indefinitely because of COVID.

This would be the last in-person service in which I would be able to say Kaddish, or present a poem, for the foreseeable future. Our nest of prayers, as Bialik put it, was being emptied out and abandoned—an unimaginable occurrence to me then, given my many straight months of worshipping daily in that building.

Later that week, Zoom services began. Soon enough, the practice became second nature. The *Shir Ḥadash* tradition continued too, but now, instead of handouts, there was screen share, and a follow-up email, comprised of short interpretive essays, that over the course of weeks and months would coalesce into the heart of this book.

Like Kaddish recitation, the *Shir Ḥadash* project transformed and translated into a self-conscious effort to carry over private experience into public, shared spaces for constructive theological purposes. There is nothing lonelier or more personal than loss. The Kaddish ritual, woven into the fabric of communal prayer, nevertheless insists on stitching people together in their respective bereavements for the sake of retaining and refashioning a positive relation to God. Similarly, I hoped, the *Shir Ḥadash*, set in the context of a morning prayer service attended by many mourners, would both reinvigorate our collective prayer practice and make this poetry accessible and useful to my religious community.

Over the course of time, which included the loss of both my parents, the varied stages and faces of prayer life with COVID, the headline events of 2020, 2021, and 2022 (including the Black Lives Matter movement, the 2020 presidential election, the January 6 insurrection, and the attenuated public grip on Truth), and my mother-in-law Dvora's descent into Alzheimer's dementia all found expression in the poem selections and interpretations for the *Shir Ḥadash*. This thick tangle of seemingly unprecedented happenings would induce personal as well as shared communal reflection on what each of us was undergoing, and how contemporary liturgy and religious life and practice ought to register such experiences.

PART 2 Transitions and Translations

2 Picturing God in Grief and Prayer

Beginning to Mourn with Lea Goldberg

My dad, David Zierler, grew up in a small immigrant Jewish community in Western Ontario, where he experienced only a modicum of formal Jewish education and little positive peer pressure to pray. Somehow, though, he became a lifelong daily *davener* (prayer).

During the week he typically did his devotions at home. Every morning, he'd go downstairs to the den, take out his tallit (prayer shawl) and tefillin (phylacteries), sit in the old wooden rocking chair or stand by the patio window facing our backyard and the green park behind it to the east, and *daven*. For years he used the same old *Tikkun Meir* siddur (Hebrew prayer book), which he repaired over and over again using red duct tape. When that siddur became too tattered to fix anymore, he switched to an ArtScroll version, which he marked up in various places with cues as to where to chime in and where to stop, so he'd be ready if asked to lead services at shul. On Shabbat he went to services on Friday night, Saturday morning, and again on Saturday afternoon, faithfully attending all of the prescribed prayer services for the day.

I had many more Jewish educational advantages than my dad. From the time I was five years old, I was sent to a Jewish day school, and I had an extensive post-secondary school Jewish education, too. Still, when I was not in school or camp or some other organized Jewish framework, I had often flagged in my daily prayer discipline. During those first few months of saying Kaddish for Dad, however, I committed to be more like Dad, praying to connect to and continue his deeply established Jewish ways and habits.

Michelle Zauner writes in *Crying in H Mart* about crying by the freezer in the Korean H Mart grocery store, in the aftermath of her

Korean mother's death to cancer. I suppose I could have titled this book *Sobbing in Synagogue*, for that was what it was like, certainly during the first few months after his death. The more attentive I was to the words in the siddur, the more I experienced my mourning as acutely and painfully alive.

One morning, while saying the third blessing of the *'Amidah* with its praise of a God who "with great compassion revives the dead, supports the fallen, heals the sick," I started picturing my now dead dad. Precious, painful images. How, in recent years, because of arthritis in his fingers, he often asked me to help him button his shirt, zip his zipper, and buckle his seat belt. Yet, on the day of his tragic accident, no one had been there to protect him from his fall. God had not revived him from the dead, and now he was gone. "For there is no praise of You among the dead; in Sheol, who can acclaim You?" (Ps. 6:6), I read one Tuesday in the daily *Taḥanun* (post *'Amidah* supplications), and wept, my head on the table. And, on another random early morning, this thought punched like a blow to the head: *Kaddish Yatom* means "Orphan's Kaddish"; I am now an *orphan*.

When I was not praying, I was busy tending to my mother, Marion Zierler, and her adjustment to New York life, the ups and downs of her moods, and my own acclimation to this new proximity and responsibility. For twenty-five years my mother and I had lived in different countries. Now we were a block away from each other, with the day-to-day running of her life my new remit—all this while trying to keep up my teaching and research in the fields of Hebrew and Jewish literature.

The choice of poet Lea Goldberg (1911–1970) as the first poet of the *Shir Ḥadash shel Yom*, my in-shul poetry teaching, grew naturally from this new reality.

Decades earlier, as a graduate student in Hebrew and comparative literature, I had been attracted to Goldberg as a model of all that I aspired to be: a scholar, translator, editor, writer, and artist. I still remember that feeling of awe and rapture, during the first week of a Fulbright doctoral fellowship at the Hebrew University: going to the library to borrow a book of poems assigned for a course in modern Hebrew poetry and discovering an ex libris drawing by Goldberg herself, affixed to the

FIG. 5. Ex libris of Lea Goldberg. Courtesy of the Administrator of the Estate of Lea Goldberg and the Leah Goldberg Collection, The National Library of Israel.

inside cover—attesting that this volume had been part of Lea Goldberg's own personal library. My own reading would be melding with hers.

In the fall of 2019, however, there were specific points of biographical convergence that drew me specifically to Goldberg—beginning with the fact that Goldberg grew up in Kovno, Lithuania, which my husband, Daniel, and I had visited just that summer on a Jewish literary tour.

Goldberg had also lost her own father, Abraham Goldberg, under tragic circumstances, in her case, to mental illness. During World War I, the Kovno Jewish community was exiled to Russia on the specious accusation that the Jews were spying for the Germans. Upon the Goldberg family's return to Lithuania in October 1919, Lithuanian authorities at the Russian border arrested and imprisoned her father on similarly false charges of being a communist, and threatened him daily with execution. All this precipitated a lasting mental breakdown. For the rest of his days, Abraham Goldberg never truly reintegrated into the life of his family. When Lea and her mother Cilia (who divorced Abraham in 1931) immigrated to Mandatory Palestine, he stayed behind in Europe; the date of his death remains unknown.

All this was a serious blow to Lea Goldberg. As a young girl exiled with her family in Russia, she had been very close to her father, an insurance director and one of the founders of the Lithuanian Social Security Service. Among her favorite memories of him were the business trips he took her on, including a cruise along the Volga River. Their moments of father–daughter togetherness came to a cruel end as a result of his torture by the Lithuanians and his subsequent unremitting psychological challenges.[1]

Almost exactly a hundred years later, as I was mourning my own father's death, I found myself turning to Goldberg's poetry and to this story of loss. And not just that, but to her relationship with her mother, too. In the absence of her father, Goldberg developed an intensely close relationship with her mother, one of mutual admiration and total loyalty. Cilia recognized Lea's poetic and intellectual talent early on, and for good reason.[2] Goldberg began publishing Hebrew poems at age fifteen. Attending the universities of Kovno, Berlin, and Bonn, she received a PhD in Semitic languages in 1933 when she was only twenty-two.

In 1935, she moved to Palestine; the same year saw the publication of *Taba'ot 'Ashan* (*Smoke Rings*), her first book of poems. Goldberg's mother followed her to Palestine the following year, and from then on these two adult women lived together—first in Tel Aviv, where Goldberg served on the editorial staff of the newspapers *Davar* and then *Mishmar*, and from 1952 in Jerusalem, where she helped found the department of comparative literature at the Hebrew University (where I studied in 1991–92). In effect she lived with her mother almost her entire adult life. Considering her mother a barometer of good taste, she consistently shared her poetry and consulted with her about it—and also about clothing, furniture, and all things aesthetic.

With her mother's encouragement and support, Goldberg wrote (and edited) prolifically and was a dedicated professor. She composed plays and prose fiction, and translated works by Shakespeare, Petrarch, Ibsen, and Tolstoy. Nine books of poetry, six works of literary criticism, two novels, twenty children's books, and three plays of hers were published during her lifetime, and more works would be published posthumously. An accomplished visual artist as well, she illustrated several of her own works in addition to several ex libris bookplates.

This first *Shir Ḥadash* selection, a poem Goldberg wrote about her mother in 1933, while she was away at university, brought to my mind my own mother, whom I was now seeing every day, sometimes several times a day. While I did not share my writing or intellectual interests with Mom, who had left college in New York after one year to move to Sarnia, Ontario (Canada) and marry my furniture businessman father, the older I got, the more I came to respect her fierce intelligence and people smarts. Mom's taste, too, was impeccable: frugal in the way she spent money (sometimes painfully so), but always to exquisite effect. Her lovely, classy wardrobe accentuated her beautifully self-curled hair and her tall and striking stature. She had a big broad smile and an easy way with people. She walked fast, as if knowing there was no time in this life to waste. Perhaps she is the reason I became a sprinter on my high school track team? When I was growing up, my friends liked coming to our house—not just to visit with me, but also with my mother, who fed them delicious food and spent hours talking with them in the kitchen. To this day, when people in my Riverdale community remember Mom, they praise her style and slender beauty, her social gifts, and her wide-armed warmth.

In the midst of my Kaddish journey, I found myself thinking about Mom as well as Dad, wondering what it might mean to view the God approached in prayer not only as a Father, as is the traditional liturgical practice, but also as a Mother, like Goldberg's or my own.

Jewish feminist theologian Mara Benjamin looks at the experience of adults caring for young children as a "template for abstract theological and social attachments."[3] For me, Goldberg's poems provided a template to reflect on the theological experience of having my mother nearby, of caring for her as an adult and being cared for in return, and then losing her so much sooner than I expected. My siblings and I had gone to heroic lengths to bring our mother to New York. I myself spent weeks finding and setting up her apartment and arranging the many parts of her medical care, including her Access-a-Ride transportation to and from dialysis. I experienced a mix of exasperation and elation over having her so nearby: the impossible weight of her daily frustration-turned-fury with her dialysis regimen, and the dream-come-true of having a parent nearby who loved me and my children with such happy ferocity, who knew how to look at my kids (especially my eldest daughter) and see right into their hearts, and who always understood exactly what to say. Goldberg's relationship with her mother, showcased in the first poem I taught by her for the *Shir Ḥadash*, became an emotional touchstone.

Over the next five months, I presented a different poem by Goldberg every Tuesday morning, choosing as I went, depending on what seemed most relevant and necessary for both my community and me in any given week. Ten of these poems have made their way into this book.

The period in which they were presented coincided not just with my Kaddish observances for my father, and my mother's move to New York and her illness, but also her death and the beginning of the COVID lockdown that March. Some of the poems engaged the experience of that COVID spring—the way it, too, shook my sense of the natural order of things. Other poems and their analyses resonated with my teaching at the Hebrew Union College–Jewish Institute of Religion (HUC-JIR), as well as with my own rabbinical studies at the Yeshivat Maharat, as the textual explorations reimagined classical Jewish sources from a modern feminist point of view.

"To Mother's Portrait"

To Mother's Portrait	לִתְמוּנַת אִמָּא[4]
Your picture's so tranquil. You're other:	תְּמוּנָתֵךְ כֹּה שְׁלֵוָה. אַתְּ אַחֶרֶת:
A bit proud and confused you're—my mother.	קְצָת גֵּאָה וּנְבוּכָה עַל שֶׁאַתְּ—אִמִּי.
You guide with tear and conceding smile too	מְלַוָּה בְּדִמְעָה וּבְחִיּוּךְ מְוַתֶּרֶת
And never do you question, "Who?"	וּמֵעוֹלָם אֵינֵךְ שׁוֹאֶלֶת: "מִי"?
Never wondering, never raging, when I came	לֹא תָּמַהְתְּ, לֹא רָגַזְתְּ, עֵת בָּאתִי אֵלַיִךְ
To you saying, "Give!" Each day, the same,	מִדֵּי יוֹם בְּיוֹמוֹ וְאָמַרְתִּי: "תְּנִי"!
Bringing me all with your own hand	אֶת הַכֹּל הֵבֵאת לִי בְּמוֹ יָדַיִךְ
Just because I am—what I am.	רַק מִפְּנֵי שֶׁאֲנִי—אֲנִי.
And today better than I, you recall	וְיוֹתֵר מִמֶּנִּי אַתְּ הַיּוֹם זוֹכֶרֶת
My childhood sorrow, how your mind solved it all:	אֶת יְגוֹן־יַלְדוּתִי, וְנַפְשֵׁךְ כְּבָר פָּתְרָה:
When your grown-up daughter would come home	עֵת תָּבוֹא אֵלַיִךְ הַבַּת הַבּוֹגֶרֶת,
She'd bring sorrow's despair fully grown.	הִיא תָּבִיא אֶת יֵאוּשׁ תּוּגָתָהּ שֶׁבָּגְרָה.
Without greeting I came home shattered.	כֵּן. אָבוֹא רְצוּצָה וְלֹא אֶשְׁאַל לִשְׁלוֹמֵךְ
Without crying in your arms or whispering: "Mother!"	לֹא אֶבְכֶּה בְּחֵיקֵךְ, לֹא אֶלְחַשׁ: "אִמִּי"!
You'd know:	אַתְּ תֵּדְעִי:
He who left me was dearer to me than you,	זֶה שֶׁעֲזָבַנִי הָיָה לִי יָקָר מִמֵּךְ
Yet, you'd never ask me: "Who?"	וְלֹא תִּשְׁאָלִינִי: "מִי"?

The poet stares at a photograph of her mother and calls attention to the act of representation: that in picturing someone, we create and distill the image we ourselves have in mind.

Goldberg portrays a mother who is tranquil, contained, and yet Other. However perplexed by her daughter, she is empathetic and ready to concede for her daughter's sake, without violating boundaries and asking too many questions. Despite her awareness that her daughter cares more about her various lovers, gained and lost, than she does about her, and irrespective of her daughter's consistently thoughtless demands upon her, she gives unconditionally. She stands by her daugh-

FIG. 6. Portrait of Marion Zierler as a young girl.
Acrylic painting by Wendy Zierler.

ter in her times of pain, accepting it all in line with the old Yiddish adage: *Kleyne kinder, kleyninke tsures; groyse kinder, gresere tsures* (small children, small troubles; big children, big troubles).

All this evoked my images of my own mom: How when I was small, if I woke up in the middle of the night because of a bad dream and went to my parents' room, she'd hear me even before I made it to her bedside, immediately calling out, her eyes still closed, "What's wrong?" How when I was grown up and we spoke on the phone, she could automatically tell if I was bothered about something and would spend hours talking it through with me. How patiently she listened to me—much more patiently than I would listen to her, and anyone else, for that matter. Unlike the mother depicted in Lea Goldberg's poem, who never violates boundaries and never asks "Who," my mother always knew "Who," whether I told her or not. She always knew, well before I ever did, if a friend I had chosen or a boy I was dating was not to be trusted—an often-exasperating form of maternal omniscience.

My father's death altered this dynamic. More than ever before, Mom now looked to my siblings and me to care for her and fill a hole that no one could quite fill. Even then, though, if she saw me worrying about one of my kids, she'd say, "Leave it to me; I'll do the worrying for you." As long as she was there, I could come to her, shattered or whole, and she'd give me what she could.

What, then, if God were a mother? What would it mean to go to shul and address prayers and petitions to a divine Mother who is Other and transcendent, but also immanent and deeply present, even needy, like my own mother? What would it mean to laud and to beseech a Mother who cries over our tears and swells with pride over our accomplishments, who sits with us in our trials, and also manages to give us the latitude to err, lose, falter, grow, and mature? And what would it mean to honor with all of one's being a Mother who always allows us to "come home" to Her in all of our thoughtlessness and self-absorption, knowing full well that as flawed human beings, we are often more concerned with ourselves than with Her?

Every so often, during prayer, the feminine gender peeked out to me from the clefts of the *siddur*, such as in the second blessing of the

'Amidah prayer: ***Mi** khamokha ba'al gevurot u-mi domeh* ***lakh***, "Who is like You, Master of might, who is likened to You" (using the feminine form of the last Hebrew pronoun)?[5] What might it mean, then, if in reciting this line, we pictured an incomparable Mother (like Goldberg's, or mine), who knows us intimately, and yet never asked ***Mi***, allowing us to come before Her just as we are? What if in saying Kaddish we were to herald the great Name and Ultimate Peacemaker God—the *'oseh shalom*, as God is described in the concluding line of the Kaddish—picturing a Mom who somehow lovingly accepts our constant "gimme" and the asymmetry of our relationship, never looking at us strangely, or asking us, "Who?"

"By Three Things"

By Three Things	**עַל שְׁלֹשָׁה דְבָרִים**[6]
Said the fisherman going down to the sea:	אָמַר הַדַּיָּג הַיּוֹרֵד לַיָּם:
The world is sustained by objects three—	עַל שְׁלֹשָׁה דְבָרִים הָעוֹלָם קַיָּם—
By the waters of seas,	עַל מֵי־הַיַּמִּים,
By the banks of the shore,	עַל חוֹפֵי־הַיַּבֶּשֶׁת,
And by deep-sea fishes caught by the score.	וְעַל דְּגֵי הַמְּצוּלָה הָעוֹלִים בָּרֶשֶׁת.
Said the farmer pushing the plow:	אָמַר הָאִכָּר הַמּוֹבִיל מַחְרֵשָׁה:.
The world stands on three things right now—	עוֹמֵד הָעוֹלָם עַל דְּבָרִים שְׁלֹשָׁה—
On the soil of the fields,	עַל אַדְמַת הַשָּׂדוֹת,
On the rains of the sky,	עַל גִּשְׁמֵי שָׁמַיִם,
And on bread that's baked by the sweat of one's brow.	וְעַל לֶחֶם מוּצָא בְּזֵעַת־אַפַּיִם.
Said the artist in his solitary space:	אָמַר הָאָמָן בְּבֵיתוֹ הַבּוֹדֵד:
In these three things the world takes place—	עַל שְׁלֹשָׁה דְבָרִים הָעוֹלָם עוֹמֵד—
In the human heart,	עַל לִבּוֹ שֶׁל אָדָם,
In natural splendor,	עַל יְפִי הַטֶּבַע,
In expressing things in sound and color.	עַל בִּטּוּי הַדְּבָרִים בִּצְלִיל וָצֶבַע.
Said the human being, open-eyed:	אָמַר הָאָדָם הַפּוֹקֵחַ עֵינָיו:
The riches of this world, how wondrous and wide—	עָשְׁרוֹ שֶׁל עוֹלָם מַה נִּפְלָא וּמָה רַב—
Every morning	בֹּקֶר־בֹּקֶר
Caught in my heart like a net,	נִלְכַּד בְּלִבִּי כְּבָרֶשֶׁת,
Are the world and its fullness,	הָעוֹלָם וּמְלוֹאוֹ,
The shore and the depth,	הַמְּצוּלָה, הַיַּבֶּשֶׁת,
And light and shade,	וְאוֹרוֹת וּצְלָלִים
Holidays and weekdays,	וְחַגִּים וְחֻלִּין,
Terms and tones,	וּמִלִּים וּצְלִילִים
Fields of maize,	וּשְׂדוֹת־שִׁבֳּלִים
And the whole rainbow palette.	וְכָל צִבְעֵי הַקֶּשֶׁת.

All this picturing of the God in Kaddish and prayer got me thinking and reading about the requirement to say Kaddish in the presence of a minyan and the world of devotion it has sustained. As Orthodox rabbi Maurice Lamm writes in his popular guide to Jewish mourning, "[T]he recitation of Kaddish had united the generations in a vertical chain, father to son, while the requirement to gather a minyan has united Jews on a horizontal plane. Kaddish, miraculously, has brought together parents and children and also man and his neighbors."[7]

A moving picture, to be sure, but missing a crucial component: What about women, like me, who came morning and afternoon, day after day, to "unite [with] the generations"? What about the connections between father, mother, and *daughter*; and between *woman* and her neighbors? What chain has linked us vertically and horizontally and sustained *our* ties?

Lea Goldberg's children's poem "By These Three" met me in this line of questioning. If the tradition's *Pirkei 'Avot* (literally "chapters of the fathers") lays out an exclusively male chain of transmission from Moses to Joshua, to the elders, to the prophets, to the men of the Great Assembly, "By Three Things"—which comments upon two of the most famous *mishnayot* from the opening chapter of *Pirkei 'Avot*—provided the beginnings of a contemporary *Pirkei 'Imahot*, "chapters of the mothers," for my searching soul.

Chapter 1 of *Pirkei 'Avot* includes not one but two rabbinic statements on the three core principles that sustain the world. The first comes in the second *mishnah* of the chapter in the name of Shimon the Just, a High Priest during the Second Temple period and one of the last members of the Great Assembly, those scholars and leaders who presided in Jerusalem during the period between the biblical prophets (fifteenth through sixth centuries BCE) and the development of rabbinic Judaism (second century CE): "Says Shimon the Just: The world stands on three things—Torah, *'avodah* (service to God), and *gemilut ḥasadim* (deeds of lovingkindness)." Torah, the enterprise of Jewish study, links the legacy of Moses, as well as Ezra, the priest and scribe who recited the Torah of Moses before the entire people (Neh. 8) and founded the Great Assembly, of which Shimon the Just was a part. *'Avodah*, the cultic service of the Temple, was later repurposed by the rabbis as service of the heart—namely, prayer. The ethical practice of *gemilut ḥasadim*, doing good deeds (such as visiting the ill and consoling the bereaved), bridged the ethical concerns of the biblical prophets with those of the early rabbis.

For Shimon ben Gamliel, however, whose life coincided with the Jews' failed rebellion against the Romans and the traumatic destruction of the Second Temple, Shimon the Just's particularistic values-set appears to have been unsustainable. According to this second Shimon, as recorded in *Pirkei 'Avot* 1:18, the world exists (*kayam*) by dint of three very different, more universalistic principles: *din* (justice), *emet* (truth), and *shalom* (peace). That he was one of the ten rabbinic martyrs the Romans cruelly executed attests to the tragic absence in his world of the very universal values he deemed so crucial for Jewish and human continuity.

The two Shimons of this first chapter of *Pirkei 'Avot* thus set a traditional precedent both for defining and redefining core principles in times of major historical change. The creation of the State of Israel in 1948 was one such epochal transition, leading Lea Goldberg to compose not just her own version of the things that sustained the world but also to replace the rule of three, evocative of the biblical forefathers (Abraham, Isaac, and Jacob), with a principle of four (the fisherman, the farmer, the artist, the human), evocative of the biblical foremothers (Sarah, Rebecca, Leah, and Rachel). To this day, Goldberg's poem figures prominently in Israeli school curricula, as teachers encourage students to determine and defend their own core principles.

For the fisherman, farmer, and artist featured in the first three stanzas, the concept of *'avodah* is transformed from divine service to productive labor. For all three, in fact, one thing sustains their world: work. What is most important to them? Their occupations. We learn where and how their work takes place and what it yields. Goldberg's inclusion of the artist in this worker trio underscores her conviction about the crucial role of art and culture in the fledgling State of Israel.

So much, then, for study and religious devotion. Even ethical deeds are absent in the labor-centered value system of the first three stanzas.

The fourth stanza, longer and differently rhymed, shifts from specific laborers to *ha-'adam* (humankind), and it seems closer in tenor to Shimon ben Gamliel's more universalistic values-set—and yet, one finds in it traces of the previous stanzas, and hints of Shimon the Just's values, too. The fisherman, farmer, and artist work and live alone; the human being opens their eyes to a broader world. *Ha-'adam*, created in the image of God and designated (in Genesis 1:27) as both male and female, is caught in a net of interconnected human emotions and concerns. Goldberg's Adam/Human, like the farmer, refers to fields and their yield; and, like the artist, to light, shadow, sounds, and words—but additionally to God and prayer as service of the heart.

The description of *ha-'adam ha-pokeaḥ 'einav* (the human being who opens their eyes) brings to mind the daily morning blessing that praises God for opening the eyes of the blind (*pokeaḥ 'ivrim*), except here it is the human being who is doing the opening, not God. *Ha-'adam* expresses wonder over the vast beauty of the created world, "the earth . . . and all it holds" (Ps. 24:1). The reference to "holidays [and] weekdays" highlights the Jewish calendar, now renewed in the Jewish state. Finally, *ha-'adam*'s egalitarian recognition of the importance of all work, physical as well as spiritual, can be understood as a form of ethical awareness and lovingkindness.

Feminists have long taught the importance of appreciating the values of interconnectedness and attachment. For me, my time of grief was marked by a quest for connections, both across time and across the synagogue *meḥitzah* (the partition separating the men from the women). "By Three Things" modeled a new way of "uniting with the generations." I carried this with me, from then on, as I opened my own eyes before heading out to daily morning services. And I took pride in sharing this Torah of renewal and interconnection with fellow prayers and *Shir Ḥadash shel Yom* learners.

"In My Prayer Book"

In My Prayer Book	בְּסִדּוּר שֶׁלִּי[8]
Master of the world,	רִבּוֹנוֹ שֶׁל עוֹלָם,
If You force Your day on me like an inherited throne,	אִם כָּפִיתָ עָלַי אֶת יוֹמְךָ כְּמַלְכוּת,
And heavy on my shoulders is its gold,	וְכָבֵד עַל כְּתֵפַי זְהָבוֹ,
Then let it be my pardon, glory, and merit	וְהָיָה לִי סְלִיחָה וְתִפְאֶרֶת וּזְכוּת
When the last hour finally tolls—	בְּשָׁעָה אַחְרוֹנָה כִּי תָבוֹא—
Master of the world,	רִבּוֹנוֹ שֶׁל עוֹלָם,
If Your nights have become my footrest[9]	אִם הָיוּ לֵילוֹתֶיךָ הֲדוֹם־רַגְלַי
And their stars—dewdrops to slake my want,	וְכוֹכְבֵיהֶם—רְבִיבִים לְהַשְׁקִיט צִמְאוֹנִי,
Then plant a white moon at my behest	וְנָטַעְתָּ יָרֵחַ לָבָן בִּשְׁבִילַי
In the window of my poor dream haunt—	מוּל אֶשְׁנַב חֲלוֹמִי הֶעָנִי—
For I	וַאֲנִי
Never secreted my tears and woe,	דִּמְעָתִי לֹא שָׁמַרְתִּי בְּסוֹד,
Never knew a muted prayer,	לֹא יָדַעְתִּי תְּפִלּוֹת הָאִלְּמִים,
But my weary heart has fallen low	וְלִבִּי הַיָּגֵעַ נָמוֹךְ עַד מְאֹד
Amid the rising grain	בַּקָּמוֹת
And aftergrowth laid bare.	עִם סְפִיחֵי שִׁבֳּלִים.

After months of repeated prayers and Kaddish recitations, set against the experiences of longing and loss, I was easily drawn to "In My Prayer Book," the title of an earlier Goldberg poem—and to the idea, now percolating within me, of creating "my own prayer book." Were I to compile my own siddur, I wondered, what would I include? In putting together my own book of merits, pardons, longings, dreams, and things laid bare—some of the key words in the poem above—what would I add or omit? And what prayers would I myself want to invent?

"In My Prayer Book" begins with an allusion to a famous midrash (from BT Shabbat 88a) about the giving of the Torah at Sinai. In an attempt to understand the biblical description of the people standing *under* the mountain (Exod. 19:17), Rabbi Avdimi (Land of Israel, third-fourth centuries) depicts God as lifting up Mount Sinai, turning it upside down, and threatening to drop it onto the people underneath—that is, unless they acquiesce to accepting the Torah. In direct contrast to the commonly celebrated idea that the people eagerly volunteered to observe the Torah's dictates (Exod. 24:7), Rabbi Avdimi suggests that God threatened and forced (*kafah*) the Israelites into compliance.

Goldberg's prayer-poem turns this idea of divine coercion into a quid pro quo opportunity for covenantal mercy: If You, God, have forced (*kafita*) the glory of daylight onto me, then give me credit for doing my best to carry the heavy burden of that light. Similarly, if You have given me the rest and relief of nighttime, with stars to slake my longings, why not do me the additional favor of hanging a white moon in my window, lending a bit more illumination and inspiration to my (poor) dreams?

The poet's petition for help in managing the light of day and night spoke to me in my own need to make sense of what I was saying at synagogue, every morning and evening, during that time of grief. More than that: the off-set אני (*'ani*, "I") that opens the third stanza spoke to my need to find some way to pray not just in the first-person plural voice of the traditional siddur, but also in my own individual voice. The poet-speaker doesn't even attempt to hide or mute her tears. The after-growth of grain growing tall—symbolic perhaps of the world outside her own mind and heart—sharply contrasts with her sense that she is sinking ever lower, a feeling I often had while praying with others who seemed given over to everything they were saying, while I felt angry, distracted, or sad. Presumably, Goldberg's speaker is praying for God to notice this and lift her up.

I related. Getting up early every morning for services—the Hebrew word for "getting up," *lakum*, shares the same root as the noun *kamot*, "tall grain"—was a weighty and onerous task, its own form of being coerced into the light. Nighttime, when it finally rolled around, brought the welcome respite of sleep. Shouldn't those of us in the depths of mourning also be able to stand before God with openness and honesty about the abject sadness and emotional exhaustion we feel? Fate had dumped a mountain of sadness on top of me with the tragic death of my father, and now my mother was facing new, grave health challenges. *If all of this has been forced on me, God,* I prayed, *Let it be my pardon and merit. Loosen my nervous clutches. Straighten my back, open my heart, calm my head. And let me find a way to put all of this into this volume, my own, new prayer book,* which Goldberg's "In My Prayer Book" was coaxing me to fashion.

"Let Winter Be Blessed"

Let Winter Be Blessed	יְהִי הַחֹרֶף מְבֹרָךְ![10]
The air is clear and purely dressed,	הָאֲוִיר צָלוּל וְזַךְ,
White sky, its radiant best,	זֹהַר, לֹבֶן, שַׁחַק צַח,
Cool sun, snow soft, our guest.	שֶׁמֶשׁ קַר וְשֶׁלֶג רַךְ.
Let winter be blessed!	יְהִי הַחֹרֶף מְבֹרָךְ!
Didn't you just yesterday swear,	הַאֻמְנָם נִשְׁבַּעַתְּ אֶתְמוֹל,
That sorrow had struck everywhere,	שֶׁיָּגוֹן תָּקַף הַכֹּל,
That the heart had fallen ill	וְהַלֵּב הָיָה דַוָּי
You said it wasn't worth the bill?	וְאָמַרְתְּ כִּי לֹא כְּדַאי?
I don't remember and do not know.	לֹא אֵדַע, לֹא אֶזְכֹּר.
But to the past I shall not go	אֶל עָבָר לֹא אֶחְזוֹר
And today there's joy and glow.	וְהַיּוֹם חֶדְוָה וָאוֹר.
Boundless bliss, from high to low,[11]	גִּיל בְּלִי גְבוּל, בְּלִי מַעֲצוֹר,
And thus forgotten is the rest,	וְלָכֵן הַכֹּל נִשְׁכַּח,
The skies so see-through dressed,	הַשְּׁחָקִים שְׁקוּפִים כָּל כָּךְ,
Cool sun, soft snow, welcome guest—	שֶׁמֶשׁ קַר וְשֶׁלֶג רַךְ—
Let the winter be blessed.	יְהִי הַחֹרֶף מְבֹרָךְ.

January 2020. A tough winter's beginning for my family, colored by my mother's hospitalization and her prolonged stay in the ICU. From day to day, we felt unsure where her treatment was going. But every so often something happened that turned the winter mood around and ushered in new hope: an encouraging doctor's report, a heartwarming conversation, a sunny day.

So too, in this Lea Goldberg poem, where the conventional association of winter with darkness, gloom, and death is completely overturned. Goldberg heralds winter as a blessed, joyous time—a welcome guest, as underscored in my translation; a happy occasion and exhortation, like the morning and evening *Barekhu* call to blessing and prayer.

Goldberg blesses winter specifically for the opportunity it affords to white out the past and present a clean slate. Having written elsewhere about her nostalgia for the pine trees of her native Lithuania, here she celebrates European winter and puts a positive face on past sorrow.[12] To be sure, there's pain at the heart of this poem: in the second stanza, the reiterative AAAA rhyme scheme of the first stanza (the last syllables of the first four lines all rhyming with each other) temporarily gives way to a BBCC form, with lines 8 and 9 onomatopoetically rhyming with the *-ai* sound of pain. Isn't it true, the speaker asks herself there, that just yesterday, you succumbed to despair, and wondered whether it was even worth trying to persevere?

In the third stanza, however, she commits to putting all that out of mind, to covering over despair with winter snow, and reveling in the shining day. With that resolve, the initial rhyme scheme resumes, the final stanza reprising the *-aḥ* rhyme of the first stanza with its onomatopoeic sound of laughter: hahahah! *Nishka**ḥ**, ka**kh**, ra**kh**, Yehi ha-ḥoref mevora**kh***! Let the winter be blessed!

Sometimes happiness comes all on its own. Sometimes it needs to be conjured up magically. In this case, the conjuring happens in the alchemic mixture of poetry and prayer, itself a reminder of how both can transform us, if just for a morning or a brief moment.

“Blessing”

Blessing	**בְּרָכָה**[13]
Sun like this never shone again upon our heads,	שֶׁמֶשׁ גְּדוֹלָה שֶׁכָּזֹאת לֹא זָרְחָה עוֹד מֵעַל לְרָאשֵׁינוּ,
Seven bright days, seven days,	שִׁבְעָה יָמִים בְּהִירִים, שִׁבְעָה יָמִים,
Good tranquil sun upon our heads.	שֶׁמֶשׁ טוֹבָה וּשְׁלֵוָה מֵעַל לְרָאשֵׁינוּ,
We went our quiet way.	הָלַכְנוּ דְמוּמִים.
When great night comes and knocks on the door,[14]	לַיְלָה גָּדוֹל כִּי יָבוֹא וְדָפַק עַל הַדֶּלֶת,
We’ll bow and curtsey and bow.	נִשְׁתַּחֲוֶה וְנִקֹּד, וְנִשְׁתַּחֲוֶה.
Seven days it waited silently at the door,	שִׁבְעָה יָמִים חִכָּה דוּמָם מוּל הַדֶּלֶת,
Seven blazing days.	שִׁבְעָה יְמוֹת הַיְקוֹד.
Blessed is the Creator of blessing, blessed the Creator of joy,	בָּרוּךְ בּוֹרֵא הַבְּרָכָה, בָּרוּךְ בּוֹרֵא הָאֹשֶׁר,
Blessed is the Giver of hurt,	בָּרוּךְ נוֹתֵן הַמַּכְאוֹב,
We knew the hurt was good, and good was the joy	יָדַעְנוּ כִּי טוֹב הַכְּאֵב, יָדַעְנוּ כִּי טוֹב הָאֹשֶׁר
We knew it was good.	יָדַעְנוּ כִּי טוֹב.

My mother passed away on January 26, 2020. I got up from shivah on a Thursday, and the next Tuesday I taught this poem.

I’d spent two weeks burrowing in with family—the week with Mom in the hospital, and then the shivah week of retreating into the inside space of familial memory. After the close of shivah, seven days of solely indoor lighting, I stepped out the door to perform the post-shivah ritual walk around the block and face the sun.

All this came to life for me in “Blessing.”

The original publication date of the poem, June 22, 1945, sets it in the context of a larger global experience of reemergence into the light. That day marked the end of the battle of Okinawa on the Pacific front, the last major battle of World War II. Earlier that month, on June 5, the United States, the USSR, Britain, and France signed the Berlin Declaration confirming the legal dissolution of Nazi Germany. The entire world was thus finally coming out of the prolonged, harrowing darkness of the Second World War and squinting at a great, good sun, for the first time in close to six years.

Seven days. This motif evokes contradictory associations: the seven-day biblical Creation of the world, the seven blessings of the Jewish wedding ceremony (a new world for the married couple)—and also the first seven days of mourning after death, a world newly destroyed. The first stanza's depiction of seven days of good tranquil sun accords with Genesis 1 and all the positive associations with the number seven. But then, in the second stanza, the seven scorching days and the image of genuflecting before the coming of the great night point to the long night of death.

There is relief in death to those in pain and those who have to watch their loved ones suffer. In the case of Mom, death came quietly at night. We literally bowed before it, bending over Mom's bed to say goodbye, and then leaning into one another. More than any other poem I knew, "Blessing" reflected what our family experienced around Mom's deathbed and thereafter.

The final stanza, which blesses God as giver of pain and pronounces this pain good, echoes the mourning ritual of *Tzidduk Hadin* (Justifying the Divine Decree), derived from Job's resigned declaration: "God has given, and God has taken away; blessed be God's name" (Job 1:21). Of course, the book of Job doesn't extol his suffering or call it good. Rather, the poet ties together unlike things to bring something new to light. In death, days and nights get stitched together, just as the light of life ebbs into the darkness of death. Ideally, too, a Jewish family or community become stitched together through the experience of shared loss and pain. Togetherness in the aftermath of death is not happiness, but it is caring and meaningful, and in that sense, it is good—a sorely needed source of blessing.

From "One Spring"

One Spring

5

As of today, I don't know any prayers,
But that night
I imagined it might be possible to kneel down
On the floor of the room (how cold
a stone floor is under one's knees!)
And say this:
Magnified and sanctified is the Name of years
    That raised and brought me
    To this time.
Forgive me, Eternal God,
That I conceived only poems.
Pardon me, Eternal God,
That I had no loyal lapdog,
And that no human or animal
Ate fresh bread from my hands,
Absolve me, because that single one You sent
Never knocked on my door.
And I was righteous in all my sufferings.
And I shall forgive, pardon and absolve
You, Eternal God,
For I knew how to love with my soul
And my flesh, with all my 248 limbs,[16]
And I loved flesh as soul,
And bit the mezuzah of my closed door
As one bites the naked shoulder of a man.
I forgive You for all of it.
So perhaps, Master of all worlds,
You have one spring left for me
In the hidden trove of Your numerous springs,
A small, dry-hot spring.

אָבִיב אֶחָד[15]

ה

כַּיּוֹם אֵינִי יוֹדַעַת שׁוּם תְּפִלָּה,
אַךְ בְּאוֹתוֹ הַלַּיְלָה
דִּמִּיתִי כִּי אֶפְשָׁר אוּלַי לִכְרֹעַ
עַל הָרִצְפָּה בַּחֶדֶר (מַה קָּרָה,
רִצְפַּת הָאֶבֶן תַּחַת הַבִּרְכַּיִם!)
וְכַךְ לוֹמַר:
יִתְגַּדַּל וְיִתְקַדֵּשׁ שֵׁם הַשָּׁנִים
    שֶׁנְּשָׂאוּנִי וְהִגִּיעוּנִי
    עַד הַזְּמַן הַזֶּה.
סְלַח לִי, רִבּוֹנוֹ שֶׁל עוֹלָם,
כִּי לֹא הָרִיתִי אֶלָּא שִׁירִים.
מְחַל לִי, רִבּוֹנוֹ שֶׁל עוֹלָם,
כִּי לֹא הָיָה לִי כֶּלֶב נֶאֱמָן
וְשׁוּם אָדָם וְשׁוּם בְּהֵמָה
לֹא אָכְלוּ לֶחֶם רַעֲנָן מִיָּדַי.
כַּפֵּר לִי, כִּי לֹא דָּפַק עַל דַּלְתוֹתַי
הַהוּא הַיָּחִיד שֶׁשָּׁלַחְתָּ.
וְכִי צָדַקְתִּי בְּכָל יִסּוּרַי.
וַאֲנִי אֶסְלַח, אֶמְחַל וַאֲכַפֵּר
לְךָ, רִבּוֹנוֹ שֶׁל עוֹלָם,
כִּי יָדַעְתִּי אֱהֹב בְּנַפְשִׁי
וּבִבְשָׂרִי וּבְכָל רְמַ״ח אֵבָרַי,
וְכִי אָהַבְתִּי בָּשָׂר כֶּאֱהֹב נֶפֶשׁ,
וְכִי נָשַׁכְתִּי אֶת מְזוּזַת דַּלְתִּי הַסְּגוּרָה,
כִּנְשֹׁךְ כָּתֵף עֵירֻמָּה שֶׁל גֶּבֶר.
הַכֹּל אֶסְלַח לְךָ.
וְאוּלַי יֵשׁ לְךָ, רִבּוֹן עוֹלָמִים,
בְּגִנְזֵי אֲבִיבְךָ כִּי רַבּוּ
אָבִיב אֶחָד לְמַעֲנִי,
אָבִיב קָטָן וַחֲמְסִינִי.

Grant it to me as a keepsake	תְּנֵהוּ לִי לְמַזְכֶּרֶת,
For I am sung unto him.	הֲרֵי אֲנִי מְזֻמֶּרֶת לוֹ.
Perhaps You have—	אוּלַי יֵשׁ לְךָ—
Just one.	רַק אַחַת.

This fifth poem in a cycle titled "One Spring" was the first *Shir Ḥadash* I presented to my Bayit prayer community on Zoom—marking the pivotal moment when my private mourning melded with the communal trauma of COVID.

The poet begins by saying that in her current, disbelieving moment she knows nothing about prayer. When I presented this poem on March 16, 2020, on Zoom in response to the newly imposed COVID lockdown, our prayer community, too, knew nothing of how to pray together in the midst of a pandemic. In times BC—Before COVID—it had been entirely natural to pray in the physical presence of others, but now we could no longer gather safely in person.

In her state of "not knowing prayer," Goldberg nostalgically looks back at a time gone by when it seemed possible to kneel in prayer, even on a cold stone floor, and offer a version of the Kaddish, or of the *Sheheḥeyanu* blessing, which marks the advent or use of something festive or new. Her alterations of the traditional liturgy mark her own unnatural times. Goldberg's modified Kaddish and *Sheheḥeyanu* prayers invoke not the great Name of God, but the Name of Years, *she-nesa'uni ve-higi'uni*, that lifted *me* and brought *me* (not *us*, as in the traditional blessing) to this time.

Goldberg insists on speaking to God in the first person—not a common usage in the traditional prayer book—even as she employs the conventional epithet of *Ribbono shel 'olam*, "Master or the universe" (or "Eternal God," as I have translated here). That her modified Kaddish/*Sheheḥeyanu* prayer is also indented, set off from the rest of the poem, accentuates it as an exceptional personal utterance. We, too, in our Zoom *tefillah* were now all speaking to God in the first person, praying on our own, and yet also, somehow, together.

The poet seems to be taking stock of and apologizing for all that she has and hasn't accomplished in her work and personal life. Having never married or had children, she acknowledges with regret giving birth only to poems. Having lived a solitary life of words rather than of collective, agricultural labor, she begs forgiveness for not taking care of other living creatures.

As the poet-speaker attempts to atone for all this, she also points out God's own sins of omission. As it turns out, "the one" who God promised would knock on her door never actually appeared—an allusion to Song of Songs 5:2, where the Shulamite hears her beloved knocking on her door but gets out of bed too late to greet him; the poet, by contrast, doesn't even experience the knocking. No one comes a-wooing in springtime, and as such, she holds God to account. Nevertheless, she insists she has loved with all of her 248 limbs, a number associated in BT Makkot 23b with the number of positive commandments of the Torah. Thus Goldberg elevates love to the level of all the positive mitzvot, including the injunction to love God with all of one's heart, soul, and might (Deut. 6:5), as inscribed on the *mezuzot* affixed to one's doorposts.

Protestations of having loved notwithstanding, traces of frustration or of unrequited love linger between the lines. This sense is underscored by the speaker's recollection of biting (*nashakhti*) rather than kissing (*nashakti*) the mezuzah on the doorpost.

Goldberg's frustrated speaker thus entreats God for one little spring—a fitting theme for that first COVID week at the beginning of the spring of 2020. A *mezameret* (singer or poet), she petitions God for one little keepsake spring, because as a poet she is *mezumeret lo*, "sung unto" spring—a play on *mekudeshet lo*, the liturgical phrase used to mark a woman as sanctified to her husband in marriage. She needs the one God to grant her that one little spring, so that she can write its poetry and sing its praises.

Like Goldberg, we, too, wanted a warm, keepsake 2020 spring, one that would allow each of us to be sung into, and receive some sense of providential protection. "One Spring" became an opportunity to mark this need and moment.

From "My Silences"

My Silences	**דְּמָמוֹת שֶׁלִּי**[17]
2	ב
The ripened silence within me stands	הַדְּמָמָה שֶׁבָּשְׁלָה בִּי, עַל סַף נִשְׁמָתִי
At my soul's doorstep, like a tree full of fruit.	כְּאִילָן כְּבַד־פֵּרוֹת הִיא נִצֶּבֶת.
She has folded my life and death in her hands.[18]	הִיא קִפְּלָה בְּתוֹכָהּ אֶת חַיַּי וּמוֹתִי
Upon my grave she'll mount a tribute.	עַל קִבְרִי הִיא תִּהְיֶה מַצֶּבֶת.
My prayers are to her alone, every letter and jot.	תְּפִילּוֹתַי רַק אֵלֶיהָ—כָּל תָּג וְכָל אוֹת,
I've summoned her—for she's a delight.[19]	קְרָאתִיהָ אֵלַי—כִּי טוֹבָה הִיא.
And she's with me simply, on this spot,	וְהִנֵּה הִיא אִתִּי: בְּפַשְׁטוּת שֶׁכָּזֹאת
Like a home-lit lamp at night.	כְּמוֹ אוֹר שֶׁהֻדְלַק בַּבַּיִת.
That kind wind touching my face—	זֶה הָרוּחַ הַטּוֹב שֶׁנָּגַע בְּפָנַי—
What's it making me forget?	מַה הוּא בָּא, מַה הוּא בָּא לְהַשְׁכִּיחַ?
In the silence, God, it's but Your psalm's trace,	בִּדְמָמָה הוּא רַק הֵד מִזְמוֹרְךָ, אֲדוֹנָי,
Detached from heavenly depths.	שֶׁנִּפְרַד מֵעָמְקוֹ שֶׁל רָקִיעַ.

Death is a long silence. And COVID had moved all of our lives to an almost intolerably quieter place. This next *Shir Ḥadash*, Goldberg's "My Silences," afforded me the chance to consider silence as a feature of poetry and prayer, especially in the strange new prayer format of Zoom.

The poem builds on God's revelation to the prophet Elijah in 1 Kings 19. After killing all the prophets of Ba'al in the previous chapter, Elijah has fled angry King Ahab and Queen Jezebel to the desert, consigning himself (suicidally) to death on account of their failure to heed his prophetic message, though God repeatedly sends angels to feed and sustain him. After forty days and forty nights in the desert (evocative of Moses's sojourn atop Mount Sinai), God's word comes to Elijah at Horeb, asking him, "Why are you here, Elijah?" Elijah answers: "I am moved by zeal for the ETERNAL, the God of Hosts, for the Israelites have forsaken Your covenant, torn down Your altars, and put Your prophets to the sword. I alone am left, and they are out to take my life" (19:10). God responds to Elijah's declaration of zeal by exposing him first to a dramatic wind (*ruaḥ*), then to an earthquake (*ra'ash*), and finally to a fire (*'esh*), but contends that the Divine resides in none of these. Then comes a *kol demamah dakah*, a still small voice, suggesting that God is best found not in clamorous, noisy phenomena or loud, dramatic behavior but rather in calm small silences.

In exposing Elijah to the "still small voice" God aims to precipitate a change in Elijah, one that might allow him to adopt a subtler, quieter, less zealous approach to leadership. Fire-and-brimstone Elijah fails, however, to learn the lesson. After exposing Elijah to the "still small voice" God asks Elijah once again, "Why are you here, Elijah?" As if impervious to the very ideas of silence and change, Elijah answers exactly as he had before: "I am moved by zeal for the ETERNAL, the God of Hosts; for the Israelites have forsaken Your covenant, torn down Your altars, and have put Your prophets to the sword. I alone am left, and they are out to take my life" (19:14). Despite divine schooling, Elijah cannot see the spiritual value of quiet.

By contrast, Goldberg presents silence as a ripe fruit and a powerful, personified force that guards and stores the very essence of the poet's life. Silence is an affirmative presence, akin to the white space surrounding a poem on a page, or moments of unguided prayer left for each of us to fill or leave blank as needed—so much so that in the second stanza, the poet-speaker asserts that all of her prayers, every letter and jot, are directed toward this personified, feminine, beneficent silence. Silence is as easy and straightforward as turning on a light at home. Unlike words that have to be chosen carefully, silence is godly simplicity.

The last stanza shifts, however, to something far less simple. A wind touches the speaker's lips, and she wonders what this wind wants to make her forget—an allusion to the talmudic legend that every Jew learns the entire Torah as a fetus in the womb, but upon birth an angel touches of us on the lips and makes us forget.[20] In this context, forgetting stands for the loss of prior, foundational knowledge, something precious previously given but then taken away.

The wind or spirit touching the poet's lips also suggests inspirational *ruaḥ*. However we ourselves may understand this (prophecy? religion? theological yearnings? . . .), the poet insists it's but an echo of the real thing, namely, the quiet of God. To be touched by that spirit is thus to sit at the very nexus of divinely inspired creativity and inherent human limitation.

Reading Goldberg's poetic tribute to silence during those early days of COVID proved to be a challenge and a provocation. COVID felt unbearably quiet—formerly busy streets now empty and still, mourners sitting shivah alone at home without the din and envelopment of supporting visitors. None of this conjured up God's still small voice, only emptiness and lack. Our prayer community wondered aloud about God's role in the world—how, after biblical postdiluvian promises, God could allow this plague—and not just this one, but so many other plagues in human history. Then, and now, divine silence seemed at best a signal of absence, and at worst, of assent. *Shetikah ke-hoda'ah*, the rabbis instruct: Silence constitutes admission, even acceptance.[21]

And yet, Psalm 65:2 teaches: "For You, praise is silence." In his *Guide of the Perplexed* Maimonides adduces this verse to explain the idea of apprehending God through negation:

> We are dazzled by [God's] beauty, and [God] is hidden to us because of the intensity with which [God] becomes manifest, just as the sun is hidden to eyes that are too weak to apprehend it. . . . The most apt phrase concerning this is the dictum occurring in Psalms: "For You, praise is silence," which interpreted signifies: silence with regard to You is praise.[22]

With this in mind, I asked my Zoom *tefillah*-mates to consider the choreography of the *'Amidah* in a normal communal prayer context—the interplay of the silent *'Amidah* with the responsive chanting of the *Kedushah*, congregants calling out together "Holy, holy, holy, God of Hosts!" And the combination of "mute" and "unmute" on Zoom—the times when people's lips may have been moving, but no actual voices could be heard, or perhaps we heard only one voice against the background of respectful silence, which had been so hard to achieve back when we were all together chatting in the synagogue pews. And poetry, with its meter and rhyme, its careful measurement of sounds, silences, and white spaces around the words, all meant to inspire and reach that which exists beyond words. Marshaled properly, I suggested, silence allows us to hear better and learn. It teaches us humility: that we don't always have the right words at our disposal. Silence guides us to sit with other people in their grief without easy consolations. And it also opens us to imagine, optimistically, something beyond what we ourselves are experiencing, something fuller and truer than the troubling sounds of our own times.

"Night Psalm"

Night Psalm	מִזְמוֹר לַיְלָה[23]
He hid away every star,	אֶת כָּל הַכּוֹכָבִים טָמַן,
Wrapped the crescent moon in night[24]	אֶת הַסַּהַר עָטַף בִּשְׁחוֹר,
Due North to Yemen far[25]	מִצָּפוֹן וְעַד תֵּימָן
No ray of light.	אֵין קֶרֶן אוֹר.
And the morning's a mourning spouse	וְהַבֹּקֶר אַלְמָן נֶאֱמָן
Gray sack to his waist tied tight	שַׂק אָפֹר עַל מָתְנָיו יַחְגֹּר,
Due North to Yemen South	מִצָּפוֹן וְעַד תֵּימָן
No ray of light.	אֵין קֶרֶן אוֹר.
In the black tent of my soul[26]	הַדְלִיקָה־נָּא נֵר לָבָן
Kindle a candle white	בְּאֹהֶל־לִבִּי הַשָּׁחֹר,
From North to South Pole	מִצָּפוֹן וְעַד תֵּימָן
Shine forth the light.	יִזְרַח הָאוֹר.

I had lost both my parents in under eleven months. After Dad's tragic passing, I'd undertaken the heroic task of moving Mom to New York, only for all that work to be undone five months later by her illness and death. Within weeks of her death, that personal experience of loss was subsumed and eclipsed by COVID, a shocking new communal reality. There were days when it all seemed too much, when my outlook turned wholly dark. "Night Song" helped me acknowledge that gloom and envision a transition into some form of light.

Our liturgy prescribes daily psalms (*Shir shel Yom*) but no nightly ones. Goldberg's poem thus expands the daily psalm tradition to nighttime—and not just literal night, but also those emotionally dark times, when we find ourselves groping for hope.

Personification and conflict in the poem emphasize these ideas. The speaker's emotional experience is pitted against the doings of someone else. Who is the "He" who "hid away every star, / Wrapped the crescent moon in night"? "Night" is a masculine noun in Hebrew. So is the "He" a personified night? Or a masculinely personified God? In consonance with the lack of illumination and object definition in the poem, Goldberg keeps this ambiguous.

"Due North to Yemen (South)" comprises a merism, the invocation of polar opposites as a way of capturing everything in between and establishing a sense of total eclipse. The Hebrew direction markers, *tzafon* (north) and *teiman* (south), also play on the words *tzafun* (hidden) and *taman* (hid), further underscoring the blackness. The poet (as stand-in for all of us) seems mired in this darkness.

Indeed, the second stanza portrays the all-enveloping darkness not just of night but also of day. *Veha-boker 'alman ne'eman*, "morning is a faithful widower"—or, as I have translated it here, to preserve the wordplay and rhyme: "And morning is a mourning spouse." As if lamenting a spouse, the widower-morning wears gray sackcloth, an embodiment of pre-dawn gloom. *'Alman ne'eman* also calls to mind the liturgical phrase *'El melekh ne'eman* (God is a faithful king), which precedes the traditional recitation of the morning and evening *Shema'* when one prays alone—reinforcing a sense of a world widowed both of light and a faithful divine presence. Day and night meld indistinctly. Darkness extends everywhere, always.

But then the poem turns from description to command: "In the black tent of my soul / Kindle a candle white." The use of the term *'ohel libi*, "the tent of my heart," calls to mind the biblical tent of meeting, a revelatory site where God gave commandments through Moses to the people Israel. The elevated, cohortative grammatical form of *hadlikah*, expressing a wish, request, or a form of self-encouragement, keeps the object and gender of the one being commanded unclear. Is it God? The grammatically androgynous sun, given that in Hebrew the word *shemesh* (sun) is gendered both masculine and feminine? The poet herself? Or the poem? Or, as in merism—all of the above? How the poet desperately desires to turn toward a hopeful light *somewhere* and transition to *something* other than overarching pessimism!

On many occasions before the COVID outbreak, I had walked to synagogue for morning prayers when it was still dark out, only to see day break through the window during the middle of prayers. Now, of course, I was not walking to synagogue. Instead, early in the morning I was logging on to Zoom at my kitchen table, the windows in this room still wrapped in black. And I taught "Night Psalm" to my community as a prayer for some new light in this impossibly dark time for us all.

He Passed Over Our Door and There Was Light	עַל דַּלְתֵּינוּ פָּסַח וַיְהִי אוֹר[27]
He passed over our door and there was light,	עַל דַּלְתֵּינוּ פָּסַח וַיְהִי אוֹר,
And the door opened wide.	וּפְתוּחָה לִרְוָחָה הַדֶּלֶת.
Don’t turn your head, don’t glance behind,	אַל תַּחֲזִיר אֶת רֹאשְׁךָ, אַל תַּשְׁקִיף לְאָחוֹר,
Learn, learn to see the blue outside.[28]	לְמַה, לְמַד מֵחָדָשׁ לְהַבִּיט אֶל הַתְּכֵלֶת.
Learn, learn anew to smell, feel, and peer,	לְמַה, לְמַד מֵחָדָשׁ לְהָרִיחַ, לָחוּשׁ וְלִרְאוֹת,
(Behold the sun is dipping her rays in the deep,)	(הִנֵּה הַשֶּׁמֶשׁ בַּיָּם אֶת קַרְנֶיהָ טוֹבֶלֶת,)
In your eyes, even now, are untainted tears,	בְּעֵינֶיךָ עֲדַיִן דְּמָעוֹת טְהוֹרוֹת,
So long as you’re young, you’ll easily weep.[29]	עוֹד יִרְוַח בִּכְיְךָ, עוֹדְךָ יֶלֶד.
At night I knew they’d return, they’d return one and all,	בַּלֵּילוֹת הֵם יָשׁוּבוּ, יָדַעְתִּי, יָשׁוּבוּ כֻּלָּם,
In the dream they’d strangle, vilify,	יַחַנְקוּ בַּחֲלוֹם, יְדַבְּרוּ בָּנוּ דֹּפִי,
And you’d lie down wide-eyed, attentive to their call:	וְתִשְׁכַּב בְּעֵינַיִם קְרוּעוֹת וְתַקְשִׁיב לְקוֹלָם:
“Blood darkness, blood darkness, pass by!”	״חֲשֵׁכָה שֶׁל דָּמִים, חֲשֵׁכָה שֶׁל דָּמִים, חֲלֹפִי!״
Learn, learn anew to distinguish night from day—	לְמַה, לְמַד מֵחָדָשׁ לְהַבְדִּיל בֵּין לַיְלָה וְיוֹם—
(Here grinning girls return home from school,)	(הִנֵּה יְלָדוֹת שׂוֹחֲקוֹת מִבֵּית סֵפֶר חוֹזְרוֹת לְבֵיתָן)
Hatred hasn’t been weaned, you haven’t loved your full,[30]	עוֹד לֹא גָּמְלָה הַשִּׂנְאָה, עוֹד לֹא אָהַבְתָּ עַד תֹּם,
You’re still a child at play.	עוֹדְךָ נַעַר קָטָן.

More New Yorkers died in April 2020 than in any other month during the entire pandemic.[31] Against this grim backdrop, and with my first Passover without my mother and second without my father around the corner, I taught Lea Goldberg's "He Passed Over Our Door and There Was Light," with its intimations of a providential "Passover."

The "He" who "passes over" the open door of the speaker's home is unspecified. Goldberg's Lithuanian background and her years studying in Germany in the early 1930s seem to point to the Nazi threat, which Goldberg and her mother managed to escape by immigrating to Palestine in the nick of time, in 1935 and 1936, respectively. The poem can thus be seen to engage the question of survivor guilt. How does one look ahead and forge ahead, knowing that so many others stayed put, and thus perished?

The words "and there was light" in the very first line recall the earliest moments of the Creation story in Genesis 1, and seem to beckon the speaker, who has somehow eluded the menacing "He," to embrace this new world. Line 3's admonition not to look back recalls God's warning to Lot's family (in Genesis 19): Flee Sodom and don't look back. Both biblical references indicate the need to press on at all costs, without misgiving, keeping one's eye on the future, as symbolized by the blue (*tekhelet*) skies overhead.

And yet the Bible also commands us to look at the blue (*tekhelet*) thread of the *tzitzit* (fringes on a prayer shawl) in order to remember the past—the Exodus from Egypt, the covenant at Sinai—and remain faithful to God. Likewise, the repeated order to "Learn, learn anew" is reminiscent of the Passover Haggadah's command to "Go out and learn what Laban the Aramean attempted to do to our forefathers." Our tradition urges us to face the future by turning to the past. The poet is thus caught between two seemingly antithetical imperatives.

In the second stanza, the speaker reasserts a here-and-now approach, which proves exceedingly difficult. At night the past haunts her in technicolor: images of people being suffocated—victims of Hitler's gas chambers?—and figures who berate her, possibly for leaving them behind and surviving somewhere else. Night descends as bloody darkness, like the biblical plagues of blood and darkness.

In the fourth stanza, the process of reeducation resumes, as the speaker struggles to separate blood-dark night from day. The daily evening *Ma'ariv* liturgy speaks of God as separating day from night. The reordering here, with night preceding day, evokes how night weighs down her psyche.

In April 2020, the parallels between the poem and our COVID experience seemed at once obvious and elusive. We, too, were hovering in a liminal space. If we were lucky enough to have avoided contagion and were now sheltering in place, COVID, too, had "passed over our door." I thought often of Mom, and even wrote her a letter in my journal, asking her (as if she could respond): "Did you know? Did you know this was coming, and therefore that late January 2020 was the right time to die? Is that where your decisiveness about discontinuing dialysis came from—some preternatural knowledge that if you had stayed alive a little longer, you wouldn't have died with all of us around you, but on a ventilator, all alone?"

My mother had died but had been spared the experience of COVID. The rest of my family and I had made it thus far into the pandemic, but the COVID angel of death was still lurking outside our doors, threatening future harm, while a dark cloud of guilt hovered, knowing that others were suffering or placing themselves in harm's way to serve, help, and heal.

Unlike the Passover story, we could not view our present-day plague as a form of divine punishment. COVID was striking with no regard for nation, religion, ethnicity, or ethics. But we were learning and doing whatever we could to bring some meaningful community solidarity to our COVID lives. Every night at 7:00 p.m., we went out onto our porches and balconies to clap, hoot, and clang out our gratitude to the frontline medical staff and essential workers who were increasing the likelihood that infection would continue to pass over our homes, enabling us to train our gaze onto the future.

From “Ending”

Ending

1

I saw a leaf at night with my eyes sealed.
Just a leaf—and I knew it was good.
And the rivers go to the sea and the sea
is never filled,
And thus, I knew it was good.

Somewhere on the graves of my dead,
soft grasses frilled
Soft green grass, fresh and wet.
And their blood flowed to the sea and
the sea isn’t filled,
My God, Grower of tree and leaf,
Creator of worlds,
My God, is it indeed good?

סִיּוּם[32]

א

בַּלֵּילוֹת בְּעָצְמִי אֶת עֵינַי רָאִיתִי עָלֶה.
רַק עָלֶה—וְיָדַעְתִּי כִּי טוֹב.
הַנְּהָרוֹת הוֹלְכִים אֶל הַיָּם וְהַיָּם אֵינֶנּוּ מָלֵא,
וְלָכֵן יָדַעְתִּי כִּי טוֹב.

אֵי בָּזֶה עַל קִבְרֵי מֵתַי דֶּשֶׁא רַךְ עוֹלֶה
דֶּשֶׁא רַךְ וְיָרֹק רַעֲנָן וְרָטֹב.
וְדָמָם זָרַם אֶל הַיָּם וְהַיָּם אֵינֶנּוּ מָלֵא,
אֱלֹהֵי הַבּוֹרֵא עוֹלָמוֹת, הַמַּצְמִיחַ אִילָן וְעָלֶה,
אֱלֹהַי, הַאֻמְנָם זֶה טוֹב?

It was the season of *siyyumim*, the Hebrew term for graduations. HUC-JIR, where I teach, had just ordained a new class of rabbis, cantors, and educators; our middle daughter, Yona, had graduated from Washington University in St. Louis; and the most recent class at Yeshivat Maharat, where I was studying for rabbinic ordination, had been ordained, too. All of these long-awaited ceremonies, however, took place not in person, but online. It was a season of irregular celebrations, of culminations that weren’t quite complete. Lea Goldberg’s “Siyyum”—originally published in the socialist Hebrew women’s paper *Davar Po‘elet* on 4 Iyar / May 13, 1948, the day before the declaration of the establishment of the State of Israel, and in the midst of the Israeli War of Independence—matched the mixed mood of these 2020 graduations.

In the first stanza, the speaker describes a vision reminiscent of nighttime prophecies from the Bible: She sees an *‘aleh*, which can be translated either as “leaf” or “piece of paper.” Goldberg appears to mobilize both possible meanings. If one reads *‘aleh* as a tree leaf, then this vision, together with the repeated phrase "and I knew it was good," conjures up the biblical Creation story, in which God deems each stage of Creation good but then complicates matters by placing the Tree of the Knowledge of Good and Evil in the midst of the Garden.[33] The phrase "I knew it was good" also recalls one of many moments in Ecclesiastes where the speaker, butting up against the seeming pointlessness of life, nonetheless attempts to offer guidance on how best to live: "Thus I realized that the only worthwhile thing there is for them is to enjoy themselves and do what is good in their lifetime" (3:12).

If, however, *'aleh* points to a piece of paper, or to writing on a page, then the poem seems to address the idea of seeing the world through a poet's eyes. Perhaps goodness comes from a sense of endless creative and interpretive possibility, the sea of poetry always refilling and replenishing. That's one way to read the verse, "All streams flow into the sea, yet the sea is never full" (Eccl. 1:7)—a view of the sea as half full, rather than half empty.

The second, longer stanza satirically undermines this sense of goodness by invoking the graves of "her dead" and the flow of blood, not water, into the sea. As long as one lives, there is always more to accomplish—all good. But running alongside that is a bleak counter-reality: The sea of life never fills, because life is too short. And, as the poet suggests, war consumes so many lives before their time. A veritable river courses through the heart of life on earth.

My Kaddish recitation was a thrice-daily reminder of this, concomitant with questions raised by the poem. If the world God created includes vegetation that grows and flourishes on the fertilized soil-bed of death, is this good? Is it possible to reconcile this image with that of God as cultivator of redemption?

All of these questions are intensified in light of the publication date and Zionist context of the poem, as underscored by its repeated play on the relationship between the word *'aleh* (leaf/page) and the Hebrew verb *la'alot* (meaning "to rise, ascend," or in Zionist parlance "to immigrate to the Land of Israel"). This wordplay, highlighted in the Hebrew text above, resonated within me in the particular context of an alternative, secular kibbutz version of Kaddish composed by Oved

Sadeh (1925–2008), one of the founders of Kibbutz Keshet. Both texts contain the same play on the verbal root *ʿayin-lamed-dalet*: "Magnified and sanctified / Be the clod of earth / That falls apart / In the plow's segmenting / Hard earth. / **Elevated be the leaf** [*yitʿaleh he-ʿaleh*] / That sprouted and turned green, reddened—and fell off."[34]

This alternative secular Kaddish, which calls for the exaltation (*yitʿaleh*) of a plant leaf (*he-ʿaleh*), reminds us that like Goldberg, this now-departed agricultural worker might very well have made *ʿaliyah* to help build the Jewish state. If Goldberg's *ʿaleh* can be understood as celebrating the Zionist agriculturalist project of *ʿaliyah*, the violence and death accompanying the state from its inception have surely undercut the celebration. How can all this be deemed good?

Despite Goldberg's title, "*Siyyum*" ("Ending"), she ends the work with a question mark, with everything open, unresolved.

I shared "Ending" as part of the *Shir Ḥadash* in late May 2020, four months after my mother's funeral. Soft young grasses were growing over the new graves of those who had died from COVID. Graduates, including my own daughter, were entering a dark, uncertain world, eager to make their contributions but uncertain if their own seas of opportunity would be half full or half empty. Reflecting on the final words of the poem ("My God, is it indeed good?") offered us a chance to pray that even if things were not yet good in the ways we always hoped, they would somehow get better, before too long.

3 Facing an Absent God

Grief and God Struggle in the Poetry of Avraham Ḥalfi

It was six months after my mother died before I realized that aside from the first seven days, I hadn't had a proper chance to mourn her passing. After the shivah, there had simply been too much *to do*. First came the task of packing up and cleaning out Mom's apartment. After all the previous packing and unpacking to move her from Toronto to New York City over the summer of 2019, here we were again: armed with boxes, bubble wrap, and packing tape, boxing up or bagging her belongings—this time distributing them among the children and grandchildren, or giving them away to the local thrift shop.

There is a certain painful poignancy to doling out and disposing of a loved one's precious things, carefully chosen and amassed over a lifetime. There was nothing but frustration and anger, however, in the various bureaucratic tasks and reams of paperwork attached to settling Mom's estate. There were surprise medical bills: first, unexpected out-of-network charges, and then a shocking letter from Empire Blue Cross Blue Shield, which, after paying $248,000 for her hospitalization, was now demanding that money back. Repeatedly I asked myself why I had even thought to move her from Canada, with its free, universal health care, to the patchwork dysfunction of the American system. As executor of her estate, it would take me a full year and a half, and the intervention of New York's attorney general, to get that insurance debacle sorted out. All the while, I fielded repeated requests for death certificates, wrote an ever-dizzying array of checks—and faced inscrutable tax bills from Canada Revenue, too. Both her U.S. and Canadian tax returns had somehow been incompletely or incorrectly filed. Wasn't it enough that I had lost both of my parents so quickly, in such a cruel way? Did my family have to be plagued by ongoing bureaucracy, too? Was this not the meanest, cruelest joke of all?

And then there was the pandemic, which gobbled up all private grumbling and grieving, assimilating it into a general churn of worry.

Several of the poems I would teach for the *Shir Ḥadash* during these months reflected this experience of collective trauma eclipsing personal pain. If the first stage of grief is denial, I was certainly experiencing it—not in the sense of refusing to accept my mother's loss, but in *being denied* the emotional space truly to process it. This led, in part, to the next stage of grief: anger, over everything my family had experienced over the past year and half; and, in part, to the last stage of grief, acceptance—because, really, what could any of us do? COVID fate had thrown my family, my community, America—the whole world, in fact—all together in a common crisis. We had no choice but to confront it together.

The poetry of Avraham Ḥalfi (1906–1980) met me exactly where I was. According to Israeli scholar Tzvi Luz, Ḥalfi was a modern mystic, insofar as a hoped-for image of God stands at the center of the quest that is his work. But this quest occurs in a modern, deeply flawed, skeptical world, characterized by heresy and the absence of revelation.[1] Throughout his poetic career Ḥalfi remained obsessed with seeking and addressing a God he was angry and disappointed with but whom he passionately loved. Haim Rechnitzer, a Reform rabbi, poet, and professor of Jewish thought, writes in his study of Ḥalfi's poetic theology that his poems picture "a broken, wretched, and evasive God who requires first and foremost our forgiveness for His shortcomings."[2]

Teaching Ḥalfi helped me channel some of my own feelings of anger, loss, and religious struggle. As our synagogue moved from lockdown to socially distanced, in-person meetings, Ḥalfi's poems mirrored my own vexed but dogged efforts to find a way back to routine as well as to renewed devotion. Amid ongoing COVID fears and rising racial tensions, Ḥalfi's poems also captured a personal and collective quest for a guiding providential Presence that we could not yet quite locate.

Ḥalfi is not very well known in the United States, but in Israel his work has enjoyed mainstream popularity ever since Israeli rock star Arik Einstein (1939–2013) and various musical collaborators discovered his poetry and set it to music. Born in Lodz, Poland, Ḥalfi grew up in Uman, Ukraine, where he learned about Breslover Hasidism and became interested in acting. In 1924 he immigrated to Palestine, working as a farmer and road builder and joining the newly founded Ohel Theater troupe. In 1953 he became part of the Cameri Theater troupe, there originating some sixty different roles. He also joined a circle of poets and writers, including Lea Goldberg, who were associated with the journal *Ketuvim* (*Writings*, a play on the name of the third section of the Hebrew Bible). Over the course of his career he published twelve volumes of poetry and two children's books. Several of his poems have recently made their way into Reform and other liberal Jewish prayerbooks in Israel, as part of an effort over the past three decades to infuse secular Israeli identity and Zionist Hebrew culture with a new form of Jewish religious expression: a mix of questing and doubting, yearning and frustration. How consonant Ḥalfi's fraught poetic search felt with my own spiritual state in the summer and early fall of 2020!

My journal from that time includes a series of letters that I wrote to my departed parents—efforts to reach out and connect to them beyond the impassable breach of death, to feel some hint of their presence nonetheless. "Dear Mom and Dad," I wrote, giving them a report on my classes and the doings of each of my kids: "All these things, I would have called to tell you about, if only I could. I continue to deal with the estate. And it's annoying. But when it is all over and done, it will be one more thread broken." "Dear Dad, It's your birthday today and if it weren't bad enough that I can't call you, my cellphone dropped out of my handbag while I was crossing the street on my way home from shul and was run over by a car. Could the impossibility of ever reaching you be any clearer?" "Dear Mom and Dad, We're starting to convene once again at shul, outside on the terrace, sitting six feet apart. But people are still being infected in droves by Corona. Changes and stasis, all at the same time. Wish us all luck."

Penning these letters to them into the void, knowing they could never be sent or received except in my own mind, was at once an act of desperation, determination, and love. The same combination, leavened with skepticism and doubt, characterizes the poetry of Avraham Ḥalfi.

I decided to begin the *Shir Ḥadash* foray into Ḥalfi with "Dream of Your Footsteps," one of his best-known poems, given its setting to music by Arik Einstein and Yitzḥak Klepter. Looking for any trace of a sign of my Mom and Dad in my continuing life, knowing full well that many of the traces were already fading in my mind, I would follow Ḥalfi's own poetic footsteps, as he set about to recover the dream and trace of God's elusive, ever-disappearing, providential presence.

“Dream of Your Footsteps”

Dream of Your Footsteps	**חֲלוֹם עִקְבוֹתֶיךָ**[3]
I sought You and couldn’t find You,	חִפַּשְׂתִּי אוֹתְךָ וְלֹא מְצָאתִיךָ.
I sought You, in cloud cover dark.	חִפַּשְׂתִּי אוֹתְךָ הַלּוּט בְּעָנָן.
Soul-brimming, I gathered honey from within You,[4]	מְלֹא נֶפֶשׁ אָרִיתִי הַדְּבַשׁ מִנִּי פִּיךָ.
Saw the dream of Your footsteps in the park.[5]	רָאִיתִי חֲלוֹם עִקְבוֹתֶיךָ בַּגָּן.
I knew You’d fled from us to the far ends.	יָדַעְתִּי, כִּי נַסְתָּ הַרְחֵק מֵעִמָּנוּ.
You commanded we die mystified.	עָלֵינוּ צִוִּיתָ לָמוּת נְבוֹכִים.
You planted a world—our world like a garden,	נָטַעְתָּ עוֹלָם—עוֹלָמֵנוּ כְּגַן הוּא,
Your dream ascends, scent of flowers outside.	עוֹלֶה חֲלוֹמְךָ בּוֹ כְּרֵיחַ פְּרָחִים.
But who are You? Who? What’s Your image incarnate?	אַךְ מִי אַתָּה? מִי? וּמַה דְּמוּת גִּלְגּוּלֶיךָ?
And how many are there, in time’s infinity?	וּמַה מִּסְפָּרָם בְּאֵין־סוֹף הָרְגָעִים?
Reveal Your face to me, to a lost wanderer	גַּלֵּה לִי פָּנִים, לַתּוֹעֶה בַּמַּמְלֶכֶת
In the saddest kingdom that ever could be.	הָעֲצוּבָה מִנִּי כֹּל בַּחַיִּים.
I’ll love You if You’re You, unlike me,	אֲנִי אוֹהַבְךָ, אִם הִנְּךָ לֹא כָּמוֹנִי,
And shall not hate You if You are sorrow.	וְלֹא אֶשְׂנָאֶךָּ, אִם עֶצֶב אַתָּה.
See: our daylight is the sun of affliction.	רְאֵה: אוֹר יָמֵינוּ הוּא שֶׁמֶשׁ הָעֹנִי.
Feel: Our nights are darkened clods of woe.[6]	הַרְגֵּשׁ: לֵילוֹתֵינוּ רִגְבֵי עֲלָטָה.
And the space gapes empty—(Our window’s	וְרֵיק הֶחָלָל—(חַלּוֹנֵנוּ פָּתוּחַ
Open to empty space all around).[7]	לְמַעַן נִרְאֶה בּוֹ, מָה רֵיק הֶחָלָל).
I sought You at night and in windblow,	חִפַּשְׂתִּי אוֹתְךָ בַּלֵּילוֹת וּבָרוּחַ,
In heat wave and dew on the ground.	חִפַּשְׂתִּי אוֹתְךָ בַּשָּׁרָב וּבַטָּל.

For the year and a half I had been saying Kaddish, I had been striving to connect to my parents and to the beyond—to God—often stumbling and failing on both counts. Wasn’t Kaddish recitation, with its aim that “God’s great name be praised throughout all eternity, glorified and celebrated, lauded and praised, acclaimed and honored, extolled and exalted . . . far beyond all song and psalm, beyond all hymns of glory which mortals can offer," a form of thrice-daily delusion? If prayer is a quest for the Infinite, then death and its aftermath had been marking the crushing limits of my all-too-human quest. "Dream of Your Footsteps" perfectly captured this sense of Kaddish questing, with its attendant frustrations and disappointments.

Ḥalfi's poem echoes a long-standing convention of Hebrew poetry in which the poet seeks God, night and day, and despairs over ever finding the Divine. Written in the traumatic shadow of World War II, the poem grieves that God has abandoned the world, leaving behind but a dream of God walking in our world. It alludes repeatedly to the Song of Songs, but it is tinged all over not with the giddy love of the biblical Song but rather with confusion and unanswered questions.[8] The poet doubts that God actually exists, and yet insists on praying to that dubious God.

Haim Rechnitzer identifies in this poem the imprint of Jewish mysticism.[9] In the context of the *Shir Ḥadash*, I chose to read this poem, with its quest language and references to dreams and infinity, as a response to one of the most famous recorded dreams of the Ḥasidic master, storyteller, and mystic, Rebbe Naḥman of Breslov:

> *I heard from one of ours that the rebbe told him this story on eve of Yom Kippur after the Kapparot ceremony.* He saw himself walking in a forest, and the forest was huge and thick, seemingly without end. And he wanted to retrace his steps [but couldn't], but just then [some]one came and told him that this forest indeed had no end, and that all the tools in the world were made from this forest. And he showed him the way out of the forest. After this he came to a river, and he wanted to reach its end [but could not]. And once again [some]one came to him and told him that it is impossible to get to the end of this river, for this river has no beginning or end. And everyone in the world drinks from the waters of this river, and he showed him the way, and so forth. And then he came to a mill that stood on that same river. And [some] one came to him and said that these millstones grind the flour for the entire world. And then he returned to the woods and there he saw a blacksmith sitting in this forest and working at his craft. And he was

told that this blacksmith was forging tools for the entire world. And these words are very obscure and closed off to us.[10]

Evoking Rebbe Naḥman, who gets lost in the infinite forest and attempts to retrace his footsteps, Ḥalfi's "Dream of Your Footsteps" returns to this image at the end of the poem. In Rebbe Naḥman's dream, an unidentified One—God? a heavenly guide?—appears in four different sites to help lead the dreamer out of the thicket of infinity. At the end of Ḥalfi's poem, the night, wind, heatwave, and dew—all places where the speaker seeks God—point to all of the sites in Rebbe Naḥman's dream: the night represents the thick, shady forest; the wind evokes the windmill that grinds the world's wheat; the heatwave recalls the blacksmith's fiery forge; and the moist dew points to the river's waters.

In the poem, however, no divine guide appears to show the speaker the way home or answer his questions. The poetic speaker tries to entice God to appear with human promises of love and acceptance, to no avail. If God fills the world of Rebbe Naḥman's dreams endlessly and awesomely, Ḥalfi's world teems with empty spaces—a reality he describes, but also protests and mourns. It is 1939; Ḥalfi's speaker has reason to be angry and disappointed by God's absence, and to express persistent perplexity.

In late May 2020, in the midst of my second year of mourning, and with the U.S. death toll due to COVID having reached 100,000, Ḥalfi's portrayal of an evasive God who condemned human beings to die in a state of sadness and confusion spoke straight to my discouraged, angry heart.[11] Where was God at all in our world of grief and woe?

Even as Ḥalfi's poem asked these questions, it also modeled a commitment to follow the "Dream of God's Footsteps" wherever they led: the parks; the evening breeze; the sad, glad rays of the sun; and the morning dew that would greet us once we finally met again in-person for socially distanced communal prayer.

I Know Not the Words	**אֵינֶנִּי יוֹדֵעַ מִלִּים**[12]
I know not the words	אֵינֶנִּי יוֹדֵעַ מִלִּים
From which prayer is born.	מֵהֶן נוֹלֶדֶת תְּפִלָּה.
All the words have gotten lost in my voice	כָּל הַמִּלִּים אָבְדוּ בְּקוֹלִי
And have become a dark muteness.	וְהָיוּ כְּאִלְּמוּת אֲפֵלָה.
But my eyes still see	אַךְ עֲדַיִן רוֹאוֹת עֵינַי
The radiance in the eyes of a child.	זוֹהַר עֵינָיו שֶׁל יֶלֶד.
And my eyes still see:	וְעוֹד רוֹאוֹת עֵינַי:
A star that has no peer in its radiance	כּוֹכָב אֵין דּוֹמֶה לוֹ בַּזֹּהַר.
And worried-faced mothers	וְאִמָּהוֹת דְּאוּגוֹת־פָּנִים
Guide their small children toward the light.	נוֹהֲגוֹת אֶל הָאוֹר יַלְדֵיהֶן הַקְּטַנִּים.
What will be upon them? What will be?	מַה יִּהְיֶה עֲלֵיהֶם? מַה יִּהְיֶה?
Hear their joy that's breathing	שִׁמְעוּ שִׂמְחָתָם הַנּוֹשֶׁמֶת
Like a spring it seems never subsides.	כְּאָבִיב, שֶׁנִּדְמֶה כִּי לֹא יַחֲלֹף עַד עוֹלָם.
Surely, I shall kneel before God's image	כָּרוֹעַ אֶכְרַע לִפְנֵי דְּמוּת אֱלֹהִים
Though vanished from my eyes.	אַף אִם מֵעֵינַי נֶעְלָם.
Wrong not the innocents, please.	אַל־נָא תָּרַע לַתְּמִימִים,
They know not why	הֵם אֵינָם יוֹדְעִים מַדּוּעַ
Lightning strikes a tree	בָּרָק פּוֹגֵעַ בְּעֵץ
That innocently bears its fruit.[13]	הַנּוֹשֵׂא אֶת פִּרְיוֹ לְתֻמּוֹ.
Wrong not the innocents, please.	אַל־נָא תָּרַע לַתְּמִימִים.
They know not	הֵם אֵינָם יוֹדְעִים מַדּוּעַ
Why a person betrays their image.	אָדָם מְחַלֵּל אֶת צַלְמוֹ.
I know not the words	אֵינֶנִּי יוֹדֵעַ מִלִּים
From which prayer is born.	מֵהֶן נוֹלֶדֶת תְּפִלָּה.
All the words have gotten lost in my voice	כָּל הַמִּלִּים אָבְדוּ בְּקוֹלִי
And have become a dark muteness.	וְהָיוּ כְּאִלְּמוּת אֲפֵלָה.

In grief and in prayer alike, words often miss their mark. And yet, what else do we have to pray with and articulate our grief, if not words?

Consider this scene: A few weeks after my father's tragic accident, my husband and daughter are sitting around the Shabbat table at the home of dear friends who have extended hospitality at our family's time of need. (I'm in Toronto, helping out my mother.) Another couple around the table asks my husband about the circumstances surrounding my father's death (a truck struck him dead) and then about his age at the time of the accident (ninety). "Better a ninety-year-old than an eleven-year-old," tosses out the wife. "It must've been even worse for the driver who hit him," adds the husband. My daughter walks away from the table in shock and disgust; my husband resolves that it would be best not to tell me anything about the conversation that everyone else around the table sorely wishes had not happened. When the story gets back to me, nonetheless, it takes me days—months, really—to simmer down. Who says such things, however philosophically "interesting," to a grieving family—to anyone, for that matter? Better not to say anything than to say something so hurtful and wrong.

Often, in this angrier mode of my mourning, I lashed out at words: the ones people said to make me feel better and that I was being asked to pray, too. Words like those in the *Taḥanun* (supplication) prayers, that viewed *magefah u-gezeirah kashah* (plague and harsh decree, like those we were currently undergoing as a result of COVID) as an expression of divine wrath and punishment for our sins. If not outright objectionable, the traditional words of prayer—finite sounds and symbols—often fell short of moving my spirit. And yet I was tied to them nonetheless. Might words of a more modern, poetic sort abet my quest for meaning and connectedness in prayer?

In expressing exasperation as well as determination, Avraham Ḥalfi's "I Don't Know the Words" answered a major need. The most famous of Ḥalfi's "liturgized" poems, it has been included in at least one liberal prayerbook under the title "Tefillah" ("Prayer"), even though that title never appears in any of Ḥalfi's published works.[14] The poem begins and ends with professions of ignorance and disavowal about prayer, its origins and its words. And yet it rings throughout with prayer-words and their beginnings. The poetic speaker who claims no knowledge of prayer nevertheless prays. He professes not to know the words from which prayers are born, but uses prayerful words to portray the mystical radiance found on the faces of children and in starlight. When he sees worried mothers shepherding their children toward the light, he poses ambiguously worded, theologically resonant questions. *Mah yihyeh 'aleihem*? What duties will press down upon them? Will God watch over them? Who will worry and oppress them? Even as the poet refrains that he doesn't know the words from which prayer is born, *this is precisely* how prayer is born: out of fear and hope for our world, our children, their future.

The poet then kneels before an image of the very God he claims has disappeared, asking this absent, biblical God—who planted a Tree of Knowledge of Good and Evil in the middle of the Garden of Eden—not to harm the vulnerable and the innocent. The references to Adam, a tree, and a fruit, and the use of the verb "to know" all substantiate this threat—as God's planting of the tree prepared the ground for Adam and Eve's loss of innocence and their expulsion from Eden.

To be sure, in the poet's eyes God is hardly the only source of harm or wrong. The speaker's twice-uttered plea not to wrong the innocents recalls two harrowing, human-centered biblical episodes that feature that same plea. In Genesis 19:7, a mob of Sodomite men beat on Lot's door, demanding to "know" the angels or messengers who have come to save Lot and his clan, only to be beseeched by Lot not to "commit such a wrong" and to be offered Lot's virgin daughters as a (sacrificial) substitute. And in Judges 19:23, a mob is similarly instructed, "Please, my friends, do not commit such a wrong," only to be offered a virgin daughter and a concubine to do with what they will. The mob ends up seizing the concubine, "knowing" her, and abusing her all night long. Subsequently, a Levite dismembers the body of his gang-raped and murdered concubine "and cut[s] her up limb by limb into twelve parts" (Judg. 19:29) in order to send a message of outrage to the twelve tribes.[15]

Ḥalfi's allusion to these two stories underscores the violence that underlies the sacrificial system. Even more saliently, "I Don't Know the Words" emphasizes the endemic violence of human society, and the way wars are waged against individual, innocent, human bodies. The reference to radiant innocent children and worried mothers and the post-1967 publication date of the poem all speak to the Israeli reality of sending innocent, perfect children off to the army to fight in Israel's wars. Repeated references, at the beginning and end of the poem, intimate this too: The word *'ilemut* (muteness) is a near homophone of the word *'alimut* (violence).

Ḥalfi's plea not to wrong innocents reverberated in my experience of how one can be wronged and wounded even by those with good intentions. It also sounded a clarion note in June 2020, as Americans were reckoning with the police murder of George Floyd and the failure of those in power to protect the innocent and vulnerable. In the midst of COVID, despite our general avoidance of group gatherings, we took to the streets, calling on those in charge of safeguarding our laws: *"Wrong not the innocents!"* Protect our businesses and property, but also our Black and Brown citizens and our peaceful protesters. Harm not, tear gas not, bayonet not, knock-down not the innocents. Let not the worst, most mendacious, violent, bigoted version of our society prevail.

"I Don't Know the Words" reminded me: *Don't ever lose hope and faith in words. Keep your sense of light and right in the forefront, even as you fear its extinction.*

“Crowned Is Your Forehead with Black Gold”

Crowned Is Your Forehead with Black Gold

Crowned is your forehead with black gold.
(I don’t remember if they wrote this in a poem.)
Your forehead rhymes with eyes and light.
(I don’t remember if they wrote this in a poem.)
But whoever you’re with—
His life’s filled with poems.

Your pink robe is soft and fluffy.
Come night you always wrap yourself in it.
Your brother, I never wanted to be,
Nor a monk praying to angel thee
Seeing sad dreams of sanctity—
With a real woman in front of me.

You love to be sad and silent,
Listening to stories about close and far.
And I, who watches often in quiet,
Without voice or words,
Forgetting everything about everyone else.

My spirit dwells within the walls of your house.
Captive within your walls, apart from me,
When my body is apart from you.

Spread out is my dream like a rug at your feet
Beloved, tread your paces on its blooms.
Wear your pink robe come night.
In just a bit, I’ll come to your rooms.

And your forehead,
Crowned with black gold
Will near my lips like rhyme to sound.

עָטוּר מִצְחֵךְ זָהָב שָׁחוֹר[16]

עָטוּר מִצְחֵךְ זָהָב שָׁחוֹר.
(אֵינֶנִּי זוֹכֵר אִם כָּתְבוּ כָּךְ בְּשִׁיר.)
מִצְחֵךְ מִתְחָרֵז עִם עֵינַיִם וְאוֹר.
(אֵינֶנִּי זוֹכֵר אִם חָרְזוּ כָּךְ בְּשִׁיר.)
אַךְ לְמִי שֶׁתִּהְיִי—
חַיָּיו מְלֵאֵי שִׁיר.

חֲלוּקֵךְ הַוָּרֹד צַמְרִירִי וָרַךְ.
אַתְּ בּוֹ מִתְעַטֶּפֶת תָּמִיד לְעֵת לַיִל.
לֹא הָיִיתִי רוֹצֶה לִהְיוֹת לָךְ אָח,
לֹא נָזִיר מִתְפַּלֵּל לִדְמוּתוֹ שֶׁל מַלְאָךְ
וְרוֹאֶה חֲלוֹמוֹת עֲגוּמִים שֶׁל קְדֻשָּׁה—
וּלְמוּלוֹ אַתְּ, אִשָּׁה.

אַתְּ אוֹהֶבֶת לִהְיוֹת עֲצוּבָה וְשׁוֹתֶקֶת,
לְהַקְשִׁיב לְסִפּוּר עַל קָרוֹב, עַל רָחוֹק.
וַאֲנִי שֶׁלֹּא פַּעַם אַבִּיט בָּךְ בְּשֶׁקֶט,
אֵין קוֹל וּדְבָרִים,
שׁוֹכֵחַ הַכֹּל עַל אוֹדוֹת אֲחֵרִים.

שׁוֹכֶנֶת נַפְשִׁי בֵּין כָּתְלֵי בֵּיתֵךְ.
וּשְׁבוּיָה בֵּין כְּתָלַיִךְ מִמֶּנִּי נִפְרֶדֶת
עֵת אֲנִי בְּגוּפִי נִפְרָד מִמֵּךְ.

פָּרוּשׂ חֲלוֹמִי כְּמַרְבָד לְרַגְלַיִךְ.
צַעֲדִי, אֲהוּבָה, עַל פְּרָחָיו פְּסִיעוֹתַיִךְ.
לִבְשִׁי חֲלוּקֵךְ הַוָּרֹד לְעֵת לַיִל.
עוֹד מְעַט וְאָבֹא אֵלַיִךְ.

וּמִצְחֵךְ
הֶעָטוּר זָהָב שָׁחוֹר
יִקְרַב אֶל שְׂפָתַי כְּחָרוּז אֶל שִׁיר.

Then I'll whisper in your ear, 'til morn,	אָז אֶלְחַשׁ בְּאָזְנַיִךְ עַד בֹּקֶר,
'Til light	עַד אוֹר,
Pours a round:	כְּשִׁכּוֹר:
With black gold your forehead is crowned.	עָטוּר מִצְחֵךְ זָהָב שָׁחוֹר.

Like the beloved in Ḥalfi's "Crowned Is Your Forehead with Black Gold," my tall, beautiful mother wore a pink fluffy housecoat at home; she, too, was often sad and depressed, while also active and friendly, and fiercely devoted to our family. A yoking as strange and beautiful as black gold. As the months wore on after her death, I missed the realness of it all: The visits and phone calls as regular as morning and night. Her jagged bony hugs. Her listening. Her love.

To be sure, Ḥalfi is not writing here about his mother. By one theory, Ḥalfi fell in love with the wife of a fellow actor and wrote this poem for her. "Crowned Is Your Forehead with Black Gold" thus seems an unlikely choice for a parent- or prayer-centered *Shir Ḥadash*. Then again, love poetry addressed to an unattainable beloved is hardly foreign to liturgy or grief.

Much of Ḥalfi's imagery and word order is eccentric, unusual, surprising, and yet not without biblical or liturgical precedent. Consider the opening line (and refrain), "Crowned is your forehead with black gold." The speaker's description of his lover's head recalls Song of Songs 5:11, where the Shulamite describes her lover: "His head is finest gold / His locks are curled / And black as a raven." But whereas the biblical writer keeps the gold and black somewhat apart in the form of a simile (using "as"), Ḥalfi mixes them entirely: the "black gold" suggests, at the same time, a strange alloy, the glint of stars at night, and, perhaps, an erotic vision of the tefillin worn on one's—on this case, a woman's—head.

The imagery in the third line is similarly unusual: "Your forehead rhymes with eyes and light." Not literally—the word *mitzḥekh* (your forehead) doesn't at all rhyme with *'einayim* and *'or*. Rather, the rhyming is figurative. The experience of beholding the beloved's shining, gold, black forehead is itself synonymous with sight and light.

But in the second stanza, the speaker reassesses his beloved. The radiant, celestial being he adulates is now an earthly woman wearing a fluffy pink housecoat whom he very much wants to touch. And so it is throughout the poem: the speaker oscillates between the desire to view his beloved in tangible terms and his countervailing desire to experience her as numinous, other, and peerless.

In the third stanza, the beloved listens to stories about "close and far," an intimation of both her immanence and transcendence. In the process of observing her, the speaker forgets everything and everyone else. His soul dwells only in her house—like God's Presence in the Tabernacle. His body may depart her home—like what some say happens to a soul after death: separating out from one's body—but his soul stays put, with her.

All this suggests a purely spiritual love, yet the next stanza imagines a physical union. The poet's dreams spread out at the feet of his beloved like a flowered carpet, upon which he bids her to tread. Soon enough, he declares, he'll come to her rooms and unite with her in love.

Returning to the opening image, the final stanza portrays the black-gold-crowned forehead approaching the lips of the poet in order to be kissed. Her forehead's proximity to his lips is again likened to poetry and rhyme. A kiss as a rhyme: this is textual intimacy, a drama of mind and heart as well as body, a product of giddy imagining and drunken desire.

Reading this poem evoked familial intimacy. Mom used to stretch her arms out wide before hugs. I imagined kissing her forehead, and Dad's, too. Could I feel such physical, emotional, and spiritual intimacy with God as well?

As part of my teaching, I played Arik Einstein's gorgeous musical setting of the poem, considered one of the most beautiful Israeli pop love songs of all time, for my *Shir Ḥadash* community, inviting everyone to pray along with it.[17] And, I wondered, what might it mean for each of us, individually and collectively, if, when we recited prayers such as *'Ahavah Rabbah* and *Ve-'ahavta* (which describe the mutual love of God and Israel), we felt the forehead of God, adorned with black gold, approach our lips so as to be kissed by our prayers?

Here a Person Believed	אָדָם הֶאֱמִין פֹּה[18]
Here a person believed in the whisper of evening,	אָדָם הֶאֱמִין פֹּה לְלַחַשׁ הָעֶרֶב,
Kissed stars with a blurry gaze,	נָשַׁק כּוֹכָבִים בְּמַבָּט מְעֻרְפָּל.
Left their house	הָלַךְ מִבֵּיתוֹ
And stood along the way	וְעָמַד בַּדֶּרֶךְ
To see a star fall in the haze.[19]	לִרְאוֹת אִם כּוֹכָב מֵרָקִיעַ נָפַל.
A silent breeze rolled the grass,	רוּחַ־דְּמָמוֹת גִּלְגְּלָה אֶת הָעֶשֶׂב,
In the dream, the horizon closed stretches of sky.	הָאֹפֶק קֵרֵב מֶרְחַקִּים בַּחֲלוֹם.
The dreamer raised a prayer to this wonder	נָשָׂא תְּפִלָּתוֹ הַחוֹלֵם אָז עַל נֵס זֶה,
As if evening had wished them goodbye.	כְּאִלּוּ הָעֶרֶב בֵּרְכוֹ לְשָׁלוֹם.
Behold, the heavens have a thousand wings,	הִנֵּה לָרָקִיעַ יֵשׁ אֶלֶף כְּנָפַיִם,
Hence, of dying in song there's no fear.	עַל כֵּן אֵין כָּל פַּחַד לִגְוֹעַ בְּשִׁיר.
But if eyes sometimes see	אֲבָל אִם רוֹאוֹת לִפְעָמִים הָעֵינַיִם
A falling star—	כּוֹכָב שֶׁנּוֹשֵׁר—
That's death, bright and clear.	זֶה מָוֶת בָּהִיר.
Here a person believed in the whisper of evening,	אָדָם הֶאֱמִין פֹּה לְלַחַשׁ הָעֶרֶב,
Heard an airy chorale from on high,	שָׁמַע מַקְהֵלַת הָאֲוִיר בַּמְּרוֹמִים,
Left their house	הָלַךְ מִבֵּיתוֹ
And stood along the way	וְעָמַד בַּדֶּרֶךְ
To see if star and death are alike.	לִרְאוֹת אִם כּוֹכָב וְהַמָּוֶת דּוֹמִים.

In late June 2020, many if not all of us in the Bayit daily minyan community began venturing outside each morning and evening for outdoor prayer, hoping to recover the feeling and regularity of shared ritual space. Yet tentativeness and insecurity marked our steps, our seating, our movements. We were together, but still masked and distanced. We struggled in the summer heat to hear each other and the prayer leader on the synagogue terrace, amid the whirring of the Henry Hudson Parkway, the chirping of birds, and the voice delay of Zoom-generated sound—the Zoom still on not only for those of us too vulnerable to attend in person, but for everyone sitting right there. Many of us came to shul equipped with headphones just to hear above the traffic.

"Here a Person Believed," Ḥalfi's portrayal of a faith experience, was the first poem I presented to our community after our return to in-person services. In Jewish liturgy the verb *le-ha'amin* (to believe or have faith in) typically appears in relation to God, Moses, or the coming of the Messiah, but here it captures an experience in nature: a mystical encounter under the stars, the breeze rolling the grasses. Viewing the horizon line—that optical illusion where sky and land appear to touch each other in the distance—is likened to a dream and a miracle, to an evening's greeting, to kissing the stars.

Insofar as the speaker wants to maintain an uplifting outlook, to hang on to this notion of the heavens having a thousand wings—With so many wings, why would anyone or anything fall from the sky? Why would anyone ever die?—he then encounters a falling star, which shakes his faith to the core.

The Mishnah specifies the blessing to be said over exceptional (natural) phenomena, such as a meteor, comet, or falling star: "Blessed is the One whose strength and might fill the world." Upon receiving good news, one is to say, "Blessed is the One who is good and who grants good." And if one receives bad news, such as a death, one says, "Blessed is the True Judge."[20] All of these diverse experiences provide occasions for affirming God's place in the world.

"Here a Person Believed" echoes but also subverts the Mishnah's teachings. The speaker never says a prescribed blessing, rather simply stands, looks at the falling stars, and ponders the meaning of what they are seeing. Are human experiences really echoed in the cosmos? Popular mythology would have us believe that falling or shooting stars are good luck omens or opportunities to make a wish. Judaism would have us believe that these are signs of God's ongoing involvement in the created world. The speaker merely witnesses and wonders.

So, here we were: together, out in the open, on the synagogue terrace. No grasses rustled, but a multitude of cars rushed by on the parkway. It was morning, not evening, so we saw no falling stars. Nevertheless, we "people who believed" stood, looked, wondered, and prayed. We drew all we'd been experiencing—our sense of danger and insecurity about a future with COVID, our desire to see life return to normal, our countervailing fear of rushing into anything too soon—toward the horizon line of our prayers. Our eyes kissed the clouds and the sky.[21]

“And Songs Are the Dust of Antiquities”

And Songs Are the Dust of Antiquities

☆ ☆
☆

And songs are antiquity dust
In the sanctuary of God’s world.
And ministers bear the torches they must,
Lighting stars in nights unfurled.

And those who long for spring along the way
Flee from the graves of their dead.
And the dead not forgotten that day
Guard the doors of their homes instead.

וְהַשִּׁירִים הֵם אֲבַק עַתִּיקוֹת[22]

☆ ☆
☆

וְהַשִּׁירִים הֵם אֲבַק עַתִּיקוֹת
בְּמִקְדַּשׁ אֱלֹהֵי הָעוֹלָם.
וְהַשָּׁרִים הֵם נוֹשְׂאֵי אֲבוּקוֹת,
מַדְלִיקֵי כּוֹכָבִים בְּלֵילָם.

וְהַכְּמֵהִים לְאָבִיב בַּדְּרָכִים
נָסִים מִקִּבְרֵי מֵתֵיהֶם.
וְהַמֵּתִים שֶׁאֵינָם נִשְׁכָּחִים
שׁוֹמְרִים בְּפִתְחֵי בָּתֵּיהֶם.

Mid-summer 2020. We were back praying in person, but could not sing. COVID had turned singing, especially indoors, into a super-spreader activity. How could something so beautiful have become so toxic and deadly? If we could no longer freely sing, how could we retain a sense of galvanizing, participatory prayer?

Ḥalfi’s “And Songs Are the Dust of Antiquities” spoke to the ongoing role of song in prayer even at that time when we couldn’t actually sing. The poem’s repeated use of the conjunctive *ve-* (“and”) suggests a string of answers to a series of ongoing, shared questions: What is the purpose of poems or songs (the same word in Hebrew), especially at a time of major disruption? And what is our role as these poems’ singers?

With a seeming prescience of our COVID-era understanding of talking and singing as emitting tiny, aerosol (potentially infectious) particles, Ḥalfi refers to songs/poems as tiny dust specks. But not just any specks: those of the ancient past. And not just any ancient past, but that of the Temple. Writing as part of a Hebrew poetic tradition, Ḥalfi is reminding us: Even though the actual physical Temples were destroyed and modernity has silenced many traditional notes, the purported psalms of those Temples live on in the form of modern Hebrew poetry and song.

The liturgical tradition of the *Shir Shel Yom* (Psalm of the Day), as specified in BT Rosh Hashanah 31a, underscores this idea. Each day at the end of the morning service, Jews announce the day of the week and recite the biblical psalm that was reportedly sung on that particular day of the week during Temple times. As such, through the prayers that have come to replace the sacrifices and through the poems/songs that recall the Temple service, we keep the Temple service alive.

Ḥalfi, though, doesn't limit his definition of poetry/song to Temple or traditional liturgy. For him, modern poems/songs are the dust or residue of a universal sanctuary. And so, to write a poem or sing a song in Hebrew is to remake ancient biblical letters—the dust of antiquity—anew, the present reforging the past all over the world. In the third line Ḥalfi models this re-creation through wordplay: *'avak* (dust) becomes *'avukot* (torches), and the *sarim*—the ministers in this everlasting sanctuary—become the torchbearers of the dust/word particles of the past. Ḥalfi's reference to the *sarim* brings to mind a midrashic passage in the eleventh-century century Midrash Vayosha 8:4, where *sarim va'avadim* (ministers and servants) are seen bearing lit torches to illuminate the path for those they serve, as well as a passage in Mishnah Sukkah 5:4, which describes the *simḥat beit hasho'eivah* (the Water Drawing Celebration) in the Temple on the festival of Sukkot, with *ḥasidim* and *'anshei ma'aseh* (the pious and the people of action) singing *divrei shirot vetishbeḥot*, words of song and praise, with flaming torches, *'avukot.* With these torches, the *s[h]arim* light up stars in an otherwise dark world, forming a line with what came before, tying us to it.

And so it was that our *tefillah* group, too, was managing, against all COVID odds, to "go out with devotional (k)nots." Assembling carefully, many of us in tallit and tefillin, with prayer books but without singing, we were bearing the torch of connectedness, civic responsibility, and mutual care.

And those final two lines, imagining the dead as guardians of their houses! Kaddish, I realized, was our own antiquity-dust. An ancient poem replete with rhythms and rhymes, Kaddish calls for the full acknowledgment and reverence of God's name, and for imagining the best possible world. Saying—albeit not singing—Kaddish together with my community was helping me conjure up a formerly illuminated world, if only for a few dusty moments.

From "Heretic's Prayers"

Heretic's Prayers

2

Exalted above all!
I am tied to You by a worn shoelace
Found at the Dung Gate
By a rummaging angel in the city of Your
Godliness.

Exalted above all!
I don't know who told Your High Holiness
That I dwell in the midst of Your city[24]
And there are none standing on guard on her wall
By day and by night.[25]

Now You know:
I too exist.
And my name resembles all those
Who so resemble each other.

All those so expect for You to be
Like one of them
Or for them to be
Like You in Your many heights.

Exalted above all!
Pour out Your exalted nothingness[26]
Upon the dreams of those who seek You
day and night.

Will Your living dead awaken to
A pale blue morning prayer
And will a "let there be great light"
Arise from Your mouth to greet them?

I look at You mute, both my eyes torn wide open.

מִתּוֹךְ תְּפִלּוֹת כּוֹפֵר[23]

ב

הַנַּעֲלֶה מִכֹּל!
אֲנִי קָשׁוּר בְּךָ בִּשְׂרוֹךְ שֶׁל נַעַל מְרֻפֶּטֶת
אוֹתוֹ מָצָא בְּשַׁעַר הָאַשְׁפּוֹת
מַלְאָךְ נוֹבֵר בְּעִיר אֱלֹהוּתְךָ.

הַנַּעֲלֶה מִכֹּל!
אֵינִי יוֹדֵעַ מִי סִפֵּר לִקְדֻשָּׁתְךָ שֶׁל מַעְלָה
כִּי יוֹשֵׁב אֲנִי בְּתוֹכֵכִי עִירְךָ
וְאֵין עוֹמְדִים שׁוֹמְרִים עַל חוֹמָתָהּ
יוֹמָם וָלֵיל.

עַכְשָׁו יָדַעְתָּ:
גַּם אֲנִי יֶשְׁנִי.
וּשְׁמִי כְּמוֹ שֶׁל אֵלֶּה הַדּוֹמִים כָּל־כָּךְ
פְּנֵי אִישׁ לִפְנֵי רֵעֵהוּ.

כָּל אֵלֶּה מְצַפִּים כֹּה לִהְיוֹתְךָ
כְּמוֹ אֶחָד מֵהֶם
אוֹ לִהְיוֹתָם
כֻּלָּם כָּמוֹךָ בִּמְרוֹמֶיךָ הָרַבִּים.

הַנַּעֲלֶה מִכֹּל!
שְׁפֹךְ אֵינוּתְךָ הַנַּעֲלָה
עַל חֲלוֹמָם שֶׁל מְבַקְשֶׁיךָ יוֹם וָלֵיל.

הַאִם מֵתֶיךָ הַחַיִּים יֵעוֹרוּ לִתְפִלָּה
שֶׁל שַׁחֲרִית תְּכֻלָּה
וְיַעֲלֶה יְהִי שֶׁל אוֹר גָּדוֹל
מִפִּיךָ לִקְרָאתָם?

אֲנִי מַבִּיט בְּךָ אִלֵּם וּקְרוּעַ שְׁתֵּי עֵינַי.

If personal mourning and COVID weren't enough, Tisha B'Av (the fast of Ninth of Av) thrust us all into the lap of the Jewish communal catastrophe. There we all were, seated on the floor, reciting biblical and medieval poems of lament over the destruction of the First and Second Temples and consequent Jewish exile. That week of Tisha B'Av I taught Avraham Ḥalfi's "Heretic's Prayer," with its distinctive modern mixture of heresy, anger, and devotion, as a way of processing a triple sense of grief.

In the poem, a man identified as the lowest of the low addresses God, Highest of the High. This lowly speaker ties himself to exalted God with a worn shoelace found by a (homeless) angel at the Dung Gate, the repository of trash in Temple times. The speaker's connection to God is so tenuous and degraded it seems primed to snap. And yet somehow, from this compromised position, he reels God into conversation. In the second stanza, he asks God, "Who told You I was here, dwelling in Your city? And, contra Psalm 122:2, no one stands on guard in Your city." In other words, none of the promised, biblical visions of providence and protection seem operative anymore in Your world. Do You recognize any of us anymore, God, (Ḥalfi asks) and do we recognize You?

Ḥalfi's speaker then paradoxically petitions an absent God to pour out exalted nothingness over the people—to show them something, even if that something is nothing we can define. What does he mean by this? Is this all a bitter taunt? Or a desperate plea? Or an acknowledgment of the impossibility of ever capturing the infinity that is God?

A bit more clarity comes in the next stanza, where Ḥalfi wonders and questions the possibility of there being *something* better, some form of reawakening of "the living dead," a renewal of light, and a greeting from God. Might such a renewal be possible?

Reading this poem the week of Tisha B'Av 2020, amid the ongoing health and economic crises of COVID, I wondered along with Ḥalfi about the possibility of such a resurrection, all the while tapping into his tone of heretical, trouble-making protest. The only way our world will get better is if we push, prod, and demand it be so. The poet's decision to sit in the very midst of God's city and to level these insistent—in some instances, taunting—words to God about a world devoid of God's presence and protection brought to mind the activism and teachings of Congressman John Lewis (1940–1920), whose funeral had taken place that same week. Lewis's stubborn determination as a young man to sit down at segregated lunch counters and buses and march on the Edmund Pettus Bridge in the very heart of the segregated South, and his later years of service in Congress alongside many representatives bent on thwarting his civil rights agenda, were all in service of nudging America toward a better tomorrow.

The last line of the poem, in which the poet declares, "I look at You mute, both my eyes torn wide open," conveys both dumbfounded shock and wide-eyed, expectant wonder. Ḥalfi and Lewis alike understood the need to call attention to what is shocking and upsetting in our world—not as an end in itself, but as a goad, a call to action. Hence Lewis's (unwitting) last words, published as a *New York Times* op-ed on the Ninth of Av: "[W]alk with the wind, brothers and sisters," and get into "good trouble, necessary trouble."[27]

“At Night Birds Fell”

At Night Birds Fell

☆ ☆
☆

At night birds fell from the nest,
And the trees shook in the night.
And the great life became small
And wept to live.

Perhaps there was never anything else
in the heavens.
Perhaps in heaven there never was anything.
Only, that someone,
Like a bird fallen from the nest,
Pretended to find something there.

And the weeping is good since it’s still weeping,
And it’s good for tears—to be tears.

At night,
Always at night,
A mighty storm roars
And strikes at the heart of the branches
And the branches are reminded that their
heart aches.
And someone who fell like a bird from the nest
And like a broken branch,
Who doesn’t know who he is, who he is,
who he is—
He falls too.

בַּלַּיְלָה נָפְלוּ צִפֳּרִים[28]

☆ ☆
☆

בַּלַּיְלָה נָפְלוּ צִפֳּרִים מִן הַקֵּן,
וְעֵצִים רָעֲדוּ בַּלַּיְלָה.
וְהַחַיִּים הַגְּדוֹלִים נִהְיוּ קְטַנִּים
וּבָכוּ לִחְיוֹת.

אוּלַי לֹא הָיָה עוֹד דָּבָר בָּרָקִיעַ.

אוּלַי מֵעוֹלָם לֹא הָיָה בָּרָקִיעַ דָּבָר.
וְרַק מִישֶׁהוּ,
כְּצִפּוֹר שֶׁנָּפְלָה מִן הַקֵּן,
דִּמָּה לִמְצֹא בָּרָקִיעַ דָּבָר.

וְלַבְּכִי הָיָה טוֹב כִּי עוֹדֶנּוּ בֶּכִי,
וְטוֹב לַדְּמָעוֹת—כִּי דְּמָעוֹת הֵן.

בַּלַּיְלָה,
תָּמִיד בַּלַּיְלָה,
שׁוֹאֵג סַעַר אֵיתָן
וּמַכֶּה עַל לֵב הָעֲנָפִים.
וְנִזְכָּרִים הָעֲנָפִים כִּי לִבָּם כּוֹאֵב.

וּמִישֶׁהוּ כְּצִפּוֹר שֶׁנָּפְלָה מִן הַקֵּן
וּכְעָנָף שָׁבוּר,
שֶׁאֵינוֹ יוֹדֵעַ מִי הוּא, מִי הוּא, מִי הוּא–
נוֹפֵל גַּם הוּא.

In August 2020 Tropical Storm Isaiah knocked down trees and downed power lines throughout New York City, heaping physical devastation onto our already traumatized communal landscape. “At Night Birds Fell” captured this scene.

During the night, the poet tells us, something shook the trees and toppled baby birds from the safety of their nest. In the previous week's Torah portion, we had read the commandment to send a mother bird away from the nest before taking her baby chicks (Deut. 22:6–7). It isn't just weather that ambushes birds in trees, but human beings do, too.

Deuteronomy promises longevity to those who obey the commandment, but the Talmud relates a story told by Rabbi Yaakov that challenges this promise: A father asks his son to go up to a high place and bring down chicks. Listening to his father, the son ascends and carefully performs the commandment of sending away the mother bird, but falls tragically to his death.[29] This story raises not only the age-old problem of theodicy, but also the question of parental culpability for endangering their young. Is this any different from parents and political leaders sending the young off to battle, thereby toppling them from the safe nests of their previously protected lives?

Chicks fall from a nest; order gives way to chaos. Birds (and by extension, human beings) look to the sky for comfort, for a structuring belief system, to account for what has befallen them. Is that how religion came into being? The poet ponders and fears: Perhaps in reality, he intimates, there is no heaven and no Creator who orders the world and protects the vulnerable? Perhaps people, like fallen birds, have created heaven as a bulwark against the chaos, building a nest of belief, as it were, to substitute for other, tangible protections?

I shared these questions with my Orthodox community in the *Shir Ḥadash*, despite their obviously heretical implications, because I believe that those of us grieving a loss especially need a place within prayer to express our honest doubts and fears. The *Taḥanun* prayers of supplication, which traditionally follow the morning and afternoon *'Amidah*, offer an opportunity for pleading and tears, but within a very limited framework of divine anger and retribution. What about those of us who are tumbled from our nest by happenstance, due to no fault of our own? What if we are brought down by storms or inconceivable illness or other "acts of God," itself a preposterous term for major events that defy human understanding? What if someone, like my poor father, is struck dead by a driver too busy putting his coffee in a cup holder to pay attention to where he is driving? Family and friends of victims of such accidental losses might feel entirely abandoned by God, and by the pointlessness of their loved ones' deaths. Traditional theology has little wisdom to offer in the face of random bereavements. Ḥalfi's poem gives voice to the pain.

There is crying and there are tears. And, the poet contends, all of the lost and unmoored places in us are deep and real. The broken branches, like broken hearts, must be acknowledged.

Is there space in organized prayer to recognize this deep pain? Could our prayer community at the Bayit, or the larger, now online *Shir Ḥadash* community, envision a place in our siddur where these emotions aren't merely encased in praise, petition, thanks, and explanatory structures of punishment, but rather are thrown up to God, just as they are?

At the end of "At Night Birds Fell" we hear the repeated sad hootings of a bird—*mi hu', mi hu', mi hu'*—a seeming loss of language and identity in the aftermath of tragedy. *Mi hu', mi hu', mi hu'*—I cried along with Shem Tov Levi's musical setting of the poem, my own mourning melding with Ḥalfi's as I listened and wept "to live."[30]

"Jewish Fall"

Jewish Fall	סְתָו יְהוּדִי[31]
Jewish fall in the land of my forefathers	סְתָו יְהוּדִי בְּאֶרֶץ אֲבוֹתַי
Sends me	שׁוֹלֵחַ בִּי
Hints of Elul.	רִמְזֵי אֱלוּל.
Already running riot inside me	כְּבָר מִשְׁתַּגְּעוֹת בִּי קְצָת
Are the tiny birds, whistling with the sorrow	הַצִּפֳּרִים הַקְּטַנְטַנּוֹת שׁוֹרְקוֹת הָעֶצֶב
Of Yom Kippur.	שֶׁל יוֹם־הַכִּפּוּרִים.
Then the shofars will blast to open the gates of Heaven	אָז יִתָּקַע בְּשׁוֹפָרוֹת לִפְתֹּחַ שַׁעֲרֵי שָׁמַיִם.
And Jewish faces from the Disapora	וּפָנִים יְהוּדִיּוֹת מִן הַגּוֹלָה
In grayish sadness	בְּאַפְרַפַּר נוּגֶה
Will hover before the throne of the Eternal Lord.	יְרַחֲפוּ לִפְנֵי כִּסֵּא אֲדוֹן־עוֹלָם.
With requests and supplications and many sparks	וּבַקָּשׁוֹת וְתַחֲנוּנִים וְנִיצוֹצוֹת הַרְבֵּה
In the depth of their eyes.	בְּעֹמֶק עֵינֵיהֶן.

Summer had slid into fall, and Avraham Ḥalfi's "Jewish Fall" marked this transition.

The poem offers a view of autumn from the perspective of a once religious, now secular Israeli Jew. Hints of Elul stir up former experiences of Jewishness, observance, and inner spiritual feeling, precipitating a form of repentance or return.

In the previous poem, "At Night Birds Fell," birds falling out of a nest symbolized sudden human misfortune. Their repeated hooting of the words/sounds *mi hu', mi hu', mi hu'* holler out to the reader, signaling a crisis of faith and self, the reduction of a person to animal grief. In "Jewish Fall" birds hoot and whistle, too, but inside the poet's own head. Chirping, hooting birds are typically associated with the freedom of the outdoors; birds hooting, running riot, or going crazy (as the word *mishtage'ot* literally means); "inside," however, suggests entrapment, even horror. But while there is fear in Ḥalfi's poem, and nagging guilt, too, there is no horror. Despite the similar sounds of the Hebrew word *sherikah* and the English word "shriek," the little birds do not scream. Instead the whistling serves as the poet's gentle wake-up call: *You will soon depart from your mundane, secular ways.* Sure enough, the shofars blow, throwing open the gates of heaven, as intimated in the High Holy Day liturgy, replete with images of the opening and closing of the gates of mercy, and giving the poet a renewed sense of meaning to Jewish time and ritual.

In the third stanza, though, those who attend traditional High Holy Day services are presented negatively, as "Jewish faces from the Diaspora / In grayish sadness." Yet in the spirit of High Holy Day reconciliation, the poem then enacts and ends on another turn, transforming those gray faces into light, with sparks in the depth of their eyes.

In the fall of 2020, the metaphor of the whistling birds spoke to me in newly relevant ways. This year, like none other, I would be spending the High Holy Days without either of my parents, and outside the protective walls of the Bayit's main sanctuary—instead, in outdoor backyard clusters, amid the trees and birds. Our Jewish New Year observances would hoot and whistle with strange sadness, but hopefully they'd yield some precious sparks of light too.

4 Living with a Lesser, Closer God

Yehuda Amichai's Secular Theology of Everyday Life

It was early fall 2020, a full year after selling my parents' house in Toronto and moving my mother to New York, when the idea finally sunk in that I would never again be returning to my childhood home. For several years I'd been going to Toronto at least every other month to see my parents. Frequent visits with Carol, one of my best friends from childhood, were an extra side benefit. A friend as well as a physician, Carol had come to my mother's medical aid on many occasions, especially during a long hospitalization in 2015. I remember my distinct sense of panic when moving Mom back to the Bronx where she herself had grown up: Who would be our Carol here, when the inevitable medical crises struck?

I had always thought, somehow, that I'd be back in Toronto soon—at the very least for the unveiling of my father's headstone. But when Mom died just five months after her move, we buried her not in Toronto, with my father, but in New Jersey. Since all of us kids lived in New York, the new plan was to move my father and grandmother's remains to rest next to Mom's. And then came COVID, which made all travel over the border to Canada completely impossible.

In my mind I still saw my mother in her Toronto kitchen, wearing her pink housecoat and sitting at her regular place on the left side of the table, sipping coffee and eating a cookie or a piece of toast with jam. And Dad in his paint-splattered, work-around-the-house clothes, puttering outside, fixing this and that.

In reality, though, I learned at that time that the house where I had grown up and brought my children every summer so they could go to day camp and ride their bikes in the park behind the backyard was now being rented out as a college rooming house. The very thought of my immaculately kept childhood home being overrun by boarders provoked a sudden, visceral response: a heaviness to my gait, a burning in my chest.

Yehuda Amichai (1924–2000), who left his childhood home and the religious life of his youth and yet remained so tenderly and meaningfully connected to this past, became the featured poet of the *Shir Ḥadash* during that time of aching nostalgia, from the early fall of 2020 through the arrival of Passover in the spring of 2021. Considered the most important Israeli poet of his generation (and shortlisted for the Nobel Prize before his death in 2000), Amichai responded to the big theological and political issues of his day from the intimate vantage point of home and personal/familial relationships. His juxtaposition of childhood teachings with adult realities directly matched my emotional state, and resonated with the *Shir Ḥadash* audience too. Due to COVID, all of our worlds had become narrower and more home centered.

Born Ludwig Pfeuffer in Wurzburg, Germany in 1924, Amichai immigrated with his family to Palestine in 1935. He was raised Orthodox, but he abandoned religiosity as a young man. Serving as a soldier in the 1948 War of Independence, he lost treasured comrades. He had previously lost his best childhood friend from Germany, a young woman named Ruth who perished in the Holocaust.

These experiences of major loss colored and shaped Amichai's work. Written in beautiful, spare language belying deep emotional and theological complexity, and steeped in biblical and liturgical references, his poetry helped move us through that singular High Holy Day season of 2020/5781.

"And That Is Your Glory"

And That Is Your Glory	**וְהִיא תְּהִלָּתֶךָ**[1]
Taken from a *piyyut* for the Days of Awe	מתוך פיוט לימים הנוראים
I've yoked together my great silence and small	בִּשְׁתִיקָתִי הַגְּדוֹלָה וּבְצַעֲקָתִי הַקְּטַנָּה אֲנִי חוֹרֵשׁ
Howl. I've been through water and fire, seen it all.	כִּלְאַיִם. הָיִיתִי בַּמַּיִם וְהָיִיתִי בָּאֵשׁ.
I've been in Jerusalem, Rome, perhaps in Mecca, who knows how.	הָיִיתִי בִּירוּשָׁלַיִם וּבְרוֹמָא. אוּלַי אֶהְיֶה בְּמֶכָּה.
But now God's hiding, and man's crying, "Where are You now?"	אַךְ הַפַּעַם אֱלֹהִים מִתְחַבֵּא וְאָדָם צוֹעֵק אַיֶּכָּה.
And that is Your glory.	וְהִיא תְּהִלָּתֶךָ.
Underneath the world, God lies on His back,	אֱלֹהִים שׁוֹכֵב עַל גַּבּוֹ מִתַּחַת לַתֵּבֵל,
Always fixing and refixing the inevitable crack.	תָּמִיד עָסוּק בְּתִקּוּן, תָּמִיד מַשֶּׁהוּ מִתְקַלְקֵל.
I wanted to see Him whole, but all I can spy	רָצִיתִי לִרְאוֹתוֹ כֻּלּוֹ, אַךְ אֲנִי רוֹאֶה
Are the soles of His shoes and it's making me cry.	רַק אֶת סֻלְיוֹת נְעָלָיו וַאֲנִי בּוֹכֶה.
And that is His glory.	וְהִיא תְּהִלָּתוֹ.
Even the trees went out to choose themselves a king.	אֲפִלּוּ הָעֵצִים הָלְכוּ לִבְחֹר לָהֶם מֶלֶךְ.
A thousand times I've resolved to do some other thing.	אֶלֶף פְּעָמִים הִתְחַלְתִּי אֶת חַיַּי מִכָּאן וָאֵילֵךְ.
On the side of the street someone's counting has begun:	בִּקְצֵה הָרְחוֹב עוֹמֵד אֶחָד וּמוֹנֶה:
This one, and that one, this one and that one.	אֶת זֶה וְאֶת זֶה וְאֶת זֶה וְאֶת זֶה.
And that is Your glory.	וְהִיא תְּהִלָּתֶךָ.
Perhaps like an ancient statue without any arms	אוּלַי כְּמוֹ פֶּסֶל עַתִּיק שֶׁאֵין בּוֹ זְרוֹעוֹת

Our lives are lovelier without heroics and alarms.	גַּם חַיֵּינוּ יָפִים יוֹתֵר, בְּלִי מַעֲשִׂים וּגְבוּרוֹת.
Ungird the armor of my undershirt for this final bout.	פִּרְקִי מִמֶּנִּי אֶת שִׁרְיוֹן גּוּפִיָּתִי הַמַּצְהִיבָה,
I fought all the knights, until the power went out.	נִלְחַמְתִּי בְּכָל הָאַבִּירִים, עַד הַחַשְׁמַל כָּבָה.
And that is my glory.	וְהִיא תְּהִלָּתִי.
Rest your mind, it has raced me all the way,	תָּנוּחַ דַּעְתֵּךְ, דַּעְתֵּךְ רָצָה עִמִּי בְּכָל הַדֶּרֶךְ,
It's tired now and needs to take off for the day,	וְעַכְשָׁו הִיא עֲיֵפָה וְאֵין בָּהּ עוֹד עֶרֶךְ,
I see you standing by the open fridge door,	אֲנִי רוֹאֶה אוֹתָךְ מוֹצִיאָה דָּבָר מִן הַמְּקָרֵר,
Lit up by otherworldly light from its core.	מוּאֶרֶת מִתּוֹכוֹ בְּאוֹר שֶׁמֵּעוֹלָם אַחֵר.
And that is my glory	וְהִיא תְּהִלָּתִי
And that is His glory	וְהִיא תְּהִלָּתוֹ
And that is Your glory.	וְהִיא תְּהִלָּתֶךָ.

This poem that finds divine splendor in everyday domestic spaces precisely fit our 2020 COVID experience of observing the High Holy Days either in improvised backyard synagogues or at home.

And much more: High and low. Achievement and failure. Glory and shame. "And That Is Your Glory" is at once a work of radical God-seeking and radical God-skepticism, a "theological hybrid"—much like its opening image of the poet yoking together large silence and small outcry (a reference to the biblical prohibition against yoking together an ox and an ass and against mixing linen and wool; Deut. 22:10). The poet claims that he's experienced almost all the religious options, and now the categories have become confused. He's been in Jerusalem and in Rome—the centers of Judaism and Christianity—and perhaps one day, he'll even get to Mecca to experience what Islam has to teach—peace should come speedily in our days. But all of this has yielded him little theological insight. In a reversal of Genesis 3:9, here it is God who hides away in shame, and Adam/humankind who calls, "Where are You?" To all of this, the poet sardonically refrains *ve-hi' tehilatekha* ("And this is Y/your Glory"), a repeating yet ever-changing chorus.

The phrase *ve-hi' tehilatekha* alludes to two different Yom Kippur *piyyutim* (liturgical poems), both of which employ this refrain: *'Omnam 'Ashamnu* (Indeed We Have Sinned) by the fifth-century liturgical poet Yose ben Yose, identifies God's glory in the divine willingness to quell anger and forgive; and *'Asher 'Eimatekha* (You Whose Dread), attributed either to Yannai (fifth/sixth-century, Palestine) or to his disciple, Eliezer Ha-Kallir (570–640 CE, Byzantium), which pays repeated tribute to God's fearsomeness.[2] For example, the latter *piyyut*'s depiction of the *'er'elim* (angels associated with tragedy and mourning) as knights of courage is echoed in Amichai's reference to having done battle with all of the knights. So too, its picturing of God's fearsomeness in fire and water is echoed again by Amichai's description of having been in fire and water. All the more, both *'Asher 'Eimatekha* and (as we will see) Amichai's poem allude to divine *ziv* (splendor) and *zohar* (radiance).

And yet, undermining this ancient liturgical attestation of God's glory, Amichai presents one of the most memorable theological metaphors in the history of modern Hebrew poetry: the image of God as a car mechanic, working in a garage under the car that is the world. The speaker yearns to see all of God but can visualize only the soles of God's feet (perhaps a reference to conventional liturgy's sometimes unfruitful attempts to make God visible in our lives through the metric "feet" of poetry).[3] But, Amichai is saying, we humans are not unique in our limitations. In fixing the automobile that is this world, only for it to break down over and over again, God too demonstrates a finite corrective capacity. As if criticizing God behind God's back, but also making God look more and more like everyday us, the chorus shifts to the third person, intoning, "And that is H/his glory"—referring either to God or to humans, with deliberate ambiguity.

Traditionally, on Rosh Hashanah and Yom Kippur we crown God as King. In keeping with this kingship theme, Amichai's poem quotes from the parable of Jotham, about a group of trees that set out to anoint themselves a worthy king but end up with the least worthy arboreal candidate—essentially a polemic against the choice of corrupt Abimelech as king of Shechem (Judg. 9:8–20). Amichai's poem implies opposition to the coronation of God, too!

He also remakes the image of God in the *Unetaneh Tokef* (Let Us Ascribe Holiness, a central High Holy Day *piyyut*) from *sofer u-moneh* (a counter and enumerator [of all God's creatures]) to standing on a street corner and counting the passersby, one by one. As such, Amichai dares to depict God as homeless, or perhaps cast out of home.

Where, then, do we find true glory in the poem—and in the world? For the poet-speaker, who has been to war and found no grandeur there, the real glory resides at home, in relationship, and in love.

In this domestic context the poet relinquishes cynicism and discovers divine revelation in the unlikeliest of places: in the kitchen, in front of the refrigerator.

Looking at his beloved standing by the open fridge, he sees H/her illuminated, as if by a divine light. Amichai doesn't buy the conventional images of the High Holy Day season. And yet he doesn't renounce divine splendor, either.

This COVID Rosh Hashanah of 2020, missing my parents, my childhood home, and my regular seat by the south wall of the Bayit main sanctuary, I was grateful for Amichai's homebound transformation of garage and refrigerator into revelatory sites. A backyard tent, then, could be revelatory as well.

FIG. 7. Glowing refrigerator. Courtesy of W. Carter, Wikimedia Commons.

"In the Morning I Stand by Your Bed"

In the Morning I Stand by Your Bed	**בַּבֹּקֶר אֲנִי עוֹמֵד לְיַד מִטָּתֵךְ**[4]
In the morning I stand by your bed.	בַּבֹּקֶר אֲנִי עוֹמֵד לְיַד מִטָּתֵךְ.
My shadow falls on your face	צִילִי נוֹפֵל עַל פָּנַיִךְ
And deepens your sleep	וּמַעֲמִיק אֶת שְׁנָתֵךְ
And adds on to your night.	וְעוֹשֶׂה לָךְ תוֹסֶפֶת לַיְלָה.
Like fingers of a smoker, your soul	כְּאֶצְבָּעוֹת מְעַשֵּׁן, נַפְשֵׁךְ
Has darkened, addicted to love.	כָּהֲתָה, מְכוּרָה לְאַהֲבָה.
I love you	אֲנִי אוֹהֵב אוֹתָךְ
With all my might and with all my light.	בְּכָל מְאֹדִי וּבְכָל אוֹדִי.

After Sukkot, the days got shorter. When I walked to shul for morning prayers, it was still dark outside, as it had been back in March before we moved the clocks forward. Like Lea Goldberg's "Night Psalm," Yehuda Amichai's "In the Morning I Stand by Your Bed" spoke to that recurrent experience of walking to shul in the dark, and sometimes even wondering what this running back and forth to synagogue was all about.

The poet speaker stands in the morning next to his lover's bed, his body casting a shadow over hers, the darkness of this shadow offering her the gift of more nighttime sleep—a loving gift I would have been delighted to receive on those mornings when I dragged myself out of bed to make it to synagogue in time for the first Rabbis' Kaddish of the day.

The shadow cast over his lover in bed is then compared to a darkening of her soul due to an addiction to love, which itself is likened to the stains of nicotine on a smoker's fingers. These are dark similes, indeed: love's comparison to a pathological compulsion we can't stop acting upon even though it endangers us.

But the compulsive lover here doesn't love in isolation. That she is loved in return should surely mitigate any potential harm. As the speaker says in the final stanza, evoking the *Ve-'ahavta*, "I love you with all my might" (*be-khol me'odi*).[5] And then, playing on that phrase, he adds *be-*

khol odi. Left unvocalized the word אודי can be read either as *'odi,* my thanks, or as *'udi,* "all of my firebrand or spark," that is, all that is left of passion's fire, or as *Udi,* a common diminutive nickname for Yehuda, the poet's own name. For many Israelis, born to Holocaust survivors, the word *'ud* (ember) also invokes Zechariah 3:2, "For this is an *'ud* [brand or ember] plucked from the fire"—a poetic expression often used to describe Holocaust survivors. German-born Amichai himself was one such "ember," arriving in Palestine as a child and thereby averting the fate of so many German Jews, including his best friend, Ruth. The love in the poem is yet another ember, kept aglow against all odds despite darkness everywhere.

In her memoir about addiction and recovery, author Leslie Jamison describes addiction as "a narrowing of the repertoire, all of life contracting around the booze or the drugs or the high."[6] Might daily prayer and, by extension, Kaddish be a kind of addiction? I wondered. Every morning and evening I walked to one destination for one purpose. Every morning and evening I recited the *Shema'* with its injunction to love God with all my heart and all my soul and all my might: Was this not a kind of narrowing of the repertoire?

Of course, the *Shema'* is preceded in the morning by the words *'ahavah rabbah 'ahavtanu* ("You have loved us greatly"), and in the evening by *'ahavat 'olam beit Yisra'el 'amekha 'ahavta* ("You have loved Your people, the house of Israel, an eternal love")—both reminders that God loves us back. Taken together, these prayers constitute a form of lovespeak between us and God, and a widening rather than a narrowing of the aperture of light.

With this in mind, I revisited Amichai's poem from a daily prayer's point of view. It was early in the morning. A loving God stood by our beds as we savored last minutes of sleep. We then pulled ourselves out of bed; grabbed our coats, bags, and masks; and either drove or walked to synagogue. It was a habit we could not seem to break; it had us tied up in knots. But the commitment—a more positive way of referring to deeply ingrained habits—was not one-sided. Tough as it was to believe, God loved us back. And our commitment every morning and night to encounter that love was the very thing keeping the fire alight.

"Half the People in the World"

Half the People in the World	מַחֲצִית הָאֲנָשִׁים בָּעוֹלָם[7]
Half the people in the world	מַחֲצִית הָאֲנָשִׁים בָּעוֹלָם
Love the other half,	אוֹהֲבִים אֶת הַמַּחֲצִית הַשְּׁנִיָּה,
Half the people in the world	מַחֲצִית הָאֲנָשִׁים
Hate the other half,	שׂוֹנְאִים אֶת הַשְּׁנִיָּה,
Because of these and those must I	הַאִם בִּגְלַל אֵלֶּה וְאֵלֶּה עָלַי
Go out and wander and constantly adapt,	לָלֶכֶת וְלִנְדֹד וּלְהִשְׁתַּנּוֹת בְּלִי הֶרֶף,
Like rain in its cycle, and sleep between rocks	כַּגֶּשֶׁם בַּמַּחֲזוֹר, וְלִישׁוֹן בֵּין סְלָעִים,
And be rough like the trunks of olive trees,	וְלִהְיוֹת מְחֻסְפָּס כְּגִזְעֵי זֵיתִים,
And hear the moon bark over me,	וְלִשְׁמֹעַ אֶת הַיָּרֵחַ נוֹבֵחַ עָלַי,
And camouflage my love with worries,	וּלְהַסְווֹת אֶת אַהֲבָתִי בִּדְאָגוֹת,
And sprout like timid grass between the tracks,	וְלִצְמֹחַ כָּעֵשֶׂב הָרָהוּי בֵּין פַּסֵּי הָרַכֶּבֶת,
And live beneath the earth like a mole,	וְלָגוּר בָּאֲדָמָה כַּחֲפַרְפֶּרֶת,
And endure with roots but not branches,	וְלִהְיוֹת עִם שָׁרָשִׁים וְלֹא עִם עֲנָפִים,
Without my cheek against the cheek of angels,	וְלֹא לֶחֱיִי עַל לְחִי מַלְאָכִים,
To love in the first cave	וְלֶאֱהֹב בַּמְּעָרָה הָרִאשׁוֹנָה
And carry my wife under a canopy	וְלָשֵׂאת אֶת אִשְׁתִּי תַּחַת חֻפַּת
Of poles bearing the earth,	הַקּוֹרוֹת הַנּוֹשְׂאוֹת אֲדָמָה,
And always act out my death	וּלְשַׂחֵק אֶת מוֹתִי, תָּמִיד
Until the last breath and last	עַד הַנְּשִׁימָה הָאַחֲרוֹנָה וְהַמִּלִּים
Words without ever understanding,	הָאַחֲרוֹנוֹת וּבְלִי לְהָבִין,
And put flagpoles high on my house	וְלַעֲשׂוֹת בְּבֵיתִי עַמּוּדֵי דְּגָלִים לְמַעְלָה
And a bomb shelter below. And go out on roads	וּמִקְלָט לְמַטָּה. וְלָצֵאת בַּדְּרָכִים
Made only for returning and traverse	הָעֲשׂוּיוֹת רַק לִשִׁיבָה וְלַעֲבֹר
All the terrible stations—	אֶת כָּל הַתַּחֲנוֹת הַנּוֹרָאוֹת—
Cat, stick, fire, water, butcher,	חָתוּל, מַקֵּל, אֵשׁ, מַיִם, שׁוֹחֵט,
Between the kid and the angel of death?	בֵּין הַגְּדִי וּבֵין מַלְאַךְ-הַמָּוֶת?

Half the people in the world love,	מַחֲצִית הָאֲנָשִׁים אוֹהֲבִים,
The other half hates.	מַחֲצִית שׂוֹנְאִים.
And where is my place between such well-matched halves	וְהֵיכָן מְקוֹמִי בֵּין הַמַּחֲצִיּוֹת הַמֻּתְאָמוֹת כָּל־כָּךְ
And through which crack will I see	וְדֶרֶךְ אֵיזֶה סֶדֶק אֶרְאֶה אֶת
The white housing projects of my dreams,	הַשִּׁיכּוּנִים הַלְּבָנִים שֶׁל חֲלוֹמוֹתַי,
And the barefoot runners on the beach	וְאֶת הָרָצִים הַיְחֵפִים עַל הַחוֹלוֹת
Or at least the waving	אוֹ לְפָחוֹת אֶת נִפְנוּף
Of a girl's kerchief, beside the tel?	מִטְפַּחַת הַנַּעֲרָה, לְיַד הַתֵּל?

What an abrupt shift to move from a poem celebrating the mutuality of love to one lamenting a world split in half by hate. Late at night on November 3, 2020, watching the returns of the then still inconclusive 2020 U.S. presidential election, I found myself struggling to understand how America could be divided into such vociferous, opposing halves—and how, in light of these deep divisions, a world of things fallen apart, we could ever hope to recover a sense of shared national values.

Yehuda Amichai's "Half the People in the World" perfectly illustrated the embattled American condition during that post-election week, and which continues to this day. The poem depicts a starkly divided world riven with enmity where human beings hide underground, flee and wander, develop hard protective shells, and raise up marriage canopies that seem to bear the weight of the entire world.

There's a fatalistic quality to this divided world. The allusion to the *Ḥad Gadya'* song from the Passover Haggadah introduces Jewish specificity and an endless cycle of violence to this deterministic portrayal. The cat, stick, fire, water, *shoḥet* (ritual slaughterer), goat (kid), and angel of death are all present—with the conspicuous absence of the Holy Blessed One.

And where is my place, asks Amichai's idiosyncratic speaker, amid these tidily divided halves? Is there a crack in this system that can allow for the dream of individuality as well as solidarity? The Hebrew word *maḥatzit* (half) echoes the biblical commandment to every man to contribute a half-shekel toward the building of the tabernacle (Exodus 30:13), highlighting the significance of every individual contribution as well as the challenge of asserting individuality in such a collective framework.

Amichai further depicts this mix of collective and individual aspiration through the metaphor of the Zionist white housing project, symbolic of all the white stucco new towns and neighborhoods created in the new State of Israel, and in a more private image of barefoot runners on the beach. As for the final hoped-for picture of a girl waving a kerchief: Is this a gesture of greeting or surrender? Is her position beside a tel suggestive of the newness and promise of Israeli cities such as Tel Aviv, or of the ancient cycles of violence and destruction built up over the centuries in the form of archaeological tels? "Half the People in the World" remains ever divided between these possibilities. And so, in a sense, were we: as divided citizens of America, awaiting the post-election chapter.

“God’s Hand in the World”

God’s Hand in the World	**יַד אֱלֹהִים בָּעוֹלָם**[8]
[1]	[א]
God’s hand in the world	יַד אֱלֹהִים בָּעוֹלָם
Like my mother’s hand in the guts of a slaughtered chicken	כְּיַד אִמִּי בִּמְעֵי הַתַּרְנְגוֹל הַשָּׁחוּט
On Sabbath eve.	בְּעֶרֶב שַׁבָּת.
What does God see through the window	מָה רוֹאֶה אֱלֹהִים מֵעֵבֶר לַחַלּוֹן
While His hands reach into the world?	בְּעֵת יָדָיו נְתוּנוֹת בָּעוֹלָם?
What does my mother see?	מָה רוֹאָה אִמִּי?
[2]	[ב]
My pain is already a grandfather:	כְּאֵבִי כְּבָר סָב:
It has birthed two generations	יָלַד שְׁנֵי דּוֹרוֹת
Of identical pains.	שֶׁל כְּאֵבִים הַדּוֹמִים לוֹ.
My hopes put up white housing projects	תִּקְווֹתַי הֵקִימוּ שִׁכּוּנִים לְבָנִים
Far from the congestion within me.	הַרְחֵק מִן הַדֹּחַק שֶׁבִּי.
My girlfriend forgot her love on the sidewalk	נַעֲרָתִי שָׁכְחָה אֶת אַהֲבָתָהּ עַל הַמִּדְרָכָה
Like a bicycle. All night outside, in the dew.	כְּמוֹ אוֹפַנַּיִם. כָּל הַלַּיְלָה בַּחוּץ וּבַטָּל.
Children sketch my life story	יְלָדִים רוֹשְׁמִים אֶת תּוֹלְדוֹת חַיַּי
And the story of Jerusalem	וְאֶת תּוֹלְדוֹת יְרוּשָׁלַיִם
With moon chalk on the street.	בְּגִיר יָרֵחַ עַל הַכְּבִישׁ.
God’s hand in the world.	יַד אֱלֹהִים בָּעוֹלָם.

From the political to the personal. And, once again, a burial.

After months of planning and repeated COVID delays, as America awaited official polling results in the week after the presidential election, my siblings and I were finally reinterring the remains of my father and grandmother, previously buried in Toronto, next to my mother in New Jersey. Once again, I found myself ritually tearing my shirt and sitting on a low chair. My two sisters, brother, and I were joining the fewest number of Jews ever to sit *shemonah* (eight days of mourning)—the reinterments adding an eighth day of ritual mourning to the seven previously observed.

And the very morning before the reinterments, I taught "God's Hand in the World," in which Amichai reflects on the coexistence of life and death in our world, and God's hand in it all.

Like many of Amichai's poems, this poem opens with a provocative simile linking God with a mundane—in this case, gruesome—task. God's hand in the world is likened to the poet's mother's hand in the bowels of a slaughtered chicken on Sabbath eve. How are we meant to interpret this analogy? Does it mean that like a mother with her hands in the guts of a slaughtered chicken, God handles death casually, wordlessly, and without sentiment? Or that like a mother who prepares chicken for Shabbat to feed her family, God gets Her hands dirty to create a bountiful Shabbat feast? Or both?

Amichai's speaker asks what his mother and God each see as they stick their hands into the guts of the chicken and of the world, but leaves the question unanswered. He then shifts to his own pains and hopes, saying that these are like a grandfather who has begotten two generations of similar pains.

All too aware of the impending reinterments of my father and grandmother, I mused about the painful familial patterns recurring throughout Genesis, which we had been reading in shul over those autumn weeks: choosing one son over another, fleeing or being driven from a familial household, and burying a family member.[9] Relatedly, I reflected on my dad's tragic death on March 12, 2019; my mother's passing fewer than eleven months later; New York's COVID lockdown on March 12, 2020—exactly a year after my father's death; and now, this additional double-reburial. Our familial pain felt like a great-great grandfather, an accumulation of acute, intergenerational grief. Yet we also felt hope and peace, having gathered ourselves together in life and brought our deceased loved ones together in death.

Which brings us to the next image in Amichai's poem. As if to counter the generations of pain, Amichai once again invokes the Zionist white housing project. In this spanking white neighborhood the poet's girlfriend leaves her love overnight like a bicycle on the sidewalk. Is this a sign of benign (or not so benign?) neglect? Or is it the confidence that love will still be there the next morning—not stolen or spoiled by the nighttime dew?

Which, in turn, leads to the writing of *toledot,* a word that refers at once to both generations and history. In the final stanza, children inscribe the poet's *toledot* (his personal life story) and the *toledot* (history) of Jerusalem not with chalk but with moonlight. There's a heavenly, providential tint to the inscription, but also a sense of impermanence: moon drawings are sure to disappear come morning. This, together with the recurrent image of God's hand in the world, suggests an ongoing but ephemeral Divine Providence.

But better something than nothing. Indeed, the final line, "God's hand in the world," brings us back full circle to the opening image of the poet's mother's hand in a slaughtered chicken. Pictures of children and moon drawings on the sidewalk return the poet to his earliest notions of God and religion, to his childhood and his mother. Amichai seems to suggest that this mundane image of a maternal hand in the slaughtered chicken, representative of everyday—messy, gory, but also loving—care, is the truest, most relatable image of God's role in the world.

And so, like the poem, I returned to where I began: with the gathering of my father and grandmother's bones. All that day until sundown, I thought of my father, my mother, and my grandmother: the way they had often moved from place to place to be closer to one another. Decades ago, in 1952, my mother left her childhood home in the Bronx to marry my father and take up a life, first in Sarnia, Ontario, and then in Toronto. Upon being widowed, her mother (my grandmother Shirley) moved to Toronto to live near our family. Some thirty years later, I moved with my own family from Hong Kong to the Bronx, and upon my father's tragic death, we moved my mother back to the Bronx to live near us. Now, with the reinterments, my siblings and I were gathering our father, mother, and grandmother together again in death. All three had put their hands to work in the guts of our lives, to nurture us and leave their mark. It wasn't all perfect, or pleasant, or harmless, but it was abiding, real, and good: God's hand in the world.

A Sort of End of Days	**מֵעֵין אַחֲרִית הַיָּמִים**[10]
The man under his fig tree phoned the man under his vine:	הָאִישׁ תַּחַת תְּאֵנָתוֹ טִלְפֵּן לָאִישׁ תַּחַת גַּפְנוֹ:
“Tonight they definitely might come in time.	״הַלַּיְלָה הֵם בְּהֶחְלֵט עֲלוּלִים לָבוֹא.
Armor-plate the leaves, tightly close the tree,	שַׁרְיֵן אֶת הֶעָלִים סְגֹר הֵיטֵב אֶת הָאִילָן,
Call the dead home and be ready in three.”[11]	קְרָא לַמֵּתִים הַבַּיְתָה, וֶהֱיֵה מוּכָן.״
The white lamb said to the hungry wolf:[12]	הַכֶּבֶשׂ הַלָּבָן אָמַר לַזְּאֵב:
“People are bleating and my heart aches enough.	״בְּנֵי אָדָם פּוֹעִים וְלִבִּי כּוֹאֵב:
Over there they’ll soon come to bayonet blows.	הֵם יַגִּיעוּ שָׁם לִידֵי קְרָבוֹת כִּידוֹן.
At our next meeting the issue will be disclosed.”	בַּפְּגִישָׁה הַבָּאָה בֵּינֵינוּ, הָעִנְיָן יִדּוֹן.״
All the nations (united) will stream to Jerusalem to perceive	כָּל הַגּוֹיִים (הַמְאֻחָדִים) יִנְהֲרוּ לִירוּשָׁלַיִם
Whether the Torah has taken leave.	לִרְאוֹת אִם יָצְאָה תּוֹרָה, וּבֵינְתַיִם,
Meanwhile, since spring has started to sprout,	הֱיוֹת וְעַכְשָׁיו אָבִיב
They’ll gather flowers from all about.	יִלְקְטוּ פְּרָחִים מִסָּבִיב.
And they’ll beat swords into plowshares and plowshares into swords,[13]	וְכִתְּתוּ חֶרֶב לְמַזְמֵרָה וּמַזְמֵרָה לְחֶרֶב
Again, forfend, and back and forth.	וְחוֹזֵר חֲלִילָה וְשׁוּב בְּלִי הֶרֶף.
Perhaps from beatings and honings galore,	אוּלַי מִכִּתּוּתִים וְהַשְׁחָזוֹת הַרְבֵּה,
The iron of quarrel will vanish, evermore.	בַּרְזֶל הָרִיב בָּעוֹלָם יִכְלֶה.

It was the day before Thanksgiving. That time when American families traditionally gather to give thanks and enjoy each other’s company. When we recall the Puritan pilgrims and renew our sense of the fundamental decency and comity of America. To be sure, that story about the pilgrims and the Native Americans sharing a meal together in peace and thanks has always been mere myth. But myths shore up our ideals and prod us to actualize them.

In November 2020 the ideal of Americans gathering as a national family seemed particularly mythical and impossible. A few weeks earlier, Joe Biden had been declared the forty-sixth president of the United States, yet increasingly more Republicans were casting doubt on the election result. Meanwhile, COVID cases, hospitalizations, and deaths were spiking nationwide. Every day we watched newscasters and public health experts stand before electronic boards displaying maps covered with red dots corresponding to COVID cases—a kind of public-health prophetic-Apocalypse in the making. Dr. Anthony Fauci issued a "final plea" for Americans to follow COVID-19 guidelines and avoid large gatherings, and still many Americans refused to listen.[14]

The day before Thanksgiving, I taught "A Sort of End of Days," Amichai's poem addressing the issue of myth and unrealizable promises by revisiting the prophetic descriptions of future redemption.

If the prophet Micah envisions "the End of Days" as a time in God's world when each man can sit securely under his vine and fig tree without fear of being attacked, Amichai situates this image alongside the other elements of the apocalypse, including the climactic battle of Gog and Magog meant to precipitate messianic redemption.[15] He imagines a man sitting under his fig tree telephoning a man sitting under his vine: Prepare for the Great War. Batten up the hatches, fortify the leaves, and seal up your sheltering tree, gather up your family's resurrected dead into your home, and hunker down for the bloody duration of Judgment Day. Without pause, the poet adds, in the language of committees and bureaucracies, "At our next meeting this matter will be disclosed." Such is the coldness and matter-of-factness of modern war.

And yet, the next stanza tries to coax the "End of Days" in a more redemptive direction. Alluding to biblical visions of how the nations will stream to Jerusalem at the end of days (Mic. 4:1, Isa. 2:1–3), Amichai imagines the actual arrival of these pilgrims in Jerusalem, a stream of spectators who come, as if to a sporting event, to see whether the Torah is about to go out from Jerusalem (Isa. 2:3) or if it will simply depart from the world completely. After the various nations arrive, they busy themselves gathering flowers—to adorn themselves, or the graves of the dead? As they continue to wait, they beat their swords into plowshares (Isa. 2:4), signifying the end of war. But their wait doesn't end there. The wait is in fact so prolonged that they beat their repurposed farm tools back into implements of war—plowshares back into swords, and then the swords back into plowshares, and plowshares back into swords—in a never-ending cycle of wars and temporary truces, all the prophetic promises of peace notwithstanding.

Hoping for something better, Amichai then imagines a modest end to the cycle. Perhaps the iron of strife and war will simply wear out from all the effort to precipitate redemption. This might be the best we can hope for: an end-time when people are simply too exhausted and enervated to perpetuate war.

In 2020, weren't we already too tired? Tired of being stuck inside, and of bracing ourselves for even tighter lockdown measures? Tired of the warring news narratives and of comity blown apart? Tired of the conspiracy theories and lies? Tired of COVID case numbers and death tolls, of those who weren't taking COVID seriously, of school shutdowns and the closing of businesses, like the closing up of trees in the poem's first stanza?

That week before Thanksgiving, I presented Amichai's poem as a reminder of what we could be thankful for even if we could not gather as we wished: our sense of irony and humor, and our capacity to cling to myth and tradition, even as we quarreled with it. We had not reached the End of Days. Even had the nations wanted to stream to Jerusalem, COVID restrictions would never have let them past Israel's borders. And since we were tired of it all, might the continued wearing down of our spirits also help dull the metal of enmity and strife and bring us closer to the way we hoped this country and the world might be? It was a mythic notion, to be sure, but worth clinging to. We gave thanks for that lesser but higher hope.

“My Mother Baked Me the Whole World”

My Mother Baked Me the Whole World	**אִמִּי אָפְתָה לִי אֶת כָּל הָעוֹלָם**[16]
My mother baked me the whole world	אִמִּי אָפְתָה לִי אֶת כָּל הָעוֹלָם
In sweet cakes.	בְּעוּגוֹת מְתוּקוֹת.
My beloved filled my window	אֲהוּבָתִי מִלְאָה אֶת חַלּוֹנִי
With raisins of stars.	בְּצִמּוּקֵי כּוֹכָבִים.
And my yearnings are sealed up inside me like air bubbles	וְהַגַּעְגּוּעִים סְגוּרִים בִּי כְּבוּעוֹת אֲוִיר
In a loaf of bread.	בְּכִכַּר הַלֶּחֶם.
On the outside I am smooth and quiet and brown.	מִבַּחוּץ אֲנִי חָלָק וְשָׁקֵט וָחוּם.
The world loves me.	הָעוֹלָם אוֹהֵב אוֹתִי.
But my hair is sad like reeds in the drying swamp—	אַךְ שְׂעָרִי עָצוּב כַּגֹּמֶא בַּבִּצָּה הַמִּתְיַבֶּשֶׁת וְהוֹלֶכֶת –
All the rare, lovely-feathered birds	כָּל הַצִּפֳּרִים הַנְּדִירוֹת וִיפוֹת הַנּוֹצָה
Flee from me.	נָסוֹת מִמֶּנִּי.

It was Tuesday. It was Ḥanukkah. And it was my last day of Kaddish for my mother. I had been saying Kaddish for twenty-two straight months, minus five days. After some eighty-eight weeks, it had become second nature for me to say that set of rhyming Aramaic words eight times a day. How would I ever stop saying it? How would I stay silent during the Kaddish recitation at morning *tefillah* the following day?

Because it was also Ḥanukkah, I kept thinking of “Likhvod ha-Ḥanukkah,” a children’s song by the great poet Ḥayyim Naḥman Bialik (1873–1934), which I had learned as a child—especially the third verse, which mentions a mother:

> My mother gave me a latke [*levivah*],
> A latke warm and sweet.
> Do you know in honor of what?
> In honor of Ḥanukkah.[17]

Levivah, the Hebrew term for the Yiddish latke (pancake), is a wonderful, heartwarming word that evokes the Hebrew word *lev* (heart), thereby embodying the very idea of maternal love and care.[18]

This song—and this stanza in particular—might very well have been on Yehuda Amichai's mind, too, when he wrote the poem "My Mother Baked me the Whole World." Their opening lines certainly seem close: Bialik's *'imi natenah levivah li* (my mother gave me a latke) and Amichai's *'imi 'afetah li 'et kol ha-'olam* ("My mother baked me the whole world").

In the children's song by Bialik, the child receives all that's needed for Ḥanukkah: a candle from Father, a dreidel from Teacher, a latke from Mother, and a coin from Uncle. A whole Ḥanukkah world.

In Amichai's poem, the mother gives the speaker all he needs, too: not just a holiday's worth, but an entire world. As such (and in keeping with Amichai's secular theology of everyday life), the mother becomes a Mother/Baker/Creator God This mother bakes an entire delicious universe for her poet-son. In his sweet treat cosmos even his longings are accounted for, tucked in, saved, and protected like air bubbles in nourishing, freshly baked bread. Because his mother loves him, everyone else will love him—or so the speaker expects.

Yet the last three lines undercut the speaker's sense of security. Suddenly he sees a gap between his expectations for love, as conditioned by his mother, and the way others treat him. If he previously perceived himself as smooth, quiet, and brown on the outside, like well-baked bread, he now compares his sad, unruly hair to reed papyrus in a drying swamp. The reference to *gome'* (reed papyrus) brings to mind baby Moses in his *teivat gome'*, the reed basket in which his mother places him before (unable to protect him) she sets him afloat on the Nile (Exod 2:3). The use of reed papyrus in the production of paper suggests that the speaker's poems, which are written on paper and which hang down over his face like sad hair, induce discomfort in those around him. The rare lovely birds, a metaphor for the beautiful people around him—those with social, political, or literary power, perhaps—avoid and shun him, threatening the secure, loving world of his mother's baking.

The word nostalgia literally means "an aching for home." Reading and teaching this poem on Ḥanukkah and on the last day of my Kaddish recitation for my mother was nostalgic in the most aching sense. When I was little, my mother would protect me and account for my every need. She would stay up until all hours of the night talking with me, if that's what I needed. My relationship with my mother was never perfect; she suffered from depression, and as the youngest child I often tried to fix things, to coax her out of her sadness in ways she didn't always appreciate. Still, until the very end of her life, I lived with the recognition that there was a person in the world who knew me from the time I was born, who stood firmly in my corner, who cared about each and every aspect of my life and my family's life, and who never tired of hearing about any of it. When she passed away, that whole world of care disappeared. The sad awareness that my parental world had vanished had not lessened with the passing months. Knowing that my formal mourning period was ending made the sadness even more acute.

And yet it was Ḥanukkah, a time when Jews are enjoined to place limits on sadness. The *halakhah* (codified law) as stated in the Shulḥan Arukh (*Oraḥ Ḥayyim* 670:1) forbids one from fasting or offering eulogies for the dead on Ḥanukkah, but allows for work. The Shulḥan Arukh also notes that it was common practice for women not to work while the Ḥanukkah candles were burning, because of women's special role in the Ḥanukkah story. According to the Rema (Rabbi Moses Isserles, 1530–1572), some people eat cheese on Ḥanukkah to commemorate the story of Judith giving milk to the Greek general Holfernes as a way of seducing and defeating him—the milk here adding a particularly maternal aspect to the Ḥanukkah victory.[19] To be maternal in the context of the Ḥanukkah story is not just to nurture, but to go to battle for one's children (as in Judges 5, where Deborah is identified as a "Mother in Israel" and gives Sisera milk before impaling him with a tent peg).

My mother was that kind of Mother, a fierce protector of and advocate for her kids. When we moved to a new neighborhood in Toronto right before I began first grade, I was placed in the only class at school with space left for another student. As soon as it became clear that I was not suited academically for that class, Mom undertook a relentless campaign to secure me a more appropriate class placement. By Ḥanukkah of that year she had me ensconced in the right class, where I took my first steps toward becoming fluent in Hebrew and I made my first lasting friends, including my childhood best friends, Carol and Debbie.

Mom loved and appreciated these friends of mine, and had so many deep friendships of her own. She was a specialist in gratitude: the sort of person who always sent thank-you cards and gave hostess gifts and made phone calls to acknowledge kindnesses. "It doesn't cost anything to make someone feel good," she would say.

With my mother's specialty in mind, I offered words of gratitude to the Bayit community, whose members had held me in a tight circle of extra-familial care and continued to give me a platform to teach the idiosyncratic brand of Torah that would eventually become this book. I also thanked my HUC-JIR students, who had arranged in-person and Zoom minyanim throughout my long period of mourning. As I prepared to step outside the Kaddish circle, I acknowledged my relief in knowing I would soon be released from a thrice-daily, twenty-two-monthlong obligation. At the same time, I confessed my sadness and trepidation about the impending moment of release. I knew that, like the speaker in Amichai's poem, the bright plumage of joy would likely elude me for some time, but the love and fierce protectiveness of my Bayit and HUC-JIR prayer communities would surely accompany me during the times ahead. My fellow prayers had baked a world of care for me: *levivot* of shared intention and prayer, for which I would be forever grateful.

That night we ate cheese *levivot* in honor of Ḥanukkah, my mom, and all moms.

"Whoever Wrapped in a Tallit"

Whoever Wrapped in a Tallit	**מִי שֶׁהִתְעַטֵּף בְּטַלִּית**[20]
Whoever wrapped in a tallit in youth will never forget:	מִי שֶׁהִתְעַטֵּף בְּטַלִּית בִּנְעוּרָיו לֹא יִשְׁכַּח לְעוֹלָם:
Taking it out of the soft velvet bag, opening the folded tallit,	הַהוֹצָאָה מִשַּׂקִּית הַקְּטִיפָה הָרַכָּה וּפְתִיחַת הַטַּלִּית הַמְקֻפֶּלֶת
Spreading it out, kissing the length of the neckband (some neckbands embroidered,	פְּרִישָׂה, נְשִׁיקַת הַצַּוָּארוֹן לְאָרְכּוֹ (הַצַּוָּארוֹן לִפְעָמִים רָקוּם
others trimmed in gold). After that, with a great unfurling overhead	וְלִפְעָמִים מֻזְהָב). אַחַר כָּךְ בִּתְנוּפָה גְּדוֹלָה מֵעַל הָרֹאשׁ
Like a sky, a wedding canopy, a parachute. And then winding it	כְּמוֹ שָׁמַיִם, כְּמוֹ חֻפָּה כְּמוֹ מַצְנֵחַ. אַחַר כָּךְ לִכְרֹךְ
Around your head as if playing hide- and-seek, and then wrapping	אוֹתָהּ סְבִיב הָרֹאשׁ כְּמוֹ בְּמַחֲבוֹאִים, אַחַר־כָּךְ לְהִתְעַטֵּף
Your whole body in it, so close, tucking into it like the cocoon	בָּהּ כָּל הַגּוּף, צְמוּדָה צְמוּדָה, וּלְהִתְכַּרְבֵּל כְּמוֹ גֹּלֶם
Of a butterfly, then opening up, as if with wings to fly.	שֶׁל פַּרְפַּר וְלִפְתֹּחַ כְּמוֹ כְּנָפַיִם וְלָעוּף.
And why is the tallit striped and not checkered black and white	וּמַדּוּעַ הַטַּלִּית בְּפַסִּים וְלֹא בְּמִשְׁבְּצוֹת־שָׁחֹר־לָבָן
Like a chessboard? Because squares are finite and hopeless,	כְּמוֹ לוּחַ שַׁחְמַט. כִּי הָרִבּוּעִים הֵם סוֹפִיִּים וּבְלִי תִּקְוָה,
Stripes come from endlessness and go to endlessness	הַפַּסִּים בָּאִים מֵאֵין־סוֹף וְיוֹצְאִים לְאֵין־סוֹף
Like runways in an airport Where angels land and take off.	כְּמוֹ מַסְלוּלֵי הַמַּמְרָאָה בִּשְׂדֵה תְּעוּפָה לִנְחִיתַת הַמַּלְאָכִים וּלְהַמְרָאָתָם.
Whoever has wrapped in a tallit will never forget,	מִי שֶׁהִתְעַטֵּף בְּטַלִּית לְעוֹלָם לֹא יִשְׁכַּח,
When you climb out of the swimming pool or the sea,	כְּשֶׁהוּא יוֹצֵא מִן הַבְּרֵכָה אוֹ מִן הַיָּם
You wrap in a large towel, spread it out again Over your head, and again, tuck into it so close	מִתְעַטֵּף בְּמַגֶּבֶת גְּדוֹלָה וּפוֹרֵשׂ אוֹתָהּ שׁוּב מֵעַל רֹאשׁוֹ וְשׁוּב מִתְכַּרְבֵּל בָּהּ, צָמוּד צָמוּד
And still shiver a bit, and laugh and bless.	וְרוֹעֵד עוֹד קְצָת וְצוֹחֵק וּמְבָרֵךְ.

I did not stop attending morning services after the completion of my Kaddish cycle. I had become used to the routine and the community, to the rhythms of the walk and the protected time to pray, and was eager, together with my Kaddish buddy Lisa, to guard the few parts for women in the service that we had secured together: leading the *Mi Shebeirakh* prayers for healing and for the well-being of IDF soldiers; reciting the *Yehi Ratzon* (Let It Be Your Will) prayers after the Monday and Thursday Torah readings; returning the Torah to the ark; and reciting the customary *mishnah* of Rabbi Ḥananyah before the final Rabbis' Kaddish.

So there I was the next morning, maintaining one habit, but trying, somehow, to detach from another. Three times, I started reciting Kaddish with all of the other mourners. Each time, I had to stop myself. This persisted for several days. After some five thousand recitations, saying Kaddish had become reflexive, a tough habit to kick.

I taught "Whoever Wrapped in a Tallit" that week because it depicted the impossibility of breaking certain ritual routines or forgetting their impact.[21]

The speaker, like Yehuda Amichai himself, seems to have left the religious fold of his youth long ago, and yet all the intimate sensations of childhood religious observance and their theological implications remain with him. Not just that: they open up, ramify, and transmute into other forms.

In this sense, I realized, the poem was not just about ritual, but about transition and translation, the carrying over of a feeling and a meaning: an experience of intimacy, of being swaddled and protected, and then of opening up, and lifting off. The sensation and memory of wrapping in a tallit is translated from youth to adulthood, from the holy to the mundane, from cocoon to butterfly, from geometry (squares and lines) to physics (motion) and aeronautics (the landing and takeoff of a plane), and then to metaphysics, mysticism (the concept of *'ein sof*, divine infinitude), and religion (belief in angels), and then back to Amichai's theological comfort zone: everyday life.

Amichai's poetry, flourishing in translation, explicitly engages the very themes and theories of translation. A basic issue addressed in translation theory is fidelity. Is a given translation—say, my translation of Amichai's poem as it appears above—faithful to the original? Is faithful translation between languages really feasible, given differences between national and linguistic cultures and fundamental disagreements between human beings? More broadly, is authentic communication between diverse people and cultures even possible?

Amichai's poem attempts to answer these questions by exploding or blurring the distinction between faithfulness and faithlessness. The poem hinges on the speaker's departure from childhood faith, but nevertheless demonstrates his ongoing fidelity to its rituals—or, at least, the feeling thereof. The sensation of being wrapped in a tallit and holding it overhead is recapitulated, simulated, and translated into other activities and objects: a child's game of hide-and-seek, the young adult's spreading of wings and flying away from home, a parachute, a wedding canopy, and other everyday experiences of transcendence—including the exhilaration of swimming, of moving through and then emerging from water, and then drying off. I thought too of parents and children at the beach: kids running into the water and then coming out, shivering, to be swiftly wrapped in a towel by caring parents.

But what if those parents are no longer in this world to wrap you up?

There are fundamental dissimilarities between the elements compared in the poem: synagogue and airport, child and larva, tallit and beach towel. But the fabric of metaphors and associations sews up those holes, stitching them together in a seemingly seamless whole. The poem seems to be chronicling continuity in the midst of rupture, persistence in the face of obstacle. Taken together these similes—*like a sky* (a metonymy for God), *like a wedding canopy* (marriage), and *like a parachute* (skydiving)—suggest, on the one hand, an unraveling of faith (has the marriage you thought was made in Heaven come to a crashing end, necessitating the parachute of a divorce?), and on the other hand, the ultimate demonstration of faith (isn't parachuting the very embodiment of faith in the continuity of sky and ground?).

That week, I was all the more drawn to "Whoever Wrapped in a Tallit" because its choreography, like that of the ritual donning of the tallit, entails an unfurling, but then a wrapping up. The poet retreats into the striped cocoon and then spreads his wings. These movements alternate but never disconnect from one another. There may be a shiver in the aftermath of one of these acts, but there is also laughter, joy, and blessing.

My own childhood ritual experience did not match Amichai's. I could not reimagine earlier memories of wrapping in a tallit. In adopting the practice of wearing a tallit—and, more recently, of putting on tefillin—as an adult woman, I had innovated rather than continued established familial practice. No woman in my family had ever before performed these rituals.

I had begun using my father's tefillin during the shivah for my mother as a conscious, ritualized way of differentiating between the first eleven months of Kaddish for Dad and the next eleven months of Kaddish for Mom. Taking on this new commitment was a way to add other ritual fastenings to my parents and to God that, I anticipated, would outlast the months of formal mourning. My son Amichai, named with the poet in mind, was the one who taught me what to do: how to place the boxes on arm and head and wrap the straps, what to say, and how to put them away.

Now, Amichai the poet had reminded me that metaphor—like translation, like communication, and like my laying of tefillin—brings together disparate elements to create something new. And more than that: his poem held out the promise of continuity in the face of the gut-wrenching end of my formal mourning. Some days and doings act as connectors; others, I knew, mark beginnings or ends. My many consecutive days of reciting Kaddish had concluded, but there would be annual yahrzeits and *Yizkor* memorial commemorations on each of the major Jewish holidays, and the responsibility to say "Amen" in response to the Mourners' Kaddish of others.

So, too, because my morning recitation of Kaddish had come every day on the heels (or fringes) of taking out my father's tallit (and tefillin) from their respective painted leather bags, the memory knots tying me to the ritual would not easily unravel.

The new regimen had taken a lot of getting used to. At first the boxes and windings would refuse to stay in place, and kept sliding down my arm, or tilting askew on my head. But, in time, laying tefillin became my new morning default setting. Every day I would reconnect through the act of carefully winding those straps that used to be Dad's, counting the windings, placing the first box on my arm in proximity to my heart, and the second box on my forehead between my eyes. And then, at the end of prayers, I would wrap it all back up, stacking each winding of the strap on top of the previous one, the way one straightens a pile of written pages.

Whoever has walked to synagogue daily in the dark, entered the building and found their seat, dug out their prayer props from a bag, suited up with tallit and tefillin, joined in the discordant chorus and choreography of Kaddish, sat down and stood up, bowed, sang, and finally returned to the same Rabbis' Kaddish with which they had begun, will never forget.

And so it is that as of this writing, more than three years since I taught "Whoever Wrapped in a Tallit," my daily realignment and check-in continues, for what I expect will be all of my days. A remedy for my longings. Going out with knots.

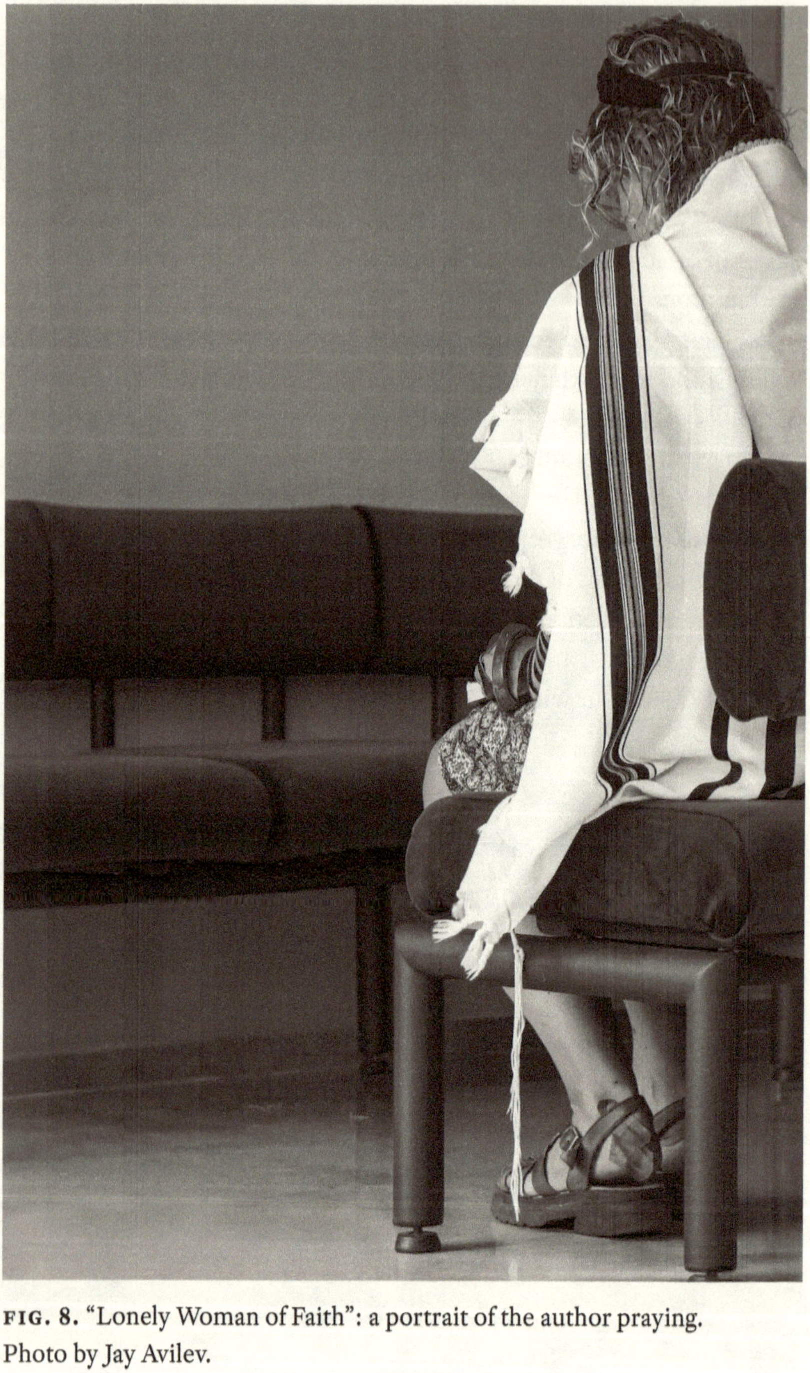

FIG. 8. "Lonely Woman of Faith": a portrait of the author praying. Photo by Jay Avilev.

Men, Women, and Children	אֲנָשִׁים נָשִׁים וָטַף[22]
Men, women, and children,	אֲנָשִׁים נָשִׁים וָטַף,
Jews, Christians, and Muslims,	יְהוּדִים נוֹצְרִים וּמֻסְלְמִים,
I want to belong to something	אֲנִי רוֹצֶה לִהְיוֹת שַׁיָּךְ לְמַשֶּׁהוּ
To receive special treatment and discounts,	וּלְקַבֵּל יַחַס מְיֻחָד וַהֲנָחָה,
Officers, soldiers, and students,	שׁוֹטְרִים, חַיָּלִים וּסְטוּדֶנְטִים,
Widows, orphans, and bereaved parents,	אַלְמָנוֹת, יְתוֹמִים וְהוֹרִים שַׁכּוּלִים,
The disabled, schoolchildren, seniors,	נָכִים, יְלָדִים, פֶּנְסְיוֹנֶרִים,
And to be without responsibility,	וְלִהְיוֹת בְּלִי אַחֲרָיוּת,
Deaf-mute, imbecile, and minor.	חֵרֵשׁ, שׁוֹטֶה וְקָטָן.
Love, part, and die,	אוֹהֲבִים, נִפְרָדִים וּמֵתִים,
I want to be part of some triangular order:	אֲנִי רוֹצֶה לִהְיוֹת בְּתוֹךְ אֵיזֶה סֵדֶר מְשֻׁלָּשׁ:
Prayer, Repentance, and Charity,	תְּפִלָּה, תְּשׁוּבָה וּצְדָקָה,
Blood, Sweat, and Tears,	דָּם, יֶזַע וּדְמָעוֹת,
Equality, Liberty, and Fraternity,	שִׁוְיוֹן, חֹפֶשׁ וְאַחֲוַת עַמִּים,
Sea, Land, and Air,[23]	יָם, יַבָּשָׁה וַאֲוִיר,
Something permanent:	מַשֶּׁהוּ קָבוּעַ:
Holy, holy, holy,	קָדוֹשׁ, קָדוֹשׁ, קָדוֹשׁ,
Quiet, quiet, quiet.	שֶׁקֶט, שֶׁקֶט, שֶׁקֶט.

Every so often one reads a poem that gives a glimpse of one poet's connection with another, a literary version of "going out with knots." This beautiful connection unites Yehuda Amichai's "Men, Women, and Children" and the 1948 children's poem "By Three Things" written by Amichai's poetic "parent," Lea Goldberg.

Goldberg's influence on Amichai was extraordinary. For hundreds of years women were entirely absent from the annals of Hebrew literature. Scholars do not know of a single book authored by a woman in the Hebrew language from the end of the biblical period through the end of the nineteenth century. One might have expected, along gender lines, that in setting out to be a poet, Amichai might have sought tutelage from some of the preeminent modern male poets of the prior generation, say

Avraham Shlonsky (1900–1973) or Natan Alterman (1910–1970). That Yehuda Amichai took inspiration from Goldberg—who, in addition to being a professor at the Hebrew University where Amichai studied and the convener of a writer's workshop that he attended, was also one of the first modern Hebrew women poets to achieve canonical status—constituted a paradigm shift.

Goldberg also seems to have been instrumental in helping him get his first poems published. On March 22, 1949, when he was still a soldier, Amichai mailed Goldberg some of his poems using his military address. "I've been writing more or less continuously for about four years," he wrote her, but "I've decided that it the time has come for my work to undergo a more general, expert critique."[24] We have no record of Goldberg's reaction or critique of these particular poems, or which exactly they were, only that three months later three of his poems appeared in the literary supplement *'Al ha-Mishmar*, where Goldberg was a columnist.[25] When his first book of poems, *'Akhhsav uve-Yamim 'Aḥerim* (*Now and In Other Days*), was published in 1955 to scathing critique by members of the poetic old guard, including *Davar* literary critic Shlomo Tzemaḥ ("A kind of mockery and profanation hovers before your eyes. . . . You can't draw anything from the word combinations on account of the emptiness of the picture, the triviality and the lack of taste. . . . A form of upside-down logic that contains nothing"[26]), Goldberg wrote a counter-review, defending the new generation that Amichai represented, his use of everyday language, and his "surprising originality," proclaiming, "This poet has a *partzuf* (distinct countenance)!"[27] Amichai would later reflect on Goldberg's importance to him in "Lea Goldberg Metah" ("Lea Goldberg Has Died"), a poem published a week after her death, in which he refers to carrying around a tattered copy of her book *Mi-beiti ha-Yashan* (*From My Old Home*) in his backpack throughout the 1948 War of Independence battles in the Negev.[28]

Israeli literary historian Gidon Ticotsky suggests why Amichai was particularly drawn to Goldberg. Both had strong roots in German language and culture. Both experienced firsthand the rise of the Nazis and immigrated to Palestine in the same year (1935). As poets, both were drawn to traditional forms and rhymes, and welcomed the influence of European modernism as well as the Hebrew poetry of medieval Spain.[29] Amichai's first published poems—sonnets that meditate on a seaside scene in Tiberias against the backdrop of war, and include a string of metaphors for memory and loss—read like variations on the themes and style of Goldberg's *Mi-beiti ha-Yashan*. Later in his career, he moved toward more colloquial and accessible language, but Goldberg's influence and sensibility remained formative.

With all this in mind, I could feel the reverberations of Goldberg's "By Three Things" in Amichai's "Men, Women, and Children." It was as if I was overhearing a conversation between the two poets on the subject of cardinal threes.

Goldberg had offered a new take on the rabbinic notion of core values, as articulated in *Pirkei 'Avot* 1:2 and 1:18 (see chapter 2). Her three workers—the fisherman, farmer, and artist—identify three things upon which the world stands, all of which relate to their particular fields of work. But a fourth speaker, *ha-'adam*—an androgynously gendered human being—insists that the world's riches are too manifold and wondrous to be relegated to the workplace or reduced to three. Goldberg's message is broad, universalist, and pluralistic. It encompasses religious and secular values, work, worship, wonder, the natural and human spheres, all the senses and colors.

If Goldberg's "By Three Things" busts up the rule of three and suggests a broader rule of four, Amichai's "Men, Women, and Children" hankers nostalgically for the simplicity of the triad. His poem is a veritable catalog of trios, including the three major Western religions and also *'anashim, nashim, va-taf* (men, women, children), the triad used in Deuteronomy 31:12 for the three classes of participants in the septennial commandment of the *Hakhel* or National Assembly. The poet craves to join a trio, however mundane—"I want to be part of some triangular order," he declares—implying that as a secular Israeli Hebrew poet, he doesn't belong anywhere.

His desperation to join a threesome is so acute that he even includes among his coveted trios "sea, land, and air" (the three sites of service and danger for Israeli soldiers, which hearken back to his hard army days), "widows, orphans, and bereaved parents" (socially vulnerable people in need of care and sympathy), and "blood, sweat, and tears" (emblematic of overall human suffering). He seeks membership even in onerous groups, laden with pain and responsibility.

Yet, he also wants to be absolved of responsibility, as exemplified by the halakhic trio of *ḥeresh shoteh ve-katan* (the deaf-mute, the cognitively or psychologically impaired, and the minor), who according to rabbinic law are exempt from positive mitzvot (commandments).

All the while, I observed, the tragic nature of some of the groups the poet claims to desire to belong to casts some doubt on the sincerity of his claims. Since he longs to fold himself into some collective category, his repeated assertion of *'ani rotzeh* (I want) does not suggest communal connection but persistent individual desire.

That is, until the last stanza, where the pronoun *'ani* disappears and the poet leaves us with two new trios: "Holy, holy, holy" and "Quiet, quiet, quiet."

Thus, both poems conclude in a liturgical modality: Goldberg's, a psalm-like declaration about the wonders of (God's) world, and Amichai's, a kind of sacred chant, evocative of the *Kedushah* prayer ("Holy, holy, holy"). If the poet's closing declamation of "Quiet, quiet, quiet" is understood, say, as an order issued by an irate teacher to a class of unruly students, it suggests an emptying out of holiness. Or it reflects the ultimate silence of death, like an earlier set of threes: *'ohavim, nifradim, u-metim,* "love, part, and die."

As it turns out, "Men, Women, and Children" consists of eighteen lines, the *gematria* (numerology) of the Hebrew word חי/*ḥai* (life) being eighteen, and thus pointing symbolically to the idea and sweep of a person's life. As such, the poem reflects the hope that our lives amount to something. They are meant to be tales of companionship and family, as represented by Ecclesiastes's teaching, "the threefold cord doesn't easily break" (4:12)—pointing in this case to the familial "cord" of father, mother, and child. This braided cord cannot guarantee permanence—nothing in life can—but it has a better chance of staying tied and unfrayed than a single or double cord.[30]

As for me and my grief journey, Amichai's poem provoked consideration of the threefold cords that were affording me meaning and a sense of connection to my family and community now that my formal mourning period was done:

Wife, husband, kids.
God, Torah, Israel.
Siddur, tallit, tefillin.
Shir, Ḥadash, Yom.
Reading, writing, teaching.
Presence, absence, memory.
Mom, Dad, me.

God Has Mercy on Kindergarten Children	אֱלֹהִים מְרַחֵם עַל יַלְדֵי הַגַּן[31]
God has mercy on kindergarten children,	אֱלֹהִים מְרַחֵם עַל יַלְדֵי הַגַּן,
Less on schoolchildren.	פָּחוֹת מִזֶּה עַל יַלְדֵי בֵּית־הַסֵּפֶר.
And on grown-ups, none at all,	וְעַל הַגְּדוֹלִים לֹא יְרַחֵם עוֹד,
He leaves them alone,	יַשְׁאִירֵם לְבַדָּם,
And sometimes they're forced to crawl on all fours	וְלִפְעָמִים יִצְטָרְכוּ לִזְחֹל עַל אַרְבַּע
On burning sand,	בַּחוֹל הַלּוֹהֵט,
In order to reach the first aid station	כְּדֵי לְהַגִּיעַ לְתַחֲנַת הָאִסּוּף
All the while dripping blood.	וְהֵם שׁוֹתְתֵי דָּם.
Perhaps He'll bestow mercy on those who love in truth[32]	אוּלַי עַל הָאוֹהֲבִים־בֶּאֱמֶת
And will cast caring shade	יִתֵּן רַחֲמִים וְיָחוּס וְיָצֵל
As a tree does on a person sleeping	כְּאִילָן עַל הַיָּשֵׁן בְּסַפְסָל
On a public street bench.	שֶׁבַּשְּׁדֵרָה הַצִּבּוּרִית.
Perhaps we'll give them	אוּלַי לָהֶם גַּם אֲנַחְנוּ נוֹצִיא
The last coins of our compassion,	אֶת מַטְבְּעוֹת הַחֶסֶד הָאַחֲרוֹנוֹת
Bequeathed to us by our mothers,	שֶׁהוֹרִישָׁה לָנוּ אִמָּא,
So that their happiness can protect us	כְּדֵי שֶׁאָשְׁרָם יָגֵן עָלֵינוּ
Now and on other days.	עַכְשָׁו וּבַיָּמִים הָאֲחֵרִים.

It was now March 2021. My father-in-law, Ephraim, had passed away on election night, Tuesday, November 3, 2020—the third parent to pass away in only eighteen months. Immediately following his death in Florida, we had moved my mother-in-law, Dvora—a woman formerly of great fortitude and intelligence, who was now suffering from Alzheimer's—to Riverdale to live near us, so we could be involved in her care. Some five months later we had signed a contract to sell her house, and so my husband, Daniel, and I found ourselves driving down to Boca in the midst of the still pre-vaccine pandemic to clean out the house in preparation for the closing. It was the third time in under two years that I had to pack up a parental home, and it proved to be a pitiless, back-breaking task—one we had but a week to complete before it was necessary to drive back home.

Begging for divine mercy is fundamental to prayer. Embedded in this request, in the very etymology of the word *raḥem* (have mercy), is the desire to be mothered, to be returned to and be sheltered in God's merciful *reḥem* (womb). The older we get, though, the farther we naturally move from that warm, embodied, sheltering place. How much the more so when one is compelled to leave the safety of one's home and city, drive across several states, assume the responsibilities of an incapacitated mother, and pull apart her once-sheltering home.

So it felt fitting and necessary that Tuesday morning in March to teach, by Zoom from Boca Raton, "God Has Mercy on Kindergarten Children," Amichai's poem measuring the distance between the *reḥem/raḥamim* (womb/mercy) of childhood and the harsh realities of adulthood.

The poem opens with the assertion that divine mercy seems to be operative or recognizable only when one is a small child. The older you grow, the less mercy you see.

Yet the next two stanzas hold out hope for compassion, even for us adults. The poet suggests that God's mercy might extend to those who "love in truth," which the poet compares to a tree casting shade on a person sleeping on a park bench—a seemingly ironic simile, given the limited scope of the mercy of a bit of shade to a plausibly impoverished, homeless human being. Still, the small kindness of shade offered by an otherwise impassive (Mother) Nature can be seen as a very real, tangible act of mercy in the world.

From compassionate Mother Nature, the poet moves to lessons of mercy imparted by our human mothers. Perhaps, like the tree that shades the anonymous sleeper, we will learn from this compassionate example and donate "the last coins of our compassion / bequeathed to us by our mothers." This image evokes the long-standing practice of mothers giving their children coins to put in a tzedakah (charity) box at school—a form of compassionate parenting and nurturing of citizenship, too. I thought of my own intergenerational connection to this practice: how my mother would give me a nickel or a dime to put in the blue-and-white JNF (Jewish National Fund) box at Associated Hebrew Schools in Toronto; how I gave my own kids quarters (for inflation!) to deposit in the tzedakah box at SAR Academy in Riverdale; and how when I started going to daily minyan to say Kaddish, I brought along a change purse with coins and individual dollar bills so I could contribute to the tzedakah box placed midway between the women's and men's sections.

In a community prayer context, the term *matbe'ot ḥesed* (coins of compassion) also evokes rabbinic statutory prayer and the *matbe'a she-tave'u ḥakhamim,* the rabbinic liturgical coinage for the various blessings, including the opening blessings of the *'Amidah* that address God as a merciful bestower of compassion.[33] Amichai, though, transforms the rabbinic blessing formula and its implicit theology in two crucial ways: by feminizing the compassionate divine parent and by having this divine Mother transmit to us the responsibility of bestowing compassion on others.

The notion of divine as well as maternal compassion (or the lack thereof) was on our minds that week as Daniel and I cleared out his mother's Florida house. We dared not even step into a grocery store in a state that had forsworn the basic COVID precautions to which we had become accustomed. Inside the house we found challenges, too. For one, my mother-in-law's dementia had resulted in an excess accumulation of duplicate items that needed to be pared down. With that, though, came the opportunity to give out coins of compassion in the form of Goodwill donations that allowed us to recycle rather than dispose—a small act of kindness to the environment and world, too.

Reading and teaching "God Has Mercy on Kindergarten Children" provoked many connections. Amichai's poem traverses temporal, physical, and experiential distances, from childhood to adulthood, from the battlefield to a park bench, all in the hope of rediscovering mercy not just for children but for adults, too. We, too, had traveled geographical and psychic distances: New York to Florida (and back), two different COVID worlds. We had immersed ourselves in artifacts of Dvora's earlier and later years—some of them poignant (albums and framed photographs of her Holocaust survivor grandparents and of Daniel's father, who died when Daniel was a baby), and some of them preposterous (several sets of "Fiddler on the Roof" butter knives). In confronting the need to throw or give away so much of what we found, we prayed that all of it—the time, the work, the donations—might be reckoned as "coins of compassion" to protect us, as Amichai writes, "Now and on other days."

I Filtered from the Book of Esther	סִנַּנְתִּי מִתּוֹךְ מְגִלַּת אֶסְתֵּר[34]
I filtered from the book of Esther the dregs	סִנַּנְתִּי מִתּוֹךְ מְגִלַּת אֶסְתֵּר אֶת מִשְׁקַע
Of vulgar joy, and from the book of Jeremiah	הַשִּׂמְחָה הַגַּסָּה וּמִתּוֹךְ סֵפֶר יִרְמְיָהוּ
The wail of pain in the guts. And from	אֶת יִלְלַת הַכְּאֵב בַּמֵּעַיִם. וּמִתּוֹךְ
Song of Songs the endless quest	שִׁיר הַשִּׁירִים אֶת הַחִיפּוּשׂ הָאֵין סוֹפִי
For love and from the Book of Genesis	אַחַר הָאַהֲבָה וּמִסֵּפֶר בְּרֵאשִׁית אֶת
The dreams and Cain and from Ecclesiastes	הַחֲלוֹמוֹת וְאֶת קַיִן וּמִתּוֹךְ קֹהֶלֶת אֶת
The despair, and from the Book of Job, Job.	הַיֵּאוּשׁ, וּמִתּוֹךְ סֵפֶר אִיּוֹב אֶת אִיּוֹב.
And from the leftovers I pasted myself a new Bible.	וְהִדְבַּקְתִּי לִי מִן הַשְּׁאֵרִיּוֹת סֵפֶר תַּנַ"ךְ חָדָשׁ.
Now I live censored, pasted, constrained, and tranquil.	אֲנִי חַי מְצֻנְזָר וּמֻדְבָּק וּמֻגְבָּל וּבְשַׁלְוָה.
Last night on the darkened street a woman	אִשָּׁה אַחַת שָׁאֲלָה אוֹתִי אֶמֶשׁ בָּרְחוֹב
Asked me about the well-being of another woman	הֶחָשׁוּךְ עַל שְׁלוֹם אִשָּׁה אַחֶרֶת
Who had died before her time, and anyone's time.	שֶׁמֵּתָה לֹא בְּעִתָּהּ וְלֹא בְּעִתּוֹ שֶׁל אַף אֶחָד.
I answered out of great exhaustion:	מִתּוֹךְ עֲיֵפוּת גְּדוֹלָה עָנִיתִי לָהּ:
She's fine, she's fine.	שְׁלוֹמָהּ טוֹב, שְׁלוֹמָהּ טוֹב.

Another COVID Purim loomed: a grim anniversary. Exactly a year before, we began retreating from regular activities due to COVID. We had "attended" the Purim reading of the book of Esther by Zoom. We had refrained from giving out *mishloaḥ manot*, the food-baskets traditionally gifted to friends and neighbors on the holiday. We had held festive meals but without guests, a harbinger of a stripped-down pandemic life.

"I Filtered from the Book of Esther" seemed a fitting teaching for this second COVID Purim because of its depiction of a censored Bible as a metaphor for a stripped-down life.

The censoring begins with the Purim story. Much like the traditional noisemaking to blot out the name of Haman during the ritual chanting of Esther, the poet sets out to filter out the objectionable parts from the book of Esther—its vulgar joy, drunkenness, triumphalism, and violence—and, in turn, filter everything disturbing from just about every book of the Bible: the howling pain of Jeremiah, the unfair suffering of Job, the unconsummated love of Song of Songs, the despair of Ecclesiastes, Cain's murder of his brother Abel, and so forth. The result of all this is a Bible, and by extension, a life, with no troubling aspects and no friction.

This filtered Bible serves as a coping mechanism, a means of evading pain, danger, and longing: rubber padding for a beaten psyche. But what's left in the end is nothing short of absurd. What, after all, is the book of Job without Job, or Ecclesiastes without philosophical hand-wringing and despair?[35]

This stripped-down life is fundamentally fake and dishonest, too. In the second stanza, the speaker replies "She's fine, she's fine" to the question posed about the woman who has just died an untimely death. By this point in my mourning and pandemic journey, I completely understood the impulse to lie and say "Fine, thanks" when feeling the opposite of fine. More often than not it was easier to mask up, both literally and figuratively, than to reveal how I really felt.

That Purim of 2021, though, we were beginning to witness a Purim-like reversal. After all, the Purim story is all about the overturning of a threat of annihilation into a triumph and an occasion for celebration. The numbers of COVID cases and deaths were still high, but there were signs of things turning around: a decrease in infection rates and death tolls, and a reversal of the previous year's filtering out of life. More of us gathered in person in shul on that 2021 Purim to hear the book of Esther. More of us headed out on the streets to deliver *mishloaḥ manot*. Many of us had already been vaccinated and so felt prepared to hold a festive Purim meal with at least a few loved ones. Given the massive death toll that COVID year had witnessed, it would have been obscene to answer the collective question *Mah shelomeinu* (How are we?) with *Shelomeinu tov* (We're fine, thanks). We were far from fine, but we were recovering the sense of what it might mean to return to our former, unfiltered lives.

“My Father on Passover Eve”

My Father on Passover Eve	**אָבִי בְּעֶרֶב פֶּסַח**[36]
On the final evening I gave you the example	בָּעֶרֶב הָאַחֲרוֹן הִמְשַׁלְתִּי לְךָ
Of my father, who on Passover eve	אֶת מְשַׁל אָבִי, אֲשֶׁר בְּעֶרֶב פֶּסַח
Would punctiliously cut bread	הָיָה חוֹתֵךְ לֶחֶם בְּהַקְפָּדָה
In exact cubes and place them	לְקֻבִּיּוֹת מְדֻיָּקוֹת וְשָׂם
On the window sill in order	אוֹתָן עַל אֶדֶן־הַחַלּוֹן כְּדֵי שֶׁיּוּכַל
To find them with his dimmed eyes	לִמְצוֹא אוֹתָן בְּעֵינָיו הַכְּבֵדוֹת
By candlelight dancing a good deed dance.	לְאוֹר הַנֵּר הָרוֹקֵד רִקּוּדֵי מִצְוָה.
And so that his blessing for burning the leaven not	וְלֹא תְּהִי בִּרְכַּת בִּעוּר חָמֵץ שֶׁלּוֹ
Be in vain.	לְבַטָּלָה.
To live like this:	כָּךְ לִחְיוֹת:
Directors of ourselves,	בַּמָּאִים שֶׁל עַצְמֵינוּ,
Directors of duplicity	בַּמָּאִים רַמָּאִים
With almost perfect faith,	בֶּאֱמוּנָה שְׁלֵמָה, כִּמְעַט,
So as not to	וּלֹא נִהְיֶה
Be in vain.	לְבַטָּלָה.

Every year before Passover, my father would receive a *bedikat ḥametz* kit from one or another of the Jewish benevolent associations that he used to support. The kit came in a manila envelope equipped with everything needed to perform the search for leaven: a paper bag, wooden spoon, candle, feather, and a printed card with the required blessings for the ritual. On the night before Passover, every year throughout my childhood, I would lay out little pieces of bread on foil for Dad to find. The hiding-of-the-bread component of the *bedikat ḥametz* ritual was a legal fiction meant to ensure that some leaven would actually be found, and therefore no blessing (in this case, the blessing for burning the leaven) would be recited in vain. Dad and I would turn off the lights, and he would set about finding the pieces.

In the process of packing up my parents’ house in Toronto, I found and packed in my own bags a few yet-to-be-used *bedikat ḥametz* kits. Two years later, in preparation for my third Passover without Dad, I stumbled upon one of these kits, and the discovery coaxed back wonderful memories of this sacred hide-and-seek game. How Dad would use that kit: carefully searching every corner of the house by candlelight, upstairs and downstairs, until he'd scooped up every last cube of *ḥametz* with that spoon, sweeping away any remaining crumbs with that feather, and setting it all aside in that paper bag for burning the next day.

How remarkable it was, then, in searching for a pre-Passover *Shir Ḥadash*, to stumble upon Yehuda Amichai's "My Father on Passover Eve," which engages the very same images!

The difference between my own memories and Amichai's poem, though, is that while I readily hid the bread cubes for my dad and delighted in his finding them, Amichai's father cuts and hides them and plays the hide-and-seek game all on his own. His *bedikat ḥametz* is self-choreographed as a quasi-performance, replete with lighting, dance, and script—presumably because his son has grown up and has left the world of religious observance they once shared.

Amichai's speaker recalls relating the parable of his father searching for leaven *ba-'erev ha-'aḥaron*, on the "last evening" (of what: a holiday? a military operation? a trip? a course of study?). "Last evening" brings to mind Jesus's Last Supper, which many identify with a seder, while the expression *himshalti lekha 'et meshal 'avi* (I gave you the example or told you the parable of my father) summons up the same expression in Ezekiel (18:2): "What do you mean by quoting this proverb [*moshelim 'et ha-mashal*] upon the soil of Israel, 'Parents eat sour grapes and their children's teeth are blunted?'"

In Ezekiel, this exclamation comes to reject the idea of intergenerational punishment—and yet, in the Haggadah, the expression *hak'heh et shinav* (blunt his teeth) serves as advice on how to respond to the questions of the wicked son. The poet's use of this same expression reveals a certain anxiety: as a religiously alienated "wicked son," do his teeth deserve blunting?

At the end, the poet's adduced example of his father's hiding the bread suggests that he has in fact absorbed his father's lessons. Like his father, he does not want to act in vain. Like his father, he wants, paradoxically, to be a *bamai ramai be-'emunah shelemah* (duplicitous director in perfect faith)—that is to say, one who suspends disbelief for the sake of cultivating what philosopher Paul Ricoeur calls a "Second Naiveté": a new kind of modern faith achieved through criticism and reinterpretation.[37]

This idea, too, resonated with me: the poem's implicit suggestion that parables and poetry can help us cultivate that second innocence, by allowing us to integrate our childhood memories and lessons into our adult lives, even in the wake of rupture or loss. And so I shared this message, and my memories of Dad, not only with the *Shir Ḥadash* community, but also at our family's Passover seder, hoping in my own way to inculcate the textured, honest values of the *bamai ramai be-'emunah shelemah* to my own children, too.

5 Searching for Female Liturgical Voices

Mourning and Studying with Rachel Morpurgo

Spring 2021. I was nearing completion of my twentieth year of teaching at the Reform rabbinical seminary, Hebrew Union College–Jewish Institute of Religion (HUC-JIR). And in mid-June I was scheduled to be ordained myself by Yeshivat Maharat, the first Orthodox Jewish seminary to ordain women. After two decades of training cantors and rabbis, I was finally becoming a rabbi myself. My grandfather, after whom I was named, was a cantor; my uncle and brother both served as rabbis; and because I had taught for years at a rabbinical school, many Reform leaders and community members who invited me to speak and teach in their congregations and conventions had long assumed that I was a rabbi, too. I had a drawer full of "Rabbi Wendy Zierler" name tags prepared for me for such occasions that I could never in good conscience don—but all that was about to change.

Six years earlier, when I was inaugurated as Sigmund Falk Professor at HUC-JIR, my parents were unable to attend the ceremony. Mom was in the hospital at the time in Toronto, recovering from a broken hip and shoulder as well as an antibiotic-resistant C-Difficile infection she'd picked up from the hospital. So she and Dad watched the ceremony over and over again on her iPad, and shared their giddy pride with me and anyone else who would listen.

Now, as my Maharat ordination drew near, it hit me that this would be the first academic or career milestone I would be celebrating without any parents there in any way to cheer me on. The prospect of marking this event without them occasioned a fresh, resurgent sense of grief, a heightened awareness of all the occasions going forward that my parents would miss: my kids' graduations and weddings, the births of our first grandchildren (God willing), and so many more holidays and birthdays.

My halakhically prescribed mourning period was officially over, but because my rabbinical studies had begun with both my parents alive and were coming to a close with both of them gone on to the next world, the lead-up to my ordination, with its final examinations and assignments, was emotionally fraught. Add to this the ongoing frustration I often had with the rabbinic tradition that I was working so hard to master and join, beginning with the way it restricted the role of women in public prayer. Even in my own Bayit community, women were not counted in a minyan (prayer quorum) or allowed to lead the central prayers in the service. Because women are considered exempt from timebound commandments such as wearing a tallit or putting on tefillin, I was usually one of very few women at shul—if not the only one—suited up with such accoutrements, and "going out with knots" in this particular, ritual manner.

The impending conclusion of my rabbinical studies; my twenty-two months of reciting Kaddish and two-plus years of regularly attending daily *tefillah* with few (if any) other women present, and without a single woman's voice represented in the liturgy; the ongoing COVID crisis—all of this sent me looking for a role-model-woman-poet to present in the next unit of the *Shir Ḥadash*. Who could accompany me and my community at this time? Whose poetry could be studied like complex talmudic texts, and even prayed?

I found my model in Rachel Morpurgo of Trieste, a devout Orthodox woman scholar and the first modern Hebrew woman poet. Born Rachel Luzzatto in 1790 in Trieste, Italy, Morpurgo was a descendant of an eminent line of rabbis, among them the kabbalist and philosopher Rabbi Moshe Ḥayyim Luzzatto (1706–1746), author of the influential ethical tract *Mesilat Yesharim* (*The Path of the Just*). She also had an especially close relationship with her younger cousin and study partner, the poet, philosopher, biblical commentator and rabbinical school professor Shmuel David Luzzatto (1800–1865, best known by the acronym ShaDaL). Though traditional in religious practice, ShaDaL was also a dedicated *maskil* (proponent of Jewish Enlightenment, and the scientific study of Judaism). It was he who sent Morpurgo's Hebrew poems to the *maskilic* journal *Kokhevei Yitzḥak* (*Stars of Isaac*), resulting in her becoming the only female contributor to its pages.

Morpurgo's poetry is a rare early example of Hebrew poetry that is female-authored, scholarly and religious. As a woman about to be ordained as an Orthodox rabbi, I was inspired but also saddened by the model she set more than two centuries before my birth: of vast erudition and literary creativity, and of simmering sadness and frustration, too. Unlike the scholarly men in her family Rachel Morpurgo could not become a rabbi or communal leader, but she brilliantly modeled a life of Torah learning, spiritual leadership, and proto-feminist literary vision. She showed by example the importance and power of an expanded Jewish bookshelf, one that included her own modern forms of *piyyut* (liturgical poetry) as well as occasional verse, written for specific occasions in the lifecycle of her family and community. All the more for me, her poetry voiced authentic moments of grief and loss.

Rachel Luzzatto Morpurgo studied Talmud as a teenager and the *Zohar* as a young adult, and remained devout throughout her life despite the secularizing trends sweeping through Europe over the course of her long lifetime. Some of her poems were sincere and fervent prayers, offered in response to challenging or galvanizing events. Others were veiled sardonic responses to the inordinate and inadvertently insulting praise male colleagues heaped upon her as an "exceptional woman," so much more admirable than the regular run of women.

Looking back at my weekly notes and reflections on her poems, as I prepared to teach them for the *Shir Ḥadash*, I see a record not just of my learning but of my life during that sad, maddening, fearful, and yet truly exciting time. Each poem, with its strict meter, form, and rhyme, was part of the soundtrack of my prayer and study life as I prepared for my final exams with all the detail and minutiae that entailed, and participated in the countdown toward my ordination as a rabbi among the people of Israel.

“Behold the Letter”

Behold the Letter	**הִנֵּה זֹאת הָאִגֶּרֶת**[1]
A Passover Offering Relayed	קרבן פס״ח אשר יפסח על בתי
to My Dear Relatives	קרובי היקרים
Behold this letter	הִנֵּה זֹאת הָאִגֶּרֶת
Stores truth for the getter	דִּבְרֵי אֱמֶת אוֹגֶרֶת
With graceful trimming[2] better	עִם לִוְיַת חֵן חוֹגֶרֶת
And all without fetter.	לָזֹאת אֵינָהּ סֻגֶּרֶת.
Should it my relations meet	אִם קְרוֹבַי פּוֹגֶשֶׁת
It will warmly greet	אֶת שְׁלוֹמָם דּוֹרֶשֶׁת
With declaration complete;[3]	אֶת לְבָבִי פּוֹרֶשֶׂת;
If trapped not were my feet	אִם כַּצִּפּוֹר בָּרֶשֶׁת
Like a captive bird	רַגְלַי לֹא נִלְכָּדוּ,
I'd stride over undeterred	לָבֹא אֶצְלָם יִצְעָדוּ,
But my ankles have been hurt.[4]	קַרְסֻלַּי מָעָדוּ,
Therefore let my muse be heard,	לָכֵן עֵת כִּי יִסְעָדוּ,
When you sit down to dine	אֶת בַּת הַשִּׁיר אָעִירָה
And from afar I'll entwine	וּמֵרָחוֹק אַחְבִּירָה
With Padovians mine.	אֶל פַּאדוֹבָה הָעִירָה.
May God's blessing array	בְּרָכוֹת יִתֵּן הָאֵל
For all those who pray;	שֶׁפַע טוֹב אֶל כָּל־שׁוֹאֵל;
And may the redeemer come our way![5]	יִשְׁלַח לָנוּ הַגּוֹאֵל!
The voice of Rachel chirping, may	קול צפצוף רחל
It raise walls and ramparts of salvation today	ישועה ישית חומות וחל
Saturday night after the Great Sabbath 5610	מוצאי שבת הגדול בשנת חותנו ית״ר

It was our second COVID Passover, my second Passover without my mother, the third without my father, and a few short months before my expected ordination. "Behold the Letter," a Passover poem-letter sent by Morpurgo to her relatives in Padua (including her dear cousin Shmuel David, then a professor at the Padua rabbinical academy), elicited many thoughts, wishes, and emotions in me: love and longing for faraway loved ones, regret over not being able to share the holiday with them, poetic and intellectual ambition, gender-based frustrations—all of this conveyed through Morpurgo's canny layering of classical references (more typically seen in male-authored *piyyut*).

The Hebrew literary scholar Tova Cohen, who authored a monumental 2016 Hebrew biographical and literary study and collection of Morpurgo's poetry entitled *'Ugav Ne'elam* (*A Silenced Harp*), describes Morpurgo's poetry through American feminist critics Sandra Gilbert and Susan Gubar's metaphor of the palimpsest: a manuscript page from which the text has been scraped or washed off so that the page can be reused for another document.[6] Like palimpsests, which bear the distinct traces of prior writings, Morpurgo's poems are built upon the strata of prior classical Hebrew texts, often making her work difficult to fully understand. Upon first reading, as Cohen suggests, they seem "'suitable' for a modest Jewish woman who submissively accepts being shunted to the margins. Yet this socially acceptable surface conceals another level of submerged meaning, one that gives voice to the poet's sense of double marginality."[7] It takes work to uncover the layers of meaning and the composite artistry of her poems.

Indeed, upon first reading, "Behold the Letter" reads simply like a rhymed note of apology and greeting to her relatives. The awareness that this poem was shared not just with her Padovian relatives but also with the readers of *Kokhevei Yitzḥak* reveals it to be a great deal more.

The poem's subtitle declares it to be a *korban Pe"saḥ* (paschal offering). The acronymic spelling of the name of the holiday, however, introduces the wordplay of *peh saḥ*, "a speaking mouth," an image often brought forth to explain how the Passover (Pesaḥ) seder, with all of its storytelling and talk, came to substitute for the *korban pesaḥ* after the destruction of the Jerusalem Temple. Implied is Morpurgo's hope that her poem will speak and pass over the geographical and generic distance from Trieste to Padua and beyond, thereby emulating none other than God in the Exodus story.

Morpurgo identifies her poem as an *'iggeret* (letter or scroll), a word that conjures up a host of historical and literary associations. The scroll of Esther was an *'iggeret*, and so Morpurgo's letter connects her with one of the two only instances in the Bible where a woman writes.[8] Judaism has a long history of masculine rabbinic epistolary writing, including the whole corpus of rabbinic responsa (legal rulings, often written in response to letters from community members). By the eighteenth and nineteenth centuries, in Jewish and general culture alike, letter writing served as an important medium for spreading Haskalah (Jewish Enlightenment) ideas, and one of the few in which aspiring women writers or scholars could get an audience.[9] As such, I understood the titular word *'iggeret* as inscribing "Behold the Letter" onto a canvas of prior and contemporary associations with Jewish and secular letter writing. It also highlighted Morpurgo's unique position as a female scholar and writer of Hebrew letters, and her awareness of her social limitations. Her younger cousin and former study partner Shmuel David could sit at the center of Jewish learning, teaching, and writing in Padua; she could not. She seemed to be expressing regret over several forms of absence—literary, intellectual, familial—and also determination to transcend these limitations through whatever genres or means were available to her.

A similar plurality of meanings can be teased from the second line, where Morpurgo refers to *divrei 'emet* (words of peace). This phrase, too, points to the book of Esther, as the books/letters Esther and Mordechai send to one another are referred to as *divrei shalom ve-'emet*, "words of peace and truth" (9:30). Closer to Morpurgo's own time, German-Jewish Hebraist and educational reformer Naphtali Hertz Wesseley penned what would become a famous *maskilic* tract entitled *Divrei Shalom ve-'Emet* (*Words of Peace and Truth*, 1782) encouraging the Jews of the Austrian Empire (of which Trieste was a part) to acculturate and enlighten, a work which had great influence on the Trieste Jewish educational system. Morpurgo's "letter" seems to have been part of an unfolding library of Jewish "words of peace and truth"—all this while also inquiring after the wellbeing and welfare (*doreshet shelomam)* of her relatives. She'd folded the personal and communal into one literary unit.

In line 3 Morpurgo refers to the poem's *livyat ḥen,* its "ornament of grace" (a grammatically feminine term). The term *livyat ḥen* originates from Proverbs 4:9, in association with the femininely personified *ḥokhmah* (wisdom). And yet, Tova Cohen notes, Morpurgo attaches *livyat ḥen* to the verb *ḥogeret,* usually associated in the Bible with the (masculine) girding of loins in preparation for battle or a difficult task.[10] In referring to the poem's ornament of grace, Morpurgo insists on being identified with the kind of feminine beautifying wisdom that also packs a punch.

Likewise with the image of the captive bird at the end of the second stanza. The Hebrew word *tzippor* is grammatically feminine; Morpurgo connects the feminine bird with her own poetic voice in signing the poem with *kol tziftzuf Raḥel* (the chirping voice of Rachel).[11] As a bird, however, she finds herself involuntarily trapped in a net. If she hadn't been so trapped, if her feet hadn't been caught or bound—think of the Chinese custom of female foot binding—she would have been free to travel to Padua to see her beloved relatives and join in their learned conversation and celebration. That the word *regel* also means a poetic foot (a unit of prosody) adds an element of resistance against the literary limitations imposed upon her by her gender.

The enjambment at the ends of stanzas two and three, continuing the sentence without pause from one line to the next, emphasizes the poet's determination to go beyond both geographical and typographical limits and hence conventional boundaries. The couplet signature to the poem, which diverges from the formal rhyme scheme, further accentuates this boundary-crossing aspiration.

All in all, the poem stakes a bold claim. It celebrates the poet's capacity to awaken her muse not just for the sake of bestowing love on her relatives, but also to shower them with blessing. And it accomplishes all this using strict meter and rhyme: Each of the stanzas refrains the same rhyme sound in all four or three lines: AAAA, BBBB, CCCC, DDD, EEE.

In the context of my rabbinical studies, which included the study of not a single book or canonical piece of writing written by a woman, this learned, crafted, and liturgically resonant poem was nothing short of a godsend. My more than two years of daily *tefillah* attendance had made me keenly aware of the general lack of female representation—not just in public leading of Orthodox prayer services, but also in the prayers themselves. The few biblical poems authored by women are conspicuously absent from traditional liturgy—for example, the lines traditionally attributed to Miriam in the Song of the Sea (Exod. 15:21) had somehow been lopped off from the daily morning recitation of the Song.

No traditional Jewish prayers speak in a woman's voice. We often ignore the plain fact that the prayers in the *siddur* had authors and editors, and they were all men.

Teaching "Behold the Letter" served a potent testament to the fact that claiming a voice for women in traditional Jewish prayer was a task still yet to be accomplished, and that my Maharat studies and the *Shir Ḥadash* were furthering that cause.

“And Thus Sang Rachel about Her Wedding”

And Thus Sang Rachel about Her Wedding	**וזאת אשר שרה רחל על חתונתה**[12]
Thanks to God above	תּוֹדָה לָאֵל נוֹרָא
No longer am I forsaken;[13]	לֹא־עוֹד אֶהְיֶה שׁוֹמֶמֶת:
Casting off all fear for love,	אַשְׁלִיךְ אֶת־כָּל־מוֹרָא,
From silence I’ll awaken.[14]	לֹא־עוֹד אֶהְיֶה דוֹמֶמֶת.
A man lovely to regard[15]	בָּחוּר יְפֵה עֵינַיִם
Will be my crowning glory:	יִהְיֶה פְּאֵר רֹאשִׁי:
God in heaven gave a reward	נָתַן אֲדוֹן שָׁמַיִם
The one who does adore me.[16]	שֶׁאָהֲבָה נַפְשִׁי.
Bless our day of delight,	בָּרֵךְ יוֹם שִׂמְחָתֵנוּ,
Turn our darkness to light.[17]	הַגִּיהַּ אֶת חָשְׁכֵּנוּ.
Hasten our right end.[18]	חִישׁ נָא קֵץ הַיָּמִין.
Build our Temple strong,	כּוֹנֵן בֵּית הַמִּקְדָּשׁ,
And we shall sing a new song:	אָז נָשִׁיר שִׁיר חָדָשׁ:
Salvation God did send.[19]	הוֹשִׁיעָה־לּוֹ יָמִין.

In 1816 when Rachel Luzzatto was twenty-six years old, her younger cousin Shmuel David Luzzatto took her to task, in a sixteen-line Hebrew sonnet, for her refusal to marry any of the men suggested to her by her parents. She replied to her cousin with a sonnet of her own devising, one that mimicked his phrasing and retorted each of his points. She had already found a worthy man whom she wanted to marry, but her parents had refused to accept the match (for reasons unknown to us). Moreover, she declared, even had her parents suggested she marry the Messiah, she would have refused and held out for her chosen groom.[20]

Rachel held her ground, and eventually her parents relented. In 1819, she was finally granted permission to wed her chosen (*baḥur*) mate, Jacob Morpurgo. “And Thus Sang Rachel about Her Wedding” is the poem she wrote to celebrate her wedding.

I taught this poem to add a celebratory note to the Passover season, and also to deepen my own understanding of it as a wedding poem. When I was ordained and would be able to officiate at wedding ceremonies (in the near future!), might I suggest this text to couples looking to add a woman's voice to the traditional ceremony? I began to explore this idea with great excitement.

Morpurgo adduces her love and her wedding as a model not just of personal but also of communal salvation. Now that she has wed, she, like a future redeemed Jerusalem, will no longer be *shomemet* (desolate or forsaken). She has also ceased being *domemet* (silent), suggesting some connection between her marriage and her poetry. Indeed, "And Thus Sang Rachel about Her Wedding" was among the first poems her cousin submitted on her behalf to *Kokhevei Yitzḥak*.[21] In a very real sense—not merely as allegory—her personal life had become a communal matter.

In depicting her groom, Morpurgo recalls the biblical description of the young David as *yefeh ʿeinayim* (handsome to the eyes, 1 Sam. 16:12), linking her wedding (and writing) to the messianic Davidic line. And, she says, with the coming of messianic redemption, we shall sing a new song with the words *hoshiʿah lo yemin*—notably not *hoshiʿah lo yemino*, "**His** right hand won Him victory," as stated in Psalm 98:1, but, rather *hoshiʿah lo yemin*, the (feminine) right hand has won him." Morpurgo seems to suggest that it was her own forceful, stubborn persistence that saved her beloved Jacob Morpurgo and their marriage prospects—and that her own writing hand was playing a crucial role in strengthening God's nation and language. This interpretation itself may seem presumptuous, hinging as it does on the minuscule omission of a *vav*. But Morpurgo appreciated the significance of small, incremental changes and of working within the system to effectuate a redemptive end.

This literary reminder of the power of subtle change, coming during the last months of my rabbinical studies—which often focused on ways in which tiny legal nuances could be harnessed for humane, progressive, legal decision-making—helped strengthen my focus and resolve. The poem's traditional language and its integration of personal as well as communal perspectives made it eminently suitable for recitation by a Jewish bride. Given the lamentable lack of women's liturgical voices in the traditional prayer book and wedding ceremony, "And Thus Sang Rachel about Her Wedding" offered a meaningful resource and remedy. A new, inclusive liturgy was in the making.

See, This Is New	**ראה זה חדש הוא**[22]
If upon cedars a flame should fall,[23]	אִם בַּאֲרָזִים נָפְלָה שַׁלְהֶבֶת
The elect women of the world would be a sign[24]	מִבְחַר נְשֵׁי תֵבֵל לְאוֹת תִּהְיֶינָה
If these were charged with error[25] malign[26]	אִם תָּהֳלָה הוּשַׂם וְשַׁל בָּהֵנָּה
Who else in their stead would stand up tall?	מִי זֹאת לְעֻמָּתָן תְּהִי נִצֶּבֶת?
I have no power to repair the breach[27]	לֹא יֵשׁ לְאֵל יָדִי לְחַזֵּק בֶּדֶק
Only to seek peace and rightly judge	כִּי אִם דְּרֹשׁ שָׁלוֹם וְלִשְׁפֹּט צֶדֶק
Behold, Deborah a judge she was[28]	הִנֵּה דְבוֹרָה שׁוֹפְטָה הָיְתָה
I shan't do wrong;[29] so she would preach.[30]	לֹא אֶעֱשֶׂה עוֹלָה וְלֹא יָאָתָה.
Adoration, praise, precious acclaim	שֶׁבַח תְּהִלָּה עִם יְקָר תִּפְאֶרֶת
Every year, she's remembered by name (Haftarah for Be-shallaḥ)	אַף הִיא בְּכָל שָׁנָה בְּשֵׁם נִזְכֶּרֶת (הפטרת בשלח)
Hence on women's heads she's a crown of fame.—	לָכֵן לְרֹאשׁ נָשִׁים תְּהִי כוֹתֶרֶת.—
You may ask, then, why do you mourn[31]?	שָׁאוֹל יִשְׁאֲלוּ בְּאָבֵל לָמָּה?
For I sit silent dreaming like a stone.	כִּי אֵשְׁבָה דוּמָם כְּמוֹ אַחְלָמָה—(מלשון חלום)!
What can a worR.M. do! Like a dumb ewe shorn![32]	מַה־תַּעֲשֶׂה רִמָּה! כְּרָחֵל נֶאֱלָמָה

The previous three years had brought so many unprecedented changes and challenges to my life. Before March 2019, I had known nothing of personal tragedy. But now, everything was different. I had buried two parents and a father-in-law, had disinterred and reburied a parent and a grandparent, and was now taking care of a mother-in-law with Alzheimer's. And over it all hovered the protracted fear and threat of COVID. It all seemed thoroughly unprecedented, and yet the quickest glance back at my father's family history reminded me that we Zierlers were no novices to tragedy and loss. While commemorating my paternal uncle's yahrzeit, which happens to coincide with Yom ha-Shoah, I had a stunning realization: All of the children in my father's family had died in some tragic way. His eldest brother Sam drowned in Lake Huron at age fourteen; his older brother Isaac (whose yahrzeit I was commemorating), an RCAF Navigator in World War II, was shot down over Leipzig at age twenty-three; my father was struck dead by a distracted truck driver. And Dad's mother, my grandmother Lea, had been hit by a car and killed, too.

Pandemic literature also made clear just how commonplace our COVID experiences of the past year were in the context of human history.[33]

How new, then, was anything we had been experiencing? Were there actually *any* new experiences in our world, any truly novel ideas or thoughts?

"See, This Is New" linked these questions to issues of feminism, leadership, social organization, authorship, and liturgical responses to tragic loss. The fact that I had written about this poem in my first book, *And Rachel Stole the Idols*, added the additional element of reinterpretation and revision to *Shir Ḥadash* teaching, too.[34] It took us three sessions to get through the elements in this complex intertextual poem, but by the end it was clear that this poem was a novel form of female-authored poetic Torah.

The title refers to Ecclesiastes 1:10, which seems at first blush to reject the very idea of newness: "Is there a thing about which it can be said: 'See, this is new'?—It has always and already been this way for eons, before any of us."[35] And yet, the title is the only part of the poem that seemed to address directly this verse and issue of newness. What, then, was the connection between the title and the rest of the poem?

The appearance of the prophet Deborah in the second stanza suggests, perhaps, that the poem aims to challenge the purported novelty of women's leadership and writing. If the biblical Deborah was a prophet, judge, and poet, was there really anything counter-traditional and new about women such as Morpurgo being leaders or poets?

Beyond this, however, what did any of this have to do with flames falling on cedars, or the other descriptors in the poem?

Pointing to the poem's original publication in the maskilic journal *Kokhevei Yitzḥak*, scholar Tova Cohen suggests that two poetic tributes to Morpurgo, published in the prior volume, ignited Morpurgo's ire and provoked the writing of this poem. The poem's surface tone may appear appreciative and deferential, but closer inspection reveals fire and fury.[36]

The first of the tribute poems, "Tehillah le-Raḥel" ("Praise for Rachel" or "Psalm of Rachel") by Leopold Winkler, purports to laud Morpurgo but in the process slurs and diminishes the rest of womankind, including all the biblical matriarchs and female prophets.[37] Winkler portrays Morpurgo as a wondrous, aberrant exception to the rule of feminine intellectual and creative inferiority. Like the biblical Rachel, he says, women were short on intelligence, long on temper, and creatively barren. Like Hannah, they were perennially jealous of their female rivals. Like Miriam, whose Song at the Sea is a mere echo of Moses's, they lacked the capacity to lead or originate. It was "the way of women" to spend their days on chasing wind, the kind of vain pursuits decried by Ecclesiastes.[38]

Morpurgo, in contrast, has eluded the general failings of womankind. Her poems represented something utterly unprecedented: They are "new every morning" (*ḥadashim la-bekarim*, Lam. 3:23), says Winkler, adding: "You are such a wondrous woman that *ḥadal heyot lakh oraḥ ka-nashim* (you have ceased to follow the ways of women)." This same expression is used in Genesis 18:11 to describe the elderly, menopausal Sarah. But whereas Sarah's miraculous post-menopausal pregnancy is literal and biological, the now-elderly Morpurgo has birthed both ideas *and* poems.

The same issue of *Kokhevei Yitzḥak* featuring Winkler's poem included another poetic tribute to Morpurgo: a sonnet, titled "To Rachel Morpurgo," by the journal editor Mendel Stern.[39] His poem was less blatantly misogynist; since Morpurgo had not contributed recently to the journal, he sought to encourage her to continue writing and publishing there. But Stern's poem still proved to be a source of consternation for Morpurgo. Stern accosts her: "Why suddenly silent, like a dumb *raḥel* (ewe)?"—comparing Morpurgo's poetic silence to the people of Israel in their most sinning, obtuse, and degraded feminine state. (In Isaiah 53:7, they are likened to dumb ewes led to the shearing, akin to sheep led to the slaughter.) And Stern exhorts: "Has the flame of poetry burning within her suddenly extinguished, quelled by still waters?"—evoking the "still waters" (*mei menuḥot*) of Psalm 23:2, a psalm associated with funeral liturgy. This, together with the image of quelled poetic fire (*shalhevet*) and the expression *sha'ol yish'alu be-'avel* ("My readers ask and seek without consolation") in Stern's first line, all make their way into Morpurgo's poetic rejoinder.

Put simply, in "See, This Is New" Morpurgo stands up to defend all the women both Winkler and Stern's poems insult (herself included). Her main focus is the prophet Deborah, whom Winkler berates for being arrogant and undeserving of praise. Judges 4:4 depicts Deborah as *'eshet lapidot*, a "woman of torches." If flame is tossed onto the reputation of such a revered woman leader as Deborah, what chances do regular women have of being taken seriously? If Winkler sees Deborah as an example of feminine vice ("in the exultation of her song she raised herself up arrogantly"), Morpurgo makes her a fiery, regal exemplar of feminine virtue and capacity: "Adoration, praise, precious acclaim / Every year, she's remembered by name (*Haftarah* for *Be-shallaḥ*) / Hence on women's heads she's a crown of fame." If Winkler's praise for Rachel Morpurgo hinges on casting *tohalah* (reproach) on the biblical Deborah—that in Judges 5, she heaped praise upon herself when the victory was really owing to God—Morpurgo insists *lah ya'atah*, "for her [Deborah] it [praise] is fitting." Deborah truly deserves praise and glory.

Morpurgo's opening reference to flames falling on cedars indirectly evokes Deborah ("woman of torches"), but the exact wording of that opening actually comes from the talmudic story (BT Mo'ed Katan 25b) of the funeral of Ravina, a leading sage who collaborated with Rav Ashi in compiling the Babylonian Talmud:[40]

> When the soul of Ravina went into repose, a certain orator opened [his funerary oration] thus:
>
> "Ye palms, sway your heads [and deplore]
> A saint, a noble palm that is no more,
> Who days and nights in meditation spent;
> For him, day and night, let us lament."
>
> Said Rav Ashi to Bar Kipok, "What would you have said on such a day [about me]?"
>
> He responded thus:

"If upon cedars a flame should fall,
What becomes of the moss on the wall?
If Leviathan by hook be hauled to land,
What hope have fishes of a shallow strand?
If fish in rushing stream by hook be caught
What death may in marshy ponds be wrought!"

Said Bar Abin to him: "God forbid that I should talk of 'hook' or 'flame' in connection with the righteous."

[He asked:] Then what would you say?

I would say:

"Weep for the mourners,
Not for what is lost:
He found him rest;
'Tis we who are left distressed?"

Rav Ashi was offended by them, and their feet were turned.

On that day [of Rav Ashi's demise] they did not come to make a lament for him, and that is what Rav Ashi had said: "Neither shall Bar Kipok nor shall Bar Abin take his shoes off [for me]."

One might have expected the various speakers at Ravina's funeral to focus on him and his passing. Instead, Ravina's funeral turns into an occasion for his survivor-colleague Rav Ashi to criticize the funeral speaker, who pictures the grief over Ravina's death through the seemingly hackneyed image of swaying palms. Rav Ashi asks the other professional funeral poets in attendance what they might have said instead (either at Ravina's funeral or at Rav Ashi's), and a man named Bar Kipok responds first with a string of metaphors alluding to the predicament of lowly mourners in the aftermath of this great man's death. If a great cedar succumbs to fire, how will the mere moss on the wall survive? And so on, with shallow-water fish who survive the death of a whale, or the marsh fish who survive the death of those who live in rushing waters. Bar Abin, the other poet bystander, objects to Bar Kipok's use of fire and hook imagery but agrees with the focus on the mourners' plight rather than Ravina.

For his part, Rav Ashi is offended and dismayed, either because these sample eulogies imply that compared to Ravina he is but a small fish or mere moss on the wall, or because of their focus on the mourners rather than on the departed rabbi. Cursing both Bar Kipok and Bar Abin, he brings about a "turning of their feet," either an actual foot defect that prevents them from removing their shoes in order to mourn, or a defect in their "poetic feet"—a kind of writer's block, perhaps—which disables them from being able to perform their professional functions as funeral orators.

Nothing in this story presents the sagacious male establishment in a good light. None of it shows good pastoral modeling. R. Ashi focuses on himself and on rhetorical critique instead of the death of his close colleague. Bar Kipok and Bar Abin take Rav Ashi's "bait," auditioning in the midst of a funeral, and evincing no awareness of Rav Ashi's psychological fragility and vulnerable ego. Rav Ashi proves especially vindictive: It's one thing not to appreciate someone's work, but quite another to curse him and prevent him from making a living at his chosen profession.

Invoking this talmudic story as an object lesson, Morpurgo juxtaposes Winkler's poetic assertion of female inferiority (and, by extension, masculine superiority) with the insensitivity (and tone deafness) of an eminent male sage and two male poets. With all this in mind, the purported newness of women's writing becomes less a violation of sacred tradition than a means of rescuing and strengthening it, by bringing new voices and perspectives to the fore in the arenas of Torah study and the pastoral care of mourners.

In the second stanza, Morpurgo strengthens this critique of the male establishment by asserting that she has no power to repair the breach.[41] The expression *le-ḥazek bedek* (to repair the breach) alludes to 2 Kings 12, where King Jehoash discovers that powerful priests who had long been collecting funds for the sake of repairing/renovating the Temple have instead used this money for some other purpose, presumably to enrich themselves. Given a choice between a corrupt, money-obsessed masculine elite and justice-seeking Deborah, Morpurgo easily chooses Deborah.

Which brings us to the poem's unexpected, self-denigrating final stanza, with its strange first line, *sha'ol yish'alu be-'avel* ("They shall surely ask counsel in Abel," from 2 Sam. 20:18), which, as previously mentioned, appears in the first line of Mendel Stern's "tribute" to Morpurgo. Her self-description as a *raḥel ne'elamah* (a "dumb ewe," or silenced Rachel) also serves as a response to Stern, who uses the same exact phrase.

But why would Morpurgo call herself a dumb/mute ewe and a *RiMaH* (the Hebrew word for "worm"), as an acronym for *Rachel Morpurgo Ha-ketanah*, little Rachel Morpurgo?

Cohen points to the biblical origin of the phrase *sha'ol yish'alu be-'avel*. In the midst of David and Joab's bloody war with the Benjaminite rebel Sheba son of Bichri, a wise woman from the city of Abel cannily uses this folk idiom to defend the honorable, peace-loving nature of her city from potential attack (2 Sam. 2:17).[42] By saying *sha'ol yish'alu be-'avel*, Morpurgo is likely (1) uplifting yet another biblical wise woman, (2) offering a diplomatic response to Stern's provocative questions about her literary silence, and (3) suggesting that in the case of misogyny masquerading as admiration, perhaps the best tack is simply to stay silent like a dumb ewe and let readers discern her message of protest from her learned references.

For me, reading, writing, and teaching about this poem was an emotional as well as an intellectual delight. I was amazed by Morpurgo's learning, her ability to fashion such a mosaic of classical and contemporary references, as well as her dedication to working within the system to nudge forward the change she wanted to see. I thought about my own experience studying for *semikhah* (rabbinic ordination), reading texts written by male rabbis who had never imagined a woman studying what they wrote and never considered how insulting their words might sound. To Morpurgo, Winkler and Stern's poems distilled and concentrated the insult. And so, since I was heartbroken to see how she suffered at the hands of her so-called admirers, I also relished her astute depiction of this suffering through allusions to a talmudic story about mourning for a beloved dead sage.

The poem's title, "So, This Is New" ("*Re'eh Zeh Ḥadash Hu'*"), offers some hope: The rabbis and later halakhic writers use this very phrase in contrasting ways, either to argue that Moses had already anticipated all novelty in Torah study, or conversely, to dismiss creative interpretations as too novel, and therefore beyond the pale.[43] Yet another later usage of this term appears, however, in the introduction to the *Keli Yakar*, a popular commentary on the Torah by Rabbi Shelomo Ephraim ben Aaron Luntschitz of Prague (1550–1619). Rabbi Luntschitz confesses his sense of despair over the sinful behavior of the people of his generation, but finds personal consolation in uncovering new insights about the Torah, which he likens to breasts overflowing with milk:

> For her [the Torah's] breasts overflow and at any time one can find within new things that ears have never heard and eyes have never seen, and these insights are pleasant and lovely to those seeking cover under a new dress, leading one to say *See this is new*, never considered by the ancients, and if because of evil contrary ways of this generation, one becomes morose, in seeing that they have no power *to fix and repair the breach* in the house of Israel for it is great, this is my consolation in my suffering to interpret God's book, and have it be my amusement day in and day out, and in this way the heart's worry will be diverted from the vanities of the world, and replaced with the toil of Torah that gladdens the human heart "and the envy of Ephraim will depart" (Isa. 11:13).[44]

Like Morpurgo, Rabbi Luntschitz uses the phrase "See this is new" as well as the term *le-ḥazek bedek* (repair the breach) from 2 Kings. Might Morpurgo have read this introduction and identified with Luntschitz's frustrations? If so, she might have similarly concluded that it was beyond her power to repair the breach in other people's thinking. Accordingly, she might have resolved, just like Rabbi Luntschitz, to take comfort in her own ability to "nurse from the breasts of the Torah"—to cull novel insights from old texts and to shape them into something new, whether her readers understood these new insights or not. Learning all of this from Morpurgo assuaged some of my own frustrations and sadness, and provided newfound momentum to what I had set out to do in the *Shir Ḥadash* and my future rabbinate, too.

“On Those Fleeing the Cholera Epidemic”

On Those Fleeing the Cholera Epidemic	**על הבורחים מקטב הקאלערא**[45]
How precious is Your faithful care, O God! Humankind shelters in the shadow of Your wings. (Psalm 36)	מה יקר חסדך אלהים ובני אדם בצל כנפיך יחסיון (תהלים ל"ו)
I see runners dash toward runner, from whom do they flee?	אֶרְאֶה רָץ לִקְרַאת רָץ, מִמִּי יִבְרַח?
Souls all in God’s hands, native and stranger, equally;	נַפְשָׁם בְּיַד אֵל כְּגֵר כְּאֶזְרָח;
He’ll crush and deaden a luxuriant native tree,[46]	יִמְחַץ וְיָמִית רַעֲנָן אֶזְרָח,
The righteous will heal, a palm flowering free.	צַדִּיק יֵרָפֵא, כְּתָמָר יִפְרַח.
Therefore all His creatures, each in its spot[47] Will dwell in security and trust in God It is senseless to escape the fear of God Let all cling to His hand and draw near to God.	לָכֵן כָּל יְצוּרָיו אִישׁ עַל יָדוֹ (מקום) יִשְׁכֹּן לָבֶטַח יִבְטַח עַל יָדוֹ (כח ה׳) לָנוּס אֵין שׁוֶה מִפַּחַד יָדוֹ (מכה) יִגַּשׁ יִקְרַב וְיַחֲזִיק יָדוֹ. (יד)
Gracious and Merciful One, please take pity on us From anger and fury, please bring a cure to us We’ll grant thanks to Your Name for saving us.	חַנּוּן וְרַחוּם חוּסָה נָא עָלֵינוּ מֵאַף וּמֵחֵמָה רְפָא נָא לָנוּ נוֹדֶה לְשִׁמְךָ אֲשֶׁר הִצִּילָנוּ.
Please turn our mourning into happiness And together we’ll rejoice in gladness For You and not for us, God, not for us	הֲפָךְ־נָא לְשָׂשׂוֹן יְמֵי אֶבְלֵנוּ וְנִשְׂמַח וְנָגִיל יַחַד כֻּלָּנוּ לְךָ, לֹא לָנוּ אֲדֹנָי לֹא לָנוּ
For your sake and not for ours, deliver us. —Rachel Morpurgo 5 Av 5656[48]	עשה למענך אם לא למעננו עשה למענך והושיענו. —רחל מורפורגו ה׳ לחדש מנחם תרט"ו.

When I stumbled upon Rachel Morpurgo’s “On Those Fleeing the Cholera Epidemic,” it felt as though I was opening a liturgical time capsule.

Morpurgo wrote her poem as a poetic response both to the 1855 cholera epidemic in Trieste and, as Tova Cohen shows, to a prayer composed by Trieste Chief Rabbi Shabbetai Elhanan Treves in response to an earlier 1836 cholera outbreak.[49] Historians of medicine identify both plagues as part of a multigenerational cholera pandemic. In the spring of 2021, well into our second year of COVID and with no real end to the pandemic in sight, the poem took on heightened relevance, speaking to our mounting fears that with vaccine denialism and the failure to reach herd immunity, COVID and other such illnesses would persist among us for generations.

Rabbi Treves's prayer sought healing from God not just for the Jewish community of Trieste but for the entire city, the Habsburg Empire, and the world. Cohen believes Morpurgo was deliberately adopting a less ecumenical approach in her poem, dividing those afflicted with cholera between righteous Jews, who deserved to be saved in some ultimate, redemptive sense, and sinning gentiles, who deserved to perish. Cohen finds proof for this reading in the date of the poem, 5 Av (a traditional mourning period for the destruction of the two Jerusalem Temples), as well as from the phrase "Runner dashes to meet runner" (an allusion to Jeremiah 51:31, where Babylonian messengers are seen running to spread the message of the Babylonian downfall, just retribution for the suffering they have brought upon the people of Israel). She points as well to antisemitic incidents in Morpurgo's hometown of Trieste and to Morpurgo's tendency in other poems to distinguish Jews from gentiles.[50] Given the history of scapegoating Jews during other historical times of plague such as the Black Death, Morpurgo may well have been voicing concern here for the plight of her fellow Jews.[51] The poem certainly prays for the end of Jewish suffering and looks forward to a time of redemption.

In teaching this poem during our second pandemic spring, however, I chose to read it not as an exclusivist call for (only) Jewish healing, but rather as an exhortation to Morpurgo's community to listen to sage medical advice and to trust in God. From my vantage point, the Jewish, first-person plural focus of the poem modeled how taking care of one's own helps the larger world. Perhaps this was wishful reading on my part. Perhaps I didn't want to view this poet, whom I admired, as a bigot. I preferred to see "On Those Fleeing the Cholera Epidemic" as a woman poet's effort to provide encouragement and guidance for the common good.

To this end, I focused on the title and impetus for the poem—namely, the phenomenon of people fleeing from cholera, which Morpurgo was suggesting risked even more death. In 1855 there was still no consensus about the cause of the disease, but many believed in the miasma theory, which attributed the illness to noxious air; hence, they believed the best way to stay safe was to escape the foul air. By 1849, however, Dr. John Snow of London had published the tract "On the Mode of Communication of Cholera," proving that the disease was caused not by noxious air but by contaminated water. Snow republished his findings in greater detail—he'd traced a cholera outbreak in the Broad Street area of London to a single Broad Street water pump—in 1854.[52] It is unclear whether Morpurgo knew of Snow's findings, though her family did include physicians. With all this in mind, I read the poem's fourth line ("the righteous will heal, will flourish like a palm") as promoting trust in the uprightness of healing professionals. In teaching this poem, I reflected with gratitude on the many heroic doctors, public health officials, and researchers of our own day who had advised us all to stay put to avoid spreading infection, and who had managed in less than a year to develop healing vaccines and therapies for our contemporary plague.

Asking people to trust doctors at a time of great uncertainty and death is never easy. It's almost impossible to sit still when a threat looms. Perhaps for this reason, Morpurgo accompanies her poetic request not to flee with a prayer to shore up trust. Her fourfold reiteration of the word *yado* (his arm/hand) at the end of every line in the second stanza, expressing faith in various manifestations of the Divine, in God's strong arm as well as in human agency, also reminded me in the spring of 2021 of the power of vaccinated arms to ensure public health. Many of us were now fully vaccinated, but many others were resisting or refusing to take the shot, disparaging the vaccines on a variety of bogus grounds. In countries like India the disease was still running rampant. In the long term, our own safety could only be ensured if theirs was, too. Morpurgo's poem thus came as a message from the past to look after our own in the broadest possible sense, as a means of ensuring universal healing and well-being.

“A Voice Is Heard in the Heights”

A Voice Is Heard in the Heights	קול ברמה נשמע[53]
My God, my God, Rock and Salvation[54]	אֵלִי אֵלִי צוּר גֹּאֲלִי
Look, see and hear my intonation.[55]	הַבֵּט וּרְאֵה וּשְׁמַע קוֹלִי,
I cry and wail in supplication	אֶבְכֶּה אֶזְעַק וְאֶתְחַנֵּן
Take pity and spare a troubled nation.	חוּס נָא חֲמוֹל עַל עַם נִפְעָם.
Set up my tent, consent to my plea	הוֹאֵל הָקֵם אֶת אָהֳלִי
For no one helps or cares about me.[56]	כִּי אֵין דּוֹרֵשׁ אֵין עוֹזֵר לִי.
Sons will return to their frontiers[57]	בָּנִים יָשׁוּבוּ לִגְבוּלָם
In boundless joy for endless years.[58]	עֲלֵי רֹאשָׁם שִׂמְחַת עוֹלָם.
Please bear the weight of what they’ve transgressed	אָנָּא שָׂא נָא כֹּבֶד פִּשְׁעָם
Hasten, raise up the chosen best.	חִישׁ נָא הָרֵם בְּחִיר הָעָם.
Weep no more for God’s grace is blessed.[59]	לֹא עוֹד תִּבְכִּי, כִּי אֵל חָנַן:
If he tarries I shall surely wait.	אִם יִתְמַהְמַהּ לוֹ אֲיַחֵל
His house shall be rebuilt, wall and barricade	בֵּיתוֹ יִבְנֶה חוֹמוֹת וָחֵל
And in new song Rachel shall celebrate.	וּבְשִׁיר חָדָשׁ תָּשִׂישׂ רָחֵל.
Let the heavens be glad, and the earth rejoice[60]	ישמחו השמים ותגל הארץ
Rosh Ḥodesh Ḥeshvan 5654[61]	ליל ראש חדש בול ה'תרט"ו.

If you’re a Hebrew woman poet studying and writing in the absence of female poetic peers, or a female rabbinical student casting about for models of female leaders in a Jewish denomination where the idea of women rabbis is still not broadly endorsed, the biblical foremothers assume great significance. They become your imagined study and conversation partners in your scholarly and creative work. They offer you a sense of grounding in tradition, despite the seeming novelty of your work. When a poet shares a name with a biblical foremother, this relationship takes on even greater importance. That was certainly true with poet Rachel Morpurgo and the biblical Rachel. Over and over again, Morpurgo adopted her biblical namesake's story for her own times.

Morpurgo's identification with the biblical Rachel is especially evident in "A Voice Is Heard in the Heights," a prayer-poem that builds on the image of the biblical Rachel on Ramah ("the heights," some six miles north of Jerusalem), bewailing the fate of her exiled sons (Jer. 31:14). As Morpurgo's speaker cries, wails, and supplicates, fusing her own voice with the biblical Rachel's, she vocalizes personal and communal lament simultaneously.

The poem also references the preface to Lamentations Rabbah 24 and related midrashic traditions, in which Jeremiah, Amram, Abraham, and Moses all entreat God to end the exile, but God rejects their pleas.[62] Only when Rachel steps forward and speaks of her selfless willingness to help her sister Leah marry Jacob first, sharing with Leah the signs that she and Jacob had prearranged to avoid being tricked by Laban, does God assent.[63] Of course, all of this assumes that both Rachel and Leah want to marry the same man and are willing parties to this deceit; and that God is the sort of deity who rewards such duplicity. I remain troubled by these assumptions. But I am also moved by the rabbis' suggestion that sisterly solidarity might actually have the power to end the exile and bring the Jewish people home.

The second-person address in the eleventh line, "Weep no longer for God's grace is blessed," echoes God's answer to Rachel: "Thus said GOD: Restrain your voice from weeping, Your eyes from shedding tears; for there is a reward for your labor—declares GOD: They shall return from the enemy's land" (Jer 31:16). Yet, I also saw it as Morpurgo's own attempt to comfort the weeping biblical Rachel, and the biblical Rachel's reciprocal attempt to reassure and shore up her nineteenth-century descendant. And so I read the closing line, "And in new song Rachel shall celebrate," as Morpurgo's deliberate conflation of two Rachels, herself and her biblical namesake—and then the poem itself as a turning of an ancient woman's lament into a celebratory song for a nineteenth-century woman's own day.

Reading and teaching this poem during this lead-up to my ordination, when I was studying for exams and missing my parents especially acutely, offered needed comfort and strength. It reminded me of my own privilege to be one of a cohort of women trying to change the face of Jewish leadership and Jewish ritual life. And it encouraged me to imagine how poems such as these might make their way, one day, into mainstream, traditional *siddurim*, where they deserve to be.

“This One Shall Be Called ‘My Delight Is with Her’”

And this poem is for the aforementioned bride, upon her leaving Trieste to join her groom in Padua:	וזה השיר לכלה הנ"ל ביום צאתה מטריאסטי ללכת עם חתנה אל פאדובה:
This One Shall Be Called “My Delight Is with Her”	**לְזֹאת יִקָּרֵא חֶפְצִי־בָהּ**[64]
Rachel and Rachel are connected Like a necklace to a neck Your love is my laurel, On my head a crowning glory.	רָחֵל עִם רָחֵל נִקְשֶׁרֶת כְּעָנָק עֲלֵי גַּרְגֶּרֶת, אַהֲבָתֵךְ לִי תִּפְאֶרֶת עַל רֹאשִׁי הִנָּךְ כּוֹתֶרֶת.
To me your good sense is prized above all[65] Dessert, but you’re leaving our small Cohort, to be lifted tall On a ladder[66] in another capital.	טוֹב טַעְמֵךְ מִכָּל־פַּרְפֶּרֶת לִי יִנְעַם, אַךְ אַתְּ סוֹתֶרֶת הַחֶבְרָה, לִהְיוֹת נִבְחֶרֶת מִסֻּלָּם אֶל עִיר אַחֶרֶת.
This poem is a memento Of love now absent Longingly I chant.[67]	שִׁירָה זֹאת הִנָּהּ מַזְכֶּרֶת אַהֲבָה מִהְיוֹת נֶעְדֶּרֶת הוֹמִיָּה אֲנִי שׁוֹרֶרֶת.
Daily shall I send mail, Bearing greetings to regale Solomon and his jewel Rachel.[68] 1847	יוֹם אֶל יוֹם אֶשְׁמַע אִגֶּרֶת דִּבְרֵי שָׁלוֹם, גַּם אוֹגֶרֶת לִשְׁלֹמֹה רָחֵל עֲטֶרֶת: ה'תר"ז

In late May 2021 I attended our middle daughter Yona’s graduation from Washington University in St. Louis. Because of COVID, Yona and her graduating class had waited a year for this commencement ceremony. There we were, finally, on a Sunday morning, celebrating the class of 2020, an exercise in continuity after the prolonged social, emotional, and occupational disruption of COVID.

Upon my return home after only five days away, I was giddy and overjoyed to find my shul dramatically transformed—restored almost entirely to the way it had been before the pandemic. The blue upholstered chairs, piled up along the walls for months to allow for socially distanced seating pods, were mostly back in their former places, with the exception of a few rows stacked against the south window. No one was wearing a mask. For the first time in over a year, I saw people's complete faces at shul.

Unmasked as well, and unmuffled, I rose to the podium to teach, "This One Shall Be Called 'My Delight Is with Her,'" a sonnet that Rachel Morpurgo wrote for her cousin Rachel Luzzatto Sulam. A tribute to female kinship, the poem offers the hope for continued love and connection—for going out with knots—despite the change and dislocation occasioned by her cousin's marriage to Solomon Sulam and her resultant move from Trieste to Padua.

The first Hebrew poem written by a woman for another woman, it is filled with biblical references to love, albeit transformed from their original usage to depict the love shared between female cousins/friends.[69] The poem's title is taken from Isaiah 62:4, where it serves as a metaphorical declaration of spousal love between a (masculine) God and a (feminized) people of Israel, but Morpurgo deftly recasts the classical meaning into to a declaration of loving kinship between women. Her opening comparison of the two cousins' connection to a necklace around a neck similarly transforms the tradition's teaching about holding tight to one's parents' wisdom ("For they are a graceful wreath upon your head, a necklace about your throat," Prov. 1:9) into a celebration of female wisdom.[70]

All this recalled a concept I had just learned in my rabbinical studies: *serakh bitah*, "the lace (or: knot) of the daughter." A gendered counterpart to the concept of sons going out with knots, this phrase is discussed by the rabbis in the Talmud in the context of family purity laws. The rabbis suggest that mothers and daughters are so mimetically knotted to one another that a daughter will automatically (and wordlessly) emulate her mother, often to a halakhic fault.[71] The rabbis thus forbid a woman (presumably a mother) from immersing in a *mikveh* during the day (rather than at night) on the thirteenth day of her menstrual cycle, even though she is legally permitted to do so, lest her daughter see this and erroneously infer that one may immerse on the twelfth day during the day as well—although it would be too early to do so at that time.

All of this was arcane law, to be sure. What especially caught the attention of me and my *ḥavruta*, Lindsey, was the rabbis' assumption that daughters would somehow reflexively imitate their mothers without talking about it first, without asking for clarification or explanation. As daughters ourselves, and mothers of daughters, both of us had more often than not experienced daughters doing the very opposite of their mothers. In those (rare) cases where a daughter might be inclined to over-emulate her mother, couldn't the mother and daughter simply have a conversation to clarify what was right? And anyway, didn't mother-daughter closeness imply communication, commiseration, and conversation rather than wordless imitation? Why was it, then, that the rabbis imagined the intimate "lacing together" of mothers and daughters—and women in general—as assuming a nonverbal, reflexively mistaken form?

All in all, the tradition seemed to offer precious little depiction of friendships or warm familial conversations between women. Midrashic traditions aside, Leah and Rachel's relationship in Genesis was limited to rivalry over Jacob's affections and the ability to provide him with sons. The co-wife or wife-handmaid stories of Sarah/Hagar and Hannah/Penina emphasized bitter competition and complaint over loving support.[72]

The rabbinic notion of *serakh bitah* thus highlighted for Lindsey and me the classical tradition's general lack of understanding, let alone representation, of female friendship—the magnetic, compelling, verbal connections enjoyed between women. During our own years of study, conversation, and laughter, Lindsey and I had benefited from what I came to call *serakh ḥavruta* (the lace or knot of the study partner): a shared intellectual sensibility about what we were studying and an ability even to predict how the other would react to each of the texts we were assigned to prepare. Morpurgo's poem to her cousin thus offered a welcome literary glimpse at this kind of female lacing of minds.

Morpurgo also calls attention to the two close cousins' sharing of one name, added evidence of their strong bond. I imagined that writing *Raḥel 'im Raḥel niksheret* (Rachel is tied to Rachel) consoled her as she faced the impending loss of her cousin's daily presence. Her consistent rhyming reiteration of the sound *-eret* at the end of every Hebrew line in the poem (*niksheret, gargeret, tif'eret, koteret,* and so on)—her only poem with such a consistent AAAA rhyme scheme—spoke to me of persistent connection and abiding love.[73] I envisioned Morpurgo praying herself into a sense of nurturing continuity by repeating the same sound, line after line, using words and sound to effect an enduring link.

So, too, had I connected with my parents during those many months of rhyming Kaddish recitation. So were we, my *Bayit* prayer community, using the words of prayer to tie ourselves, day after day, to one another—even when COVID restrictions had kept us at a remove from each other.

And, at last, here we were again, in seats ever closer together, with our full faces visible to one another, from shin to crown.

"I, Leah, Was So Very Tired"

Upon the Death of the Righteous Mrs.	אל מות החסידה מרת לאה אשת
Leah, Wife of Avraham Cohen, Adar 5651	אברהם הכהן, אדר תרי"א
I, Leah, Was So Very Tired	**אֲנִי לֵאָה לָאָה הָיִיתִי**[74]
I, Leah, was so very tired[75]	אֲנִי לֵאָה לָאָה הָיִיתִי
Only toil and sorrow I descried	כִּי רַק עָמָל יָגוֹן חָזִיתִי,
And in quiet times I aspired	וּבְעֵת שַׁלְוָה קַוֹּה קִוִּיתִי;
To an early death, my soul withdrawn.	מָוֶת קָדַם נַפְשִׁי לָקַחַת.
Hush my daughter, your soul has flown	דֹּמִי בִתִּי נַפְשֵׁךְ פּוֹרַחַת
In my Garden of Eden you shall be sown	וּבְגַן עֶדְנִי תִּהְיִי צוֹמַחַת
The afterlife is a fire, glowing,	דֹּמָה דוּמָה אֶל אֵשׁ קוֹדַחַת
Meant to atone and cleanse offense.	אוֹתָךְ לִצְרֹף וּלְכַפֵּר פֶּשַׁע.
Speedily shall I send deliverance	אֲבָל מַהֵר אֶשְׁלַח לָךְ יֶשַׁע,
No guilt-slag have you, nor malevolence,	סִיגִים אֵין בָּךְ אַשְׁמָה וָרֶשַׁע,
May you traverse the fiery stream[76]	נְהַר דִּי נוּר אָנָא עֲבֹרִי
And be cleansed of the world's impurity	לְטַהֵר טֻמְאַת הַחֶלֶד
For your light has come, arise, gleam;[77]	כִּי בָא אוֹרֵךְ קוּמִי אוֹרִי;
The door's open to you, already.	כְּבָר לָךְ נִפְתַּח הַדֶּלֶת.
Open the gates and let in a righteous nation[78]	פתחו שערים ויבוא גוי צדיק
The lowliest of creatures Rachel Morpurgo	הנקלה שבבריות רחל מורפורגו

A dialogue beyond death between the departed Mrs. Leah, Wife of Abraham Cohen and Almighty God, this next poem I taught, "I, Leah, Was So Very Tired," broadened Morpurgo's sense of identification not just with her biblical namesake, but also with her sister-rival Leah—and with God, too.

The first line ("I, Leah, was so very tired") plays on the meaning of the Hebrew word *le'ah* and hence the biblical name as "tired" or "fatigued."[79] The now deceased Leah tells God how worn out she had been at the end of her life and how she came to long for the respite of death. In response, God (as ventriloquized by Morpurgo) promises her many measures of solace: her separated soul will be replanted in God's own Garden of Eden, she will be cleansed of the impurities of the living world, the door of the afterlife will be open to her as a reward for her righteousness, and she'll be invited to reawaken and gleam with this future promise.

This last promise, "For your light has come, arise, gleam," alludes to Isaiah 60:1, where the prophet speaks on God's behalf to exhort a femininely personified Jerusalem to rise and shine: "Arise, shine, for your light has dawned; the Presence of God has shone upon you!" Here, Morpurgo inhabits the prophetic/divine voice but de-allegorizes it; instead of a feminized Jerusalem, she uses Isaiah's words to refer to a specific, individual, deceased woman.

So often in the liturgical and midrashic tradition, women appear as allegories for the feminized people of Israel, in a way that bypasses real women's actual lived experiences and hopes—if not for outright redemption, then for something better than the current reality. Morpurgo pushes back against this allegorical habit, insisting instead on letting women be subjects in their own right. In beginning her poem in the first person, with the word *'ani* (I), she expresses direct personal identification with the weariness the deceased Leah experienced while she was still alive. The closing images of open doors and gates suggest an effort on Morpurgo's part to open a poetic gate to shared female sympathy and mutual understanding.

And for female eulogizing, too. Reading Morpurgo's poem as I approached the date of my rabbinical ordination, I suddenly saw Morpurgo not just as a scholar and poet but as a kind of proto-woman rabbi presiding at Leah's funeral, reassuring Leah's family that if Leah had suffered so much that she yearned to die, she had now been delivered to a better place. I saw Morpurgo's own sense of exhaustion, sitting there alone in Trieste, doing such groundbreaking work. And I imagined myself reassuring her, across generations and lifetimes, that her life's work had survived long past her death. In fact, it had arisen to gleam anew for my community and my readers in the form of the *Shir Ḥadash shel Yom*.

"Fount of Wisdom from a Flowing Stream"

In honor of the lauded, glorious, clever,
wise, and respected rabbi and teacher,
Dr. Bernhard Beer from Dresden:

לכבוד המשֻבח והמפואר החכם והנבון
כמו"ה [כבוד מורינו הרב] **דאקטאר**
יששכר בעער מעיר דרעזדען:

Fount of Wisdom from a Flowing Stream

מנחל נובע מקור חכמה[80]

A fount of wisdom from a flowing stream[81]
A WORM's tongue laps water cool and clean

מִנַּחַל נוֹבֵעַ מְקוֹר חָכְמָה
מַיִם קָרִים תִּשְׁתֶּה לְשׁוֹן רִמָּה

A well of living waters before my eyes[82]
With four columns surrounding the spot[83]
In their splendor its beauty I recognize,
And on my face, its faithful waters, its entire lot.

בְּאֵר מַיִם חַיִּים נֶגֶד עֵינַי
וְהֵן "אַרְבָּעָה טוּרִים" סָבִיב לָהּ,
בְּזִיוָם אַכִּיר יָפְיָהּ, וּבְפָנָי
בְּמַיִם נֶאֱמָנִים כָּל גּוֹרָלָהּ:

Along the "Path of Life" he strives to tread,
"Wisdom's Rule," too, does he truly teach
"The Stone of Help," too, is part of his trade,
And with "Breastplate of Judgment" he repairs
every breach.

בְּטוּר "אֹרַח חַיִּים" נִסָּה לָלֶכֶת
וְגַם "יוֹרֶה דֵעָה" הוּא מוֹרֶה צֶדֶק,
וְ"אֶבֶן הָעֶזֶר" אֶצְלוֹ כִּמְלָאכֶת,
בְּ"חֹשֶׁן הַמִּשְׁפָּט" חִזֵּק כָּל בֶּדֶק:

From the heights[84] the waters spray: behold.
Its source shall not disappoint, its portion
twofold;
And with his graceful wife an edifice will be made
And with God's blessing, this fountain be arrayed.

הִנֵּה מָקוֹר הַזֶּה מֵרָמָתַיִם
לֹא יִכְזָבוּ מֵימָיו כִּפְלֵי כִּפְלָיִם;
וּבְאֵשֶׁת חֵן אִשְׁתּוֹ יִבָּנֶה בִּנְיָן
מִבִּרְכַּת אֵל חֻצַּב זֶה הַמַּעְיָן.

Thus says his handmaiden, lowly
maggot and WORM
Trieste 20 Shevat 1859

כֹּה תֹאמַר שִׁפְחָתוֹ רִמָּה וְתוֹלֵעָה
טריאסטי כ' שבט תרי"ט

"Fount of Wisdom from a Flowing Stream" helped me mark the moment of the eve of my rabbinical ordination: Tuesday, June 15, 2021.

Morpurgo wrote a number of poems honoring relatives, friends or acquaintances: her niece, Rachel Luzzatto; the newborn son of her cousin, Yitzḥak Luzzatto; her close friend, the poet and scholar Yosef Almanzi; and the rabbi-educator Meir Redenger, who lived in and taught in Trieste and also published an Italian translation of the Passover Haggadah by his daughter, which he shared with Morpurgo, to name but a few examples. This particular poem "in honor of the lauded, glorious, clever, wise, and respected rabbi and teacher, **Dr. Bernhard Beer** from Dresden" stands out, however, in that Beer wasn't a relative or rabbi of local acquaintance, but rather a community leader and scholar in another country.

For more than two decades Bernhard Beer (1801–1861) served as the head of the Dresden Jewish community and its schools. He was a political activist for civic equality for Saxony's Jews. He founded various charitable organizations as well as a Mendelssohn Society for the furtherance of scholarship, art, and trades among Jewish youth. He wrote numerous articles on Bible, midrash, Jewish philosophy, halakhah, and other Jewish topics. He also advocated for moderate reforms in Jewish liturgy and was the first Jew to deliver a sermon in German (not Hebrew) in a Dresden synagogue. He had a lifelong close friendship with Rabbi Zacharias Frankel (pioneer of the positive-historical approach to Judaism, which later came to be known in the United States as Conservative Judaism), and early founders of the German Reform movement such as Abraham Geiger respected him, even as Beer himself adhered to Orthodox standards of observance.[85]

We don't know exactly what prompted Morpurgo to write this poem of tribute to him two years before his passing, but we can speculate.[86] Beer was an active contributor to *Kerem Ḥemed*, a periodical that published letters between *maskilim*, thus helping to create intellectual community among Jewish scholars in Germany, Galicia, and Italy, including Morpurgo's cousin, Shmuel David Luzzatto. Morpurgo likely read that journal. Perhaps in traditional circles Morpurgo felt the need to defend Beer from criticism over of his friendship with Reformers, his promotion of Haskalah, and of moderate liturgical change. As Tova Cohen suggests, Morpurgo's reference to the halakhic legal code 'Araba'ah Turim and her insistence on Beer's dedication to all four of its halakhic pillars might be read as a form of defense of Beer's halakhic bona fides in the face of possible disparagement.[87]

I thought, in this context, of the innovations spearheaded by rabbis and layfolk in the modern or open Orthodox community of which I was a part. In 1985 Rabbi Irving (Yitz) Greenberg cofounded CLAL-the

National Jewish Resource Center, with rabbinic faculty representing all the major Jewish denominations—at the time the only national organization offering educational programming with such a pluralistic composition. In 1997, his wife Blu Greenberg helped found the Jewish Orthodox Feminist Alliance. In 2009, Rabbi Avi Weiss ordained Rabba Sara Hurwitz, the first Orthodox woman rabbi in the United States, and subsequently the two of them founded Yeshivat Maharat, the first Orthodox yeshiva in North America to ordain women. All these leaders absorbed immense flack for their innovations. On many occasions when I myself had spoken with members of other, less open Orthodox communities, I had defended their work in the face of stinging criticism.

Morpurgo's poem thus became a safe harbor for me, shoring up the values and innovations I held dear. The poem's two central motifs are columns (*turim*) and water (*mayim*), the former a symbol of solidity and immovability and the second of everchanging flow. Thus I saw Morpurgo as uplifting Beer as an exemplar of tradition as well as change, who drew on the best ideas from the varied Jewish approaches of his day. Beer's Torah, as Morpurgo avers in the second stanza, is a well of living waters (the Hebrew word *be'er*, meaning a well, is a clear play on Beer's surname). Beholding this *be'er*, Morpurgo (writing in the first person) sees the true beauty of Torah.

I read Morpurgo's poem as paying homage to Beer's influence on her, too. The Latin word *influere* originally referred to the flowing of ethereal fluid that affected human destiny. Water imagery coursed through this poem, its fluidity and ongoing, progressive movement capturing a sense of generative, fateful influence.

Even more, in Morpurgo's referencing of the halakhic canon—the four pillars of the 'Araba'ah Turim remain the mainstay of the Orthodox rabbinic curriculum to this day—I saw Morpurgo as proclaiming her own desire to contribute to that unfolding tradition. Her second stanza said it best: And in my face, reflected in the sure waters, is the destiny or fate of the Torah. A well of living waters before my eyes. In my face, upon its sure waters, its entire lot. Professions of modesty and self-diminution aside—twice she refers to a (רמה / *RiMaH* / WORM), an acronym seen in other Morpurgo poems for "Rachel Morpurgo Ha-ketanah, the lowly Rachel Morpurgo"—she also opens and closes with exultant enthusiasm over what this same *RiMaH* / worm has lapped up from Beer's "well" of Torah. Infused with learning and liturgical innovation, "Fount of Wisdom from a Flowing Stream" clearly demonstrated a desire to assume a similarly learned and leaderly voice.

Scholars don't know whether Morpurgo presented the poem publicly to Beer or to others, either in speech or in writing. (It would make its first written appearance in her posthumously published collection, *'Ugav Raḥel.*) Yet it feels like a public reflection on her own capacity and necessity as an individual and as a woman—and hence a call to other women too—to draw from but also contribute to the ever-flowing fount of Torah. Teaching this poem on June 15, 2021—a professor at a Reform rabbinical seminary on the eve of her own rabbinical ordination by the Orthodox Yeshivat Maharat, the culmination of several years of studying primarily halakhic texts—I thought about my own learning and teaching journey: my desire to draw from many Jewish wells of Torah and especially, to champion Hebrew literary creativity.

I was so moved by Morpurgo's prescient poetic leadership. More than 160 years ago, she sought out inspiring models and allies, and took it upon herself to live a life of Jewish devotion, scholarship, and public writing. Her tribute to Beer exemplifies an attitude of gratitude to those who taught her throughout Europe and across the nascent Jewish denominations, splendidly devoid of the rancorous sectarianism that has become so common in our current Jewish and secular worlds. In that spirit, I, too, offered thanks: to the faculty and students of Yeshivat Maharat; to the Bayit's rabbinic staff and 6:45 morning *tefillah* attendees; to my colleagues and students at HUC-JIR and in the broader Jewish studies world, including Professor Tova Cohen, whose work on Rachel Morpurgo has been so instrumental to my engagement with Morpurgo's legacy; and to the Hebrew poets and scholars of yesteryear, who provided the coursing waters for a living tradition. And I acknowledged my late parents, paragons of pluralism, who gathered friends from multiple denominations of Judaism—Reform, Conservative, Orthodox, Ultra-Orthodox, secular Yiddishists—without judgment and with much love, who I passionately wished could have been here to share this day with me.

"Buried Here Is the Lady"

The burial monument of the honored grandame Sarah, widowed wife of the physician-sage Raphael Luzzatto, who went to her eternal rest on 5 Nissan 5618, may her soul be bound up in the bonds of life; she should rest and arise:	מצ"ק הזקנה הנכבדת שרה אלמנת החכם הרופא כמ"ר רפאל לוצאטו תנצב"ה אשר הלכה למנוחות ה' ניסן תרי"ח ותנוח ותעמוד:

Buried Here Is the Lady	**פֹּה נִקְבְּרָה הַגְּבִירָה**[88]
Buried here is the lady	פֹּה נִקְבְּרָה הַגְּבִירָה
Her profits bested all other commodities	טוֹב סַחְרָהּ מִכָּל־סְחוֹרָה
Named Sarah, a woman of valor	אֵשֶׁת חַיִל שְׁמָהּ שָׂרָה
Forever will her memory be hallowed.	לָעַד בְּטוֹב יְהִי זִכְרָהּ.
1858	ה'תרי"ח.

"The Monument Is a Witness"

The Monument Is a Witness	**עדה המצבה**[89]
That buried here is blameless man	כִּי פֹּה נִטְמַן גֶּבֶר תָּמִים
Who served the Rock his whole lifespan	עָבַד הַצּוּר כָּל הַיָּמִים.
Swift in his labors in his younger years,	מָהִיר בִּמְלַאכְתּוֹ בִּנְעוּרָיו
A merchant in his later career.	נָשָׂא נָתַן בִּשְׁאָר יָמָיו.
Seventy were the years that he did live	שִׁבְעִים הָיָה מִסְפַּר שָׁנָיו
To his sons a good name he did give.	שֵׁם טוֹב קָנָה לִשְׁנֵי בָּנָיו.
Yitzḥak Luzzatto the Turner, may his soul be bound in the bonds of life.	יצחק לוצטו המעגל תנצב"ה.
Born on Yom Kippur Eve 1792. Passed away first night of Rosh Hashanah 1863.	נולד ליל כפור שנת "רחם ארחמנו" [תקנ"ג] נפטר ליל א' ראש השנה תרכ"ג.

“This Is the Burial Monument that Rachel Morpurgo Prepared for Herself in Her Youth”

This Is the Burial Monument that Rachel Morpurgo Prepared for Herself in Her Youth

Turn away, away, out from thence[91]
Lest you succumb to any sin,[92]
Only don't charge me with any sin,
My idol did these things and did succumb;[93]
Wrongdoing, I've none, and no offense,
I shall drink the wine of the righteous some.[94]

My body sinned and not me (my soul), and the body has already perished, and I am cleansed of wrongdoing and sin, therefore I shall merit to behold God's goodness in the land of the living and shall drink of the wine reserved for the righteous, a parable on the reward of the world to come.

**וזאת מצבת קבורת רחל מורפורגו
אשר הכינה לעצמה בימי נעוריה**[90]

סוּרוּ סוּרוּ צְאוּ מִשָּׁם
פֶּן־תִּסָּפוּ בְּכָל־חַטָּאת,
אַךְ בִּי אַל תִּתְּנוּ חַטָּאת,
עָצְבִּי עָשָׂם וְהוּא נִסְפָּה;
פֶּשַׁע אֵין בִּי וְאֵין אָשָׁם,
חַמְרָא אֶשְׁתֵּי קָבֵל אַלְפָּא.

גופי הוא שחטא ולא אני (הנשמה), והגוף כבר נספה ומה ואני נקיה מפשע וחטאת, לכן אזכה לראות בטוב ה' בארץ החיים ואשתה היין המשומר לצדיקים, משל על שכר לעולם הבא.

At long last, on July 11, 2021—the day before what would have been my father's ninety-third birthday—we held the unveiling for my father, mother, and grandmother's tombstones. This was no normal unveiling, and not just because it had been delayed for so many months by COVID, but because it involved three monuments for three people, whose deaths had occurred years and countries apart.

It was a source of some comfort and surprise for me to discover, in preparing for this event, that the original biblical context for the idea of erecting a stone monument for a deceased relative involves a threesome of deaths: two women and one man, just like the three people we were commemorating. In Genesis 35 Rachel dies in childbirth, and after Jacob buries her outside Bethlehem he erects a stone monument in her memory. Throughout his own life he lays down various stone markers, but his wife's tombstone is the first he erects for a human being, and a most beloved one at that. Rachel's tombstone stands alone on the road to Efrat, though in the biblical text it is narratively flanked by two other deaths: that of Rebekah's beloved nursemaid Deborah, who is buried under an oak tree (the *'alon bakhut*, the Tree of Weeping), and of Isaac, who is buried with his parents in the Cave of Machpelah. Classical commentators wonder about the flow of this chapter, which includes several weird juxtapositions: Jacob's move back to Canaan from Padam Aram; the building of an altar at Bethel; the death of Deborah the nursemaid; a divine revelation in which Jacob is told his name has changed to Israel (even though he already learned that in chapter 33); the building of another monument at Bethel; the death of Rachel, and then Isaac's as well. There is a nightmarish quality to this chapter, with events chopped up and illogically arranged, with weird transitions and repetitions. There's a realism to it, too. These things happen in life: journeys broken up by death; rituals, building projects, and relationships interrupted; monumental experiences that occur and recur without enough time in between for anyone to properly process them.

In preparing, I also delved into Morpurgo's poetry and discovered three poetic epitaphs: one for her brother, Isaac (Yitzḥak) Luzzatto; another for her aunt, Sarah Luzzatto; and yet another for herself. Here were three poetic monuments for three close family members: two women and a man, just like Genesis 35; just like my own experience that Sunday in July 2021.

The common threads didn't stop there. My grandmother, like the aunt in Rachel Morpurgo's poem, was named Sarah (later Americanized to Shirley). The inscription on the monument for my own father, like that for Morpurgo's younger brother, focuses on his integrity. Like Morpurgo's brother Yitzḥak, my father spent his life in business and, despite the moral mediocrity of many of the people he dealt with, he somehow managed to maintain a sterling reputation and to pass on to his children a pure, unblemished name.

I found Morpurgo's own rhymed epitaph particularly extraordinary. It was the first Hebrew poem she ever wrote. How astonishing that this young poet began her poetic career by contemplating her end! How bold of her to use her own future death as a pretext to admonish others and preach against sinning! There is something beyond mischievous—hubristic, in fact—to her proclamations so early in her life that in dying she will have no guilt, that everything she may have done wrong will have been the fault of her body rather than her soul, and that she was destined to drink the wine of the righteous. All this brought to my mind the biblical Rachel's own brazenness in crying out to Jacob, "Give me children or else I'll die" (Gen. 30:1).[95] And the tragic irony, as Rachel later ends up dying in childbirth (Gen 35:16–19).

Yet her soul lives on in the book of Jeremiah, and in later rabbinic sources she emerges as an activist and the apotheosis of the merit of the matriarchs. In the case of both of these Rachels, the fact of death literally shapes the contours of their lives and, I believed, their enduring impact.

As for my own family members, whose monuments we were unveiling and whose lives and enduring impact we were commemorating, drawing together three life strands into a very different sort of threefold cord: They too had been challenged and shaped by death. My grandmother Sarah/Shirley, like the Sarah memorialized by Morpurgo, was also widowed—twice over—having lost one husband, my Grandpa Zev (William), after whom I'm named, to a sudden heart attack when she was only forty-five, and a second husband, my Grandpa Joe, to a tragic car accident when she was fifty-nine. Thereafter, she was afflicted with breast cancer and underwent a mastectomy. Somehow, she picked herself up each time and carried on, moving to Toronto in her sixties to live near us and start again.

The tragic history of my father's family was even more pronounced. Except for my grandfather Abraham Zierler, who died naturally in old age, everyone else in Dad's immediate family—he, three older brothers, and his mother—had died tragically: an infant death during World War I, a drowning, a war casualty, and two car accidents. My father wore the legacy of familial loss with him always, a garment of tears. But somehow, with stubborn temerity, he also clung to the notion that life was good—and if it didn't seem that way, it was sure to get better, soon.

And then there was my mother, the only one of the three whose gravestones we were unveiling, who was given the chance to face her death on her own terms. Surrounded by her loving family, she continued doling out love and wisdom to all of us until her very last breath. Never an optimist, at least not for herself, she encouraged her children and grandchildren relentlessly, and she taught us all the meaning of a good death.

These three epitaph poems, like the three stones we unveiled, commemorated a triple loss, but also the capacity, through words, deeds, and familial connection, to leave a mark that transcends generations.

In loving memory of:

Sarah bat Yeḥiel Mikhel ha-Kohen ve-Ḥayah Hinde
David Shelomo ben Avraham ve-Leah
Miriam Esther bat Ze'ev ve-Sarah

FIG. 9. Headstone of my parents, Marion and David Zierler. Photo by Wendy Zierler.

FIG. 10. Headstone of my grandmother, Shirley Goldfarb. Photo by Wendy Zierler.

6 Retying the Knots

Learning and Relearning with Ruhama Weiss

When loved ones die and the memory of their physical realness begins to fade, their belongings take on an almost talismanic power. So much depends on those objects you can clasp around your neck or thread through your ears and, thus fortified, go out in the world as if you're still physically connected to the person.

Among the pieces of jewelry my Mom entrusted me with when she was still alive—when I was a college student and had begun to show interest in old, good things—was a pair of antique engraved, teardrop earrings that used to belong to her mother, my Grandma Shirley (née Sarah, whose second unveiling we had recently commemorated along with the unveiling of the monuments for my parents). One day I went to put them on and discovered the gold wire on one earring was broken. The very next day I brought that broken earring (along with the good one, in order to match the two) to a local jeweler for repair, and a few days later, on my way home from a run, I picked them up from the shop, stuffing the jeweler's little plastic bag in my runner's fanny pack.

When I went through the fanny pack that evening, though, the earrings were gone. Just while running from the jewelry store to my house, I had undone a precious irreplaceable tie not only to my mother, but to her mother, too.

All night, I tossed and turned. I tried to tell myself these were just earrings: *a sheyne reyne kapporeh* (a good clean sacrifice), my mother used to say about things like this. But I couldn't fall asleep. I was angry and disappointed with myself. And I was so sad, simply overcome with the feeling that I hadn't just lost a pair of antique earrings, but a legacy that my mother had entrusted me to protect.

The poetry of Ruhama Weiss, the one living poet featured in the book, met me during this transition period: when the celebration of my rabbinic ordination was done, but my executor tasks were still not wrapped up; when possessions were still being distributed, and I was still swirling in the ambient energy of sorrow.

A Talmud scholar, poet, novelist, columnist, feminist interpreter, and activist against sexual abuse, Weiss is former Associate Professor of Talmud and Spiritual Care and Director of the Blaustein Center for Pastoral Counseling at HUC-JIR in Jerusalem. I had the distinct privilege of studying with Ruhama as part of my Maharat rabbinical training in a one-on-one course called *Sugyot Ḥayyim* (Life Topics), the title playing on the notion of the talmudic *sugya* (passage) and pivotal episodes in one's life. Selecting *sugyot* both from my rabbinic studies and my recent experience as a mourner, Ruhama and I probed them for their emotional content, searching for ways to transform personal pain into a new, usable form of living Torah. Ruhama Weiss's poetry, too, reflects this commitment to unflinching, emotional encounter with biblical, rabbinic, and liturgical texts as *sugyot ḥayyim*, as a means of connecting the past to the future and carrying the burden of everyday life.

A postscript about the lost earrings: The next morning, I set out to shul, determined to retrace every part of the previous day's route and see if—hope against hope—I might find them after all. My eyes were glued to the sidewalk, but I saw nothing but concrete and grass. Later, I stopped in at the CVS where the day before I had bought myself a drink after picking up the earrings; perhaps, if the plastic bag had fallen out in the drugstore, someone had turned it into the lost and found? No such luck. Convinced the earrings were lost to me forever, I sullenly and slowly crossed the street back in the direction of my house.

Then, suddenly, only a few feet away from the corner, I noticed, in a little crevice to the left of the sidewalk, the transparent glint of a tiny plastic bag with two gold teardrop earrings! Posthaste those earrings were back in my hands, now tightly gripped.

At home, I threaded them into my ears, sighed, smiled, and prepared for the rest of my day. Retying knots.

I Throw Down My Supplication	אֲנִי מַפִּילָה תְּחִנָּתִי[1]
I want to throw down my supplication	אֲנִי רוֹצָה לְהַפִּיל תְּחִנָּתִי
For I don't know how to carry it.	כֵּיוָן שֶׁאֵינִי יוֹדַעַת אֵיךְ לָשֵׂאת אוֹתָהּ.
Its humble longing for the unattainable[2]	קָשְׁתָה עָלַי תְּשׁוּקָתָהּ שִׁפְלַת־הָרוּחַ
Has become too much for me.	אֶל הַלֹּא מֻשָּׂג.
There are those who carry their supplication into the night.	יֵשׁ הַנּוֹשְׂאִים תְּחִנָּתָם אֶל הַלַּיְלָה.
There are those who sow it in tears	יֵשׁ הַזּוֹרְעִים אוֹתָהּ בְּדִמְעָה
And know not whether they will reap	וְלֹא יֵדְעוּ אִם יִקְצֹרוּ
And if so, in singing or wailing.[3]	וְאִם בְּרִנָּה אוֹ בִּנְהִי.
And I, who bows down to the morning	וַאֲנִי, שֶׁסּוֹגֶדֶת לַבֹּקֶר
And to the neon offices,	וּלְמִשְׂרְדֵי הַנֵּיאוֹן,
Who places my faith in red-fingernailed secretaries,	שֶׁשָּׂמָה מִבְטַחִי בְּמַזְכִּירוֹת אֲדֻמּוֹת צִפָּרְנַיִם,
And in the plastic smiles of bank tellers.	וּבְחִיּוּךְ הַפְּלַסְטִיק שֶׁל פְּקִידוֹת הַבַּנְק,
I would like to throw down my supplication	אֲנִי רוֹצָה לְהַפִּיל תְּחִנָּתִי
And know, that You'll be there	וְלָדַעַת, אַתָּה תִּהְיֶה שָׁם
To grab it.	וְתַחְזִיק.

Shortly after the earrings incident, I rediscovered this poem by Ruhama Weiss, which is all about being unable to carry the burden of pleading and self-flagellation and wanting instead to throw it all down to the ground.

The poem hinges on the Hebrew metaphorical expression *le-hapil teḥinati* or *le-hapil taḥanuneinu* (to pour out my/our supplications), which appears twice in the book of Daniel as part of Daniel's lengthy Hebrew prayer to end the exile (9:18, 22). We're told that King Nebuchadnezzar had exiled him to Babylonia, and he was still living there when the Persians conquered the land. Recalling Jeremiah's prophecy that the exile would last (only) seventy years (Jer. 25:9–13), the righteous Daniel dons sackcloth and ashes, and declares in prayer:

> With You, O Sovereign, is the right, and the shame is on us to this very day, on the citizenry of Judah and the inhabitants of Jerusalem, all Israel, near and far, in all the lands where You have banished them, for the trespass they committed against You. . . . Incline Your ear, O my God, and hear; open Your eyes and see our desolation and the city to which Your name is attached. Not because of any merit of ours do we throw down our supplications [*mapilim taḥanuneinu*] before You but because of Your abundant mercies. (Daniel 9:7,18)[4]

In his prayer Daniel avers that the Jews were exiled because of their sins. Hence he makes his abject plea to God to end the exile not on the basis of Jewish worthiness, but as a testament to God's magnanimous compassion. All year long, in the Monday and Thursday post-*Amidah Taḥanun* (supplication) prayers, traditional Jews adopt Daniel's posture and language of supplication, which accepts that Jewish suffering is due to sin and appeals to divine munificence, nonetheless.

I had been struggling with these prayers since the very beginning of my mourning journey. What sin did either of my parents commit, to deserve the suffering or tragic end they met? How could anyone in good conscience invoke that system of sin and punishment after the mass Jewish suffering of the Holocaust, which sent so many pious and innocent Jews to their deaths? I could simply not subscribe to the prophet Daniel's theology of supplication.

And so, discovering Ruhama Weiss's "I Throw Down My Supplication," which voices a similar measure of frustration over the guilt and self-abasement foundational to this continuing theological mode of liturgical expression, was an alternative, munificent godsend.

Tears continue to be marshaled in the liturgical appeal for divine mercy, Weiss says, recalling the assurance of Psalm 126:5, that "they who sow in tears shall reap with songs of joy." In reality, however, as the poet tells us at the end of the first stanza, "there are those who sow it [their supplication] in tears," with no knowledge or assurance of ever reaping any joy at all. And thus, instead of casting her supplication before God and humbly begging for God's mercy, she audaciously turns the expression *le-hapil teḥinati* (to throw down my supplication) on its head, voicing the desire not to pour out one's pleas before God, but to renounce or toss out this spiritual habit entirely.[5]

In the second stanza, however, Weiss contradicts herself and levels a measure of self-criticism and recrimination for her own this-worldly concerns and daily idolatries: the worship of neon and of the here-and-now, of bank transactions and the "plastic" niceties of daily commerce. Reading this, I thought of one of my own: a perhaps outsized concern for a pair of antique gold earrings.

Weiss, I saw, had found herself caught between a cult of abject and perhaps unattainable pleas and the meaningless materialism and ephemera of everyday secular life. That very in-between, I sensed her saying, was the proper place of prayer and care—neither in selfless, self-abasing humility nor in materialistic ego, but in the middle zone of self-respect that finds expression in reasonable requests for help. After all, if we were entirely unworthy, either personally or as a historical people, why should we expect God (or anyone else) ever to care about us at all?

Put otherwise, if the prophet Daniel insists that we base our supplication not on our own merit but on an assumption of undeserved, magnanimous mercy, Weiss was both agreeing, because she didn't see herself as a paragon of righteousness, and disagreeing, because she hoped and expected to be cared for and heard not just as a function of (divine) magnanimity but because that was the way things ought to be. And so, while she opens the poem with a stated desire "to throw down her supplication," in the last three lines she declares: "I would like to throw down my supplication / And know, that You'll be there / To grab it." In laying down her burden, she expects that some kind, caring power— God, a partner, even a reader—will help her pick it back up and carry it along to another day.

I read the ending of Weiss's poem not as a permanent letting go of devotion or responsibility, but as expressing her need for temporary respite. The final word, *taḥazik* (You will hold, grasp, store, maintain, or respect) called to my mind the verse, "She is a tree of life [*'etz ḥayyim*] to those who grasp [*maḥazikim*] her" (Prov. 3:18). The "she" here is commonly understood as femininely personified Wisdom, and, by extension, the Torah, as Jews customarily recite this verse upon returning the Torah to the ark after the Torah reading. Like Jews who (figuratively) take hold of the Torah during the reading and return the scroll to the ark, knowing it will soon be opened to read from again, Weiss wants to throw down her supplication, but also wants to know that it will be picked up, respected, and maintained. Often we are able to persevere because someone is there to spell us off for a time, reminding us that we—and by extension our feelings, even those of frustration or doubt—are worthy and deserving of respect.

"I Throw Down My Supplication" offered me that needed reminder. For two and a half years I had been carrying a heavy practical and spiritual burden—not always successfully, at least in my own mind. When Blue Cross Blue Shield attempted to claw back the payment for my mother's hospitalization, I feared it was my fault: I hadn't chosen her insurance policy correctly or secured the proper authorization. (Two nervous years later I'd discover the root of this problem, a clerical error. The insurance company had accidentally sent two reimbursement checks: one to me, which I'd handed over to Allen Hospital, and another to a different hospital, and they needed to recover one of the payments—but that resolution was still far in the offing.) Similarly, when I misplaced my Grandma Shirley's earrings, that (temporary) loss seemed proof of my incapacity to safeguard familial memory. Weiss's poem prodded me to reassess. More than my own perceived inadequacies in relation to the various spiritual and practical responsibilities I had been entrusted with since my parents' deaths, I needed to remember my effort and dignity, whether I bested the bureaucracy and recovered the lost object, or not.

None of us can manage everything all the time. Sometimes things get botched or fall down. Sometimes we succeed in finding what we've lost and lifting up what we need to carry. At other times we need to throw down our burden and seek support or some other solution, from siblings, from spouses, from health advocacy organizations like the Community Service Society of New York that helped me sort out the insurance issue, and from God—not because we have no self-respect, but because we do.

"Lament for Rashi's Daughters"

Lament for Rashi's Daughters

קינה על בנות רש״י[6]

When a son has longings for his father,
the father takes a strap from his right shoe
and ties it on the boy's left.

—BT Shabbat 66b

בן שיש געגועין על אביו נוטל רצועה
ממנעל של ימין וקושר לו בשמאלו.

—בבלי שבת, סו:

Longings—Bramare (extra love), the son longs for his father and thus cannot separate from him. But this remedy does not pertain to females, as their father does not show them much fondness from the outset such that they would ever come to long for him.—*Rashi*[7]

געגועין—ברמו״ט (אהבה יתֵרה), מְגַעגע עליו ואינו יכול ליפרד ממנו, ורפואה זו לא שייכא בנקבות, שאין האב מחבבן כל כך מתחילתן שיהיו מגעגעין עליו.—רשי, שם.

How they sat, Miriam, Yokheved, and another
  daughter left nameless
That's what we learned in Girls' School
Night after night they sat after the last
  student left,
They poured hot drinks for Father, caressed
  his words
Wrote down his commentaries.
On their last legs, with yawning eyes
They wrote with love, with longing,
This last commentary, too.
And he doesn't miss them?
And he has no extra love?
And he has no remedy of relevance for females?
It was decreed that they should write and wait
With heavy hands and unrequited longing
They should wait for him finally to show them
  fondness

אֵיךְ יָשְׁבוּ מִרְיָם, יוֹכֶבֶד וְעוֹד אַחַת,
שֶׁלֹּא הֻשְׁאַר לָהּ שֵׁם
כָּךְ לָמַדְנוּ בְּבֵית הַסֵּפֶר לְבָנוֹת
יָשְׁבוּ לַיְלָה, לַיְלָה, לְאַחַר שֶׁנִּסְתַּלֵּק
אַחֲרוֹן הַתַּלְמִידִים
מָזְגוּ חַמִּין לְאַבָּא, לִטְּפוּ אֶת מִלּוֹתָיו
כָּתְבוּ אֶת פֵּרוּשָׁיו.
בְּכֹחוֹת אַחֲרוֹנִים, בְּעֵינַיִם אֲחוּזוֹת פִּהוּק
כָּתְבוּ בְּאַהֲבָה, בְּגַעְגּוּעַ,
גַּם פֵּירוּשׁ זֶה הָאַחֲרוֹן.
וְאֵינוֹ מְגַעְגֵּעַ עֲלֵיהֶן?
וְאֵין לוֹ אַהֲבָה יְתֵרָה?
וְאֵין לוֹ רְפוּאָה שֶׁשַּׁיֶּכֶת בִּנְקֵבוֹת?
נִגְזַר עֲלֵיהֶן לִכְתֹּב וּלְהַמְתִּין
בְּיָדַיִם כְּבֵדוֹת וּבְגַעְגּוּעַ שֶׁאֵין לוֹ מַעֲנֶה
לְהַמְתִּין שֶׁיְּחַבְּבֵן בְּסוֹפָן

One day, perhaps, he will long for them or hear their longings	שֶׁיּוֹם אֶחָד אוּלַי יְגַעְגֵּעַ, אוּלַי יִשְׁמַע גַּעְגּוּעַן
With the coming of his grandsons, Rabbeinu Tam and the Rashbam,	עִם בּוֹא נְכָדָיו רַבֵּנוּ תָּם וְהָרַשְׁבָּ"ם
Their merit should protect us.	זְכוּתָם תָּגֵן עָלֵינוּ.

It was like being transported back to the very beginning of my journey, to that moment in the basement of my parents' shul in Toronto when, having wrapped myself in my father's tallit for the very first time, I stumbled upon that *mishnah* from the sixth chapter of Tractate Shabbat, which says that sons may go out on Shabbat wearing their father's knots but daughters may not, because daughters don't miss their fathers the way sons do. Two Kaddish cycles and half a year later, I was astonished to find that my teacher and friend Ruhama Weiss had formulated her own poetic retort to the talmudic notion of only sons "going out with knots"—an experience akin to looking at the opaque surface of a page and somehow seeing my own reflection.

Weiss had framed her poetic take in direct response to Rashi's commentary on BT Shabbat 66b. The father of four daughters (and no sons), Rashi asserts that daughters don't miss their deceased fathers because fathers don't play an intimate role in raising daughters and thus never show their daughters the kind of affection that would lead a daughter to long for her father in his absence.

Weiss's poem highlights the bitter ironies at the heart of Rashi's gloss. Rashi doesn't just *describe* a lack of paternal fondness for daughters; he demonstrates it himself. But his seeming disdain for Miriam, Yokheved, Rachel, and a fourth daughter whose name we don't know (she seemed to have died young) fails to drive them away—his fiercely devoted daughters transcribe all of his work, including this galling teaching about daughters. By helping him produce his commentary, Weiss suggests, his daughters may have been holding out hope that he would eventually come to appreciate them (of course, once they bore him grandsons). The legend that Rashi's daughters themselves prayed wearing tallit and tefillin symbolically reflects their efforts to tie themselves to the Torah and the ways of their father.[8]

Historically, two of Rashi's grandsons, Rabbi Samuel ben Meir (Rashbam, 1085–1158) and Rabbeinu (Yaakov) Tam (1100–1171), together with other Tosafists (medieval Ashkenazic commentators on the Talmud), helped continue their grandfather's exegetical work. These same grandsons disputed several of their grandfather's rulings. During my rabbinical studies I'd often wondered about their frequently vociferous rejections of their grandfather's legal positions. Had resentment over their grandfather's treatment of their mothers possibly contributed to their exegetical opposition? Might this especially explain Rashi and Rabbeinu Tam's contentious disagreement about the order in which parchments with sections from the Torah were to be inserted in tefillin—a symbol of masculine ties or knots that in their case failed completely to bind? Or, to put it differently: Did Rashi's abrogation of connection to his daughters give rise to grandsons who were fiercely tied to their mothers, with Rabbeinu Tam's oppositional tefillin practice reflecting that maternal tie?

For me, reading Rashi's declaration that fathers don't usually treat their daughters with enough affection to occasion feelings of longing for their father only brought to the fore my own wonderfully different story with my own father. My connection to Dad had always been affectionate and close. As a girl, I loved walking with him, sitting next to him in shul, and tagging along with him as he went on his "calls" downtown as a furniture salesman (see chapter 1). We shared a love of storytelling and writing, and he was endlessly proud of my Jewish learning—all the more so because he himself didn't have an extensive Jewish education, having grown up in a small Ontario town with little Jewish educational opportunity. By claiming that my own experience was impossible, Rashi ended up shoring up my commitment to remember Dad daily, through my daily ritual of donning of his tallit and tefillin, and my commitment to a life of Torah study.

As for Rabbeinu Tam's oppositional tefillin stance, I imagined this scenario as an example of unintended (feminist) consequences. From time to time, traditional rabbis have inadvertently strengthened feminist causes while attempting to weaken them. In June 2021, for example, my Maharat study partner Rabba Dr. Lindsey Taylor-Guthartz was ordained alongside me, but instead of commending her achievement, Rabbi Mirvis, chief rabbi of the U.K., declared that she was no longer permitted to teach at the London College of Jewish Studies or any United Synagogue shul.[9] The subsequent public backlash generated by her ouster—petitions and ads congratulating her for her achievements and calling for her reinstatement—may very well have led the chief rabbi to relent and restore her to her position.[10]

With all this mind, in teaching this poem, I offered a prayer for the future: May these texts and lessons serve as a tefillin-like sign and a symbol for the future. May all our rabbis celebrate rather than abrogate their daughters. And may we go out with knots that signify strong ties to our fathers and mothers, past and present, alike.

I Am Still Praying	אֲנִי עוֹד מִתְפַּלֶּלֶת[11]
That this story will find a resolution already	שֶׁהַסִּפּוּר הַהוּא כְּבָר יִמְצָא הַתָּרָה
And not lie down like a deserted dog in my doorway.	וְלֹא יִרְבַּץ עוֹד כְּכֶלֶב עָזוּב בְּפֶתַח בֵּיתִי.
That you'll wait patiently for me to be convinced, too,	שֶׁתְּחַכֶּה בְּסַבְלָנוּת עַד שֶׁגַּם אֲנִי אֶשְׁתַּכְנֵעַ,
That I'll be convinced.	שֶׁאֲנִי אֶשְׁתַּכְנֵעַ.
That love will win over history,	שֶׁהָאַהֲבָה תְּנַצֵּחַ אֶת הַהִסְטוֹרְיָה,
That it will have a first name.	שֶׁיִּהְיֶה לָהּ שֵׁם פְּרָטִי.
That death will not come violently,	שֶׁהַמָּוֶת לֹא יָבוֹא בְּאַלִּימוּת,
That I'll accept it when it arrives.	שֶׁאֲנִי אַסְכִּים לְקַבֵּל אוֹתוֹ כְּשֶׁהוּא יַגִּיעַ.
That I'll stop believing that sadness is about to swallow me up,	שֶׁאֲנִי אַפְסִיק לְהַאֲמִין שֶׁהָעַצְבוּת תִּבְלַע אוֹתִי,
That it doesn't swallow me up.	שֶׁהִיא לֹא תִּבְלַע אוֹתִי.
That occasionally the world will justify my decision	שֶׁמִּדֵּי פַּעַם הָעוֹלָם יַצְדִּיק אֶת הַחְלָטָתִי
To bring children into it.	לְהָבִיא אֵלָיו יְלָדִים.
That at least occasionally they'll beat swords into plowshares,	שֶׁלְּפָחוֹת מִדֵּי פַּעַם וְכִתְּתוּ,
And at least, occasionally, a man will sit under his vine.	שֶׁלְּפָחוֹת מִדֵּי פַּעַם אִישׁ תַּחַת גַּפְנוֹ.
That I'll stop wanting to know.	שֶׁאַפְסִיק לִרְצוֹת לָדַעַת.
That I'll be brave enough to erase the lines of proof	שֶׁיִּהְיֶה לִי אֹמֶץ לִמְחֹק אֶת שׁוּרוֹת הַהוֹכָחָה
And stick simply with what can be found	וּלְהִשָּׁאֵר רַק עִם מַה שֶּׁנִּמְצָא
Beneath the line.	מִתַּחַת לַקַּו.

People asked me sometimes why I kept on going to morning minyan. My Kaddish period was long over. I wasn't being counted in the prayer quorum. What kept me going so early in the morning? What unfinished business was I praying to complete?

I would answer that I had come to rely on the routine. That daily minyan attendance slowed down my *davening* and gave me more focus.

That I felt responsible to my tefillah buddy, Lisa, and to Mark and Laureen, the middle-aged developmentally disabled brother and sister, who came just about every morning, and waited until the end of *davening*, just to talk to Lisa and me. Especially Laureen, with whom Lisa and I would often sing *'Adon 'Olam* or *'Ein Ke'loheinu* (two of the closing hymns) at the conclusion of services. Lately, we had also been helping Laureen practice the English alphabet using an elementary workbook, as she had never actually learned how to read.

Though I wasn't counted in the minyan in a ritual or halakhic/legal sense, if I didn't make it to shul on a given morning, I would get texts and emails from regulars, both men and women, asking me if everything was okay. If that isn't "counting," what is?

Plus, I had no end of personal and collective things to pray for: that my children would get the professional opportunities they desperately sought, that they would find and/or keep good partners, that the political situation in America and Israel would improve, that antisemitism would not continue to escalate, that my loved ones would stay healthy and well, and so on. And I had much to express gratitude for, too.

I experienced "I Am Still Praying" as Ruhama Weiss's analogous catalog of reasons to persist in prayer. The poem starts with her praying for a solution or resolution to a particular story, and since the word *hatarah* (resolution) evokes the daily liturgical praise of God as *matir 'asurim* (the One who frees captives), it suggests the ways in which we can become captive to the various twists and complications of our lives. (More recently, sadly, in the wake of October 7, 2023, we have come to understand more starkly this blessing's significance as pertaining to actual war captives.) Then she prays that "you'll wait patiently for me to be convinced," without clarifying who the "you" is—is it God, a lover, or both? She seems to be praying on two levels simultaneously: personal and collective. She prays both for historical enmities and patterns not to repeat themselves and for love to become her intimate friend. She prays not to lose hope—for tangible evidence of why she shouldn't despair about having a family in such a broken world—and also, in allusion to Yehuda Amichai's "A Sort of End of Days" (see chapter 4), she hopes that at least a few people will sit securely under their vines and beat a few swords into plowshares, a sign that the idea of redemption has not yet become defunct.[12]

Weiss and I were praying—sometimes similarly, sometimes differently—and we kept praying. One never knew what new emotional or political challenge lay around the corner. As long as one lived, one could never run out of things to fix or of reasons to pray.

And like another Amichai poem, "Men, Women and Children" (again see chapter 4), Weiss's poem has eighteen lines, signifying a kind of numerological חי/*ḥai* (eight) lifetime of prayer. It struck me, too, that "I am Still Praying" was the last poem in Weiss's 2013 book *'Eḥeta' ve-'Ashuv* (*I'll Sin and Return*)—this title itself speaking of an ongoing story. Her book was ending but her own prayers had yet to be complete.

Were mine? Were anyone's? With these questions in mind, I turned to the group at the Bayit, assembled that morning for the *Shir Ḥadash*, and asked them as well as myself: What stories still linger in your mind, in search of resolution? What decisions, for you, for your children, for other loved ones in your life, are still in-the-making? What are your unresolved collective yearnings? And how might all of this be folded into our daily *tefillot*?

In the spirit of silent prayer, I didn't expect anyone to respond to me out loud, only to spur their own thinking and awareness of the ongoing nature of the prayer-project, well beyond any individual service. The *siddurim* (prayer books) were about to be put away. The last Rabbi's Kaddish was about to be recited. But the real-life prayerbook of our hearts had certainly not been shut.

And Once Again, I'll Sin and Return	**ושוב אחטא ואשוב**[13]
Woe for me, for I've been undone[14]	אוֹי לִי כִּי נִדְמֵיתִי
By the texture of routine	מֵאֵיכוּתָהּ שֶׁל הַשִּׁגְרָה
For I've tired	כִּי עָיַפְתִּי
Of the neon lights	מֵאוֹרוֹת הַנֵּיאוֹן
Of multi-colors	מֵהַצִּבְעוֹנִיּוֹת
Of the levity of collecting.	מִקַּלּוּת הַלִּקּוּט.
My stopover in the corner store	כָּבְדָה עָלַי הַשְּׁהִיָּה
Has become too cumbersome.	בַּחֲנוּת הַמַּכֹּלֶת.
For too long I've been undone, hence	זְמַן רַב מִדַּי נִדְמֵיתִי וְעַל כֵּן
I'm closing the door.	אֲנִי סוֹגֶרֶת אֶת הַדֶּלֶת.
I'm locking up.	אֲנִי נוֹעֶלֶת.
I know I'll hurry back.	אֲנִי יוֹדַעַת כִּי אֲמַהֵר לַחֲזֹר.
I'm hanging a sign:	אֲנִי תוֹלָה שֶׁלֶט:
I've gone out to settle urgent matters	יָצָאתִי לְסַדֵּר עִנְיָנִים דְחוּפִים
(Thank-you for your kind patience)	(אָנָּא בְּטוּבְכֶם, סַבְלָנוּתְכֶם)
I'll sin	אֶחְטָא
And immediately return.	וְתֵכֶף אָשׁוּב.

It was the one-hundredth anniversary of the yahrzeit of my Uncle Sam, my father's eldest brother, who'd drowned in Lake Huron in 1921 at age fourteen, before my father was born. Now that my father was gone, it had fallen to us, his adult children, to memorialize the brother Dad had never known. If not for my sister Randi, who remembers every important family occasion, I never would have commemorated his yahrzeit. I'd somehow forgotten that it fell out in the summer, but when else would a teenager have gone swimming?

Perhaps my memory lapse was understandable. It was that time of year when so many people take vacations, leaving our everyday routines to clear our heads and recharge. But it was also Rosh Ḥodesh Elul, when Jews initiate the annual project of spiritual return. And so personal and collective imperatives converged: The need for me to return to and take responsibility for familial memory coalesced with the requirement to gear up for the yearly project of repentance.

For those Jews who viewed the whole Elul endeavor as a kind of annually issued "get out of jail free" card, wherein one can rack up lapses all year long and then on the High Holy Days simply clear one's rack and start out fresh, the last *mishnah* in Tractate Yoma (8:9) issued a clear warning: "If one has a habit of declaring, 'I'll sin and then repent, I'll sin and then repent' (*'eḥeta' ve-'ashuv, 'eḥeta' ve-'ashuv*), one [or: Heaven] does not provide this person with the opportunity to repent."

Yet Weiss's poem "And Once Again, I'll Sin and Return" offered a diametrically opposite take. The first line ("Woe is me, for I've been undone") quotes directly from the sixth chapter of Isaiah, in which Isaiah receives his prophetic commission and sees a vision of God on the heavenly throne, flanked by angelic *serafim* who call out to one another "Holy, holy, holy! GOD of Hosts" (the basis of the *Kedushah* prayer). Yet the prophet feels unworthy of having received such a vision, exclaiming: "Woe is me that I am undone [*nidmeiti*, literally, "I am dumbfounded" or, in the Revised JPS translation, "I am lost"], for I am a man of impure lips, and I live among a people of impure lips" (Isa. 6:5). In response to his declaration, one of the *serafim* touches Isaiah's lips with a hot coal to purify them, thereby enabling Isaiah to assume his prophetic voice.

Weiss, I saw, had inserted herself into this prophetic-turned-liturgical line to make a similar declaration, but no angel intercedes to cure her sense of unworthiness. No one launches her into action on God's behalf, either. Rather, her speaker's articulated "Woe for me for I am undone" provides a pretext for her taking a break: for retreating from the commercial neon lights, the errand doing, the shopkeeping, and other mundane tasks. Still, in a poetic revision of Tractate Yoma's "I'll sin and then repent, I'll sin and then repent," she adds: "I know I'll hurry back. . . . I'll sin / And immediately return."

The Hebrew word *'eḥeta'* (here translated as "I will sin") literally means "I will miss [or: step away from] my mark," a notion of sin stemming from a view of behavior as either achieving or falling short of one's targeted responsibilities or aims. Here, Weiss is equating sinning with stepping away from established daily routine and responsibility—which implies a very this-worldly relationship with God, the kind that unfolds not against a scorching seraphic backdrop, but in the hit-and-miss of everyday life. And so, in "sinning" she also promises to try and come back soon, like a shopkeeper who hangs an "out to lunch" sign on the door indicating the planned time of return.

Weiss was telling us that we all needed times to forget or get away. We needed August vacations in order to pull off the September–October project of Repentance. After all, if we never went away, we'd never need to come back. If we never made mistakes or lost track of an important date or how to mark it, we'd have nothing to fix.

I loved, too, how Weiss was using the prophetic language of Isaiah to express the psychological experience of being speechless or stuck and the desire to find some way forward. "For too long I've been undone," her speaker was saying; "hence / I'm closing the door. / I'm locking up." Whatever had stricken her had waylaid her so thoroughly that she couldn't muster another word or deed. To protect her psyche, she had no choice but hang up that "out to lunch" sign and lock up the store.

To some, "locking up" might seem arrogant or irresponsible. But given the context—the poem evoking both the language of annual repentance, culminating on Yom Kippur with the *Ne'ilah* (locking up) service, and the *Kedushah* prayer—I connected to Weiss's prayerful declaration of intention not to remain locked away forever, but to come back as soon. I saw the wisdom in her having arrived at the very opposite conclusion than Tractate Yoma does. Whoever says "I shall sin and return" may very well stand the best chance of finding the strength and courage to stand before God—or simply to face another day.

As for the task of remembering an uncle neither my father nor I had ever met, but whom Dad had nevertheless mourned throughout his days, because he so wished to have a brother to accompany him through life, *Oy li ki nidmeiti,* "Woe was I that I was [doubly] undone."[15] If not for my sister's last-minute reminder, I would have forgotten the responsibility entirely. And even upon being reminded, what really could I say? My grandparents were so broken up by Sam's death that they rarely spoke about him. All Dad could relate about his eldest brother was what he had heard, secondhand, from other relatives: Samuel was a good student, a fine, responsible boy. Then one day, while swimming with two other friends, he somehow got a cramp, and went down before his friends or the lifeguard could save him.

It was an impossible commemoration of an unspeakable tragedy. Nevertheless, it was one I had pledged to undertake for the rest of my life and to the best of my ability—and at least on this occasion, "And Once Again, I'll Sin and Return," with its image of "sinning and returning, sinning and returning," provided a helpful framing.

When it came to this task, *'eḥeta'*: I would always miss the mark—unable because of a simple lack of information, to offer a real detailed picture of Samuel Zierler, eternal peace be with him. But every year, I'd try again: *'eḥeta' ve-'ashuv*—knowing that I was connecting to a task that Dad tried his best, his whole life, to get right, too.

Chapters of the Mothers	**פִּרְקֵי אִמָּהוֹת**[16]
From Eve I learned to want and also to take a bite	מֵחַוָּה לָמַדְתִּי לַחְשֹׁק וְגַם לָקַחַת בִּיס.
From Hagar I learned to submit and afterward, to see	מֵהָגָר לָמַדְתִּי לְהִכָּנַע וְאַחַר כָּךְ לִרְאוֹת
And to find strength to save the boy.	וְלִמְצֹא כֹּחוֹת לְהַצִּיל אֶת הַיֶּלֶד.
The harshest lesson of my life I learned	אֶת הַשִּׁעוּר הֶחָרִיף בְּחַיַּי
From Lot's wife:	לָמַדְתִּי מֵאֵשֶׁת לוֹט:
Depending on the depth of the pit, so grows the prohibition	לְפִי עָמְקוֹ שֶׁל הַבּוֹר גָּדֵל הָאִסּוּר
against looking back.	לְהַבִּיט לְאָחוֹר.
From Dinah I learned to cry quietly.	מִדִּינָה לָמַדְתִּי לִבְכּוֹת בְּשֶׁקֶט.
Hannah taught me to offer too steep a price.	חָנָה לִמְּדָה אוֹתִי לְהַצִּיעַ מְחִירִים גְּבוֹהִים מִדַּי.
Michal bequeathed me the bitter desire	מִיכַל הוֹרִישָׁה לִי אֶת הַתְּשׁוּקָה הַמָּרָה
For a man who isn't my match.	לְגֶבֶר שֶׁלֹּא יַהֲלֹם אֶת מִדּוֹתַי.
From Sisera's mother I inherited wickedness.	מֵאֵם סִיסְרָא יָרַשְׁתִּי רִשְׁעוּת.
From Sarah I inherited bitterness.	מִשָּׂרָה יָרַשְׁתִּי מְרִירוּת.
From Zipporah I learned that daring and devotion exact a price.	מִצִּפּוֹרָה לָמַדְתִּי שֶׁנּוֹעָזוּת וּמְסִירוּת גּוֹבוֹת מְחִיר.
From Miriam I learned loneliness.	מִמִּרְיָם לָמַדְתִּי בְּדִידוּת.
From My Darling, My Fair One I learned the fear of commitment.[17]	מֵרַעְיָתִי יָפָתִי לָמַדְתִּי מַהוּ פַּחַד מֵהִתְמַסְּרוּת.
From the first Tamar I learned to agree to risk all.	מִתָּמָר הָרִאשׁוֹנָה לָמַדְתִּי לְהַסְכִּים לְסַכֵּן הַכֹּל.
From the second Tamar I learned that it doesn't always help,	מִתָּמָר הַשְּׁנִיָּה לָמַדְתִּי שֶׁזֶּה לֹא תָּמִיד עוֹזֵר,
And sometimes it's better to lie quietly and let him finish.	וְלִפְעָמִים עָדִיף לִשְׁכַּב בְּשֶׁקֶט וְלָתֵת לוֹ לִגְמֹר.
From Bathsheba I inherited the ability to be used wisely.	מִבַּת שֶׁבַע יָרַשְׁתִּי אֶת הַיְּכֹלֶת לְהִשְׁתַּמֵּשׁ בִּתְבוּנָה.

From Job's wife I learned to pay the price
for other people's piety.
Samson's mother taught me to be wary of
the voices of angels
and to marry / carry stupid men
with pride.

From the Shunamite woman I learned that
there is no limit to responsibility
(And this exactly is what Hagar
taught me).
From Naamah I learned that eyes that see
are power.
From Ruhama I learned that the definition
of a "Whore's Daughter" is ever changing[18]
(And that heredity is a fluid concept).
From Ruth I learned liberty.[19]

And everything otherwise
Known and described[20]
(and perhaps cruel, besides?)
And all in the male guise
Is written in the Book of the Upright.

מֵאֵשֶׁת אִיּוֹב לָמַדְתִּי לְשַׁלֵּם מְחִיר עַל
צַדְקָנִיּוּת שֶׁל אֲחֵרִים.
אִמּוֹ שֶׁל שִׁמְשׁוֹן לִמְּדָה אוֹתִי לְהִזָּהֵר
מִקּוֹלוֹת שֶׁל מַלְאָכִים
וְלָשֵׂאת בְּגָאוֹן גְּבָרִים טִפְּשִׁים.

מֵהָאִשָּׁה הַשּׁוּנַמִּית לָמַדְתִּי שֶׁאֵין גְּבוּל
לָאַחֲרָיוּת
(וְזֶה בְּדִיּוּק מַה שֶּׁלִּמְּדָה אוֹתִי הָגָר).
מִנַּעֲמָה לָמַדְתִּי שֶׁעֵינַיִם שֶׁרוֹאוֹת הֵן כֹּחַ.
מֵרוּחָמָה לָמַדְתִּי שֶׁבַּת־זוֹנָה הִיא הַגְדָּרָה
מִשְׁתַּנָּה
(וְגֶנֶטִיקָה הִיא מֻשָּׂג נָזִיל)
מֵרוּת לָמַדְתִּי חֵרוּת.

וְכָל הַשְּׁאָר
כָּל שֶׁהוּא יָדוּעַ וּמְבֹרָר
(הֲגַם שֶׁלִּפְעָמִים אַכְזָר)
וְכָל שֶׁהוּא מִמִּין זָכָר
כָּתוּב עַל סֵפֶר הַיָּשָׁר.

It was now two years since I had begun teaching the weekly *Shir Ḥadash*, a project that had started with my picking out a poem each week, translating it, and offering up a few hand-scrawled points at the end of tefillah every Tuesday morning before the final Rabbi's Kaddish. In the course of time it had expanded to include short essays on each poem, which I sent out every Tuesday morning to a large list of readers—those essay pages eventually accumulating and becoming the heart of this book.

To mark this two-year anniversary, I chose "Chapters of the Mothers," a poem that looked back and enlarged upon earlier teachings, and gave voice to some of the repercussions of growing up in a tradition without women's voices.

What, I wondered, were the possible effects on the religious psyche of an Orthodox-identified girl or woman to hear only about the merits, wisdom, and righteousness of men? To pray three times a day to a (masculine) God identified as the God of one's Forefathers, with no liturgical reference whatsoever to one's Foremothers? To study a talmudic tradition authored entirely by men, and to have that tradition ethically and ideologically encapsulated in a book explicitly entitled *Pirkei 'Avot* (*Ethics of the Fathers*)? That the entire text of *Pirkei 'Avot* appeared in the Shabbat afternoon *Minḥah* service, elevating the work to the level of liturgy and credo, only intensified this line of questioning.

Feminist scholar and critic Judith Fetterly describes this process of "exclusion from a literature that claims to define one's identity" and of "being divided against one's self" as an experience of "*immasculation* of women by men."[21] She elaborates: "Women are taught to think as men, to identify with a male point of view, and to accept as normal and legitimate a male system of values, one of whose central principles is misogyny."[22] The feminist scholarly enterprise to which I had devoted my career thus entailed three crucial parts: critical readings of male-authored canonical texts to expose this bias; the recovery of alternative feminine literary "herstories" or traditions; and, if extant traditions didn't suffice, the creation of something new.

"Chapters of the Mothers" offered our *Shir Ḥadash* community a distilled version of that tripartite feminist project, albeit not necessarily in that order. It also continued a thread of discussion on the need at various crucial junctures to redefine core Jewish values and our definition of Torah, too.

I noted, on this score, the poem's marked contrast to the linearity of the first chapter of *Pirkei 'Avot,* which sketches a chronological line of male transmission of Torah. The poem's matriarchal object lessons move not linearly but back and forth in time, in digressive and associative accumulations: from Eve to Lot's wife, Hagar, Dinah, Hannah, Michal, the mother of Sisera, Sarah, Tzipporah, Miriam, the Shulamite from Song of Songs (dubbed "My friend, my lovely"), Tamar 1 and 2 (from the books of Genesis and Samuel, respectively), Batsheva, Job's wife, Samson's mother, the Shunamite, Ruhama, and Ruth. Sadly, however, the gleaned learnings comprise more bitterness, sorrow, and pragmatic strategy than upbeat or affirmative messages. These are maternal lessons one wishes one need never learn.

In fact, only three positive or affirmative teachings emerge from the list, and even these have a darker underside. First comes the opening teaching, which credits Eve for inventing desire and the value of taking a "bite" from the fruit of the Tree of Knowledge of Good and Evil. Of course, lurking in the background of all this is the traditional Judeo-Christian excoriation of Eve for originating (carnal) sin and mortality.

Second, Weiss credits Naamah, sister of Tubal-cain (Gen. 4:22), with the positive capacity of sight. This notion is rooted in magical and kabbalistic tradition, which associates Naamah with Jewish demonology—suggesting that this power of sight is more than a little transgressive and subversive.[23]

Third and most affirmatively, Weiss plays on the rhyme of the word *me-Rut* (from Ruth) and the Hebrew word *ḥerut* (liberation) to laud Ruth for modeling freedom. Rather than recount the traditional praise of Ruth's loyalty to Naomi's people and God, Weiss offers something entirely new: a unique understanding on the etymology and meaning of Ruth's name, and by extension, the primary message of the book named for her.

The poem ends with a five-line rhymed critique of Jewish tradition as male-centered and hence sometimes harmful: "And everything otherwise / Known and described / (And perhaps cruel, besides?) / And all in male guise / Is written in the *Book of the Upright* (*Sefer ha-Yashar*)." Other than the list of object lessons gleaned from biblical women, everything else has already been repeatedly taught and discussed in the masculine gender and voice. The rhyme at the end of each of these last five lines accentuates the sense of recurrent transmission. The idea that all of this men's wisdom can be found in *Sefer ha-Yashar* (*Book of the Upright*) underscores the claim to righteousness and eternality accompanying the tradition.

And yet, disagreement among classical sources concerning what *Sefer ha-Yashar* actually is undermines this same claim.

The term *Sefer ha-Yashar* (translated as "Book of Jashar") appears twice in the Bible. In the first instance, the prophet Joshua asks God to make the sun stand still in Gibeon so as to give his army more time to defeat the Amorites. The Bible reports that "the sun stood still / And the moon halted / While a nation wreaked judgment on its foes," and that all this "is written in the Book of Jashar" (Josh 10:13). In the second, which occurs at the beginning of David's poetic lament for Jonathan, David orders the Judites to be taught a "[Song of the] Bow," as recorded in the Book of Jashar (2 Sam. 1:18). Most scholars view these two references as pointing to a lost ancient book of Hebrew poetry or military strategy. BT Avodah Zarah 25a, however, links the title *Sefer ha-Yashar* to three different, extant biblical books. Rabbi Ḥiya bar Abba in the name of R. Yoḥanan suggests that *Sefer ha-Yashar* is the book of Abraham, Isaac, and Jacob, those whom Numbers 23:10 calls *yesharim* (honest)—in other words, the book of Genesis. Rabbi Eliezer suggests that *Sefer ha-Yashar* refers to Deuteronomy, given its directive to do *ha-yashar veha-tov*, what is right and good in the eyes of God (Deut. 6:18). Finally, Rabbi Samuel bar Naḥmani suggests that *Sefer ha-Yashar* is the book of Judges, because in that book each man anarchically does *ha-yashar be-'einav*, what is correct in his own (sometimes sinning) eyes, instead of conforming to a uniform code of religious and moral conduct.

If the rabbis couldn't get the record straight or agree as to what *Sefer ha-Yashar* refers to, what did that say about the rectitude or reliability of their male-centered tradition?

As it happens, *Sefer ha-Yashar* also refers to a medieval midrashic work that purports to have been discovered in the ruins of Jerusalem after the destruction of the Second Temple. According to this book's introduction, the book is entitled "'The Correct Book' [*Sefer ha-Yashar*], because all events are chronicled within it, according to the accurate and correct time in which they really occurred, and in strict order as to what hath taken place sooner or later"—in contrast to the original biblical narrative, which often lacks detail and chronological coherence.[24]

In pointing at the end of the poem to *Sefer ha-Yashar*, then, Weiss is expressing a measure of doubt about the identity and comprehensiveness of this masculine tradition and pointing to its need for correction and amplification. As such, she also hints at the third stage of the feminist project: new, female-authored contributions to the evolving canon—namely, modern feminist midrash. If the received tradition had assumed an entirely masculine and not entirely correct voice; and if the few female characters available to Jewish women remained stuck in a world of limited agency and heartache, then it was incumbent upon us to compose alternative texts and interpretations to supplement, affirm, and liberate, as the Ruth/*ḥerut* wordplay suggests.

By now, of course, I had introduced the *Shir Ḥadash* community (those attending shul on Tuesday mornings, whether in person or by Zoom, and those who were reading my weekly emails) to three generations of modern Hebrew women poets and scholars—Rachel Morpurgo, Lea Goldberg, and Ruhama Weiss—who had done this very work. How exciting it was to see this alternative tradition come together and accrue: yet another form of "going out with knots."

7 Penning Pandemic Torah

Rachel Bluwstein's Feminist/Illness Poetry

"Mom's in the ER again," my husband, Daniel, told me on the phone. "Do you think you can get over there when you're done teaching?"

It was the third time in one week. Over the previous month, my mother-in-law, Dvora, had taken to riding up and down the elevators at all hours at the senior residence where she lived, and strewing the contents of her closet all about her apartment. She was having difficulties with basic hygiene, too. We'd recently moved her to this residence because it was close to our house and synagogue and had promoted itself as offering a continuum of memory care for people with Alzheimer's. Yet the facility's response to this new, predictable stage of her disease was simply to insist that she be assigned twenty-four-hour care. When we questioned this abrupt shift from the lowest to the highest (and most expensive) tier of care, and whether we might move her onto the memory care floor instead, they rejected the option without explanation, and followed this, two weeks later, with a letter announcing they were evicting Dvora from the facility. My lawyer husband then read though his mother's residence contract and discovered a provision allowing him to challenge the eviction, which would give us time to find her a new home offering proper memory care. The facility's (seemingly vindictive) response was to send Dvora alone by ambulance to the hospital every time she displayed a behavior they deemed new or "strange"—basically making her life there completely intolerable, and, by extension, ours too.

By the time I got to the Allen Hospital emergency department that afternoon, Dvora was sobbing so uncontrollably that it took a nurse and me more than an hour to calm her down. When we brought her to our home for Shabbat lunch the following week, she was even more agitated. "I'll never forgive you, I'll never forgive you!" she screamed over and over again at Daniel, her dumbstruck son. "How could you do it?! How could you do such a thing to your *daughter*?!"

Nothing we had experienced thus far had prepared us for this new turn of events. The otherworldly inscrutability of this illness and the cruelty of the senior residence staff who had promised to help us care for her, together with resurgent, new strains of COVID, turned the fall of 2021 and the winter of 2022 into a third, ancillary year of familial mourning—this time, though, for a parent still very much alive.

The poet I taught during this period was Rachel Bluwstein, best known by her first name, Rachel, or in Hebrew as *Raḥel ha-Meshoreret* (the poetess Rachel). Her poetry is imprinted by the loneliness and cruelty of her own experience of chronic illness.

Born in 1890 in Saratov, Russia, she and her two sisters immigrated to Palestine in 1909—initially to Rehovot, and then in 1911 to *Ḥavat ha-'Alamot* (Maiden's Farm), an agricultural school for women at Kinneret Farm, newly founded by feminist agronomist and Zionist leader Hannah Meisel. In 1913, Rachel left Palestine for Toulouse, France to study agronomy, hoping to put this knowledge to use in agricultural work back in the Land of Israel, but once World War I erupted she couldn't complete her studies in France or return to Palestine. Out of options, she returned to Russia, volunteering in a Jewish children's orphanage on the outskirts of Odessa while also seeking treatment for acute pulmonary tuberculosis, a disease that had first afflicted her when she was a child.[1] In 1919, she returned to Mandatory Palestine as part of the Third Aliyah, hoping to settle back in the Galilee as an agronomist in Kevutzat Deganiah, the first kibbutz. Bluwstein's mentor, the Zionist philosopher A. D. Gordon, whom she had met before her studies in France, had settled there, too. But her now exacerbated tuberculosis made it impossible for her to stay on the kibbutz, both because of the rigors of the work and the fear that others would get sick. Thereafter, Bluwstein spent the rest of her life either in hospitals or in apartments in Jerusalem and Tel Aviv, where she turned her attention to translation and writing poetry. She finally succumbed to tuberculosis in 1931 at the young age of forty-one.

During her own day, Rachel's poetry was often misread as simplistic and unartful, offering little more than what immediately met the eye. In the early 2000s, however, Jewish feminist scholars and literary critics began to champion her work as demonstrating modernist and feminist artistry and depth, as seen in her minimalist form and subtly subversive biblical and talmudic references. Almost a century later, I was turning to her verse as an emotional outlet and as raw material for a new kind of COVID Torah. Rachel's illness poetry became an essential part of a new HUC-JIR course on Jewish pandemic literature, which I taught in the spring of 2022. Additionally, two of her poems that had been set to music ("Ve-'ulai" and "Kinneret") became a touchstone of our family's new relationship with Dvora as she descended further into dementia and increasingly lost her capacity to communicate. If we could no longer converse with her, we could at least sing the folksong version of Rachel's poems, which Dvora knew from her youth as a member of the religious Zionist youth group Bnei Akiva and from living on Kibbutz Yavneh for a year in 1958. As she sang or hummed along with us, Rachel's poems set to song seemed, if only for a few moments, to bring her back to some trace of the person she used to be, a much-appreciated gift.

For years I had read Bluwstein's poetry as part of my feminist scholarly work on the first Hebrew women poets and prose writers. Delving deeply into her work in the context of communal and familial illness, however, I found meaning, sorrow, and spiritual resources that I hadn't discerned before. And I would share all of this new discovery—literary, intellectual and emotional— with my *Shir Ḥadash* community.

"Soul Walking"

Soul Walking	הֲלָךְ נֶפֶשׁ[2]
For A. D. Gordon	לא. ד. גורדון
The day grew ever darker	הַיּוֹם הָלַךְ וְהֶחֱשִׁיךְ,
Ever dim.	דָּעַךְ הַיּוֹם.
Dullish gold glazed the sky	זָהָב מוּעָם צִפּוּ שְׁחָקִים
And mountain rim.	וְהָרֵי רוֹם.
Around me fields stretched wide and black	סְבִיבִי הִשְׁחִיר מֶרְחַב שָׂדוֹת
A muted plain;	מֶרְחָב אִלֵּם;
My trail strayed far away alone,	הִרְחִיק שְׁבִילִי—שְׁבִילִי בּוֹדֵד,
My trail of pain . . .	שְׁבִילִי שׁוֹמֵם . . .
Still I shall not challenge fate,	אַךְ לֹא אַמְרֶה פִּי הַגּוֹרָל,
Tyrant it may be.	גּוֹרָל רוֹדֶה,
Instead I'll greet it all with joy,	אֵלֵךְ בְּגִיל לִקְרַאת הַכֹּל,
And thankfully.	עַל כֹּל אוֹדֶה!

In 1920, a year after her return to Palestine on the *Ruslan*, the first ship bound to the region after World War I, Rachel Bluwstein published her first poem, "*Halakh Nefesh*" ("Soul Walking") in the cultural Zionist journal *Ha-Shiloaḥ,* founded in 1896 by Ahad Ha'am (pen name of Asher Ginsburg, 1856–1927). It was the first poem by a woman to be published in that famed journal. It was also permeated by a mix of fear, insecurity, determination, and gratitude, which struck a chord in all of us in the *Shir Ḥadash* community.

The expression *halakh nefesh* (soul walking) derives from a declaration in Ecclesiastes (6:9) that what one sees before one's eyes is preferable to *halakh nefesh*—that is, to allowing one's soul or desire to walk about and pursue its indeterminate yearnings.[3] The title and the first two stanzas evoke longing but also disquiet: the lone speaker traveling far away on a solitary, desolate path against a darkening landscape.

What to make of the meter, with its alternating longer and shorter lines? A first reading discerned an insecure, unresolved spirit: one who ventures out but then retreats; one who dares and then doubts. Or, I thought: Perhaps one should read it the other way around, with the short lines expressing decisiveness and resolve in the face of former hesitation?

Reading this poem in the fall of 2021, our still insecure time, prompted further associations with *Lekh Lekha*, the Torah portion we'd just read the week before, given its many repetitions of the verb *lalekhet* (the infinitive of the verbal root *hei-lamed-khaf*, meaning to walk or go). Images arose of our biblical ancestors Abraham and Sarah and the "souls [*nefesh*] they made in Haran" (Gen. 12:5) on a *halikhat nefesh*, a "soul-walk," off the beaten path of the dominant culture.[4] Abraham and Sarah's going, however, was purposeful and forward-looking, undertaken with a surety born of divine command. By contrast, Rachel's early twentieth-century walk seemed tentative and insecure, at best. That is, until I considered the poem's dedication to the Zionist philosopher A. D. Gordon, and the last stanza.

Once Gordon and Bluwstein met in Rehovot, he became her lifelong mentor. In letters to her when she was studying in Toulouse, he urged her not to despair about being so far from *'Eretz Yisra'el*, and instead to make the most of every opportunity. Doubts and suffering due to great aspiration are to be appreciated, he said. And to improve your Hebrew skills while you are away, he advised, read eight to ten chapters of the Bible a day. His endorsement of following one's desires rather than accepting conventional or current reality strengthened Rachel not just during her extended sojourn in Europe, but also when she returned to *'Eretz Yisra'el* and found she could no longer do agricultural work on account of her worsened health.[5] And his directive to immerse herself in the Bible bore fruit in her poetry, beginning with this biblically resonant poem.[6]

I realized Gordon's optimistic influence was also suffusing her last stanza, the "g," "o," "r," and "d" sounds of his last name repeating and modulating in such words as ***goral*** (fate), ***rodeh*** (tyrant), ***gil*** (joy), and ***odeh*** (I shall thank, rendered here as "thankfully"). Channeling Gordon's teaching, Rachel declares that she will not allow herself to be a victim of fate; rather, she will embrace her future—however tyrannical—with joy and gratitude. Contrary to Ecclesiastes, which preaches a seemingly complacent acceptance of what exists over letting one's spirit rove, Rachel announces that her "soul will go out walking toward joy."

I thought too of *pi ha-goral* (the mouth/pronouncement of fate) in the biblical context of division of the land. On the steppes of Moab, at the Jordan near Jericho, Moses and Elazar the priest declare that upon crossing into the Land of Israel, the land should be apportioned among the people *ʿal pi ha-goral* (according to lots), with the greater numbers of people getting a greater portion of the inheritance (Num. 26:56). In Rachel's time, the Zionist movement was calling for new settlement and apportionment. By her living apart from any kibbutz (that was doing the work of settlement) and being one of the first few modern Hebrew women poets, Rachel was a solitary "number" at a distinct disadvantage in the modern Zionist "lottery."

Nevertheless, at the end of "Soul Walking" she commits to gratitude—"I'll greet it all with joy / And thankfully"—a declaration of thanksgiving drawn from deep wells of memory.[7] After all, the word *ʾodeh* (literally, "I will give thanks") first appears in the Bible in the context of Leah's naming of Judah, the namesake of the Jews (Gen. 29:35).

The poetess Rachel's offering of thanks for life and time on earth was exactly the kind of stubbornly optimistic prayer my family and community needed at that moment, as COVID dragged on, the Omicron variant surged, testing centers sprung up in doctors' driveways and backyards, and international travel protocols changed seemingly overnight. Our daughter Shara had been awarded a yearlong fellowship in Israel, but she wasn't sure from day to day whether she'd get the all clear to join her fellowship cohort in Israel. When she was finally granted an entry permit, we greeted this development with gratitude, but also concern over what it would mean for her during COVID to travel and resettle across the ocean.

Like Rachel Bluwstein, we gave thanks for whatever good news came our way at that time, for as long as it might last. Similarly, we gave thanks for every good visit we had with Dvora, and for every time that the song-versions of Rachel's poetry allowed us to reach her, if only for the duration of a few bars or rhymes.

“Barren Woman”

Barren Woman	עֲקָרָה[8]
If only I had a son! A little boy,	בֵּן לוּ הָיָה לִי! יֶלֶד קָטָן,
Clever, with curls so dark.	שְׁחֹר תַּלְתַּלִּים וְנָבוֹן.
To hold his hand and slowly	לֶאֱחֹז בְּיָדוֹ וְלִפְסֹעַ לְאַט
Stroll in the park	בִּשְׁבִילֵי הַגָּן.
A little	יֶלֶד
Boy.	קָטָן.
Uri, I’d call him. Uri, my own!	אוּרִי אֶקְרָא לוֹ, אוּרִי שֶׁלִּי!
A short name, soft and clear.	רַךְ וְצָלוּל הוּא הַשֵּׁם הַקָּצָר.
A sliver of light	רְסִיס נְהָרָה.
For my black-haired boy	לְיַלְדִּי הַשְׁחַרְחַר
“Uri!”—	״אוּרִי!״—
I’d call!	אֶקְרָא!
Still, I’ll lament like Mother Rachel.	עוֹד אֶתְמַרְמֵר כְּרָחֵל הָאֵם.
And pray like Hannah in Shiloh.	עוֹד אֶתְפַּלֵּל כְּחַנָּה בְּשִׁילֹה.
Still I’ll await	עוֹד אֲחַכֶּה
Him.	לוֹ.

Because my *Shir Ḥadash* teaching coincided not just with my mourning period but also with my rabbinical studies and ordination, the *Shir Ḥadash* became part of my new rabbinate, especially in a mourning context. And so it was that as a rabbi and a friend, I taught “Barren Woman” at the end of the morning service on the last day of the shivah for Dr. Sandy Kammerman, mother of Bayit member and close family friend Rob Ryman. A pioneering New York scientist and physician, and also an artist, devoted mother, grandmother, sister, and aunt, Dr. Kammerman had battled cancer for several years before finally succumbing at age eighty-one. In her thirties, she was already at the pinnacle of a career in academic medicine, yet she longed for more human connection in her work—that special light that comes from personal interaction and care—and so she left her research position to help found the primary care clinic at New York's Bellevue Hospital. Around the same time, she and her husband, Sy Hyman, began building a family. When their son Rob was born they named him Moshe Feivel in Hebrew, the second name Feivel being a Yiddish version of Uri, meaning "(my) light"—the name of the hoped-for son in Rachel's poem. What a fitting poem for the last day of shivah for Sandy.

On its surface, "Barren Woman" ("'Akarah") was all about wanting something personal and small. In every stanza the line length moves from longer to ever shorter, with the final line in each stanza narrowing to a point, like the mere sliver of light the speaker says she longs for in a son. Because of this content and form, the poem had been read almost exclusively through a diminishing, biographical lens: as a small poem, by a modest female poet, who published under her first name only and wanted nothing more than a small child. Beneath the cover of all of this seeming smallness, however, lay something large and ambitious.

In the third stanza, Rachel claims a spiritual kinship with such biblical barren women as Rachel and Hannah. Notably, however, she does not call her imagined little boy Joseph or Samuel, after Rachel and Hannah's eventual sons. Her imagined son's name, instead, is Uri, recalling in secular form the name of the biblical artist of the Tabernacle, Bezalel ben Uri, whose name means "in-the-shadow-of-God son-of my-light"—albeit without the (religious) "shadow of God" part. The name Uri also evokes the prophet Isaiah's calling out to a feminized Zion to awaken and rejuvenate in the aftermath of the Exile: *'Uri 'uri livshi 'uzekh, Tziyon* ("Awake, awake, O Zion! / Clothe yourself in splendor," Isa. 52:1).

Rachel says she wants a small son with a small name, but these biblical associations lend this son, this hoped-for sliver of light, a wider national significance. The final two lines, *'od 'aḥakeh / lo* ("Still I'll await / Him") underscore this point, insofar as they allude to Maimonides's twelfth principle of faith as liturgized in the siddur—namely, the belief in the coming of the Messiah and the willingness to wait for this Messiah, even if he tarries. As such, Rachel's awaiting of a son evinces collective meaning too: the undying dedication to the cause of national redemption and rebirth.[9]

And so, I read "Barren Woman" as being about many things. On the most basic level it depicted the poet's longing for a child—but in the absence of that, for bits of poetic light that might contribute to the Zionist national revival. I saw it additionally as Rachel's female/feminist rejoinder to her male poetic predecessor Ḥayyim Naḥman Bialik's bragging insistence, in his famous 1902 poem "Lo Zakhiti va-'Or min ha-Hefker" ("I Didn't Win Light in a Windfall"), that the spark of his own poetic light derived from himself alone:[10]

I didn't gain light in a windfall,
Nor through inherited will.
I hewed it from rock and granite,
Quarrying my heart every still.
One spark hides in my heart—
A small spark—wholly my own,
Neither borrowed, nor stolen—
But from me and within me alone.

When great sorrow wields its hammer,
Exploding my heart sublime;
This one spark flies, splashes my eye,
And from my eye, drips as rhyme

And then flees my rhyme to your hearts
To vanish in your burning pyre.[11]

Bialik's claim to complete and utter originality ("A small spark—wholly my own / Neither borrowed, nor stolen— / But from me and within me alone"), seemed to hinge on a contrast between himself and the "derivative" prophet Samuel, whom his mother Hannah had so named because she asked for him and "borrowed" him from God (1 Sam. 1:20). Likewise, Bialik's use of "stolen" seemed to allude to the biblical Rachel, who had stolen the *terafim* (idols) belonging to her father (Gen. 31:34).

I was now convinced that Rachel Bluwstein had read Bialik's poem this way, too. To me, "Barren Woman" read like a streamlined, modernist, feminist rewriting of Bialik's poem. Why else would she have mentioned only two of the barren biblical foremothers, Hannah and Rachel, and excluded Sarah and Rebekah, as well as the (unnamed) mother of Samson?

I reflected too on the scene where the biblical Rachel steals the *terafim*, especially her response to her father, Laban, when he comes searching for the idols in her tent. Sitting on the camel's saddle where she has hidden the *terafim*, Rachel tells her father, "I cannot rise before you because the way of women is upon me" (Gen. 31:35).[12] Laban assumes she is menstruating, and thus stands back. But the phrase "the way of women" also implies the social condition of women then, which prevents her from laying any legal claim to the monetary, religious, or cultural inheritance symbolized by the *terafim*. Instead, she has to resort to extralegal means to claim the *terafim* for herself. She was using language to mean two things at the same time—using an expression that her father would hear one way, but that other sympathetic listeners might well hear very differently. And so, I saw the biblical Rachel as both protesting the limitations placed upon women, and also modeling the kind of nimble, multivoiced language that later poets such as Rachel Bluwstein would come to use so artfully.[13]

Likewise, I noted the biblical Hannah's role in originating a new mode of silent petition. When she prays inaudibly for a child, Eli the priest mistakes her moving lips as signifying drunkenness, but the rabbis later adopt her soundless prayer as the model of how one should recite the silent *'Amidah*.[14]

If Bialik was attempting to distinguish himself as a poet by contrasting himself with these so-called derivative biblical women, Rachel Bluwstein, like Rachel Morpurgo before her (see chapter 5), was proudly asserting a direct connection to them.

At the same time, similar to Bialik, she was ambitiously registering a desire to turn longing and loss into poetry—into her own personal light, Uri. Her description of his "black curly hair" could thus be read (at least) two ways: as the actual physical hair of a dark-curled boy (like Solomon's black curls in Songs 5:11) but also as the black curls of Hebrew cursive handwriting on a page.[15] But unlike Bialik, who claimed full credit for the poetry he conceived as light quarried and split from the rock of suffering, Bluwstein willingly assigns credit for her poetic longing and light in "Barren Woman" to two matriarchal ancestors. As such, I observed with pleasure, she demonstrated her capacity to turn the *'akarah* (barren woman) of the title to the word *'ekra'* (I shall call/read Uri), which opens and closes the second stanza—that single future-tense word connoting a commitment to call forth new works for an expanded, matriarchally conscious Jewish bookshelf.

I saw Rachel Bluwstein's combination of grateful modesty and unapologetic ambition, and her immense talent, bravery, and resolve, mirrored in Dr. Kammerman's life and career. This amazingly accomplished woman had dedicated herself to family, her smaller circle, and also, with her contributions to health care, to society at large. She knew what was vital and necessary and didn't waste time. She raised generations of medical students, cared for patients who needed her care, and nurtured her family, too—including another son, Andrew, with special needs, and two granddaughters who became ill with but thankfully recovered from cancer. When she herself was battling cancer she mustered the strength and excitement to take these same two granddaughters on an African safari. An accomplished oil painter, she created scores of beautiful paintings, including portraits of individual family members. She valued other people, prized joy and good times even amid great adversity, and demonstrated great gratitude. There wasn't a single time I saw her when she didn't make a point of thanking me for helping her granddaughters prepare for their bat mitzvah celebrations. She knew how to see the light in every idea, opportunity, experience, and interaction, and make it shine even brighter.

As Rob and his family prepared to transition to the next ritual stage of mourning, I urged them to bask in the light of Sandy's remarkable legacy, and reassured them that they had already begun to carry and shine her light forward.

From "In the Hospital"

In the Hospital	**בְּבֵית הַחוֹלִים**[16]
1	א
Here, here it is, the disease! By you, exposed	הִנֵּה הִנֵּהוּ הַדְּוָי! הִנּוֹ חָשׂוּף עַל יָדְךָ
Close enough to feel, terrible enough to smart.	קָרוֹב עַד כְּדֵי לְמַשֵּׁשׁ, נוֹרָא עַד כְּדֵי לְהַרְעִישׁ.
But why the cold glance, the indifferent heart,	וְלָמָּה קַר הַמַּבָּט, לָמָּה הַלֵּב אָדִישׁ
Why doesn't brother join you in your woes?	לָמָּה בְּצַעַר הָאָח לֹא יֵחַד צַעַרְךָ?
Brother doesn't sicken for the sick! Stranger's ache is	לֹא אָח דֹּוֶה לְדוֶֹה! רָפֶה סֵבֶל נָכְרִי
Too weak to move and unsettle his bones[17]—	מֵעַנּוֹת הַסּוֹבֵל עַד־מָה, מֵהֲנִיעֵהוּ לָנוּד—
And so, a person travels life's path alone,	כָּכָה בְּאֹרַח חַיָּיו עוֹבֵר הָאָדָם גַּלְמוּד,
And so, as death nears, he's left forsaken, forsaken—	כָּכָה בְּבוֹא יוֹמוֹ הוּא מוּטָל עֲרִירִי, עֲרִירִי—

Several of Rachel's poems dealt directly with her experience of hospitalization due to tuberculosis, one of the plagues of her day. Teaching "In the Hospital" to the *Shir Ḥadash* community, I realized, would help me both prepare for my spring 2022 course in Jewish pandemic literature and also cope with Dvora's hospitalization then with COVID. All that week, Daniel and I couldn't go to the hospital, as we ourselves were in COVID isolation, having been exposed to her right before she was taken to the hospital. And even when our test results enabled us to visit, hospital rules allowed only two visitors per patient per day. If Daniel's sister had already visited that day, that meant I couldn't get into the hospital. Protocols and bureaucracies surrounding COVID had made it impossible for full families to sit together with their ailing loved ones and rally around them in their time of need.

All this was made viscerally clear to me when I finally got my turn to visit and discovered that my mother-in-law had been assigned to Field West, Room 41, the exact same room in Allen Hospital where my mother had lived her last days in late January 2020. Before COVID, my sister and I had been allowed, quite literally, to move into that same hospital room, to sit there all day and sleep there at night, so that Mom would not be left alone as she faced her last moments. Not so now. A.C.—after Coronavirus—visits were tallied and rationed, and would-be caregivers were kept at a calculated distance.

"In the Hospital" confronts the isolation of tuberculosis head-on. Illness had closed in on Rachel. Friends and comrades had become distant and cold, afraid of becoming infected themselves. The biblical allusions in the poem only accentuate the painful nature of that abandonment. The word *devai* (disease or pain) in the first line appears in Isaiah 1:5, referring to a head and heart utterly and completely stricken with illness. The verb *le-mashesh* (to feel) in the second line implies a fear of death, as it recalls the episode of Rachel's stealing her father's *terafim*, Jacob's pronouncement to Laban that "anyone with whom you find your gods shall not remain alive!" (Gen. 31:32), and Laban's consequent feeling around (*va-yemashesh*) Rachel's tent to uncover them (Gen 31:34). The word *galmud* (alone/lonely) in line 7 appears only once in the Bible, in Job 31:33, a book all about the undeserved suffering of a good man. Finally, the word *'ariri* (translated here as "forsaken") appears twice in the Bible: first, when Abram asks God what God could possibly give him when he is *'ariri* (childless) and God promises him that he will indeed have a child (Gen. 15:1); and second, in a far less hopeful context: "Thus said GOD: Record this man as *'ariri* [without succession / childless], one who shall never be found acceptable; for none of his offspring shall be accepted to sit on the throne of David and to rule again in Judah" (Jer. 22:30). That *'ariri* appears twice at the end of "In the Hospital" said to me that Rachel was intentionally bringing forth both biblical usages of the word—and ending on the hopeless, not the hopeful, note. Her short poem, written from the insider perspective of a terminally ill patient, was offering a veritable digest of biblical depictions of lonely desperation.

Underscoring all of this were rhymes, repeated syllables, and sounds evoking the feelings of chronic pain and disappointment and pulling me viscerally into the experience of her illness. *Yadkha, tza'arkha* (your hand, your pain); *nokhri, 'ariri* (stranger, forsaken), and *lanud, galmud* (to wander, lonely)—all of these sounds at the ends of lines were echoing the *ah-ee-oo* sounds of pain. The *-ish* sounds of lines two and three, like the Hebrew word *'ish* (pronounced *eesh*, meaning "man") gave voice to the speaker's sense of having been abandoned by other, would-be caring men / human beings. Spoken aloud, the words *hineh*, *hinehu*, and *hino* (grammatical permutations of "here it is") in the first line produced inhale and exhale sounds simulating labored breath, while the onomatopoetic repetition of *lamah* (why) rang out as a plaintive *mama* call for maternal care. Finally, the sound of *kakhah* (as such), repeated at the beginning of the last two lines, struck me as a double note of resignation to fate. Reading the poem, I was listening intently to Rachel's labored breathing and her troubled heart.

Novelist and podcaster John Green writes about recurrent themes in plague chronicles over the centuries: "[T]he most gutting repetition in plague accounts is the abandonment of the ill, who were often left to die alone due to contagion. . . . In fear of death and hope of survival, may left the sick to die alone."[18] I thus saw "In the Hospital," which went out into the world in Rachel's stead, as a poignant testimony to the long-standing tradition of human failure to assuage the psychic and physical agony of other human beings who were sick.

Reading Rachel's poem together with the *Shir Ḥadash* community brought us together around the experience of human vulnerability. Reading it in the context of my mother-in-law's illness also heightened my sense of an imperative: to seize the remaining moments with her, while she still had the awareness to know we were there.

“Or Maybe”

Or Maybe	**וְאוּלַי**[19]
Or maybe none of it ever happened,	וְאוּלַי לֹא הָיוּ הַדְּבָרִים מֵעוֹלָם,
Maybe	אוּלַי
I never rose at dawn	מֵעוֹלָם לֹא הִשְׁכַּמְתִּי עִם שַׁחַר לַגָּן,
In the garden to labor and sweat?	לְעָבְדוֹ בְּזֵעַת־אַפָּי?
Did I never, on harvest days	מֵעוֹלָם, בְּיָמִים אֲרֻכִּים וְיוֹקְדִים
Scorching and long,	שֶׁל קָצִיר,
From a high, grain-filled cart	בִּמְרוֹמֵי עֲגָלָה עֲמוּסַת אֲלֻמּוֹת
Lend my voice in song?	לֹא נָתַתִּי קוֹלִי בְּשִׁיר?
Did I never cleanse in the quiet perfect	מֵעוֹלָם לֹא טָהַרְתִּי בִּתְכֵלֶת שׁוֹקְטָה
Blue	וּבְתֹם
Of my Kinneret, my Kinneret	שֶׁל כִּנֶּרֶת שֶׁלִּי . . . הוֹי, כִּנֶּרֶת שֶׁלִּי,
Were you but a dream, were you?	הֶהָיִית, אוֹ חָלַמְתִּי חֲלוֹם?

It was nearing twenty-two months since the imposition of the first COVID restrictions and since I had begun formally writing up my teachings for the *Shir Ḥadash*. Twenty-two months: a mirror of my twenty-two months of mourning, first for my father, and then for my mother, months that also included the loss of Daniel’s stepfather and the marked worsening of his mother’s dementia.

Twenty-two months into COVID and thirty-four months after my father’s sudden, tragic death, I was finding it hard to remember how things used to be. Had there ever been a time when we were parented? Had there really been a time before masks and infection statistics, when we traveled, congregated, hugged, ate and sang, without fear? Perhaps the world before was merely a phantasm, or a dream?

Rachel’s “Ve-’ulai” (“Or Maybe”) brought this sense of doubt into high relief.

In the Bible, I knew, the word *’ulai* (maybe) appears in cases of desperation or of last-ditch effort. A desperate Sarai offers her handmaid Hagar as a remedy to her own barrenness, saying “Perhaps I shall have a child through her" (Gen 16:2). Abraham attempts last-ditch negotiations with God about the fate of Sodom, conjecturing: Maybe there are forty righteous men in Sodom? Or thirty? Or twenty? Or ten? (Gen. 18:24, 28, 31, 32). The prophet Zephaniah urges the people to seek righteousness and humility, because maybe this way they will secure protection against divine wrath (Zeph. 2:3). Biblical characters who vocalize *'ulai* are on the razor's edge: between yes and no, between one state of being and its very opposite.

"Or Maybe" was thus extending the uncertainty to reality and memory. Rachel the poet was questioning: Maybe my recollections of past Zionist pioneering, of working the land at dawn, of riding a laden cart and singing with my comrades, were nothing but an illusion? Maybe, after all these years of living with a contagious and terminal disease, my memories of cleansing and purifying myself in the Kinneret (Sea of Galilee) were mere fantasy?

With the quadruply repeated word *me-'olam*, her uncertainty heightened to an almost meta level. When *me-'olam* appears along with the word *lo'*, it means "never." Rachel was reckoning with "never." Maybe I never rose at dawn, never lent a voice in song. Maybe what I remember never actually happened.

In the second stanza, though, *me-'olam* appears without *lo'*, hovering on its own for three whole lines until *lo'* finally shows up at the start of line 4. On its own, *me-'olam* connotes "from way back" or "of yore," as when the biblical narrator describes a people known as the "Nephilim" as "the heroes of old [*me-'olam*]" (Gen 6:4).

So, which *me-'olam* did she mean? Never? Once upon a time? Or both?

Rachel's closing image only underscored this subtle ambiguity. The poet-speaker asks: Did you—the femininely personified Kinneret, or my past sense of myself—ever actually exist? Were you but a dream?

I was reminded, though, that in the Zionist context dreams were the opposite of flimsy; they meant prophecy, even history. Psalm 126 describes those returning to Zion as "like dreamers"—not in the sense of being unreal, but in the sense of having experienced something so wondrous that it exceeded prior hopes and expectations.[20] Likewise,

Zionist activist, journalist, and lexicographer Eliezer Ben-Yehuda (1858–1922), who almost singlehandedly helped resurrect Hebrew as a spoken language, entitled his memoir about his life's work *Ha-Ḥalom ve-Shivro (A Dream Come True)*.[21]

Rachel's dreaming thus emerged in my reading as the opposite of nothing: an experience of the superreal or ideal. Fittingly, she closed the poem with *ḥalamti ḥalom* (I dreamed a dream), the same words young Joseph uses when telling his brothers of his dream of the sun and moon and eleven stars all bowing before him—a dream that comes to be realized much later when his brothers prostrate themselves before him in his capacity as vizier of Egypt. And, this was not her sole Joseph reference. "Or Maybe" also referred to a wagon (*'agalah*) filled with *'alumot* (sheaves)—recalling Joseph's dream of bowing sheaves of wheat (Gen. 37:7) and his dispatch of wagons to bring his father and the rest of his family down to Egypt (Gen 45:19, 21).

All this suggested to me a kind of dreaming, envisioning, and planning that meant or accomplished something, even when impeded or partially foiled. COVID, Dvora's dementia, and our other parents' deaths had wiped out so much, making us wonder whether anything really lasted. Certain "nevers," losses never to be recouped, were now indelibly stamped in our minds. Never again would Dvora carry on conversations in Hebrew, English, French, Flemish, or German, all languages she once spoke fluently. Never again would I hear Mom and Dad's voices on the phone. At least until the Messiah comes, our lost memories and our dead would never revive.

Still, we held fast to our American and Zionist dreams—our memories of and yearnings for normalcy; our hopes for our Jewish children, offshoots of what our parents had dreamed for us; our convictions about how life ought to be in Canada, America, and Israel (bastions of democracy, human rights, opportunity, religious freedom, health and prosperity). That I was struggling increasingly to remember old ways of being—before funerals, hospitals, and COVID; before masks, quarantines, and testing lines winding around the block; before political fears both in the U.S. and Israel—provided all the more reason to cling ever tighter to the brighter side of "maybe."

We would have our bright surprises, too. Every Saturday morning after shul Daniel and I would walk the two-and-a-half miles to and then from Dvora's new facility in Yonkers to bring her a taste of Shabbat. By now, all her words were gone—*lo' hayu ha-devarim me-'olam*, as if they never existed, according to the talmudic expression. Miraculously, every so often, certain Israeli songs provoked an awakening and a return. Rachel's "Ve-'ulai" ("Or Maybe"), set to music, was one such catalyst. All we had to do was sing the first word and Dvora would chime in: *Lo' hayu ha-devarim me-'olam* ("Maybe none of it ever really existed").[22] The same song that considered how mortality and illness could wipe out all of one's memories, and one's very self, was temporarily bringing Dvora back to herself. A dream and a wonder, indeed.

"Ḥoni the Circle Maker"

Ḥoni the Circle Maker	חוֹנִי הַמְעַגֵּל[23]
The painful fate of Ḥoni	עִצְּבוֹן גּוֹרָלוֹ שֶׁל חוֹנִי
Clouded my spirit today:	הֵעִיב אֶת נַפְשִׁי הַיּוֹם:
"Not a person greeted him	"פָּגַשׁ בּוֹ אָדָם בַּדֶּרֶךְ
As they passed him on his way."	וְלֹא בֵּרְכוֹ לְשָׁלוֹם".
After all, they weren't of his generation,	הֲלֹא הַדּוֹר לֹא דוֹרוֹ הוּא,
He was a stranger to them all,	הֲלֹא מוּזָר הוּא לַכֹּל,
And so beneath his bitter loneliness	וְתַחַת כֹּבֶד הַנֵּטֶל
Did hapless Ḥoni fall.	שֶׁל מְרִי בְּדִידוּתוֹ יִפֹּל.
Behold, I, too, have slept	הִנֵּה גַּם אֲנִי לָבֶטַח
Soundly behind a wall;	יָשַׁנְתִּי בְּסֵתֶר חוֹמָה;
And I, too, when passing by	אָכֵן בְּעָבְרִי בַּדֶּרֶךְ
Hear no welcome call.	בִּרְכַּת שָׁלוֹם לֹא אֶשְׁמַע.
Behold, in my dreaming, friends and	הִנֵּה בְּחָלְמִי וְזָרוּ
Comrades all have turned their back.	מַכָּר וְרֵעַ גַּם לִי.
Thus Ḥoni's gloomy shadow	צִלּוֹ הֶעָגוּם שֶׁל חוֹנִי
Spreads out upon my path.	פָּרוּשׂ עַל פְּנֵי מִשְׁעוֹלִי.

Rachel Bluwstein's "Or Maybe" sent me off on a trail for other poems about the painful nexus between illness, isolation, and dreams. And so it was that I discovered and taught "Ḥoni the Circle Maker," which demonstrated that Bluwstein drew not just from biblical but from talmudic sources, too. Reading about the aspirations and imagination of a wonder-worker and the ultimate tragedy that befell him stirred up tense connections between dreams and reality, between my current experience of the world—the seemingly never-ending pandemic and Dvora's Alzheimer's-induced altered reality—and how God's world ought really to be.

The Talmud relates that at a time of great drought, the Jews petition Ḥoni, a famous wonder-worker, to pray for rain.[24] At first, his prayers bear no fruit. But Ḥoni tries again, this time isolating himself—drawing a circle on the ground and declaring before God that he will not leave that circle until God answers his prayer. At long last God relents and assents to send rain. The story suggests that working wonders entails stubborn determination, and a measure of countercultural loneliness, too.

Seeing this spectacle, Shimon ben Shetaḥ, the head of the Sanhedrin, chides Ḥoni for his temerity, saying that were he not Ḥoni—with this unique and loving relationship with God—he would be excommunicated for making such presumptuous demands of God. Nonetheless, Ḥoni emerges from this clash with a rabbinic elder unscathed. Only as the story continues, with Ḥoni depicted not just as a wonder-worker but as a talmudic sage in his own right, does his fate take a darker turn.

In this scholarly guise, Ḥoni struggles to understand the opening simile in Psalm 126, which likens the returners to Zion to dreamers. He knows it took the Jews seventy years to return from the Babylonian exile, but dreams occur only in sleep. Is it possible that the exiled people slept for seventy years?

Thereafter, he sits down to eat and nap. As he sleeps, a rock outcropping miraculously rises around him, surrounding him on all sides, and obscuring him entirely from sight—effectively placing him in the very sort of *ḥerem* (social ban) that Shimon Shetaḥ had previously told him he deserved. Sequestered in this newly drawn, rock-formed isolation circle, Ḥoni falls asleep, only to wake up seventy years later, as if transplanted into his own exegetical question about the plausibility of a seventy-year nap.

Upon awakening from a lifetime-long sleep, Ḥoni attempts to return to his prior familial and intellectual circles, but none of his descendants recognize him or believe he is Ḥoni. At the *beit midrash* where he had once been so respected and admired, he is similarly rejected and disbelieved. Wonder-worker and scholar Ḥoni thus finds himself entirely isolated from human society—and not just for a limited time, but for all time. Unlike the dreamer Jews who happily return to Zion in Psalm 126, he, an exile in his own former home in the Land of Israel, becomes stuck, as it were, in a never-ending nightmare. He thus succumbs to despair, falling back once again on his special relationship with God and praying for death. About this the Talmud, in the name of the fourth-century Babylonian sage Rava, proclaims the adage, *'O ḥevruta' 'o mituta'*—either human fellowship or death.

What did this story about exile in Zion mean to tubercular Zionist Bluwstein? And what did it mean for all of us in late fall 2021, sick and tired as we were of intermittent COVID isolations, disrupted communities, online schooling, and circumscribed social engagements? More and more we were hearing about the plague of loneliness afflicting young and old alike, about children missing the opportunity to learn crucial social cues, about lost months and years we would never recover.[25]

In her own time of illness and isolation, Rachel Bluwstein was clearly haunted by this story of a talented, wonder-working man cast out of a social circle because of a long sleep or convalescence. As a returnee to Zion in her own right, who joined the Zionist pioneering circle not just once but twice, but whose belongingness was undone by illness, she understood Ḥoni's story as an illustration of her own experience of infirmity and exile in the Promised Land. Unlike Ḥoni, however, whose estrangement turned him inward, Rachel, in nearing death, turned outward, writing this poem as a plea for understanding. If she could no longer live inside the pioneering circle as a kibbutz worker, at least she could serve as a poetic mouthpiece for her generation: a voice calling out for compassion, with Ḥoni's very name connoting the Hebrew word *ḥen,* meaning "compassion" or "grace."

I took heart that her efforts had borne fruit. More than seventy years after Rachel wrote "Ḥoni the Circle Maker," her poem was now being read in the context of the *Shir Ḥadash,* at a politically polarized pandemic time when all of us were craving every bit of compassion, understanding, and fellowship we could possibly get.

Day of Tidings	יוֹם בְּשׂוֹרָה[26]
Now there were four leprous men at the entrance of the gate . . . and they said to each other . . . this day is a day of good tidings. (2 Kings 7:3,9)[27]	וְאַרְבָּעָה אֲנָשִׁים הָיוּ מְצֹרָעִים פֶּתַח הַשָּׁעַר . . . וַיֹּאמְרוּ אִישׁ אֶל-רֵעֵהוּ: . . . הַיּוֹם הַזֶּה יוֹם-בְּשֹׂרָה הוּא (מלכים ב׳, ז, ג-ט)
Long ago when that terrible foe	בְּשֶׁכְּבָר הַיָּמִים הָאוֹיֵב הַנּוֹרָא
Besieged Samaria City,	אֶת שֹׁמְרוֹן הֵבִיא בְּמָצוֹר;
Four lepers did good tidings bestow,	אַרְבָּעָה מְצֹרָעִים לָהּ בִּשְּׂרוּ בְּשׂוֹרָה.
Tidings of freedom and liberty.	לָהּ בִּשְּׂרוּ בְּשׂוֹרַת הַדְּרוֹר.
Like Samaria, besieged, was all the land,	כְּשֹׁמְרוֹן בְּמָצוֹר—כָּל הָאָרֶץ כֻּלָּהּ,
And the famine, too heavy to bear.	וְכָבֵד הָרָעָב מִנְּשֹׂא.
But I shall not heed redemption's command,	אַךְ אֲנִי לֹא אֹבֶה בְּשׂוֹרַת גְּאֻלָּה,
Should it come from a leper's lair.	אִם מִפִּי מְצֹרָע הִיא תָּבוֹא.
The pure shall proclaim and redeem the pure,	הַטָּהוֹר יְבַשֵּׂר וְגָאַל הַטָּהוֹר,
But if his redeeming hand can't find a way—	וְאִם יָדוֹ לֹא תִמְצָא לִגְאֹל—
Then I'll fall besieged without a cure	אָז נִבְחָר לִי לִנְפֹּל מִמְּצוּקַת הַמָּצוֹר
Before the coming of tidings' great day.	אוֹר לְיוֹם בְּשׂוֹרָה הַגָּדוֹל.

By this time, it was more than apparent that Rachel the poet was tying her own experience, and in fact her very self, to texts from the ancient biblical or talmudic past, bringing her perspectives as a terminally ill woman and a former Zionist pioneer into classical stories and vice versa.[28] In doing so, in building the present on past incidents and rebuilding the past on present experiences, she was helping to forge new kinds of imaginative community and affinity. This is the best of what writing, reading, and literary study can do: help us to recognize ourselves in these texts, too.

On this last point, the literary critic Rita Felski's depiction of what it's like to recognize oneself and one's experience in a text resonated deeply: "The experience seems at once utterly mundane yet singularly mysterious. While turning a page, I am arrested by a compelling description, a constellation of events, a conversation between characters, an interior monologue. Suddenly and without warning, a flash of connection leaps across the gap between text and reader. . . . I cannot help seeing traces of myself in the pages I am reading. I see something that I did not see before."[29]

Given all of this, I found myself puzzled, even disturbed, by Rachel's lack of self-recognition in her poem, "Day of Tidings."

The poem takes its inspiration from 2 Kings 7:3–20. The biblical story tells of four *metzora'im* (people suffering from skin scale disease) sitting outside the gates of the besieged city of Samaria who bring a *besorah tovah* (good tiding) that saves the city. Precisely because they are outliers, forced to dwell beyond the city's borders, the four *metzora'im* uncover hidden good news: the soldiers of Aram who previously laid siege to and starved the city have now deserted their camp, leaving all their provisions behind for the taking. Imagine that: The people banished from the city bring salvation and sustenance to the very people who had cast them out! Their selflessness seemed almost unimaginable to me, given the increasingly polarized and selfish nature of our current culture.

In 1926, a tubercular Rachel, confined inside the walls of one or another cramped apartment, composed her own, curious, poetic response to this biblical story, one in which she assumes the role of purity enforcer, constricting the rules of the purity regime well beyond their original Levitical context. After all, the biblical purity system imagines people moving in and out of a state of ritual impurity; one didn't need to be a *metzora'* forever. More than that: the biblical story of Naaman—a military commander who was also a *metzora'*, and eventually healed by the prophet and wonder-worker Elisha (2 Kings 5:14)—suggested that one could suffer from biblical scale disease and still function at a high level in one's culture. With all this in mind, I couldn't quite understand why Rachel was saying in the poem that she'd rather succumb to the siege than accept good tidings from a *metzora'*. Having endured being set apart due to illness, why didn't she welcome the breaking down of the walls of division? Why didn't she celebrate the idea of the afflicted bringing good tidings? Was she endorsing and reinforcing the idea of strict quarantine? Did she so hate being sick that she couldn't tolerate turning her suffering into crumbs of catharsis for someone else? Or was it because, as a Zionist, she had hoped to rehabilitate her ailing diaspora Jewish body by moving to *'Eretz Yisra'el* and working the land along with the rest of her comrades, and what the Bible considered "good tidings" from a *metzora'* somehow infected, debilitated, or undermined that vision?[30]

As I considered these questions about Bluwstein's poems, I couldn't help thinking, by way of contrast, of Hebrew Nobel laureate S. Y. Agnon's 1954 story "'Ad Olam" ("Forevermore"), which also depicts *metzora'im*.[31] A scholar named Adiel Amzeh spends his life researching the history of a lost city called Gumlidata and is on the verge of publishing his life's work, when a nurse who works in a Jerusalem leper colony happens to visit and inform him about a manuscript about Gumlidata held in the leper colony library. As a consequence of this happenstance occurrence, just like the four *metzora'im* happening upon the empty camp of Aram, Amzeh foregoes the worldly rewards of publication, consigning himself to residing in the leper colony so he can read this (infected) manuscript and pursue his scholarship.

Amzeh's devotion to the lost city of Gumlidata can be read as a commentary on Agnon's own writing in the early 1950s. At the time he wrote that story, he was busy working on *'Ir U-melo'ah* (*A City and Its Fullness*), what would become his monumental posthumously published collection of stories about the Jewish community of Buczacz, his hometown, which pogroms and the two world wars had destroyed several times over.[32] Amzeh's devotion to Gumlidata paralleled Agnon's post-Holocaust commitment to imaginatively rebuilding the world of his hometown youth, despite the early Zionists' tendency to treat European Jewish life as a kind of historical Jewish sickness.[33]

Together, Agnon's story and Rachel's poem seemed to represent two ends of a spectrum of attitudes about infection as a metaphor for collective experience. On one end, Agnon's healthy protagonist readily immerses himself in the infectiousness of the leper colony in order to receive good tidings of past knowledge. On the other end, the already infected, terminally ill Rachel Bluwstein repudiates the notion that any good news can emanate from illness. To me, her "Day of Tidings" seemed to be urging a form of self-hatred, a Zionist-purist rejection of all weakness, vulnerability, and marginality. And not just that: it seemed to repudiate the power and meaning of the poetry she herself had forged out of her own experience of illness.

Then I took a step back into my own life. Two years into the pandemic, and three plus years into this project of reading grief, prayer, and community through the lens of Hebrew poetry, did I myself envision good tidings emerging from prolonged exposure to collective and personal mourning?

In the midst of all of that, I stumbled upon a dot-matrix printer copy of the first paper I wrote in graduate school, with a quotation from Yehuda Amichai, which offered its own response: "Poetry to me is a kind of remedy. It's never a poison, it's not escapist, it's not a drug. It's more like an antidote. A horse is used to produce anti-tetanus vaccine. It goes through the tetanus and recovers and becomes immune. And from the blood of the horse the serum is made. In the same way the poet uses the matter of his life to cure himself."[34]

If poetry functions as a kind of spiritual vaccine, containing concentrated doses of disease as well as its cure, then was Rachel's "Day of Tidings" a form of vaccine denialism? Or, I wondered, was it a flaring of temper over the desperate fact that there was no shot, remedy, or ritual regime capable of curing her illness?

In this instance, I opted not for the view of a Hebrew woman poet, as I often do, but instead for Yehuda Amichai's understanding of the interconnection of disease and cure in poetry. My life was mixing and jostling with these texts, their good and bad tidings alike, and they were mixing, jostling, and listening in return. "Suddenly, without warning," to adapt Rita Felski's words, "a flash of connection" was leaping across the gap between text and me, making it and me alike into something new. With this recognition in mind, I resolved to receive the vaccine-like feeling of connection and remedy that was poetry, whatever its source or form might be.

“Sorrow Song”

Sorrow Song	זֶמֶר נוּגֶה[35]
Do you hear my voice, my faraway,	הֲתִשְׁמַע קוֹלִי, רְחוֹקִי שֶׁלִּי,
A voice calling strong, in the calm,	הֲתִשְׁמַע קוֹלִי, בַּאֲשֶׁר הִנְּךָ—
Do you hear my voice, wherever you are—	קוֹל קוֹרֵא בְּעֹז, קוֹל בּוֹכֶה בִּדְמִי
Commanding blessing, above time?	וּמֵעַל לַזְּמַן מְצַוֶּה בְּרָכָה?
The world is wide with many trails,	תֵּבֵל זוֹ רַבָּה וּדְרָכִים בָּהּ רָב.
They meet for a moment, part forevermore.	נִפְגָּשׁוֹת לְרֶגַע, נִפְרָדוֹת לָעַד.
A person seeks, but his feet often fail,	מְבַקֵּשׁ אָדָם, אַךְ כּוֹשְׁלוֹת רַגְלָיו,
Never finding what he had before.	לֹא יוּכַל לִמְצֹא אֶת אֲשֶׁר אָבַד.
Maybe my last day is already close,	אַחֲרוֹן יָמַי כְּבָר קָרוֹב אוּלַי,
Already close, the day of parting tears,	כְּבָר קָרוֹב הַיּוֹם שֶׁל דִּמְעוֹת פְּרִידָה,
I shall wait for you until my life goes	אֲחַכֶּה לְךָ עַד יִכְבּוּ חַיַּי,
Out, as Rachel awaited her Dear.	כְּחַכּוֹת רָחֵל לְדוֹדָהּ.

One morning on my way to shul, I passed by this mess on the ground. A clear blue recycling bag had opened up, its contents strewn all over the sidewalk. On top of the scattered pile of magazines, newspapers, and castaway papers, in a plastic looseleaf sleeve, was a printout from the Bayit, my own congregation, with the rabbinic words of comfort for a mourner: *Ha-makom yenaḥem etkhem be-tokh she'ar 'aveilei Tziyon vi'Yerushalayim* (May God comfort you among the mourners of Zion and Jerusalem). Whoever threw out this pile of paper recycling had thrown out the formula for divine consolation, too.

A few hours later, as I entered an elevator at HUC-JIR to teach my first class of the day, I received word of the sudden death of a twenty-four-year-old cousin.

It was in light of this happenstance discovery of a tossed-out, plastic-protected call out to God for consolation, and the subsequent crushing news of my cousin's death, that I taught “Sorrow Song.”[36]

Typically this poem has been read as portraying unrequited love. A woman pledges to wait for her lover until the day she dies. And then

FIG. 11. *Ha-Makom Yenaḥem* consolation card by the recycling bin. Photo by Wendy Zierler.

she dies. Before her death, she vacillates between her desire to speak to and be heard by her unnamed faraway lover and her recognition of the futility of these efforts.[37] This vacillation expresses itself in the first stanza's pattern of statement and counterstatement, the second half of each line countering the first. Her question, "Will you hear my voice," is undercut by the epithet, "my faraway one." The strong, repeated "Will you hear my voice" is muffled by the silent weeping in "wherever you are." If this is love, it is tenuous—and still she persists. She resolves to wait ("I shall wait for you until my life goes / Out, as Rachel awaited her Dear")—possibly an allusion to the biblical Rachel awaiting either her beloved Jacob or her yet unborn child. Tragically, of course, this Rachel ends up dying in childbirth with her second son, and is buried on the side of the road.

Still, I thought, there was a theological way to read the poem, too: as a depiction of the effort through the Jewish centuries, at times of illness or bereavement, to be heard and answered by God/*Ha-makom* (the Place). Our traditional mourning formula insists that consolation will come from the omnipresent Place that is Divine, perhaps because in these times of loss, that sense of connection to that Divine Place, and of being heard, feels especially uncertain, even illusory.

"Sorrow Song," I noted, begins with the interrogative ***hatishma'*** ("Do/will Y/you hear?"). That the letter *hei* was affixed to the beginning of the word turned the statement into a question. When praying the *'Amidah*, Jews petition God, *shema' koleinu* (hear our voices), but does this hearing actually transpire? In the poem, the woman speaks of this Place indeterminately, "wherever You are"—apparently questioning of its location and reliability as a space of comfort.

And then it dawned on me: What if I had it backward? What if the poem was enacting a dialogue between God and humanity in which *God* calls out to each one of us, wherever we are: Do you hear My voice? Do you hear My voice, **commanding blessing**? The language certainly supported this reading, given the traditional liturgical formula that repeatedly **blesses** God for sanctifying us with **commandments** (***Barukh*** *atah . . . asher kideshanu be-mitzvotav ve-tzivanu*, "**Blessed** are You . . . who sanctifies us with God's **blessings** and commands us . . .")

And what if the second two stanzas were read as a human reply from the big wide world ("The world is wide with many trails"), that sphere of fleeting ambitions and relationships ("They meet for a moment, part forevermore") and of yearning for steadiness ("A man seeks, but his feet often fail, / Never finding what he had before") in the form of eternal comfort of God?

As for the final stanza, when the woman realizes she may be at the end of her life ("Maybe my last day is already close"), her declaration, "I shall wait for you until my life goes / Out," could also be read (akin to the ending of "Barren Woman"), as alluding to Maimonides's twelfth principle of faith, which declares faith in the coming of the Messiah: *'Aḥakeh lo*, "I shall wait for him." Human beings fail; our days on earth are necessarily numbered. As long as we live, God calls out to us, we call back to God, not always in harmonious and satisfying ways. But hopefully, we keep on yearning and trying.

And so it was that the first two years of the written *Shir Ḥadash*, a discipline of translating, writing, and teaching Hebrew poetry—which began as a creative personal response to the death first of Dad, and then of Mom, and then the onset of COVID—were coming to a close. It felt fitting to cap it all this way, with a poem that hearkened back to the very beginning, offering a teaching in direct response to the death of yet another loved one, a raw calling out in a time of doubt. The problem and pain of loss remained acute; God remained difficult to locate. But the quest had certainly become less lonely, as for two years, I had enlisted creative voices from the past and present to do some of the questing with me. I had become accustomed to the comforting company of these modern Hebrew poets, to the routine of cracking open their lines, and channeling my own theological, emotional, and prayerful questions through their words. And it brought great solace to share all of it with the members of the *Shir Ḥadash* in-person and virtual community, to take the weekly risk of this kind of praying and teaching with the knowledge that there were other people there, willing and ready to listen.

"Sorrow Song," in particular, took on the quality of a culminating, personal prayer. Every so often on a Tuesday morning, after I taught the *Shir Hadash* or sent it out by email after returning from shul, I would stop and think about Dad and Mom, and wonder if they could hear what I was saying in their memory. *Ha-tishme'u koli?* "Do you hear my voice," wherever you are—commanding blessing, above time? Do you see, Mom and Dad, what I have been trying to say and do since losing you? Do you feel how I keep trying to conjure up a living, blessed connection to you that reaches beyond time and loss?

I suppose, like Rachel Bluwstein, I'll continue to wait and yearn for their answer—reading, translating, writing, and praying, meanwhile—until my own "life goes out."

Final Thoughts

Still in Knots

Sunday October 8, 2023, was Simḥat Torah, the day when Jews customarily celebrate the conclusion of the Torah reading cycle. Daniel and I awoke early that Sunday morning to begin our regular Shabbat and Jewish holiday morning routine, knowing full well that nothing was going to be regular or the way it ought to be.

By the time we arrived at shul that Simḥat Torah morning, we had already heard the terrible news about Hamas's brutal attack against Israel on the previous day, Shabbat. We don't normally watch the news or use our phones on Shabbat and holidays, but the news had reached our community right away, given our many ties to people living in Israel. I myself learned the news on Saturday soon after arriving at shul on Shabbat Shemini Atzeret, from a close friend at shul, whose daughter lived in Tel Aviv and had called her that morning in a panic. As soon as we got home from shul that Shabbat, we checked our phones and picked up a message from our daughter Shara, who had just arrived in Israel the week before to begin a social justice fellowship immediately after Sukkot. Before long, Shara would learn that her fellowship was being indefinitely postponed. None of us had expected that our jubilant end-of-Sukkot celebrations would be imprinted with such horror, fear, and uncertainty.

As fate would have it, the Bayit member preselected for the honor of *Ḥatan Torah* (the concluding *'aliyah* of the annual reading cycle) at our early morning Simḥat Torah service that Sunday was Jacob (Jack) Lew, formerly Treasury Secretary of the United States under President Barack Obama, who just a month earlier had been nominated to be the new U.S. ambassador to Israel. The leaders of the early minyan had chosen to honor Jack, a regular early morning attendee, as a way of congratulating him on this new appointment and sending him off to Israel with Bayit joy and pride. I, myself, had felt a special excitement about honoring Jack. Back in 2019, he had been a mourner like me, reciting Kaddish for his sister, while I was saying Kaddish for my father and preparing to move my mother to Riverdale. And he'd provided what felt like invaluable guidance at the time. First, he directed me to Elisabeth Benjamin and Matt Flynn of CSSNY (Community Service Society of New York), a social service agency that helped me get my mother health insurance. He later helped me work out preparations for getting Mom onto Medicare. Mom would die a mere five months after moving to New York; we would never be able to follow up on all of those plans, but it had been so appreciated, nonetheless. Now, Jack would be moving to an Israel at war, a country reeling from the worst slaughter of Jews since the Holocaust, with hundreds of civilians being cruelly held hostage in Gaza, too.

The Simḥat Torah service that Sunday morning proved to be very different from any other we'd ever experienced. Somehow, we completed the necessary *hakafot* and danced with the Torah, but our ritual circling of the synagogue felt more like a compulsive response to pain, or a marking of protective territory, than an act of celebration. When Jack was called up to the Torah for his *'aliyah*, a thick hush fell over the room, each of us imagining the burden he'd be carrying once he assumed his ambassadorial tasks as an American official, a Zionist, and an observant Jew. When our rabbi, Steven Exler, delivered his remarks to honor Jack, his voice cracked and there were tears in his eyes. In singing *siman tov umazal tov* (a good sign, a good fortune) to Jack, we were all grasping for some heavenly sign of good in the offing, for some promise of future good fortune. Who better to represent us American Jews as U.S. ambassador at this critical time than he, a man of such vast experience and integrity? But, how excruciatingly difficult was the task he was needing to undertake!

It was a somber scene—and yet, our ability to make it through the service, to sing, dance, and honor a beloved and esteemed community member at this calamitous time attested to the tremendous spiritual and creative resources of our community and the Jewish people as a whole.

And then came our regular, post-synagogue visit to see my mother-in-law, Dvora. Ever since moving her to a senior facility in Yonkers, it had become our family practice to attend the early 7:00 a.m. minyan at the Bayit, so that we could pay her a visit later in the morning. Returning home after services to make Shabbat or holiday *Kiddush* at home, we would then eat breakfast, pack up the Israeli songbooks, walk the two and a half miles to her facility to sing with her, and then walk the two and a half miles back home in time for lunch. For a time we also brought along a small bottle of wine and cookies, for a second *Kiddush* and nosh, but these days Dvora was no longer drinking wine or eating cookies, or even making much eye contact with any of us. And yet, when we sang to her, she often hummed or mouthed along, at least for a song or two. From visit to visit, we couldn't be sure anymore exactly what we would find. This weekend that sense of uncertainty felt especially thick and tense.

Our walk up to Dvora's residence later that morning was punctuated by many silences, and our singing, once we got there, by many sighs. Songs we often sang, such Natan Yonatan's 1948 War "Shayarah Shelanu" (Our Convoy) and Natan Alterman's "Shir Ha'emek" (Valley Song), with their references to sudden tragic death at the hand of the enemy, took on heightened painful meaning, especially, as Dvora hummed along. Our only solace during that visit was that she herself would never know about the attack. A Holocaust survivor and fervent Zionist, who until her illness had spent several months a year in Israel, she would have been devastated to learn of all those killed and taken hostage, and so worried about the full-on war, yet to come. And yet her inability to know and understand was its own form of heartbreak.

The Israeli poet I returned to in that pivotal post–October 7 moment was the Ukrainian-born Hebrew poet Amir Gilboa (1917–1984). Born Berl Feldman in Radziwillow (now Radyvýliv), Ukraine, he left his family behind in 1937 to immigrate to *'Eretz Yisra'el,* fought with the British Brigade in World War II while most of his family back in Ukraine was killed in the Holocaust, and then again with the Haganah in Israel's

1948 War of Independence. His first book of poems was published but a year later.

I had first delved into Gilboa's poetry in the aftermath of Russia's invasion of Ukraine on February 24, 2022. At the time, millions of refugees, among them many Jews, were streaming across the border into Poland and Hungary. A Jewish Ukrainian president and his people were making a heroic, existential stand. At that time, the entire Western world seemed tied to the fate of this beleaguered European country—a former site of grisly antisemitic persecutions and murders, but of so much Jewish culture, too. Gilboa's poetry, which often confronted this tortured past with a mix of heartbreak and survivor's resilience, seemed to fit that historic moment perfectly.

Now, once again, I was turning to Gilboa, as a figure who bridged the two worlds and wars of Ukraine and Israel. Gilboa's poetry had grown both out of the suffering of war, and the miraculous creation of the State of Israel. Somehow Gilboa had managed to turn the raw material of sorrow into spiritually strengthening song. His poem "Behold I'll Craft a Ball from the Pain," in fact, provided a kind of blueprint for precisely that sort of creative alchemy.

“Behold I’ll Craft a Ball from the Pain”

Behold I’ll Craft a Ball from the Pain	הִנֵּה אֶעֱשֶׂה כַּדּוּר מִן הַצַּעַר[1]
Behold I’ll craft a ball from the pain.	הִנֵּה אֶעֱשֶׂה כַּדּוּר מִן הַצַּעַר
Several colors will play with it in the sun	כַּמָּה צְבָעִים יְשַׂחֲקוּ בּוֹ מוּל שֶׁמֶשׁ
Several colors will cry with it when cloudy	כַּמָּה צְבָעִים בּוֹ יִבְכּוּ עִם עָנָן
With final strength I’ll throw it onward	בְּכוֹחַ אַחֲרוֹן אֲטִילֶנּוּ
From the gloom of the forest	מֵאֹפֶל שֶׁל יַעַר
From a sleepy pool.	מִבְּרֵכָה רוֹדֶמֶת
With final strength I’ll throw it onward	בְּכוֹחַ אַחֲרוֹן עוֹד אֲטִילֶנּוּ
Awake and dreaming	עֵר וְחוֹלֵם
Stormy	סוֹעֵר
And tranquil	וְשַׁאֲנָן
And the ball interlaced	וְהַכַּדּוּר שָׁזוּר
With each and every pain	כָּל צַעַר וְצַעַר
Will force open	בְּכוֹחַ יִפְתַּח
Gate	שַׁעַר
After	אַחַר
Gate.	שַׁעַר
And every onlooker	וְכָל רוֹאָיו
One to the other	זֶה אֶל זֶה
Will say	יֹאמְרוּ
Surely this is the handiwork	וַדַּאי מַעֲשֵׂה יָדָיו
Of a youth.	שֶׁל נַעַר.

After October 7, I read “Behold I’ll Craft a Ball from the Pain” as Gilboa’s effort to write metaphorically about the origins and goals of poetry, especially in the aftermath of tragedy.[2] I read it this way not just because I am a literature professor who likes to think that all literature is about literature, but because the poem explicitly alludes to—and challenges the premise of—one of the most famous Hebrew poetic reflections on the source and inspiration of poetry: Ḥayyim Naḥman Bialik’s long poem, “Ha-bereikhah” (“The Pool”), which begins:

I know of a forest, and in the forest
I know of a single, humble pool:
In the thick grove, set apart from the world,
In the shadow of a tall oak, light-blessed, storm-tossed,
Dreaming alone an upside-down dream
She raises her goldfish in secret—
And no one knows what's in her heart.[3]

In his poem, Bialik—also born and raised in the land now considered Ukraine—describes a secluded pool in the heart of a forest where the speaker spent time in as a child, and which provided him with ongoing poetic inspiration. Night and day, storm and calm, each acted upon and influenced the natural goings-on in the forest; while the feminized pool, hidden away in a grove, reflected all of it—a metaphor for the operations of the poetic eye.

The connection between Bialik and Gilboa's poems seemed obvious. Like Bialik, Gilboa speaks of a "pool" (*bereikhah*) and "forest" (*ya'ar*), as well as of the sun (*shemesh*) and storm (*so'er*). An even further thematic tie comes into view via the common roundness of a *kadur* (ball) and Bialik's pool.

But, whereas Bialik's pool existed even before the poet happened upon it, and was hidden away from sight in the recesses of the forest, Gilboa's *kadur* needed to be created and thrown into public view, in order for all to see and share in it ("Behold I'll craft a ball from the pain . . . With final strength I'll throw it onward / From the gloom of the forest"). To be activated, it required a plurality of states, emotions, and parties ("Awake and dreaming / Stormy / And tranquil / And the ball interlaced / With each and every pain . . . and every onlooker"). It was an object of tears ("Several colors will cry with it when cloudy") but also of play ("Several colors will play with it in the sun."). Thrown with all the speaker's strength, it could be a weapon (as *kadur* can also mean "bullet"), with the capacity to "force open Gate / After / Gate," and also a remedy (as *kadur* can also mean "pill"), hence the references in the title and opening line to the transformation, and by implication, alleviation of pain.

As I interpreted it, Gilboa's poem envisioned a radically participatory poetic project, initiated by the poet, but which was affected and amplified by the suffering and joy of many. The poet launches his poetic ball/bullet/remedy, but depends on others to catch and connect to it. Only then—if other people care to see, listen, and carry it forward—can poetry have impact. Only then can *tza'ar* (pain) metamorphose into a *sha'ar* (gate) of human sympathy. Insofar as *sha'ar* also means the frontispiece of a book, Gilboa's imagined opening of gate after gate points to the potential for literature in general, and poetry in particular, to cultivate a community of concern and shared understanding.

Of course, there is something extremely naive to the idea of fighting or curing pain with poetry. Which is why, in my view, the poem ends as it does: the poet predicting how his project will be understood by future generations as the work not of a *mevugar*, an adult, but rather, a *na'ar*, a youth.

Call me naive, too, but for several years now (since the fall of 2019), I had hitched my heart to the very same idea. I had translated and taught poems as a way to find and offer solace in the wake of personal and communal pain. I had insisted that poetry can heal, divert and entertain, mobilize and galvanize. In its own way, the *Shir Ḥadash shel Yom* had been my *kadur min ha-tza'ar*, a personal and communal ball, bullet, and pill, fashioned out of the pain of loss.

And so, I continue. If you're in Riverdale, New York early on a Tuesday morning, feel free to stop by. At around 7:15 a.m., I'll step up to the podium in the *beit midrash* of the Bayit. "It's Tuesday," I'll say, "and this week's *Shir Ḥadash* is . . . ." I'll read a Hebrew poem in the original and in my English translation; I'll offer some thoughts on its meaning in relation to prayer, the Torah reading, or some other matter of the day; and I'll conclude by reciting the traditional *mishnah* recited upon the conclusion of text study: "Rabbi Ḥananyah ben Akashyah says: The Holy Blessed One sought to confer merit upon the Jewish people; therefore, God increased for them Torah and mitzvot, as it is stated: 'It pleased the Eternal for the sake of His righteousness to make the Torah great and glorious.'"[4] The mourners will recite the last Rabbis' Kaddish of the service, and we'll all say amen. Hopefully, by the time we're done, you'll have a new nugget to toss up, turn around in your head, until the next week, when, if you'd like, we can do it all over again.

SOURCE ACKNOWLEDGMENTS

2.1 “To Mother’s Portrait” by Lea Goldberg

לאה גולדברג, ״לתמונת אמא״, ׳שירים׳, ספרית פועלים, 1973, כרך א׳, עמ׳ 32.

2.2 “By Three Things” by Lea Goldberg

לאה גולדברג, ״על שלשה דברים״, ׳מה עושות האיילות?׳ ספרית פועלים, 1949.

2.3 “In My Prayer Book” by Lea Goldberg

לאה גולדברג, ״בסידור שלי״, ׳שירים׳, ספרית פועלים, 1973, כרך א׳, עמ׳ 192.

2.4 “Let Winter Be Blessed” by Lea Goldberg

לאה גולדברג, ״יהי החורף מבורך!״, ׳שירים׳, ספרית פועלים, 1973, כרך ג׳, עמ׳ 101.

2.5 “Blessing” by Lea Goldberg

לאה גולדברג, ״ברכה״, ׳שירים׳, ספרית פועלים, 1973, כרך ג׳, עמ׳ 179.

2.6 From “One Spring” by Lea Goldberg

לאה גולדברג, ״אביב אחד״, שיר ה׳, ׳שירים׳, ספרית פועלים, 1973, כרך ג׳, עמ׳ 154–55.

2.7 From “My Silences” by Lea Goldberg

לאה גולדברג, ״דממות שלי״, שיר ב׳, ׳שירים׳, ספרית פועלים, 1973, כרך א׳, עמ׳ 137.

2.8 "Night Psalm" by Lea Goldberg

לאה גולדברג, "מזמור לילה", 'שירים', ספרית פועלים, 1973, כרך ב', עמ' 196.
All rights reserved by Ha-Kibbutz Ha-Me'uḥad Publishers Ltd.

2.9 "He Passed Over Our Door and There Was Light" by Lea Goldberg

לאה גולדברג, "על דלתינו פסח ויהי אור", 'שירים', ספרית פועלים, 1973, כרך ב', עמ' 226.
All rights reserved by Ha-Kibbutz Ha-Me'uḥad Ltd.

2.10 From "Ending" by Lea Goldberg

לאה גולדברג, "סיום", שיר א', 'שירים', ספרית פועלים, 1973, כרך א', עמ' 244.
All rights reserved by Ha-Kibbutz Ha-Me'uḥad Ltd.

3.1 "Dream of Your Footsteps" by Avraham Ḥalfi

אברהם חלפי, "חלום עקבותיך", 'שירים', הוצאת הקבוץ המאוחד, 1986, כרך א', עמ' 118–19.
All rights reserved by Ha-Kibbutz Ha-Me'uḥad Publishers Ltd. © Avraham Ḥalfi and ACUM.

3.2 "I Know Not the Words" by Avraham Ḥalfi

אברהם חלפי, "אינני יודע מילים", 'שירים', הוצאת הקבוץ המאוחד, 1986, כרך א', עמ' 253.
All rights reserved by Ha-Kibbutz Ha-Me'uḥad Publishers Ltd. © Avraham Ḥalfi and ACUM.

3.3 "Crowned Is Your Forehead with Black Gold" by Avraham Ḥalfi

אברהם חלפי, "עטור מצחך זהב שחור", 'שירים', הוצאת הקבוץ המאוחד, 1986, כרך א', עמ' 286.
All rights reserved by Ha-Kibbutz Ha-Me'uḥad Publishers Ltd. © Avraham Ḥalfi and ACUM.

3.4 "Here a Person Believed" by Avraham Ḥalfi

אברהם חלפי, "אדם האמין פה ללחש הערב", 'שירים', הוצאת הקבוץ המאוחד, 1986, כרך א', עמ' 46.
All rights reserved by Ha-Kibbutz Ha-Me'uḥad Publishers Ltd. © Avraham Ḥalfi and ACUM.

3.5 "And Songs Are the Dust of Antiquities" by Avraham Ḥalfi

אברהם חלפי, "והשירים הם אבק עתיקות", 'שירים', הוצאת הקבוץ המאוחד, 1986, כרך א', עמ' 202.
All rights reserved by Ha-Kibbutz Ha-Me'uḥad Publishers Ltd. © Avraham Ḥalfi and ACUM.

3.6 From "Heretic's Prayers" by Avraham Ḥalfi

אברהם חלפי, "תפילות כופר", 'שירים', הוצאת הקבוץ המאוחד, 1986, כרך ב', עמ' 52–53.

All rights reserved by Ha-Kibbutz Ha-Me'uḥad Publishers Ltd. © Avraham Ḥalfi and ACUM.

3.7 "At Night Birds Fell" by Avraham Ḥalfi

אברהם חלפי, "בלילה נפלו ציפורים מן הקן", 'שירים', הוצאת הקבוץ המאוחד, 1986, כרך א', עמ' 177.

All rights reserved by Ha-Kibbutz Ha-Me'uḥad Publishers Ltd. © Avraham Ḥalfi and ACUM.

3.8 "Jewish Fall" by Avraham Ḥalfi

אברהם חלפי, "סתיו יהודי", 'שירים', הוצאת הקבוץ המאוחד, 1986, כרך ב', עמ' 202.

All rights reserved by Ha-Kibbutz Ha-Me'uḥad Publishers Ltd. © Avraham Ḥalfi and ACUM.

4.1 "And That Is Your Glory" by Yehuda Amichai

יהודה עמיחי, "והיא תהילתך", 'במרחק שתי תקוות', הוצאת הקיבוץ המאוחד, 1958, עמ' 17–18.

All rights reserved by Ha-Kibbutz Ha-Me'uḥad Publishers Ltd. English Language and Digital Usage with permission of the Estate of Yehuda Amichai through the Deborah Harris Agency.

4.2 "In the Morning I Shall Stand by Your Bed" by Yehuda Amichai

© Schocken Publishing House Ltd., Tel Aviv, Israel. English Language and Digital Usage with permission of the Estate of Yehuda Amichai through the Deborah Harris Agency.

4.3 "Half the People in the World" by Yehuda Amichai

יהודה עמיחי, "מחצית האנשים בעולם", 'במרחק שתי תקוות', הוצאת הקיבוץ המאוחד, 1958, עמ' 35–36.

All rights reserved by Ha-Kibbutz Ha-Me'uḥad Publishers Ltd. English Language and Digital Usage with permission of the Estate of Yehuda Amichai through the Deborah Harris Agency.

4.4 "God's Hand in the World" by Yehuda Amichai

יהודה עמיחי, "יד אלהים בעולם", 'במרחק שתי תקוות', הוצאת הקיבוץ המאוחד, 1958, עמ' 11–12.

All rights reserved by Ha-Kibbutz Ha-Me'uḥad Publishers Ltd. English Language and Digital Usage with permission of the Estate of Yehuda Amichai through the Deborah Harris Agency.

4.5 "A Sort of End of Days" by Yehuda Amichai

יהודה עמיחי, "מעין אחרית הימים", 'במרחק שתי תקוות', הוצאת הקיבוץ המאוחד, 1958, עמ' 16.
All rights reserved by Ha-Kibbutz Ha-Me'uḥad Publishers Ltd. English Language and Digital Usage with permission of the Estate of Yehuda Amichai through the Deborah Harris Agency.

4.6 "My Mother Baked Me the Whole World" by Yehuda Amichai

© Schocken Publishing House Ltd., Tel Aviv, Israel. English Language and Digital Usage with permission of the Estate of Yehuda Amichai through the Deborah Harris Agency.

4.7 "Whoever Wrapped in a Tallit" by Yehuda Amichai

© Schocken Publishing House Ltd., Tel Aviv, Israel. English Language Usage with permission of the Estate of Yehuda Amichai through the Deborah Harris Agency.

4.8 "Men, Women, and Children" by Yehuda Amichai

© Schocken Publishing House Ltd., Tel Aviv, Israel. English Language and Digital Usage with permission of the Estate of Yehuda Amichai through the Deborah Harris Agency.

4.9 "God Has Mercy on Kindergarten Children" by Yehuda Amichai

© Schocken Publishing House Ltd., Tel Aviv, Israel. English Language and Digital Usage with permission of the Estate of Yehuda Amichai through the Deborah Harris Agency.

4.10 "I Filtered from the Book of Esther" by Yehuda Amichai

© Schocken Publishing House Ltd., Tel Aviv, Israel. English Language and Digital Usage with permission of the Estate of Yehuda Amichai through the Deborah Harris Agency.

4.11 "My Father on Passover Eve" by Yehuda Amichai

© Schocken Publishing House Ltd., Tel Aviv, Israel. English Language and Digital Usage with permission of the Estate of Yehuda Amichai through the Deborah Harris Agency.

6.1 “I Throw Down My Supplication” by Ruhama Weiss

רוחמה ווייס, ״אני מפילה תחינתי״, ׳אחטא ואשוב׳, הוצאת הקיבוץ המאוחד, 2013, עמ׳ 18.

All rights reserved by Ha-Kibbutz Ha-Me'uḥad Publishers Ltd.

6.2 “Lament for Rashi’s Daughters” by Ruhama Weiss

רוחמה ווייס, ״קינה לבנות רש״י״, ׳שמירה׳, הוצאת הקיבוץ המאוחד, 2004, עמ׳ 9.

All rights reserved by Ha-Kibbutz Ha-Me'uḥad Publishers Ltd.

6.3 “I Am Still Praying” by Ruhama Weiss

רוחמה ווייס, ״אני עוד מתפללת״, ׳אחטא ואשוב׳, הוצאת הקיבוץ המאוחד, 2013, עמ׳ 92.

All rights reserved by Ha-Kibbutz Ha-Me'uḥad Publishers Ltd.

6.4 “And Once Again, I’ll Sin and Return” by Ruhama Weiss

רוחמה ווייס, ״ושוב אחטא ואשוב״, ׳אחטא ואשוב׳, הוצאת הקיבוץ המאוחד, 2013, עמ׳ 53.

All rights reserved by Ha-Kibbutz Ha-Me'uḥad Publishers Ltd.

6.5 “Chapters of the Mothers” by Ruhama Weiss

רוחמה ווייס, ״פרקי אמהות״, ׳אחטא ואשוב׳, הוצאת הקיבוץ המאוחד, 2013, עמ׳ 8–9

All rights reserved by Ha-Kibbutz Ha-Me'uḥad Publishers Ltd.

Final Thoughts: “Behold I’ll Craft a Ball from the Pain” by Amir Gilboa

© Amir Gilboa and ACUM.

APPENDIX *Four Poems by the Author*

"Every poet learns to write by imitation, just as every painter learns to paint by looking at paintings," writes poet Ted Kooser. *"We teach ourselves to write the kinds of poem we like to read."*[1] Over the course of my mourning period, I wrote the following four poems (among others), bearing in mind the textual engagement, tone, play, complaint, and yearning that I admired in the poets chosen for the *Shir Ḥadash.*

"Mourning with Psalm 100"

This first poem is based on the celebratory *Mizmor le-Todah* (A Psalm of Thanks) recited on weekdays in memory of the thanksgiving offering given in Temple times. I wrote it early on in my mourning period, at a time when the biblical/liturgical call to "worship GOD in gladness" seemed like a cruel joke against mourners like me.

MOURNING WITH PSALM 100

There's too much party
In this psalm.

Too much loud whooping
By the whole wide world.
Too much worship joy
And court crowding,
When all around, daily,
Like air, is death.

Such particulates
Cannot but be breathed in,
Come mourning time.

Shout in pain to God,
All the earth, in all our
Shuttered gates
And distanced hearts.

"In Pain"

Also written early on, "In Pain" responds to Psalm 148 ("Hallelujah, Praise GOD from the heavens; give praise on high"), a sublime call to the sun, moon, sea monsters, snow, smoke, trees, animals, old and young, to praise God. This poem enlists or calls for the recognition of forces and sensations far less sublime.

IN PAIN

Halleluyah from my aching hip
Halleluyah from my numb right foot
With fear of bending down
And struggle to stand up:
All those who wince,
Praise You, alone.

Bit by bit uncoiling.
Upright.
Restored.
In praise.

"This Is Where We Take Out the Second Torah, or Reading in Place"

Written on *Ḥol Ha-mo'ed* (the intermediate days) of Passover 2020, when our Bayit's 6:45 a.m. minyan was still meeting by Zoom, this poem speaks to the sense of spiritual insufficiency I felt during the COVID lockdown. Those of us saying Kaddish had come to depend on the spiritual support of in-person prayer, and the institution of Zoom services, lacking many of the regular, tactile elements of the service, felt nowhere near equivalent. More broadly, the poem expresses frustration with words and rituals substituting for one another or for other, larger, religious goals.

THIS IS WHERE WE TAKE OUT THE SECOND TORAH, OR READING IN PLACE

Today, in this second month of COVID non-congregation,
On an intermediate Passover day,
At our morning screen synagogue,
Our regular Torah reader "returned"
After many absent weeks
And chanted the portion
from a prayer book,
The old family recipe
Of something delicious,
Familiar and lost,
Baking behind the glass
Of my computer screen.

Pausing before what would have been
The fourth *'aliyah*, he said:
"This is where we would have taken out
The Second Torah"—
Words instead of lifting,
Opening, and rolling,
And opening again.

And then more chanting
From a book
Instead of a scroll
Instead of a sacrifice
Instead of you or me.

How many substitutions will
We make
Before we arrive
At the Real
Thing.

Or, is *this* the
Real
Thing:

Forever putting
Something
In place
Of what we need
To say
To hope
To do

Until that day
Finally comes
When what we say
Is what we mean
Is what we know
Is Eternal and
True.

On that day
Will God be One
And God's name
Be One?

"Mourning Strap-Hanger: On Wearing Dad's Tefillin"

This final poem responded both to the strange newness of loss and to the COVID lockdown—a kind of double bereavement. I was endeavoring to link two kinds of straps, one having recently appeared (my then-new commitment to wearing my father's tefillin every morning) and the other having recently disappeared (my morning subway commute—a "straphanger" being the colloquial term for a New York transit rider, who hung onto once-leather straps for balance on a moving train). I was trying my best in my mo(u)rning routine to "hang on" creatively to whatever words or structures I could.

MOURNING STRAP-HANGER: ON WEARING DAD'S TEFILLIN

Every time I take those odd
Strapped boxes into my hands
I add life-lines to the
Palms of the leather.
It takes my all to get them on,

And even more to put them away.
The straps slip and
Bunch up at my wrists,
Are altogether unnatural
On this orphan daughter's arm,
A perfect fit for these unreal days
Of grief
And now, plague.
Bereft of subways, stories,
Caring, crowdedness,
Jokes, routine,
And parental reassurance—
I hang on to the straps
Of early morning
Connection,
Betrothed to loss and love,[2]
Hand, head, and heart.

NOTES

Introduction

1. Etgar Keret's story "Kavanah" ("Intention") appears in Keret, *Autocorrect*, 155–59. The remarks are summarized from "Creativity in a Time of Crisis: An Evening with Israeli Writer and Filmmaker Etgar Keret, In Conversation with Rabbi Wendy Zierler, Ph.D.," part of an HUC-in-the-Berkshires event on July 25, 2024.
2. See the Merriam Webster entry for the word "heal," accessible at https://www.m-w.com.
3. Ostriker, "Poetry and Healing," 9.
4. See, e.g., Zierler, "Anthological Poetics," 59–80. For a broader scholarly look of modern Hebrew poetry that addresses God and prayer see Jacobson, *Creator, Are You Listening?*
5. See, for example, Lawrence Hoffman's eight-volume *Prayers of Awe* series.
6. The *Shirah 'Emunit* (Poetry of Faith / Religious Poetry) movement in contemporary Israeli poetry has also been a significant cultural force. As Shachar Pinsker writes, this increased interest in Israel in religious poetry "is attested by two new major literary journals: *Dimui: A Magazine of Jewish Literature and Culture* (established in 1989), and *Mashiv ha-Ruaḥ* (established in 1994). In 1997, an ambitious anthology of poetry associated with *shira emunit* was published under the title *Shira Hadashah: shira emunit tzeira*, edited by the poets Admiel Kosman and Miron Isaacson, who brought together an impressive corpus of poems written by (among others) the two editors as well as Erez Biton, Yonadav Kaplun, Itamar Yaoz-Kest, Hava Pinhas-Cohen, Rivka Miriam, Haviva Pedaya, Binyamin Shvili, and Agi Mishol, as well as Hamutal Bar-Yosef, who is, apart from being a scholar of Hebrew poetry, a major Israeli poet associated with *shira emunit*." See Pinsker, "Never Will I Hear the Sweet Voice of God," 131.

7. Marx and Lisitsa, "This Is the Gate," Introduction to *T'fillat Ha-Adam: An Israeli Reform Siddur for Shabbat*, 13.
8. Kaufman, Rokem, and Hess, *The Defiant Muse*, and Aliza Lavie's *Tefilat Nashim* and *A Jewish Woman's Prayer Book*.
9. Murray, "All Writing Is Autobiography," 67.
10. Benjamin, *The Obligated Self*, xiv–xv.
11. See Zierler, *And Rachel Stole the Idols*; see also Zierler and Balin, *To Tread on New Ground*.
12. That a more recent bilingual anthology of Israeli poetry has not been published may be the result of market forces in Jewish book publishing, as well as the complicated place Israel has come to occupy in the academy and the English-speaking world. For English-only anthologies of Hebrew poetry see Bargad and Chyet, *Israeli Poetry* and Keller, *Poets on the Edge*.
13. Grant, *The Year of Mourning*, xx.
14. Wieseltier, *Kaddish*, 189.
15. Heilman, *When a Jew Dies*, 4.
16. Millen, "Women and Kaddish," 202.
17. The three male contributors are Mark Dratch ("Women and Kaddish: The Halacha"), Daniel Cohen ("One Kind Gesture"), and David Walk ("The Laws of Aveilut").
18. Birnbach, *A Daughter's Kaddish*, 367.
19. Birnbach, 252. In general, the volume offers a somewhat skewed, stereotypical depiction of Orthodox women.
20. Macdonald, *H is for Hawk*, 171.
21. Mention needs to be made of the world-renowned teacher of Israeli literature and Jewish educator Rachel Korazim, who teaches Hebrew poetry to English audiences worldwide. See https://www.korazim.com/about.
22. Cohen, "Peter Cole," 154–55.
23. Cohen, "Peter Cole," 154–55.
24. Tzamir, "Bein Tehom le-'Ivaron," 84.
25. Rechnitzer, *Ars Prophetica*, 7.
26. The Rabbis' Kaddish is typically recited after formal Torah study and three times a day in the context of traditional Jewish prayer with a quorum. The chosen term, "redressing," alludes to the poet Seamus Heaney's use of it in his book *The Redress of Poetry*.
27. "Weekly epidemiological update on COVID-19—29 June 2021," World Health Organization, https://www.who.int/publications/m/item/weekly-epidemiological-update-on-covid-19---29-june-2021#:~:text=Overview,recorded%20in%20early%20November%202020.

1. Learning to Mourn

1. Goldman, *Living a Year of Kaddish*, 8.
2. Goldman, 77.
3. BT Shabbat 66b: "Rather, what are knots? Like that which 'Avin bar Huna said that Rav Ḥama bar Gurya said: '[If] a son has longings for his father and has a difficult time leaving him, the father takes a strap from his right shoe and ties it on the boy's left,' in order to quell these longings."
4. Rabbeinu Ḥananel on BT Shabbat 66b.
5. Benjamin, *The Obligated Self*, xv.
6. Pirkei 'Avot 6:11 and BT Makkot 23b, quoting Isaiah 42:21 (my translation).
7. See BT Rosh Hashanah 31a.
8. Jamison, *The Recovering*, 330–31.
9. "550-Day Record Ends With Fatality," *The Windor Star*, March 29, 1960.
10. Hollyoak, *The Spider's Thread*, xv.
11. Goldberg, *Shirim*, 2:92.
12. Bialik's Hebrew poetry is available online on the Project Ben-Yehuda website. For "Take Me Under Your Wing," see https://benyehuda.org/read/5987.

2. Picturing God in Grief and Prayer

1. Bar-Yosef, *Lea Goldberg*, 31. Also Ticotsky and Weiss, *Ne'arot 'Ivriyot*, 212.
2. Bar-Yosef, 43.
3. Benjamin, *The Obligated Self*, xxii–xxiii.
4. Lea Goldberg, *Shirim*, 1:32.
5. In classical Hebrew, the masculine pronoun *l'kha*, when appearing at the end of a phrase, sometimes undergoes change of vowels and appears as *lakh*; this is known as "pausal form." However, this pausal form of the masculine pronoun is homophonous with the regular feminine pronoun, *lakh*. Thus, while grammarians might argue that *lakh* in the prayer is formally a pausal form of the masculine pronoun, I take license to hear it as the feminine form. The same principle is at play in the phrase *'anaḥnu modim* ***lakh*** *u-mevarekhim* ***'otakh*** (We thank You [pausal/feminine form] and bless You [pausal/feminine form] in the Grace after Meals and in the closing Haftarah blessing).
6. Lea Goldberg, "'Al Sheloshah Devarim," *Mah 'Osot ha-'Ayalot*, 116–17.
7. Lamm, *The Jewish Way in Death and Mourning*, 157.
8. Goldberg, "Be-Siddur Sheli," *Shirim*, 1:192.
9. This line enacts a daring reversal insofar as traditionally sources imagine the world as God's, and not humanity's, footrest. See Isaiah 66:1 and Psalm 99:5.
10. Goldberg, "Yehi ha-Ḥoref Mevorakh," *Shirim*, 3:101.
11. Literally "without bounds."

12. See Goldberg, "'Oren" ("Pine Tree"), *Shirim,* 2:143.
13. Goldberg, "Berakhah," *Shirim,* 3:179. The threefold repetition here of *ki tov* (and it was good) recalls the same threefold repetition in Genesis 1:10, 12, and 25.
14. The phrase *lailah gadol* (great night) doesn't appear in the Bible, but there are references to the great *day* of God, before which day is turned into night. See, for example, Joel 3:4.
15. Goldberg, "'Aviv 'Eḥad," *Shirim,* 3:154–55. This is the fifth poem of a cycle titled "One Spring," which includes seven poems.
16. See Mishnah 'Ohalot 1:8.
17. Goldberg, "Demamot Sheli," *Shirim,* 1:137. This is the second poem in a cycle titled "My Silences," which includes three poems.
18. Literally "within her."
19. Literally "good."
20. BT Nedarim 30b.
21. BT Yevamot 87b.
22. Maimonides, *Guide to the Perplexed* 1:59, 139; translation adapted from Pines.
23. Goldberg, "Mizmor Lailah," *Shirim,* 2:196. For Ahinoam Nini and Gil Dor's musical setting see https://www.youtube.com/watch?v=08d8kghNkLg.
24. Literally "black."
25. Meaning "from North to South." Cf. Song of Songs 4:16.
26. Literally "heart," though in the Bible, *lev* typically refers to the mind/intellect. I have combined "heart" and "intellect" into "soul" for the rhyme.
27. Goldberg, "'Al Dalteinu Pasaḥ va-Yehi 'Or," *Shirim,* 2:226.
28. Implies the pale blue of the heavens, and also evokes the *tekhelet* prescribed for the ritual fringes of a tallit (see Num. 15: 38).
29. Note the usage of the same verb in the second line of the poem, where the door is open wide, *lirvaḥah.* This line is hard to translate, because the phrase *'od yirvaḥ bikhyekha* can mean two opposite things: (1) your weeping will ease, or (2) your weeping will become more common or widespread.
30. This is an ambiguous line, as the word *gamal,* in this context, can mean either "recompense" (i.e., your hatred has been paid back) or "wean."
31. For New York death rates in April 2020, see Josh Katz and Margot Sanger-Katz, "Deaths in New York City Are More Than Double the Usual Total," *New York Times,* April 10, 2020, https://www.nytimes.com/interactive/2020/04/10/upshot/coronavirus-deaths-new-york-city.html.
32. Goldberg, "Siyyum," *Shirim,* 1:244. Emphasis added in the Hebrew original to mark the repetitions of the verbal root *'ayin-lamed-dalet.* This is the first poem in a cycle titled "Ending" that includes four poems.

33. See Genesis 1: 4, 10, 21, 18, and 25, where God repeatedly creates and deems it good. See also, in Genesis 2:7, the introduction of *tov va-ra'* (good and evil) and, in Genesis 2:18, God's pronouncement of *lo' tov*—it's not good for the human to be alone.
34. From Oved Sadeh, "Kaddish," reprinted in Dalia Marx, "Tefillat ha-Kaddish be-Tenu'ah ha-Kibbutzit," *'Atar ha-Piyyut veha-Tefillah*, https://web.nli.org.il/sites/nlis/he/song/Pages/Articles/hkadish_bakibutzim.aspx.

3. Facing an Absent God

1. Luz, *Shirat 'Avraham Ḥalfi*, 43.
2. Rechnitzer, *Ars Prophetica*, 27.
3. Ḥalfi, "Ḥalom 'Ikevotekha," *Shirim*, 1:118. For Arik Einstein and Yitzhak Klepter's musical setting of this poem, see https://www.youtube.com/watch?v=_NIIODGbGTM.
4. Literally "From your mouth." Cf. Songs 5:1.
5. Or "garden," as in the second stanza.
6. Literally "clods of gloom/darkness." License taken for rhyme.
7. Literally "So we see how empty the space is."
8. "I sought You and couldn't find You" draws on the language of Songs 3:1; "I gathered honey from inside you/ from your mouth" draws on Songs 5:1.
9. Rechnitzer, *Ars Prophetica*, 46–51.
10. From *Ḥayyei Moharan*, "Sippurim Ḥadashim" 95, accessible from Sefaria at https://www.sefaria.org/Chayei_Moharan.95?lang=he.
11. See the COVID Tracking Project, https://covidtracking.com/data/national/deaths.
12. Ḥalfi, "'Eineni Yodei-a' Milim," *Shirim*, 1:253.
13. Or: "that bears its fruit to its ripe conclusion."
14. Gottfried, *Siddur 'Erev Shabbat u-Mo'ed*, 57.
15. I have written about this poem in relation to the *'olah* sacrifice, which begins whole (*tamim*) and then is systematically dismembered. See Wendy Zierler, "On Sacrifices and Life."
16. Ḥalfi, "'Atur Mitzḥekh Zahav Shaḥor," *Shirim*, 1:286.
17. Setting by Yoni Rechter, with backup vocals by Corinne El-Al, Yehudit Ravitz, and pianist Avraham Kenner, available at https://www.youtube.com/watch?v=wcayUsa9yvw.
18. Ḥalfi, "'Adam He'emin Po," *Shirim*, 1:46.
19. Literally "fall from the sky."
20. Mishnah Berakhot 9:2.

21. For Arik Einstein and Shem Tov Levi's musical setting of the poem, see https://www.youtube.com/watch?v=4olyn65ffdU.
22. Ḥalfi, "Veha-Shirim Hem 'Avak 'Atikot," *Shirim,* 1:202. This is the first of two poems in a cycle titled "Heretic's Prayers."
23. Ḥalfi, "Tefillot Kofer, 1," *Shirim,* 2:52–53.
24. Drawing on language from Psalm 116:19.
25. Alluding to Isaiah 62:6: "Upon your walls, O Jerusalem, I have set sentries, who shall never be silent by day or by night."
26. A play on "Pour out Your Wrath" from Psalm 79:6, which is quoted in the Passover Haggadah.
27. John Lewis, "Together, You Can Redeem the Soul of America," *New York Times,* July 30, 2020, https://www.nytimes.com/2020/07/30/opinion/john-lewis-civil-rights-america.html.
28. Ḥalfi, "Ba-Lailah Nafelu Tzipporim," *Shirim,* 1:177.
29. BT Kiddushin 39b. This talmudic story attempts to reconcile the promise of long life in the biblical verse with the fact of a young life cut short by recourse to the notion of the afterlife, "that day that is all long."
30. Shem Tov Levi's musical setting of this poem is accessible at https://www.youtube.com/watch?v=QCNauA2uSlI.
31. Ḥalfi, "Setav Yehudi," *Shirim,* 2:202. See also Arik Einstein and Yoni Rechter's musical setting, accessible at https://www.youtube.com/watch?v=x2pjQdbgvj4.

4. Living with a Lesser, Closer God

1. Amichai, *Shirei Yehudah 'Amichai,* 1:88.
2. For more on allusions in this poem see Abramson, *The Writing of Yehuda Amichai,* 39–43.
3. Cf. Exod. 33:20, where Moses asks to see God's face but is only allowed to see God's back.
4. Amichai, *Shirei Yehudah 'Amichai,* 2:352. The last word of the poem has variant spellings, and I have included here the most common one, *'odi* (with an *'alef*), meaning "my thanks"—and if re-vocalized as *'udi,* "my flame" or "my spark," as I have translated it. Occasionally it is found as *'odi* (with an *'ayin*), which would mean "my everlasting" or "so long as I am / I live," as in Psalm 104:33, *'azamerah le'lohai be-'odi,* "I will sing to God as long as I live." In every later musical setting of the song, the spelling is with an *'alef,* which points to a later revision on Amichai's part. See also Yehudit Ravitz's musical setting, https://www.youtube.com/watch?v=22PZ_HHEuR4.

5. The *Ve-'ahavta* (literally "You shall love") is the liturgical passage immediately following the *Shema'*, taken from Deuteronomy. The words alluded to appear in Deuteronomy 6:5.
6. Jamison, *The Recovering*, 112.
7. Amichai, *Shirei Yehudah 'Amichai*, 1:114. See Gidi Koren's musical setting of this song, performed by Ha-Aḥim Veha-Aḥayot, which superimposes the song against the 1947 U.N. Vote to Partition Palestine: https://www.youtube.com/watch?v=uPXClM7nqkU.
8. Amichai, *Shirei Yehudah 'Amichai*, 1:80.
9. Choosing one son over another: 21:12 (Isaac over Ishmael), 25 (Jacob over Esau), 37:3 (Joseph over his brothers), and 48:14 (Ephraim over Manasseh). For fleeing or being driven from a familial household: 16:6, 21:10–21 (Hagar), 28:10, 31:21 (Jacob), and 37:23–28 (Joseph). For burying a family member: 23: 4–28 (Abraham burying Sarah) and 35:19 (Jacob burying Rachel). (All references are to the book of Genesis.)
10. Amichai, *Shirei Yehudah 'Amichai*, 1:87.
11. This is a reference to the anticipated resurrection of the dead after the coming of the Messiah, a notion anticipated in the Bible is verses such as Isaiah 26:19 and affirmed in daily prayer.
12. Alluding to Isaiah 11:6.
13. See Isaiah 2:1–4 and Micah 4:3.
14. See Audrey McNamara, "Fauci Makes Final Plea to Americans Before Thanksgiving," CBS News, November 25, 2020, https://www.cbsnews.com/news/fauci-warning-thanksgiving-2020/.
15. See Micah 4:2 for his vision, and Ezekiel 38–39 (especially 38:8) for the prophet's vision of the apocalypse.
16. Amichai, *Shirei Yehudah 'Amichai*, 1:13.
17. Ḥayyim Naḥman Bialik, "Likhvod ha-Ḥanukkah," accessible on the Project Ben-Yehuda website at https://benyehuda.org/read/3177.
18. For a far less heartwarming biblical usage of the word *levivot* see 2 Samuel 13, where Amnon asks his sister Tamar to bake him *levivot*, and uses her bringing them to him as a pretext to rape her.
19. Gloss to *Shulḥan Arukh, Oraḥ Ḥayyim* 670:2. The book of Judith is part of the Septuagint, Catholic, and Eastern Orthodox Old Testaments, and part of the Protestant apocrypha, but was not included in the canonical Hebrew Bible.
20. Amichai, *Shirei Yehudah 'Amichai*, 5:155.
21. For a recent essay that offers commentary on this poem as several others dealing with the motif of the tallit, please see Naomi Sokoloff, "The Poet's Tallit."

22. Amichai, *Shirei Yehudah 'Amichai*, 3:352.
23. Cf. the *Mi Sheberakh* prayer for the soldiers of the IDF, which asks God to bless the soldiers who stand on guard to protect the country on land, in the air, and on the sea.
24. Ticotsky, *Ha-'or be-Shulei he-'Anan*, 141–42.
25. The three-poem cycle, titled "Mi-Shirei Teveryah" ("From Poems of Tiberias"), appeared in *'Al ha-Mishmar* (July 1, 1949), 5. Two of these poems were later reprinted as sonnets 8 and 9 in a sonnet cycle entitled "'Ahavnu Kan" ("We Loved Here") in Amichai's first published collection, *'Akhshav uve-Yamim 'Aḥerim*. See Amichai, *Shirei Yehudah 'Amichai*, 1:62–63. All of this is chronicled in Ticotsky in "*Be-'Ozvi et Ḥayyai*."
26. Shlomo Tzemaḥ, "Matzevet ve-Shalakhtah."
27. Goldberg, "Gefen ha-Yayin shebe-Kharmei Zarim."
28. See Amichai, *Shirei Yehudah 'Amichai*, 2:290–92.
29. Ticotsky, "*Be-'Ozvi et Ḥayyai*," 219.
30. Perhaps the lasting threefold cord Amichai ties in this poem is that of two poets and an idea, the cord metaphorically connecting Lea Goldberg, Yehuda Amichai, and their shared modern project of secular theology.
31. Amichai, *Shirei Yehudah 'Amichai*, 1:15. See Matti Caspi and Shlomo Gronich's musical setting of this poem, accessible at https://www.youtube.com/watch?v=CpvRS7RvHXA.
32. Cf. the opening of the Haftarah blessing, which refers to the prophets' words as *ne'emarim be-'emet* (said in truth/faithfulness). The Musaf *Amidah* on Shabbat also asks of God to purify us *le-'ovdekha be-'emet* (so we can worship You in truth).
33. See BT Berakhot 40b.
34. Amichai, *Shirei Yehudah 'Amichai*, 3:211.
35. Kronfeld, *The Full Severity of Compassion*, 172.
36. Amichai, *Shirei Yehudah 'Amichai*, 2:54.
37. Ricoeur, *The Symbolism of Evil*, 351.

5. Searching for Female Liturgical Voices

1. Originally published in *Kokhevei Yitzḥak* 15 (1851): 2 and reprinted in Mopourgo, *'Ugav Raḥel*, 60, accessible on the Project Ben-Yehuda website at https://benyehuda.org/read/5801.
2. Literally "ornamental grace." See Proverbs 4:9.
3. Literally "I will spread out what is in my heart."
4. Literally "My feet have given way." See 2 Samuel 22:37.

5. See Isaiah 26:1: "In that day, this song shall be sung in the land of Judah: Ours is a mighty city; [God] makes victory our inner and outer wall."
6. Gilbert and Gubar, *The Madwoman in the Attic*, 73.
7. Tova Cohen, "The Power of Writing from the Margins," 417.
8. See Esther 9:29. The other woman, also a queen, is Jezebel. See 1 Kings 21:8, where Jezebel writes *sefarim* to seek revenge against Navot the Izraelite on behalf of her husband Ahab.
9. The journal, *Kerem Ḥemed*, for example, was dedicated entirely to letters between *maskilim*; see Moshe Pelli, "*Kerem Ḥemed*." For women's contributions to epistolary writing more generally, see The Smithsonian Postal Museum website, https://postalmuseum.si.edu/research-articles/epistolary-fiction-themes/feminism-in-epistolary-fiction.
10. See for example, 1 Kings 20:11 and 2 Kings 4:29.
11. See Cohen, *'Ugav Ne'elam*, 415.
12. Originally published in *Kokhevei Yitzhak* 10 (1847), 13 and reprinted in Mopourgo, *'Ugav Raḥel*, 52, accessible on the Project Ben-Yehuda website at https://benyehuda.org/read/5995.
13. See Isaiah 54: 1 and Lamentations 1:13. See also Leviticus 26:32 (and other verses in that chapter), in which God promises to lay waste to the land if the people disobey God's commandments. In all three of these instances a femininely personified land or city is presented as forsaken.
14. Literally "I will be quiet"; see Psalm 131:2.
15. See the description of David in 1 Samuel 16:12.
16. Literally "The one my soul loves"; see Song of Songs 3:1.
17. See 2 Samuel 22:29.
18. See Daniel 12:13.
19. Literally "the right (feminine) hand did save" (Psalm 98:1).
20. It was originally published alongside her cousin's sonnet in *Kokhevei Yitzḥak* 8 (1847): 33–34 and reprinted in Mopourgo, *'Ugav Raḥel*, 51. It is accessible on the Project Ben-Yehuda website at https://benyehuda.org/read/4807.
21. The wedding poem was published in *Kokhvei Yitzḥak* in 1847. Note, however, the twenty-eight-year time gap between the writing of the poem and its publication, owing to Morpurgo's many domestic responsibilities that left her with little time to be involved in literary or intellectual matters or to send in works for publication.
22. First published in *Kokhvei Yitzḥak* 25 (1860): 53 and reprinted in Mopourgo, *'Ugav Raḥel*, 83; accessible on the Project Ben-Yehuda website at https://benyehuda.org/read/5025.

23. BT Mo'ed Katan 25b.
24. The word *le-'ot* in conjunction with a form of the verb "to be" most famously appear in Deuteronomy 6:8 in reference to the wearing of tefillin.
25. Literally "they are charged with indiscretion." See 2 Samuel 6:7, where Uzzah is killed by God for the indiscretion (*shal*) of touching the holy ark.
26. Literally "reproach." See Job 4:18: *uve-mal'akhav yasim tohalah*, "and angels receive reproach."
27. See Laban's speech in Genesis 31:29: "I have it in my power (*yesh le'el yadi*) to do you harm." Tova Cohen notes the somewhat grammatical addition of the negative *lo'* to this biblical phrase. See Cohen, *'Ugav Ne'elam*, 472.
28. Judges 4:4.
29. See Zephaniah 3:5: "But God in her midst is righteous and does no wrong (*'avlah*)."
30. Literally "that is her due"; see Jeremiah 10:7.
31. See 2 Samuel 20:18, where a "wise woman" is quoted: "Then she spoke, saying: 'In olden times people used to say, Let them inquire of Abel (*sha'ol yish'alu be-'avel*),' and that was the end of the matter." Here Morpurgo is playing on a placename (Avel) that also means "mourning."
32. For the closing image, see Isaiah 53:7: "Like a ewe, dumb before those who shear her."
33. Green, *The Anthropocene Reviewed*, 206.
34. Upon revisiting my book nearly two decades after writing it, I now see that I barely scratched the surface of the poem's many meanings. For my earlier reading, see Zierler, *And Rachel Stole the Idols*, 90–94.
35. My translation.
36. See Tova Cohen's thorough analysis of the poem in her *'Ugav Ne'elam*, 234–42.
37. Leopold Winkler, "Tehilah le-Raḥel."
38. See Ecclesiastes 1:14.
39. Mendel Stern, "LeRachel Morpurgo," *Kokhvei Yitzḥak* 24 (1858): 95–96. The stars are a reference to Stern's own publication, *Kokhvei Yitzḥak (The Stars of Isaac)*.
40. It also alludes to Barak, whose name means "lightning," the source of many tree fires.
41. Tova Cohen notes that the doubly negative, ungrammatical expression *lo' yesh le-'el yadi* alludes to Laban's speech to Jacob in Genesis 31:29, where he tells Jacob *yesh le-'el yadi*, I have it in my power (to do you harm), but God warned me not to. Rachel Morpurgo, by contrast, renounces Laban's form of power. See Cohen, *'Ugav Ne'elam*, 473.
42. Cohen, *'Ugav Ne'elam*, 241.

43. See, for example, *Shemot Rabbah, Va-'era '* 10, *Vayikra Rabbah, 'Aḥarei Mot* 22, and *Kohelet Rabbah* 1. See also R. Isaac Sheshet (1306–1498): "And I say, 'See this is new,' and it is a forbidden notion," in *She'elot u-Teshuvot Rivash* 341. For an instance in which this phrase is positively, see *She'elot u-Teshuvot Halakhot Gedolot* 1:27.

44. Introduction to *Keli Yakar*, accessible from Sefaria at https://www.sefaria.org/Kli_Yakar_on_Genesis%2c_Introduction.2?lang=bi.

45. Originally published in *Kokehvei Yitzḥak* 22 (1856): 37–38 and reprinted in Morpurgo, *'Ugav Raḥel*, 72; accessible on the Project Ben-Yehuda website at https://benyehuda.org/read/789.

46. See Job 15:32, where the word *ra'anan* appears specifically in the context of something withering before it can properly flourish, dying before its time, as in the case of someone suddenly afflicted with cholera. See Psalm 37:35.

47. See Numbers 2:17, which describes the orderly migrations of the Israelites in the desert.

48. The word *ketev* for "plague" or "epidemic" appears in Psalm 91:6. The entire psalm appears in a 1836 Trieste plague prayer booklet.

49. Cohen, *'Ugav Ne'elam*, 244–45.

50. Tova Cohen analyzes several Morpurgo poems that respond to Christian anti-Jewish incidents in Trieste as reflecting her tendency to see an unbridgeable gaps between Jews and Gentiles. See Cohen, *'Ugav Ne'elam*, 337–47.

51. On anti-Jewish attacks and the Black Death, see Brown, *The Eleventh Plague*, 67–149. Note, however, that unlike the Black Death, the early and mid-nineteenth-century cholera outbreaks in Europe did not result in violent outbursts against Jews. For more on this, see Martin, "Outsiders on the Inside," 29–49.

52. For more on Snow and his theory of cholera transmission, see Johnson, *The Ghost Map*.

53. Originally published in *Kokehvei Yitzḥak* 22 (1856): 37–38 and reprinted in Morpurgo, *'Ugav Raḥel*, 72; accessible on the Project Ben-Yehuda website at https://benyehuda.org/read/4327.

54. Psalm 19:15.

55. Literally "heed my voice." Cf. Gen. 3:17, 21:12.

56. Psalm 142:5.

57. Jeremiah 31:16.

58. Isaiah 35:10.

59. Literally "God is gracious."

60. Psalm 96:11.

61. According to tradition the biblical Rachel died on 11 Ḥeshvan. The earliest source for this is Jubilees 32:33, which refers to Benjamin's birthdate (and

Rachel's consequent death in labor) as occurring on the eleventh of the eighth month in the first of the sixth week of this jubilee. Tova Cohen suggests that the upcoming anniversary of Rachel's death might have furnished the occasion for this poem; see her *'Ugav Ne'elam*, 441.

62. According to scholar Sarit Kattan Gribetz, "The figure of Rachel stands more prominently among matriarchs whose merit assists her descendants, parallel to Abraham's binding of Isaac as the paradigmatic event that accrued patriarchal merit." See Kattan Gribetz, "*Zekhut 'Imahot*," 263.
63. The story of Rachel sharing the signs with Leah is also found in BT Megillah 13b and Bava' Batra' 123a.
64. An epithet signifying a beloved spouse, as in Isa. 62:4.
65. This line alludes to Psalm 119:66: "Teach me good sense and knowledge, for I have put my trust in Your commandments."
66. Literally "to marry a man with the surname Sulam" (which means "ladder").
67. Literally "I exist or dwell in longing" or "of longing I do sing."
68. See Song of Songs 3:11 and Mishnah Ta'anit 4:8, where Solomon's being crowned on his wedding day is likened to the giving of the Torah.
69. Cohen, *'Ugav Ne'elam*, 406.
70. It is worth noting, of course, that relationships in the Bible between fathers, sons, and brothers are not harmonious either, though they are more commonly depicted. For more on this see Wendy Zierler, "Can Elijah Reconcile Fathers and Sons?"
71. See BT *Niddah* 67b and *Shulḥan Arukh, Yoreh De'ah* 193:3.
72. The two exceptions are Deborah's admiring praise of Yael in Judges 5 and Ruth and Naomi's relationship in the book of Ruth.
73. I was not quite able to reproduce that consistent rhyme in my translation.
74. Originally published in *Kokhevei Yitzḥak* 19 (1861): 61 and reprinted in Morpurgo, *'Ugav Raḥel*, 66; accessible on the Project Ben-Yehuda website at https://benyehuda.org/read/3372.
75. Morpurgo plays here on the name "Leah" and its literal meaning, "fatigued" or "tired."
76. Daniel 7:10.
77. Isaiah 60:1.
78. Isaiah 26:2.
79. Indeed, one way to understand the biblical description of Leah's eyes as *rakkot* ("Leah had weak eyes," Gen. 29:17) is as tender, due to tiredness. Biblical scholars have also linked Leah's name to the Akkadian *littu*, meaning "wild cow," which makes sense in light of the similar meaning of the name Rachel as "ewe." See M. Dijkstra, "Leah לאה."

80. Morpurgo, *'Ugav Raḥel,* 85 and accessible on the Project Ben-Yehuda website at https://benyehuda.org/read/3498.
81. "The words a person speaks are deep waters, a flowing stream, a fountain of wisdom" (Prov. 18:4).
82. "[You are] a garden spring / A well of fresh water / A rill of Lebanon." (Songs 4:15).
83. A reference to the 'Arba'ah Turim, the halakhic code of Rabbi Yaakov ben Asher (1270–1340). The Hebrew names means "four columns" and the poet will now refer to each of the code's four sections: *'Orah Ḥayyim* ("Path of Life," dealing with the laws of Sabbath, holidays, and the synagogue), *Yoreh De'ah* ("Wisdom's Rule," dealing with dietary laws and the laws of menstruation), *'Even Ha'ezer* ("The Stone of Help," dealing with marriage, divorce, and sexual conduct), and *Ḥoshen Mishpat* ("Breastplate of Judgment," dealing with tort and finance law).
84. The dwelling place of Elkanah, father of Samuel. See 1 Samuel 1:1.
85. Johannes Valentin Schwarz, "Max Beer."
86. Upon his passing, *Kokhevei Yitzḥak* editor Mendel Stern published a poem in his memory entitled "*'Alon Bakhut*" (Oak of Weeping), an allusion to Genesis 35:8, where Rebekah's nursemaid Deborah was buried. I discuss Genesis 35 and Deborah's death in the next and final poem discussion in this chapter.
87. Cohen, *'Ugav Ne'elam,* p. 481.
88. Mopurgo, *'Ugav Raḥel,* 80.
89. Mopurgo, *'Ugav Raḥel,* 90.
90. *Kokhevei Yitzḥak* 12 (1848): 1; reprinted in *'Ugav Raḥel,* 4; accessible on the Project Ben-Yehuda website at https://benyehuda.org/read/2734.
91. Isaiah 52: 11.
92. Cf. Number 16:26, where Moses warns the people to separate from Korah and his men lest they perish with them for their sins.
93. Isaiah 48:5.
94. Daniel 5:1.
95. My translation.

6. Retying the Knots

1. Weiss, "I Throw Down My Supplication," *'Eḥeta' ve-'Ashuv,* 18.
2. "Shefal Ruaḥ" is the title of a *piyyut* by R. Solomon ibn Gabirol (eleventh century), in which the poet describes his prayer pose as *shefal ruaḥ, shefal berekh ve-komah,* "humble of spirit, humble of knee and stature." For the text of the piyyut see https://www.nli.org.il/he/piyut/Piyut1song_010010900000005171/nli.

3. "One who goes along weeping, carrying the seed-bag, shall come back singing with joy, carrying the sheaves" (Ps. 126:5). Cf. Rachel's wailing and bitter weeping—*nehi u-vekhi tamrurim*—on Ramah (Jer. 31:15).
4. The newest JPS translation (*The JPS* TANAKH*: Gender-Sensitive Edition* or RJPS, 2023) renders this expression as "lay our plea," but the I have translated it otherwise to accord with the poem analysis. The present translation is in line with JPS's 1917 translation.
5. Poet Rivka Miriam (b. 1952) offers a similar wordplay on the expression *le-hapil teḥinati* in a 1982 poem entitled "'Elekh le-Hapil Teḥinati" ("I'll Cast Down My Plea"). See Miriam, *These Mountains*, 129–30.
6. Weiss, "Lament for Rashi's Daughters," *Shemirah*, 9.
7. This seems to derive from the Old French / German *bramer*, meaning "to roar and wail with longings."
8. While there is no written evidence attesting to Rashi's daughters wearing tefillin, Dr. Aliza Berger speculates that the legend relates to their exceptional Torah education. See Berger, "Wrapped Attention: May Women Wear Tefillin?"
9. R. Mirvis's decision to ban Lindsey from teaching at LSJS and the United Synagogue is all the more ironic and quizzical given that his niece, R. Shira Mirvis, was appointed around the same time as the sole spiritual leader of a synagogue in Efrat, Israel. See https://www.timesofisrael.com/in-israeli-first-woman-chosen-as-sole-spiritual-leader-of-orthodox-community/.
10. See for example, this JOFA (Jewish Orthodox Feminist Alliance) UK, Facebook petition, https://www.facebook.com/Plus61J/photos/a.755257981312596/1801549766683407/. And Jacob Judah, "This rabbi is working to get more women in leadership roles in Great Britain's Orthodox community," JTA (Sept. 17. 2021), https://www.jta.org/2021/09/17/global/the-rabbi-working-to-get-more-women-in-leadership-roles-in-great-britains-orthodox-community. See this article about Lindsey's reinstatement: https://www.haaretz.com/jewish/.premium-following-backlash-orthodox-female-rabbi-gets-job-back-at-top-uk-institution-1.9977589.
11. Weiss, "I Am Still Praying," from *'Eḥeta' ve-'Ashuv*, 92.
12. Amichai hopes that in the recurrent cycle of war, and all the beatings of swords into plowshares and back into swords, perhaps the metal of war will simply wear out.
13. Weiss, "Ve-shuv 'Eḥeta' ve-'Ashuv," *'Eḥeta' ve-'Ashuv*, 53.
14. From Isaiah 6:5.
15. My translation.
16. Weiss, *'Eḥeta' ve-'Ashuv*, 8–9.

17. Songs 2:10.
18. See Hosea 1:6, where Hosea's daughter, born of Gomer the prostitute, is called Lo-Ruhamah. Note that Ruhama is also the poet's first name.
19. The wordplay of Rut and *ḥerut* is not replicable in English, but the alliterative "learned liberty" is an effort.
20. Literally "clear."
21. Fetterly, *The Resisting Reader*, xiii.
22. Fetterly, xx.
23. See Amit Naor, "Introducing Naamah."
24. See Introduction to *Sefer ha-Yashar*, accessible from Sefaria at https://www.sefaria.org/Sefer_HaYashar_(midrash)%2C_Introduction?lang=bi&with=About&lang2=en.

7. Penning Pandemic Torah

1. For more on Bluwstein's tuberculosis and how it found expression in her poetry, see Yudkoff, *Tubercular Capital*, 50–78.
2. Bluwstein, "Halakh Nefesh," *Ha-Shiloaḥ* 37 (Summer 1920), accessible on the Project Ben-Yehuda website at https://benyehuda.org/read/19.
3. "Is the feasting of the eyes more important than the pursuit of desire [*halakh nefesh*]? That, too, is futility and pursuit of wind" (Eccl. 6:9).
4. My translation.
5. Gordon responded to Rachel's poem by letter with a poem of his own, "*Lekhi bishvilekh*" ("Go on Your Path"), urging her to go forth on her own path. For more on this correspondence, see https://blog.nli.org.il/rachel_poem/.
6. From A. D. Gordon's letters 15, 16, and 18, accessible on the Project Ben-Yehuda website at https://benyehuda.org/read/1904.
7. Literally "I will give thanks," modified here for the sake of rhyme.
8. Bluwstein, "'Akarah," accessible on the Project Ben-Yehuda website at https://benyehuda.org/read/5040. For Ahinoam Nini and Gil Dor's musical setting see https://www.youtube.com/watch?v=x3Pnmc_HCmE.
9. The liturgical version of Maimonides's "Thirteen Principles of Faith" as they appear in the siddur is accessible from Sefaria at https://www.sefaria.org/sheets/216717?lang=bi.
10. For more on the relationship between Bluwstein and Bialik's poetry, see Stav, "Heyeh Li 'Eim ve-'Aḥ," 213–34.
11. Bialik, "Lo Zakhiti va-'Or min ha-Hefker," accessible on the Project Ben-Yehuda website at https://benyehuda.org/read/1972.
12. My translation.

13. See Lapsley, "The Voice of Rachel," 238. See also Zierler, *And Rachel Stole the Idols*, 1–4.
14. "Now Hannah was praying in her heart; only her lips moved, but her voice could not be heard" (1 Sam. 1:13). Regarding the use of Hannah as a model of rabbinic prayer and the proper mode for the recitation of the *'Amidah*, see BT Berakhot 31b.
15. The rabbis anticipate Bluwstein's use of "curls" in this allegorical way in *Shir Hashirim Rabbah* 5:11, interpreting "His locks are curled," a description of the male beloved, as "the ruled lines" that the scribe etches to write the lines of the Torah; and "black as a raven" as "the letters" of the Torah.
16. Bluwstein, "Be-Veit ha-Ḥolim," *Safiaḥ*, 15, accesible on the Project Ben-Yehuda website at https://benyehuda.org/read/7320. This is the first poem in a cycle entitled "In the Hospital," which includes three poems.
17. Literally "to move him to wander." Cf. God's punishment to Cain in Genesis 4:12.
18. Green, *The Anthropocene Reviewed*, 209.
19. Bluwstein, "Ve-'Ulai," accessible on the Project Ben-Yehuda website at https://benyehuda.org/read/818. For the musical setting of the poem by Shelishiyat Gesher Ha-Yarkon see https://www.youtube.com/watch?v=9BDnnipllLU&t=13s.
20. My translation.
21. The title *Ḥalom ve-Shivro* is based on the use of this term in the context of Gideon's dream of victory over Midian in Judges 7:15. Ben-Yehuda's unfinished autobiography is available in English translation by T. Maraoka, under the title *A Dream Come True*.
22. See, for example, BT Yoma 83b, 'Avodah Zarah 17b, Bava' Metzi'a' 49b, and Sanhedrin 29b.
23. Bluwstein, "Ḥoni Ha-Me'agel," accessible on the Project Ben-Yehuda website at https://benyehuda.org/read/2995.
24. See BT Ta'anit 23a.
25. See, for example, Jacob Sweet, "The Loneliness Pandemic," *Harvard Magazine*, January/February 2021, https://www.harvardmagazine.com/2020/12/feature-the-loneliness-pandemic, and Maria Morava and Scottie Andrew, "The Loneliness Won't End When the Pandemic Ends," CNN.com, April 17, 2021, https://www.cnn.com/2021/04/17/us/loneliness-epidemic-covid-wellness-trnd/index.html.
26. Bluwstein, "Yom Besorah," accessible on the Project Ben-Yehuda website at https://benyehuda.org/read/8092.

27. My translation.
28. For the idea of readerly recognition see Felski, *The Uses of Literature*, 23.
29. Felski, *The Uses of Literature*, 23.
30. For Jesus's cleansing of the leper see Matthew 8:1–4, Mark 1:40–45, and Luke 5:12–16.
31. Agnon, "'Ad 'Olam," ("Forevermore"), *Ha-'Esh veha-'Etzim*, 215–34. For an English translation, see Agnon, *Forevermore and Other Stories*, 1–20.
32. This is but one of many ways—too many to fully cite here—that this enigmatic story might be read. Scholars have read this story in relation to several of Agnon's other works: his story "The Tale of the Scribe" (Arbell, *Katuv 'al 'Oro shel ha-Kelev*, 19–51); his posthumously published novel, *Shirah* (Barzel, *Sippurei 'Ahavah*, 146–73); and his novella *'Edo and 'Enam* (Zucker, "Ba'ayat ha-Peirsh"). They have also debated whether to view Amzeh, with his fanatic nostalgia for Gumlidata, as a laudable or a ridiculous figure. For an exploration of this debate, see Naomi Sokoloff, "Passion Spins the Plot."
33. On the sickness of Diaspora, see Sandy Sufian, "Mental Hygiene and Disability in the Zionist Project". For a discussion of Zionism and illness with regard to the pandemic of tuberculosis and the poetry of Rachel Bluwstein, see Yudkoff, *Tubercular Capital*, 52–78.
34. Yehuda Amichai in an interview with Howard Schwartz, "A Way to Reality," *The Jerusalem Post Magazine*, February 17, 1978, https://archive.org/details/TheJerusalemPost1978IsraelEnglish/Feb%2017%201978%2C%20The%20Jerusalem%20Post%20Magazine%2C%20%2317%2C%20Israel%20%28en%29/page/n3/mode/2up.
35. Bluwstein, "Zemer Nugeh," *Safiaḥ*, 23. Accessible on the Project Ben-Yehuda website at https://benyehuda.org/read/4548.
36. This is perhaps Rachel's best-known poem because of the musical setting by Arik Einstein and *Ha-Ḥalonot ha-Gevohim* (The High Windows). See https://www.youtube.com/watch?v=9nkCDDaMEh0.
37. According to Hebrew literature scholar Binyamin Hakhlili, the unnamed addressee here is a young man named Michael Bernstein, with whom Rachel had a romantic relationship during her studies in France. Apparently, an earlier version of the poem, written after the relationship ended, had a very similar closing line, *ke-ḥakot Solveig le-dodah*, Solveig being the loyal lover awaiting her lover in Ibsen's *Peer Gynt* and *Solveig sheli* (my Solveig), Bernstein's pet name for Rachel. Bluwstein was later encouraged to change "Solveig" to "Rachel," resulting in a play on her own name and that of the biblical matriarch. See Ḥakhlili, *Lakh ve-'Alayikh*, 11. See also Tsur, *Raḥel, Ha-ḥayyim, Ha-shirim*, 43–45.

Final Thoughts

1. See Amir Gilboa, *Kol ha-Shirim*, 2:209. Yoni Rechter's beautiful musical setting of this poem is available at https://www.youtube.com/watch?v=bQt2UOukakw.
2. The image of creating a ball out of pain seems to allude to Heinrich Heine's "Aus meinen großen Schmerzen" ("Our of my great pain I made little songs"). See Heinrich Heine, https://www.heinrich-heine.net/schmerzd.htm.
3. Bialik, "Habereikhah" ("The Pool"), accessible on the Project Ben-Yehudah website at https://benyehuda.org/read/4387.
4. Mishnah Makkot 3:16, quoting Isaiah 42:21 (my translation).

Appendix

1. Kooser, *The Poetry Home Repair Manual*, 7.
2. The use of "betrothed" is a reference to Hosea 2:21 ("I will betroth you forever . . ."), recited upon the laying of tefillin.

BIBLIOGRAPHY

Abramson, Glenda. "Amichai's God." *Prooftexts* 4:2 (May 1984): 111–26.

——. *The Writing of Yehuda Amichai: A Thematic Approach.* Albany: SUNY Press, 1989.

——, ed. *The Experienced Soul.* New York: Routledge, 2019.

Adelman, Howard. "Finding Women's Voices in Italian Jewish Literature," in *Women of the Word: Jewish Women and Jewish Writing,* edited by Judith Baskin, 62–65. Detroit: Wayne State University Press, 1994.

Agnon, S. Y. *Forevermore and Other Stories.* New Milford CT: Toby Press, 2016.

——. *Ha-'Esh veha-'Etzim.* Jerusalem: Schocken, 1978.

Alter, Robert, ed. and trans. *The Poetry of Yehuda Amichai.* New York: Farrar, Strauss and Giroux, 2017.

Amichai, Yehuda. *The Selected Poetry of Yehuda Amichai.* Translated by Chana Bloch and Stephen Mitchell. Berkeley: University of California Press, 2013.

——. *Shirei Yehudah 'Amichai.* 5 vols. Tel Aviv: Schocken, 2020.

Bargad, Warren and Stanley F. Chyet, eds. *Israeli Poetry: A Contemporary Anthology.* Bloomington: Indiana University Press, 1986.

Bar-Yosef, Hamutal. *Lea Goldberg.* Jerusalem: Zalman Shazar Center, 2012.

Barenblat, Rachel. "On Poetry and Prayer." *Crosscurrents* (March 2012): 61–70.

Bassok, Ido. *The Doubts and Loves of Yehuda Amichai: Israeli, European, and International Poet.* Translated by Mark Joseph. Lanham: Hamilton Books, 2024.

Benjamin, Mara. *The Obligated Self: Maternal Subjectivity and Jewish Thought.* Bloomington: Indiana University Press, 2018.

Ben-Yehuda, Eliezer. *A Dream Come True.* Translated by T. Maraoka. New York: Routledge, 2020.

Berger, Aliza. "Wrapped Attention: May Women Wear Tefillin?" in *Jewish Legal Writings by Women,* edited by Micah D. Halpern and Chana Safrai, 75–118. Jerusalem, 1998.

Berlowitz, Yaffa. "Rachel Morpurgo: ha-Teshukah 'el ha-Mavet, ha-Teshukah 'el ha-Shir—le-Tivah shel ha-Meshoreret ha-'Ivrit ha-Rishonah." *Sadan: Meḥkarim be-Sifrut 'Ivrit* 2 (1996): 11–40.

Birnbach, Sarah. *A Daughter's Kaddish: My Year of Grief, Devotion, and Healing.* Los Angeles: Wonderwell, 2022.

Birnbaum, David and Martin S. Cohen, eds. *Kaddish.* New York: Mesorah Matrix, 2017.

Bluwstein, Rachel. *Flowers of Perhaps.* Translated by Robert Fried. New Milford CT: Toby Press, 2008.

———. *Safiaḥ.* Tel Aviv: Davar, 1927.

Brown, Jeremy. *The Eleventh Plague: Jews and Pandemics from the Bible to COVID-19.* Oxford: Oxford University Press, 2022.

Burshaw, Stanley, T. Carmi, and Ezra Spicehander. *The Modern Hebrew Poem Itself.* New York: Holt, Rinehart and Winston Inc., 1985.

Burshaw, Stanley, T. Carmi, Susan F. Glassman, Ariel Hirschfield, and Ezra Spicehandler. *The Modern Hebrew Poem Itself* (updated edition). Detroit: Wayne State University Press, 2003.

Capps, Donald. *The Poet's Gift: Toward the Renewal of Pastoral Care.* Louisville KY: Westminster/John Knox Press, 1993.

Carmi, T. *The Penguin Book of Hebrew Verse.* New York: Penguin, 1981.

Cohen, Joshua. "Peter Cole, The Art of Translation No. 5." *The Paris Review* 213 (Summer 2015): 148–76.

Cohen, Tova. *Ke-Raḥel Ne'elamah: Raḥel Morpurgo (1790–1871), Mivḥar Ketavim.* Jerusalem: Mossad Bialik, 2024.

———. "The Power of Writing from the Margins: Assessing Rachel Morpurgo, the First Hebrew Woman Poet." *Prooftexts* 38:2 (2020): 409–32.

———. "'This Poem Is a Token of Love': Expressions of Relationships in the Poetry of Rachel Morpurgo." *Lyre* (7 October, 2023), https://biupress.org/index.php/lyre/article/view/86/66.

———. *'Ugav Ne'elam.* Jerusalem: Carmel, 2016.

Cutter, William. "Ruchama Weiss: Hebrew Poetry and Its Burdens of the Present," *CCAR Journal: The Reform Jewish Quarterly* (Summer 2014): 110–26.

Diamant, Anita. *Saying Kaddish: How to Comfort the Dying, Bury the Dead, and Mourn as a Jew.* New York: Schocken Books, 1998, 2019.

Dijkstra, M. "Leah לאה," in *Dictionary of Deities and Demons in the Bible Online,* edited by Karel van der Toorn, Bob Becking, Pieter W. van der Horst. Leiden: Brill, 1999, 505-506. Consulted online on June 3, 2021. chrome-extension://efaidnbmnnnibpcajpcglclefindmkaj/https://www.friendsofsabbath.org/Further_Research/e-books/Dictionary-of-Deities-and-Demons-in-the-Bible.pdf.

Feld, Edward. "Poetry and Prayer." *Crosscurrents* (March 2012): 71–74.

Felski, Rita. *The Uses of Literature.* Hoboken NJ: Wiley-Blackwell, 2008.

Fetterly, Judith. *The Resisting Reader*. Bloomington: University of Indiana Press, 1978.

Friend, Robert, ed. and trans, *Found in Translation: 20 Hebrew Poets, A Bilingual Edition*. New Milford CT: The Toby Press, 2006.

Gilboa, Amir. *Kol ha-Shirim*. Tel Aviv: Ha-kibbutz Ha-me'uḥad, 1987.

Gilbert, Sandra M. and Susan Gubar. *The Madwoman in the Attic*. New Haven: Yale University Press, 1979.

Gluzman, Michael. *The Politics of Canonicity: Lines of Resistance in Modernist Hebrew Poetry*. Stanford: Stanford University Press, 2003.

Gold, Nili Scharf. *Yehuda Amichai: The Making of Israel's National Poet*. Waltham: Brandeis University Press, 2008.

Goldberg, Lea. "Gefen ha-Yayin shebe-Kharmei Zarim" ("The Wine in Foreign Vineyards"). *'Al ha-Mishmar* (July 19, 1957), 5.

———. *Ha-Shirim ha-Genuzim*. Edited by Gidon Ticotsky. Tel Aviv: Sifriyat Po'alim, 2019.

———. *Lea Goldberg: Selected Poetry and Drama*. Translated by Rachel Tzvia Back. New Milford CT: Toby Press, 2005.

———. *Mah 'Osot ha-'Ayalot*. Tel Aviv: Sifriyat Po'alim, 1949.

———. *Shirim*. 3 vols. Tel Aviv: Sifriyat Po'alim, 1973.

Goldman, Ari L. *Living a Year of Kaddish: A Memoir*. New York: Schocken, 2006.

Gordinsky, Natasha. *Bi-Sheloshah Nofim: Yetziratah ha-Mukdemet shel Lea Goldberg*. Jerusalem: Magnes Press, 2016.

Gottfried, Esteban, ed. *Siddur 'Erev Shabbat u-Mo'ed*. Tel Aviv: Beit Tefilah Yisra'eli, 2015.

Grant, Lisa, ed. *The Year of Mourning*. New York: CCAR Press, 2023.

Green, John. *The Anthropocene Reviewed*. New York: Dutton, 2021.

Heaney, Seamus. *The Redress of Poetry*. New York: Farrar, Strauss and Giroux, 1996.

Ḥakhlili, Binyamin. *Lakh ve-'Alayikh—'Ahavat Raḥel u-Mikha'el: Mikhtavim, Shirim, Divrei Hesber*. Tel Aviv: Hakibbutz Hame'uḥad, 1987.

Ḥalfi, Avraham. *Shirim*. 2 vols. Tel Aviv: Hakibbutz Hame'uḥad, 1986.

Heilman, Samuel C. *When a Jew Dies: The Ethnography of a Bereaved Son*. Berkeley: University of California Press, 2001.

Hoffman, Lawrence, ed. *Prayers of Awe*. Vols. 1–8. Woodstock VT: Jewish Lights, 2011–2018.

Hollyoak, Keith J. *The Spider's Thread: Metaphor in Mind, Brain, and Poetry*. Cambridge: MIT Press, 2019.

Isaacson, Miron and Admiel Kosman, eds. *Shirah Ḥadashah: Shirah 'Emunit Tze'irah*. Ramat Hasharon: Apiryon, 1997.

Jacobson, David. *Creator, Are You Listening? Israeli Poets on God and Prayer*. Bloomington: Indiana University Press, 2007.

Jamison, Leslie. *The Recovering: Intoxication and Its Aftermath*. New York: Back Bay Books/Little Brown & Company, 2018.

Kartun Blum, Ruth and Ana Weissman, eds. *Pegishot ʿim Meshoreret*. Jerusalem: Hebrew University and Sifriyat Poʿalim, 2000.

Kattan Gribetz, Sarit. "*Zekhut 'Imahot*: Mothers, Fathers, and Ancestral Merit in Rabbinic Sources." *Journal for the Study of Judaism* 49 (2018): 263–96.

Kaufman, Shirley, Galit Hasan Rokem, and Tamar Hess, eds. *The Defiant Muse: Hebrew Feminist Poems from Antiquity to Present*. New York: The Feminist Press, 1999.

Keller, Tsippi, trans. *Poets on the Edge: An Anthology of Contemporary Hebrew Poetry*. Albany: SUNY Press, 2008.

Keret, Etgar. *Autocorrect*. Hevel Modiʿin: Kinneret Zmora Dvir Publishing House, 2024.

Kooser, Ted. *The Poetry Home Repair Manual: Practical Advice for Beginning Poets*. Lincoln: University of Nebraska Press, 2005.

Kritz, Reuven. *ʿAl Shirat Raḥel*. Kiryat Motzkin: Hotza'at Poreh, 1969.

Kronfeld, Chana. *On the Margins of Modernism*. Berkeley: University of California Press, 1996.

——— . *The Full Severity of Compassion*. Palo Alto: Stanford University Press, 2016.

Lamm, Maurice. *The Jewish Way in Death and Mourning*. New York: Jonathan David, 2000.

Lapsley, Jacqueline. "The Voice of Rachel: Resistance and Polyphony in Genesis 31:14–35." In *Genesis: A Feminist Companion to the Bible 2nd Series*, edited by Athalya Brenner, 233–48. Sheffield: Sheffield University Press, 1998.

Lavie, Aliza. *A Jewish Woman's Prayer Book*. New York: Spiegel & Grau, 2008.

———, ed. *Tefillat Nashim*. Tel Aviv: Yediʿot 'Aḥronot, 2005.

Lieblich, Amia. *To Lea*. Tel Aviv: Hakibbutz Hame'uḥad, 2011.

Luz, Tzvi. *Shirat 'Avraham Ḥalfi*. Tel Aviv: Hakibbutz Hame'uḥad, 1994.

Maimonides, Moses. *The Guide of the Perplexed*. Translated by Samuel Pines. Chicago: University of Chicago Press, 1963.

Macdonald, Helen. *H Is for Hawk*. New York: Grove Press, 2014.

Marder, Sheldon. "What Happens When We Use Poetry in Our Prayerbooks and Why." *The Reform Jewish Quarterly* (Summer 2013): 101–12.

Martin, Myrna Gene. "Outsiders on the Inside: Italian Jewish Ghettos and Cholera in the 1830's." *European History Quarterly* 49:1 (2019): 29–49.

Marx, Dalia. "Israeli 'Secular' Poets Encounter God." In *Encountering God: God Merciful and Gracious: El Rachum V'Chanun* (Prayers of Awe Series Book 7), edited by Lawrence Hoffman, 181–97, 214 notes. Woodstock VT: Jewish Lights, 2016.

———. "Tefillat ha-Kaddish be-Tenu'ah ha-Kibbutzit," *'Atar ha-Piyyut veha-Tefillah*, https://web.nli.org.il/sites/nlis/he/song/Pages/Articles/hkadish_bakibutzim.aspx.

Marx, Dalia and Alona Lisitsa, eds. *T'filat Ha-Adam: Siddur Reformi Yisra'eli*. Jerusalem: Mossad Bialik/Maram, 2021.

Marx, Dalia and Alona Lisitsa (Hebrew), and Levi Weiman-Kelman and Efrat Rotem (English), eds. *T'filat Ha-Adam: Siddur Reformi Yisra'eli le-Shabbat—A Reform Israeli Siddur for Shabbat* (Bilingual Edition). Jerusalem: Mossad Bialik/Maram, 2022.

Meiri, Gilad and Noa Shakargy, eds. *Kirvat Makom: Shirei Tefillah*. Tel Aviv: Yedi'ot 'Aḥronot, 2006.

Millen, Rochelle. "Women and Kaddish: Reflections on Responsa." *Modern Judaism* 10:2 (May 1990): 191–203.

Milman, Yoseph. "Sacrilegious Imagery in Yehuda Amichai's Poetry." *AJS Review* 20:1 (1995): 99–121.

———. "She-Hayah 'Avraham ve-Heḥzir 'et ha-Hei l''Elohav: ha-Metaforah ha-'Ikonoklastit ke-Vitui le-Yaḥaso he-Kaful shel Yehuda 'Amichai la-Yahadut." *Proceedings of the World Congress of Jewish Studies 10* (1989): 243–50.

Mintz, Ruth Finer. *Modern Hebrew Poetry: A Bilingual Anthology*. Berkeley: University of California Press, 1966.

Miriam, Rivka. *These Mountains: Selected Poems of Rivka Miriam*. Translated by Linda Stern Zisquit. New Milford CT: Toby Press, 2009.

Mishkan HaNefesh: Mahzor for the Days of Awe. 2 vols. Edited by *Edwin Goldberg, Janet Marder, Sheldon Marder, and Leon Morris*. New York: CCAR Press, 2016.

Morpurgo, Rachel. *'Ugav Raḥel*. Trieste/Cracow: Josef Fischer, 1890.

Murray, Donald M. "All Writing Is Autobiography." *College Composition and Communication* 42:1 (February1991): 66–74.

Naor, Amit. "Introducing Naamah, the 'Mother of All Demons,'" National Library of Israel, March 11, 2020, https://blog.nli.org.il/en/Naamah/.

Olmert, Dana. *Bi-Tenu'at ha-Safah ha-'Ikeshet: Ketivah ve-'Ahavah be-Shirat ha-Meshorerot ha-'Ivriyot ha-Rishonot*. Haifa: University of Haifa Press, 2012.

Ostriker, Alicia. "Poetry and Healing: Some Moments of Wholeness." *The American Poetry Review* 47:2 (March/April 2018): 9–12.

Pelli, Moshe. "*Kerem Ḥemed*: Ketav ha-'Et ha-'Ivri shel Ḥakhmei 'Italiyah ve-Galitziyah." *Kesher* 38 (Spring 2019): 77–86.

Pinsker, Shachar. "'Never Will I Hear the Sweet Voice of God': Religiosity and Mysticism in Modern Hebrew Poetry." *Prooftexts* 30:1 (Winter 2010): 128–46.

Rechnitzer, Haim O. *Ars Prophetica: Theology in the Poetry of Twentieth-Century Israeli Poets Avraham Ḥalfi, Shin Shalom, Amir Gilboa and T. Carmi.* Cincinnati: HUC Press, 2023.

———. "To See God in His Beauty: Avraham Chalfi and the Mystical Quest for the Evasive God." *Journal of Modern Jewish Studies* 10:3 (2011): 383–400.

Reif, Stephan C. *Judaism and Hebrew Prayer*. Cambridge: Cambridge University Press, 1993.

Richman, Shirel. *The North American Hazzan's Manual for the New Israeli Reform Siddur Tefilat Ha-Adam*. Rabbinic thesis, HUC-JIR, 2024.

Ricoeur, Paul. *The Symbolism of Evil*. Boston: Beacon Press, 1969.

Sagi, Avi. *Prayer after the Death of God: A Phenomenological Study of Hebrew Literature*. Boston: Academic Studies Press, 2016.

Salaman, Nina. *Rahel Morpurgo and Contemporary Hebrew Poets in Italy*. London: Allen & Unwin, 1924.

Segal, Miryam. "Rahel Bluwstein's 'Aftergrowth' Poetics." *Prooftexts* 25:3 (Fall 2005): 319–61.

Sered, Susan Starr. "A Tale of Three Rachels, or the Cultural Herstory of a Symbol." *Nashim: A Journal of Jewish Women's Studies & Gender Issues* 1 (Winter, 5758/1998): 5–41.

Shacham, Chaya. *'Al Gevul ha-'Or*. Ramat Gan: Bar Ilan University Press, 2017.

Shaked, Gershon. *Shmuel Yosef Agnon: A Revolutionary Traditionalist*. New York: NYU Press, 1989.

Shira Stav, "Heyeh Li 'Eim ve-'Aḥ," *Meḥkerei Yerushalayim besifrut 'Ivrit* 29 (2017): 213–34.

Singer, Dov. *Tikkon Tefillati: Matkonei Tefillah*. Jerusalem: Maggid, 2017.

Smart, Michal and Barbara Ashkenas, eds. *Kaddish: Women's Voices*. New York and Jerusalem: Urim Publications, 2013.

Sokoloff, Naomi. "Passion Spins the Plot: Agnon's Forevermore," in *Tradition and Trauma: Studies in the Fiction of S. J. Agnon*, David Patterson and Glenda Abramson, eds. Boulder CO: Westview Press, 1994.

———. "The Poet's Tallit: Prayer Shawls in Poems by Avraham Sutzkever, Yehuda Amichai, Myra Sklarew and Yehoshua November." *The Reform Jewish Quarterly* (Winter 2020): 73–89.

Stern, Mendel. "'Alon Bakhut." *Kokhevei Yitzḥak* 27 (1862): 6–7.

———. "Le-Raḥel Morpurgo." *Kokhevei Yitzḥak* 24 (1858): 95–96.

Sufian, Sandy. "Mental Hygiene and Disability in the Zionist Project." *Disability Studies Quarterly* 27:4 (Fall 2007), https://dsq-sds.org/index.php/dsq/article/view/42/42.

Talpaz, Sheera. "Yehuda Amichai: The Unlikely National Poet." *Prooftexts* 38:3 (2012): 623–47.

Ticotsky, Gidon. "Be'ozvi 'et Ḥayai Kara'ti Bo ve-Tov Li: Yehudah 'Amichai ha-Tza'ir Kotev le-Lea Goldberg." *'Ot* 1 (2010): 215–26.

———. *Ha-'Or be-Shulei he-'Anan*. Tel Aviv: Ha-kibbutz Ha-me'uḥad / Sifriyat Ha-po'alim, 2011.

Ticotsky, Gidon and Yfaat Weiss, eds. *Na'arot 'Ivriyot: Mikhtavei Lea Goldberg min ha-Provintziyah 1923–1935*. Tel Aviv: Sifriyat Po'alim, 2009.

Tzamir, Hamutal. "Bein Tehom le-'Ivaron." *Mikkan* 14 (2014): 82–110.

Tzemaḥ, Shlomo. "Matzevet ve-Shalakhtah." *Davar* (July 5, 1957): 5.

Tzur, Muky. *Raḥel, ha-Ḥayyim, ha-Shirim*. Tel Aviv: Hakibbutz Hame'uḥad, 2011.

Valentin Schwarz, Johannes. "Max Beer," *Encyclopedia Judaica*, 2nd ed., Fred Skolnik, ed. (Tomson Gale, 2007), 3:252–53.

Weiman-Kelman, Levi, Ma'ayan Turner, and Shaul Vardi, eds. *Ha-Avodah she-ba-Lev*. Jerusalem: Kehilat Kol HaNeshama, 2007.

Weiss, Ruhama. *Shemirah: Shirim*. Tel Aviv: Hakibbutz Hame'uḥad, 2004.

———. *Sefatai Tiftaḥ*. Tel Aviv: Hakibbutz Hame'uḥad, 2008.

———. *'Eḥeta' ve-'Ashuv*. Tel Aviv: Hakibbutz Hame'uḥad, 2013.

———. *She-'Ishah 'Einah 'Elohim*. Tel Aviv: Hakibbutz Hame'uḥad, 2019.

Wieseltier, Leon. *Kaddish*. New York: Vintage, 2000.

Winkler, Leopold. "Tehilah le-Raḥel," *Kokhevei Yitzḥak* 24 (1858): 92–93.

Yeglin, Ofra. *'Ulai Mabat 'Aḥer*. Tel Aviv: Tel Aviv University / Hakibbutz Hame'uḥad, 2002.

Yoffe, A.B. *Lea Goldberg: Mivḥar Ma'amarim 'al Yetziratah*. Tel Aviv: Am Oved, 1980.

Yudkoff, Sunny. *Tubercular Capital*. Palo Alto: Stanford University Press, 2018.

Zauner, Michelle. *Crying in H Mart*. New York: Alfred A. Knopf, 2021.

Zerubavel, Yael. "Rachel and the Female Voice: Labor, Gender, and the Zionist Pioneer Vision," in *History and Literature: New Readings of Jewish Texts in Honor of Arnold J. Band*, edited by William Cutter and David C. Jacobson, 303–18. Providence: Brown Judaic Studies, 2002.

Zierler, Wendy. *And Rachel Stole the Idols: The Emergence of Modern Hebrew Women's Writing*. Detroit: Wayne State University Press, 2004.

———. "Anthological Poetics," in *Since 1948: Israeli Literature in the Making*, edited by Nancy Berg and Naomi Sokoloff, 59–80. Albany: SUNY Press, 2020.

———. "Can Elijah Reconcile Fathers and Sons?" https://www.thetorah.com/article/can-elijah-reconcile-fathers-and-sons.

——. "On Sacrifices and Life: Wholeness Dismembered by Re-membered," *TheTorah.com,* https://www.thetorah.com/article/on-sacrifices-and-life-wholeness-dismembered-but-re-membered.

Zierler, Wendy and Carole B. Balin, eds. *To Tread on New Ground: Selected Hebrew Writings of Hava Shapiro, 1878–1943*. Detroit: Wayne State University Press, 2014.

Zucker, Shelomo. "Ba'ayat ha-Peirush" shel 'Edo ve-'Enam' ve-"Ad 'Olam' le-Shai 'Agnon, *Hasifrut* 2:2 [January 1970]: 415–17.

SUBJECT INDEX

Page numbers in italics indicate illustrations.

abandonment, 34, 35, 82, 102, 106, 226
Abimelech as king of Shechem, 109
Abraham, 25–26, 52, 208, 210, 217, 228, 269n9, 273n62
addiction and recovery, 112, 113
'Adon 'Olam, 200
affinity, 234
Agnon, S. Y., 236, 279n32
Ahad Ha'am (Asher Ginsburg), 216
'Ahavah Rabbah (prayer), 90
'akarah (barren woman), 223
'aleh, 74–76
'Al ha-Mishmar (literary supplement), 270n25
'alimut (violence), 87
Almanzi, Yosef, 178
Alterman, Natan, 134, 245
American condition, embattled and divided, 115
Amichai, Yehuda: "And That Is Your Glory," 107; background, 106; "God Has Mercy on Kindergarten Children," 138; "Half the People in the World," 114; "I Filtered from the Book of Esther," 142; "In the Morning I Stand by Your Bed," 112; "Men, Women, and Children," 133; "My Father on Passover Eve," 144; "My Mother Baked Me the Whole World," 123; "A Sort of End of Days," 120; "Whoever Wrapped in a Tallit," 127
'Amidah (prayer), 19, 22, 40, 49, 66, 101, 140, 192, 222, 240, 270n32, 278n14
"And Once Again, I'll Sin and Return" (Weiss), 202–5
"And Songs Are the Dust of Antiquities" (Ḥalfi), 94–96
"And That Is Your Glory" (Amichai), 107–11
"And Thus Sang Rachel about Her Wedding (Morpurgo), 155–57
anger, 18, 77, 78, 98; 109, 166; divine, 101; stage of grief, 78
'Ashrei, 22
"A Sort of End of Days"(Amichai), 120–22
Associated Hebrew Schools (Toronto), 140
"At Night Birds Fell" (Ḥalfi), 100–102
'avodah, 51
Avodah Zarah (Babylonian Talmud), 210

"A Voice Is Heard in the Heights" (Morpurgo), 169–71

Babylonian exile, 231
Bar Abin, 162, 163
Bar Kipok, 161, 162, 163
"Barren Woman" (Bluwstein), 219–23
Bartenura (Ovadiah Bertinoro, 1445–1515), 20
Bar-Yosef, Hamutal, 263n6
Batsheva, 208
the Bayit (Hebrew Institute of Riverdale), 23, 30, 103, 110, 201, 219, 238; close connection between community members at the, 175; closed during COVID, 34–35; member, Jacob (Jack) Lew selected as *Ḥatan Torah*, 243–44; morning services during COVID at, 33; negotiated female participation in minyan, 24; *Shir Ḥadash* presented on Zoom, 62, 102; three rabbis came to sing Mom into Shabbat from, 32; unique culture of, 27, 126; weekly Hebrew poem teachings at the, 26; words of gratitude extended to community of, 126, 181
Beer, Bernhard, 178, 179, 180, 181
"Behold I'll Craft a Ball from the Pain" (Gilboa), 247
"Behold the Letter" (Morpurgo), 150–54
Bellevue Hospital, 220
Benjamin (biblical figure), 273n61
Benjamin, Elisabeth, 244
Benjamin, Mara, 20, 44
Ben-Yehuda, Eliezer, 229
Bernstein, Michael, 279n37
Betel Senior Center (Toronto), 3, 12
Bezalel ben Uri, 220
Bialik, Ḥayyim Naḥman, 33–35, 123–24, 221, 222, 247–48, 277n10; connection between poetry of Gilboa and, 248
biblical and liturgical references, 106
biblical nighttime prophecies, 74
Biden, Joe, 121
Black Death, 167
"Blessing" (Goldberg), 59–60
Blue Cross Blue Shield (medical insurance company), 194
Bluwstein, Rachel: background, 214–15; "Day of Tidings," 234; died from tuberculosis, 215; "Ḥoni the Circle Maker," 231; "In the Hospital," 224; "Or Maybe," 227; "Sorrow Song," 238; "Soul Walking," 216
Book of Daniel, 189–90
"Buried Here Is the Lady" (Morpurgo), 182
"By Three Things" (Goldberg), 50–53, 133

Cabelly, Sharon (author's sister), 31
Cameri Theatre, 79
Camp Robin Hood, 10
Canada Revenue, 77
Carol (author's friend), 32, 105, 124
"Chapters of the Mothers" (Weiss), 206–11
cholera epidemic (1836, 1855), 166–67
CLAL—the National Jewish Resource Center, 179–80
Cohen, Abraham, 176
Cohen, Leah, 176
Cohen, Tova, 151, 153, 159, 164, 167, 179, 181, 272n36, 272n41, 273n50, 274n61

coins of compassion, 140, 141
collective experience, 236
communal salvation, 156
community, new kinds of imaginative, 234
Community Service Society of New York, 194, 244
compassion, 40, 138, 139, 140, 233; God's magnanimous, 192; maternal, 140
conflict, 68
Congregation Ramath Orah, 15
core values, rabbinic notion of, 135
The Correct Book [*Sefer ha-Yashar*], 210
COVID: basic precautions that became a part of daily life, 140; closing of the Bayit, 34–35; community solidarity during, 73; danger and insecurity of, 93; elderly vulnerability to, 34; emerging reality of, 33; influence on lives, 64; lockdown, 44, 62, 118, 258, 260; ongoing health and economic crises of, 98; pandemic literature and, 159; prayer life with, 35; private mourning melded with trauma of, 62; started journal during Kaddish and, 33–35; as worldwide crisis, 78
"Crowned Is Your Forehead with Black Gold" (Ḥalfi), 88–90
Crying in H Mart (Zauner), 39–40

darkness, 69, 71, 72, 112, 113, 155, 267n6; association with winter, 57; of death, 60; of World War II, 59
daughters: benefit also from going out with knots, 19, 20; "Lament for Rashi's Daughters" (Weiss), 195–98; less longing for their fathers according to the Mishnah, 20, 196; Lot's, 86; mothers and, knotted together according to the Talmud, 173–74
Davar (newspaper), 43, 134
Davar Po'eletI (Hebrew's women's newspaper), 74
davening, 199, 200
"Day of Tidings" (Bluwstein), 234–37
Debbie (author's friend), 10, 126
Deborah (biblical figure), 125, 158, 159, 161, 163, 184, 274n72, 275n86
demonology, Jewish, 209
denialism (COVID vaccine), 167, 237
devotion, 78, 206, 236; Jewish, 181; letting go of, 193; religious, 20, 51, 52; renewed, 78
dignity, 194
Dinah (biblical figure), 206
disquiet, 216
Divine, 64, 80, 168; consolation, 238; decree, 60; mercy, 139, 192; place, 240; presence (Shekhinah), 34; providence, 119, 168; punishment, 73; revelation, 110, 184
Doc Mann (Dr. Isadore Mann), 3
"Down Memory Lane" (with Ray Saunen), 12
"Dream of Your Footsteps" (Ḥalfi), 81–83
dreams 82, 88, 90, 97, 115, 142, 228; connection between reality and, 231; Rebbe Naḥman's, 83

earrings (grandmother's), 189; lost and found, 189–90, 193, 194
Edmund Pettus Bridge, 99
'Ein K'eloheinu (prayer), 200
Einstein, Arik, 79, 80, 90

Elazar, 217
Eliezer Ha-Kallir, 210
Elijah, God's revelation to (Goldberg), 64
"Ending" (Goldberg), 74–76
epitaphs, poetic, 184
eulogy, 6
Eve (biblical figure), 86, 206, 208; Judeo-Christian excoriation of, 209
Exler, Steven, 244

failure, 87, 108; human, 226
faith, challenges of, 20; departure from childhood, 129; ultimate demonstration of, 129; unravelling of, 129
faith and self, crisis of, 103
faith experience, 92
faithfulness and faithlessness, distinction between, 129
Fauci, Anthony, 121
fear, 7, 86, 87, 91, 101, 104, 121, 155, 206, 214, 216, 227, 229, 243, 258; community's collective, 34, of COVID, 78, 158, 166, 167; of death, 225, 226; of rushing into anything too soon due to COVID, 93; of viral transmission, 33
Feit, Amichai Zierler, (author's son), 130
Feit, Shara Zierler (author's daughter), 8, 218, 243
Feit, Yona Zierler (author's daughter), 74, 172
Feldman, Berl. *See* Gilboa, Amir
fellowship, human, 233; social justice, 243
Felski, Rita, 234
feminism, 159
feminist midrash, 210–11
Fetterly, Judith, 208
Floyd, George, 87
Flynn, Matt, 244
Forefathers, 208
Foremothers, 208
"Fount of Wisdom from a Flowing Stream" (Morpurgo), 178–81
Fox, Jeffrey, 21
Frankel, Zacharias, 178
Fulbright fellowship (Hebrew University), 40
furniture store, 3, 4, 10, 11

Geiger, Abraham, 179
gemilut ḥasadim, 51–52
Gilbert, Sandra (American feminist critic), 151
Gilboa, Amir, 247, 248–49; background, 245–46; "Behold I'll Craft a Ball from the Pain" (Gilboa), 247; connection between poetry of Bialik and, 248; poetry and signs of suffering, 246
God: depiction as homeless, 110; "God Has Mercy on Kindergarten Children" (Amichai), 138–41; "God's Hand in the World" (Amichai), 117–19; image of as a car mechanic, 109; opposition to the coronation of, 109; portrayal of an evasive, 78
"God Has Mercy on Kindergarten Children" (Amichai), 138–41
"God's Hand in the World" (Amichai), 117–19
going out with knots, 19–22, 148, 173, 211; another form of, 211; daughters not permitted, 19, 20, 131, 173, 196; literary version,133; signifying

strong ties to tradition, 198; son's permitted to wear, 21, 173, 196
Goldberg, Lea: background, 72; "By Three Things" 50; close relationship to her father, 42; "Ending," 74; "He Passed Over Our Door and There Was Light," 71; influence on Yehudah Amichai, 133–34; "Let Winter Be Blessed," 57; "My Prayer Book," 54; "My Silences," 64; "Night Psalm," 68; "One Spring," 61; relationship to her mother, 44; "To Mother's Portrait" 46
Goldfarb, Shirley (Sarah) (author's grandmother), 184, 185, 189, 194; headstone, *187*. *See also* earrings (grandmother's)
Goldman Ari L., 15–16, 23
Goodwill, 140
Gordon, A. D., 214, 216, 217, 277n5
grace, 153, 169, 170, 233, 270n2
gratitude, 73, 126, 168, 181, 200, 216, 218, 223
Green, John, 226
Greenberg, Blu, 180
Greenberg, Irving (Yitz), 179–80
grief, 17, 20, 25, 27, 53, 55, 67, 83, 85, 89, 98, 103, 137, 147, 149, 162, 237, 261; emotion of, 28; intergenerational, 118
grief, stages of, 78
Gubar, Susan (American feminist critic), 151
Guillain Barré syndrome, 5

Hagar (biblical figure), 174, 206, 207, 208, 227, 269n9
Haggadah, Passover, 72, 115, 145, 268n2635
Haimson, Dvora (author's mother-in-law): Alzheimer's, 213–14, 229, 230, 231, 245; Bnei Akiva, 215; hospitalization, 224; move to Riverdale, 138; possessions, 140–41; visits to, 218, 245
Haimson, Ephraim (author's father-in-law), death of, 138
Hakhlili, Binyamin, 279n37
halakh nefesh ("soul walking"), 216
Halevi, Yehuda, 25
Ḥalfi, Avraham: "And Songs Are the Dust of Antiquities," 44; background, 79; "Crowned Is Your Forehead with Black Gold," 88; "Dream of Your Footsteps," 81; "Heretic's Prayers," 97; "I Know Not the Words," 84; "Jewish Fall," 103; seen as a modern mystic, 78
"Half the People in the World" (Amichai), 114–16
Haman, 142
Hannah, 160, 174, 206, 208, 219, 220, 221, 222, 278n14
Ḥanukkah, 12, 123, 124, 125, 126; eating cheese on, 125; halakhah concerning eulogies on,125
Ha-Shiloaḥ (cultural Zionist journal), 216
Haskalah (Jewish Enlightenment), 148, 152, 179
hatarah (resolution), 220
hate, 81, 114, 115, 236
Ḥavat ha-'Alamot (Maiden's Farm), 214
Havdalah, 30
ḥavruta (study partnership), 3, 174
Hebrew Institute of Riverdale, 8, 23. *See also* the Bayit (Hebrew Institute of Riverdale)

Hebrew literature, 133, 279n37; modern, 25
Hebrew poetry, 9, 26, 82, 210, 263n4; female-authored, 149; as a guide to mourning, 25, *239*; history, 25; of medieval Spain, 133; modern, 25, 40–41, 94, 109; translating, writing, and teaching, 241
Hebrew Union College–Jewish Institute of Religion (HUC-JIR), 23, 28, 45, 126, 147, 181, 190, 215, 238
Hebrew University, Department of Comparative Literature, 43
Henry Hudson Parkway, 91
"He Passed Over Our Door and There Was Light" (Goldberg), 71–73
"Here a Person Believed" (Ḥalfi), 91–93
ḥerem (social ban), 232
heresy, 78, 98
"Heretic's Prayers" (Ḥalfi), 97–99
Hollyoak, Keith J, 28
"Ḥoni the Circle Maker" (Bluwstein), 231–33
human society, endemic violence of, 86; isolated from, 232
human sympathy, 9
Humber Hospital (Toronto), 23
Humility, 67, 193, 228
Hurwitz, Sara, 178
Hyman, Sam, 219

"I Am Still Praying" (Weiss), 199–201
"I Didn't Win Light in a Windfall" (Bialik), 221
"I Filtered from the Book of Esther" (Amichai), 142–43
"I Know Not the Words" (Ḥalfi), 84–87
"I, Leah, Was So Very Tired" (Morpurgo), 176–77
Ibn Gabirol, Shelomo, 25
'iggeret, 152
ignorance about prayer, 85
'ilemut (muteness), 87
illness, chronic, 214; familial, 215; genetic, 8; mental, 42. *See also* COVID
illness poetry (Bluwstein), 215
imagery, 89, 162, 180
immasculation of women by men, 208.
impurity, 176; ritual, 235
individuality, 115, 116
"In My Prayer Book" (Goldberg), 54–56
"In the Hospital" (Bluwstein), 224–26
"In the Morning I Stand by Your Bed" (Amichai), 112–13
intimacy, 128; familial, 90; spiritual, 90; textual, 90
Isaiah, 177, 203, 204, 220
isolation: 112, 231, 232; COVID, 224, 233; of tuberculosis, 225
"I Throw Down My Supplication" (Weiss), 191–94

Jamison, Leslie, 27, 113
Jewish Enlightenment, 148, 152, 179
"Jewish Fall" (Halfi), 103–4
Jewish literature, 40; modern, 9
Jewish Orthodox Feminist Alliance, 180
Jewish values, need to redefine, 208. *See also* values
JNF (Jewish National Fund), 140
Job, 60, 142, 143, 207, 208
Jonathan (biblical figure), 210
Joshua (biblical figure), 51, 209

Judith (biblical figure), 125, 269n19

Kaddish, 13, 16, 23, 31, 49, 112, 113, 148, 196, 199, 244; alternative, secular kibbutz version of, by Oved Sadeh, 75–76; annual yahrzeits and Yizkor memorial commemorations, 130; conjunction with saying, 19; as a connection to Dad, 39; connection with parents during, 81, 175; content of, 28; during COVID, by Zoom, 258; COVID lockdown during, 44; for Dad, 33, 39, 130; daily recitation, 113; desire to create own prayer book as a result of saying, 54; feelings about uncounted status, 15, 16; giving tzedakah during daily minyan, 140; Goldberg's modified version of, 62; Ḥalfi's last two lines of "And Songs Are the Dust of Antiquities," 95–96; important for connections to parent's traditions passed on, 21; journal, *18*, 33–35; *Kaddish Yatom* (Orphan's Kaddish), 40; Maurice Lamm on, 51; as a means of uniting generations, 51; for Mom, 130; observations of Ari L. Goldman in memoir of his year of, 15; obstacles assembling a minyan, 4; *'oseh shalom* verse, 49; overlap when both parents die within eleven-month period, 33, 44; in parent's community, 16; purpose of ritual, 35; questions raised by Goldberg's poem, "Ending," 74; repetitive aspects, 22; requirement to say in a minyan, 51; responsibility to say "Amen" for other mourner's recitation of, 130; routine, 23, 30; striving to connect to parents and God, 81–82; studying Mishnah in, 80

Kaddish and *Sheheḥeyanu* prayers, modified, 62

Kaddish/COVID Journal, 33–35

Kammerman, Sandy, 219, 222

Kedushah (prayer), 66, 136, 203, 204

Kerem Ḥemed (journal), 179, 271n9

Ketuvim (journal), 79

Kevutzat Deganiah, 214

Kibbutz Keshet, 73

Kibbutz Yavneh, 215

King David, 156, 164, 210, 225, 271n15

King Jehoash, 163

Kinneret, 218, 227

"Kinneret" (Bluwstein), 215

Kinneret Farm, 214

Klepter, Yitzḥak, 80, 267

Kokhevei Yitzḥak (*maskilic* journal), 149

korban pesaḥ, 151

Kranzler, Elli, 30

Laban (biblical figure), 72, 170, 222, 225, 272n41, 272n27

LaGuardia Airport, 8

"Lament for Rashi's Daughters" (Weiss), 195–98

Leah (biblical figure), 52, 170, 174, 176, 177, 218, 274n79

Leipzig, Germany, 158

Lekh Lekha, 217

"Let Winter Be Blessed" (Goldberg), 57–58

levivah (latke, pancake), 124

Lew, Jacob (Jack), 243–44

Lewis, John, 99

liturgy, traditional: lack of female authored biblical poems, 154

loneliness, 206, 214, 231, 232, 233

longing, 54, 143, 151, 191, 195, 197, 216, 221; poetic, 222–23, 274n67
Lot (biblical figure), 72, 86
Lot's wife (biblical figure), 206, 208
love: elevated to level of all positive commandments, 63; spiritual, 90
love poetry, 89
Luntschitz, Shelomo Ephraim ben Aaron, 165
Luzzatto, Moshe Ḥayyim, 148
Luzzatto, Raphael, 182
Luzzatto, Sarah, 184
Luzzatto, Shmuel David (ShaDal), 148, 155
Luzzatto, Yitzḥak, 178, 179, 182, 184

Ma'ariv, 73
Maimonides, 20, 66; twelfth principle of faith, 241
male-centered tradition, rectitude or reliability of, 210; doubt about the identity and reliability of, 210
matir 'asurim (the One who frees captives), 200
McDonald's (on Bathurst near Steeles), 6, 10
Meisel, Hannah, 214
memory, 137, 182; continuum of for people with Alzheimer's, 213; fading, 189; familial, 59, 194, 203; knots, 130; lapse in, 202; metaphors for, and loss, 135; studying Mishnah in, of a departed loved one, 18, 19, 20; uncertainty of, 228; of wrapping in a tallit, 128
"Men, Women, and Children" (Amichai), 133–37
merism, definition, 69
Messiah, 92, 155, 220, 229, 241
metaphors, 24–27, 104, 116, 124, 129, 130, 135, 142, 151, 162, 236, 248; as poetry's distinctive feature, 28
metzora'im, 235, 236
Michal (biblical figure), 206, 208
mikveh, 173
minyan (minyanim): alienating experience in parent's community, 16–17; attending as a daily routine after Kaddish period completed, 199; author's weekly Tuesday morning talk after, 24, 33; breakfast as a reward for participating, 4; challenges of Dad assembling a, 4; at Congregation Ramath Orah, 15; during COVID, 91; at the Hebrew Institute of Riverdale (the Bayit), 243–44; joined by male member, 17; meeting through Zoom, 258; morning, 15, 199; regular Bayit tefillah attendees, 23; requirement to say Kaddish in the presence of, 51; weekly Tuesday morning talk, 24–25; women attending, 15; women not counted in, 14, 15, 148, 200; women participating in, 24
Miriam (biblical figure), 154, 195, 196, 206, 208
Miriam (Rashi's daughter), 196
Mirvis, Ephraim, 198, 276n9
Mi Shebeirakh (prayers), 128
mishloaḥ manot, 142,143
modesty, 180, 223
"The Monument Is a Witness" (Morpurgo), 182
Morpurgo, Jacob, 155, 156
Morpurgo, Rachel: background, 148–149; "Behold the Letter," 150; "Buried Here Is the Lady," 182;

"Fount of Wisdom from a Flowing Stream," 178; "The Monument Is a Witness," 182; "On Those Fleeing the Cholera Epidemic," 166; "See, This Is New," 158; "This Is the Burial Monument that Rachel Morpurgo Prepared for Herself in Her Youth," 183; "This One Shall Be Called 'My Delight Is with Her,'" 172; "A Voice Is Heard in the Heights," 169
Moses (biblical figure), 51, 64, 69, 92, 124, 159, 164, 170, 218, 268n3, 275n92
mother bird and baby chicks, 101
"My Father on Passover Eve" (Amichai), 144–46
"My Mother Baked Me the Whole World" (Amichai), 123–26
"My Silences" (Goldberg), 64–67

Naamah (biblical/midrashic figure), 207, 209
Naaman (biblical figure), 235
Nebuchadnezzar, 191
Ne'ilah (locking up), 204
nephilim, 228
"Night Psalm" (Goldberg), 68–70, 112
nostalgia, 58, 106, 125, 279n32

October 7, 2023, 201
Ohel Theatre troupe, 79
"One Spring" (Goldberg), 61–63
onomatopoetic repetition, 58, 226
"On the Mode of Communication of Cholera" (Snow), 68
"On Those Fleeing the Cholera Epidemic" (Morpurgo), 166–68
"Or Maybe" (Bluwstein), 227–30
Orthodox: Jewish law, 16; Jewish Orthodox Feminist Alliance, 180; Jewish prayer, 9; pen community in Riverdale, 16, 101, 179; prayer services, 154; standards of observance, 179; synagogue, 14, 15, 16; Yeshivat Maharat, 15, 21, 45, 74, 147, 180, 181

pain, personal, 78, 190
pandemic, 24, 34, 62, 72, 73, 78, 142, 143, 167, 172, 231, 233; cholera, 167; pre-vaccine, 138 worldwide, 30. *See also* COVID
pandemic literature: Jewish, 215, 224
parables and poetry, 146
personification, 24, 68
Pfeuffer, Ludwig. *See* Amichai, Yehuda
Pirkei 'Avot (Ethics of the Fathers), 51, 52, 135, 208
Pirkei 'Imahot, 51
piyyut (*piyyutim*), 107, 109, 110, 149, 151, 275n2
poems, liturgized, 85
poetic theology, 78
poetry, interconnection of disease and cure in, 237
"The Pool" (Bialik), 247–48
"Praise of Rachel" (Winkler), 159
prayer, 84; collective, 35; communal, 3, 66, 83; daily discipline of, 39; disavowal of, 85; "In My Prayer Book" (Goldberg), 54; morning, 35; optimistic, 218; outside due to COVID, 91; participatory, 94; personal, 241; public, 15; rabbinic, 278; rabbinic statutory, 140; recognizing pain in, 102; silent, 201; soundless, 222; woman public, 148. *See also* Kaddish

prayer community, 27, 104; Bayit, 62, 102; during the pandemic, 62
prophecy, 65, 228; Jeremiah's, 191
punishment, intergenerational, 145
Purim, 16, 142, 143
purity, 235; biblical, 235; family laws, 173

Rabbeinu (Yaakov) Tam (Rashi's grandson), 197
Rabbeinu Ḥananel (Ḥananel ben Ḥushiel), 19, 20
Rabbeinu Tam, 196, 197
Rabbi Avdimi, 55
Rabbi Eliezer, 210
Rabbi Ḥananyah ben Akashyah, 24, 128, 249
Rabbi Ḥiya bar Abba in the name of R. Yoḥanan, 210
Rabbi Samuel bar Naḥmani, 210
Rabbis' Kaddish, 24, 27, 112, 128, 130, 201, 249, 264n26
Rabbi Yaakov, 101
Rabbi Yoḥanan, 233
Rachel (biblical figure), 52, 160, 170, 174, 183–84, 185, 196, 221, 222, 225, 240, 269n9, 273–74n61, 274n62, 274n63, 274n79, 276n3
Rachel (Rashi's daughter), 196
Raḥem (have mercy), 139
Rashi (Rabbi Shelomo Yitzhaki), 196–97
Rashi's daughters, 196
Rav Ashi, 161, 162–63
Ravina, 161–62
reality, 8, 25, 33, 40, 83, 101, 177, 217, 228, 231; altered reality, 231; communal, 68, 75, Israeli, 87; uncertainty to, 228
Rebbe Naḥman of Breslov, 82
Rechnitzer, Haim O, 78, 82
redemption, 122, 167; 177 201, 234; future, 121; God as the cultivator of, 75; messianic,121, 156; national, 220
Redenger, Meir, 178–79
reinterment, 117, 119; shivah for, 118
religious struggle, 78
repentance, 103, 133, 203, 204
return: "And Once Again, I'll Sin and Return" (Weiss), 202, 203, 205; spiritual concept of, 103, 202–3, 204, 230
revelation, 64; absence of, 78; divine, 110, 184
Ricoeur, Paul (philosopher), 144
ritual space, shared, 91
Riverdale, New York, 13, 14, 16, 22, 23, 44, 138, 244, 249
Riverdale Senior Center, bereavement group, 23
Riverdale Y, Mahjong group, 23
Riverside Memorial Chapel, 32
Rosh Hashanah, 95, 109, 169; 182; COVID on, 110
Rosh Ḥodesh Elul, 202
routine, 78, 128, 199, 202, 203–4, 241, 243, 260, 261
Royal Canadian Air Force, 4
ruaḥ (spirit, spirituality), 654–65
Ruhama (biblical figure), 208
Ruth (biblical figure), 208, 209, 210, 274n72
Ruth (childhood friend of Yehuda Amichai), 106, 113, 207
Ryman, Rob, 219

Sadeh, Oved, 75–76
Samson, 207, 208, 222

Samuel ben Meir (Rashbam, Rashi's grandson), 197
SAR Academy (Riverdale), 140
Sarah (biblical figure), 52, 208, 217, 222, 269n9
Sarnia, Ontario, 3, 4, 5, 10, 11, 12, 31, 43, 119
"See, This Is New" (Morpurgo), 158–65
Sefer ha-Yashar (Book of the Upright), 209–10
self-hatred, 237
self-respect, 193, 194
Serafim, 203
serakh bitah, "the lace (or: knot) of the daughter," 173, 174
Sheheḥeyanu (prayer), 62
Shekhinah (Divine Presence), 34
Shemini Atzeret, 243
Shem Tov Levi, 102
Sherwood, Ben, 4
Shimon ben Gamliel, 52, 53
Shimon ben Shetaḥ, 232
Shir Ḥadash shel Yom, 25, 27, 40, 53, 177, 249
shivah, 13, 66, 77; concluding ritual, 59; for Dr. Sandy Kammermann, 219, 220; after reinternment, 118; seven days of, 59, 60, 77; in Toronto, 16; using Dad's tefillin to during Mom's, 130
Shlonsky, Avraham, 25, 134
shul (Toronto) 196
Shulamite (biblical figure), 63, 89, 208
siddur, personal, 54–55
Siddurim, 171, 201
Sigmund Falk Professor, HUC-JIR, 147
Silber, Randi (author's sister), 8, 12, 31, 32
silence, as a feature of poetry and prayer, 64
similes, 112, 129
Simon, Joel, 32
sinning, 160, 167, 184, 203–4
Sisera (biblical figure), 125
siyyum ha-mishnah, 17
siyyumim, 74
Snow, John, 168, 273n52
solidarity, 115; community,73; sisterly, 170
"Sorrow Song" (Bluwstein), 238–42
"Soul Walking" (Bluwstein), 216–18
splendor (*ziv*), 50, 178, 220; divine, 108, 109, 110, 178
Stern, Mendel, 160–61, 164, 272n39, 275n86
suffering, 164, 165, 167, 225, 236, 249; from Alzheimer's, 138; COVID, 73; Gilboa's poetry and signs of, 246; Jewish, 167, 192, 217; Job, 60; from skin scale disease, 235
sugya (*sugyot*), 190
sugyot ḥayyim (life topics), 190
Sulam, Rachel Luzzatto, 173
Sulam, Solomon, 173
supplication, 169, 191; Daniel's posture and languageof,192; Daniel's theology of, 192; Weiss' relationship to it, 192, 193–94
survivor guilt, 72

Taḥanun (prayers of supplication), 40, 85, 101, 192; personal struggle with these prayers, 192; suffering envoked by prayer, 192 *See also* "I Throw Down My Supplication" (Weiss)
"Take Me Under" (Bialik), 33–34

tallit and tefillin, 95, 137, 266n28, 269n21; Dad's davening, 39; morning recitation of Kaddish with Dad's, 130; prepacked bag for, 23; Rashi's daughters, 197; sensation of being wrapped in a, 129; wearing Dad's for the first time, 19, 20, 196; "Whoever Wrapped in a Tallit" (Amichai), 127, 128, 129–30, 131; women wearing at the Bayit morning minyan, 148
Tamar 1 and 2 (biblical figures), 202, 206
tefillah, 23–24, 95, 200, 207; traditional, 27; weekday, WhatsApp group, 33; zoom, 62, 66, 148, 154, 181, 254
terafim (idols), 221–22
Thanksgiving, 120
theodicy, 101
theology, secular, 105
Third Aliyah, 214
"This Is the Burial Monument that Rachel Morpurgo Prepared for Herself in Her Youth" (Morpurgo), 183–86
"This One Shall Be Called 'My Delight Is with Her'" (Morpurgo), 172–75
Ticotsky, Gidon, 134
Tisha B'Av, 98
toledot, writing of, 119
"To Mother's Portrait" (Goldberg), 46–48
Tractate Shabbat, alternative reading, 21–22
Tractate Yoma, 203
transcendence, 90, 129
transition, 31, 52, 68, 69, 103, 128, 190, 223
translation, 128, 129, 130, 214–15, 274n73
translation, theories of, 128–29
trauma, collective, 78; communal due to COVID, 62; worldwide, 80
Tree of Knowledge of Good and Evil, 86, 209
Treves, Shabbetai Elhanan, 166–67
Tropical Storm Isaiah, 100
2020 election, 35, 115, 116, 121, 138
tzedakah boxes, 14, 139–40
Tzemaḥ, Shlomo, 134
Tzipporah (biblical figure), 208

United Bakers (Spadina Avenue, Toronto), 11
unveiling: father's headstone, 105; mother's, 185; reinterred, 183, 189

vacations: needed times to get away so necessity to come back, 204
vaccines (COVID), 168
validation, 9
values, 52, 146, 180; misogynistic male system of, 208; national, 115; secular, 135; Shimon ben Gamliel's universalistic, 53; Shimon the Just's, 52; universal, 52. *See also* Jewish values
Ve-'ahavta (prayer), 90, 112, 269n5
"Ve-'ulai" (Bluwstein), 215
violence, 76, endless cycle of, 86, 115, 116
vulnerability, human, 34, 226, 237

wars, 87, 236, 246; never-ending cycle of, 122
Warsh, Sylvia, 12
Washington University (St. Louis), 74, 172

Weiss, Avi, 180
Weiss, Ruhama: "And Once Again, I'll Sin and Return," 202; background, 190; "Chapters of the Mothers," 206; "I Am Still Praying," 199; "I Throw Down My Supplication," 191; "Lament for Rashi's Daughters," 195
Wesseley, Naphtali Hertz, 152
White housing project, Zionist (Amichai), 118
"Whoever Wrapped in a Tallit" (Amichai), 127–32
Winkler, Leopold, 160
winter, 30, 57–58, 214
women public prayer, restricted role of, 148
wordplay, 25, 75, 95, 151, 211, 274n75, 276n5, 277n19
world: abandoned, 82; divided, 115
worldly concerns, 193
World War I, 42, 214, 216
World War II, 59–60, 82, 159, 185, 244

Yannai, 109
Yehi Ratzon (prayer), 24, 128
Yeshivat Maharat, 15, 21, 45, 74, 147, 180, 181
Yom Kippur, 82, 109, 182, 204
Yonatan, Natan, 245
Yose ben Yose, 109

Zach, Natan, 25
Zauner, Michelle, 39–40
Zephaniah, 228
Zierler, Abraham, 185
Zierler, David Solomon: davener (prayer), 39; fixing things, 12–13; furniture salesman, 6, 11, 197; green card interview, 6–7; joke telling, 10; love of things, large and small, 12; optimistic outlook, 9–10; pet-names given to children's friends, 10; relationship with author, 197; rich vocabulary, 10; rides in furniture delivery truck, 10; romantic song sung to Marion and children, 9; synagogue friends, 12; synagogue friends, 12; *Tikkun Meir* siddur, 2; unexpected and tragic death, 13, 16, 40, 55–56, 68, 85, 118, 119, 227
Zierler, David Solomon, and Marion Zierler: different deaths, 32; tentative plans to move to New York, 7; wedding announcement (May 3, 1952), *5*
Zierler, Isaac (Buck, Bucky), 4, 28, 159, 184
Zierler, Leo, death of reported in *Windsor Star*, 28, *29*
Zierler, Marion: bleeding ulcer, 30; bureaucratic tasks to settle estate, 77; closing house in Toronto, 22; conformation of a dialysis slot for, 7; death, 32, 60, 244; emotional space being denied to process her death, 78; exceptional friend, 22; first time meeting Dad, 12; funeral, 33; habits of gratitude, 126; intelligence and people smarts, 43–44; kidney failure and dialysis, 6; move to Riverdale, 22, 68, 105; packing up and cleaning out apartment, 77; relationship with Dad, 9–10; three major life decisions, 31
Zierler, Larry, 10, 31
Zierler, Sam, 157, 204–5; one-hundredth anniversary of yahrzeit, 202

Zion, 220, 228, 232, 233, 238
Zohar, 149
zohar (radiance), 109
Zoom, 70, 91–92; combination of "mute" and "unmute" on, 66; first *Shir Ḥadash* author presented Bayit prayer community on, 62; reading the book of Esther on, 142; services on, 35, 62, 64, 66, 126, 258; teaching on, 139; three generations of modern Hebrew poets and scholars introduced to *Shir Ḥadash* community on, 211

SCRIPTURAL INDEX

Hebrew Bible
Torah
Genesis
1:4, 267n33
1:10, 267n33
1:18, 267n33
1:21, 267n33
1:25, 267n33
1:27, 53
2:7, 267n33
2:18, 267n33
3:17, 273n55
4:12, 278n17
4:22, 209
6:4, 228
12:5, 217
15:1, 225
16:2, 227–28
16:6, 269n9
18:24, 228
18:28, 228
18:31, 228
18:32, 228
19, 72
21:10–21, 269n9
21:12, 269n9, 273n55
23:4–28, 269n9
25, 269n9
28:10, 269n9
29:17, 274n79
29:35, 218
30:1, 185
31:21, 269n9
32:29, 272n27
31:32, 225
31:34, 221, 225
31:35, 222
35, 183, 184
35:16–19, 185
35:19, 269n9
37:3, 269n9
37:7, 229
37:23–28, 269n9
45:19, 229
45:21, 229
48:14, 269n9
Exodus
19:17, 55
24:7, 55
30:13, 116
33:20, 268n3
Leviticus 26:32, 271n13
Numbers
15:38, 266n28
16:26, 275n92
23:10, 210
26:56, 218
Deuteronomy
6:5, 63, 269n5
6:18, 210
Prophets
Joshua 10:13, 210
Judges
4:4, 161, 272n28
7:15, 278n21
9:8–20, 109
19:29, 86
1 Samuel
1:1, 275n84
1:13, 278n14
1:20, 221
16:12, 156, 271n15
2 Samuel
1:18, 210
2:17, 164
6:7, 272n25
20:18, 163–64, 272n31

22:29, 271n17
22:37, 270n4
1 Kings
19, 64
19:10, 64
19:14, 65
20:11, 271n10
21:8, 271n8
2 Kings
4:29, 271n10
5:14, 235
7:3, 234
7:3–20, 235
7:9, 234
12, 163
Isaiah
2:1–3, 121
2:1–4, 269n12
2:3, 121
2:4, 122
6:5, 203, 276n14
11:6, 269n12
11:13, 165
26:1, 271n5
26:2, 274n78
35:10, 273n58
42:21, 265n6(c.1)
48:5, 275n93
52:1, 220
52:11, 275n91
53:7, 160, 272n32
54:1, 271n13
60:1, 274n77
62:4, 173, 274n64
62:6, 268n25
66:1, 265n9
Jeremiah
10:7, 272n30
22:30, 225
25:9–13, 191
31:14, 170
31:15, 276n3
31:16, 170, 273n57
51:31, 166
Ezekiel
18:2, 145
38–39, 269n15
38:8, 269n15
Hosea
1:6, 277n18
2:21, 280n2
Joel 3:4, 266n14
Micah
4:1, 121
4:2, 269n15
4:3, 269n13
Zephaniah
2:3, 228
3:5, 272n29
Zechariah 3:2, 113
Writings
Psalms
6:6, 40
19:15, 273n54
23:2, 160–61
24:1, 53
36, 166
37:35, 273n46
79:6, 268n26
96:11, 273n60
98:1, 271n19
99:5, 265n9
116:19, 268m24
119:66, 274n65
122:2, 98
126, 232
126:5, 192, 276n3
131:2, 271n14
142:5, 273n56
145, 22
Proverbs
3:18, 193
4:9, 153, 270n2
Job
1:21, 60
4:18, 272n26
31:33, 225
Songs of Songs
2:10, 277n17
3:1, 267n8, 271n16
3:11, 274n68
4:16, 266n25
5:1, 267n4, 267n8
5:11, 222
Lamentations
1:13, 271n13
3:23, 160
Ecclesiastes
1:7, 75
1:14, 272n38
3:12, 75
4:12, 136
6:9, 216, 277n3
Esther
9:29, 271n8
9:30, 152
Daniel
5:1, 275n94
7:10, 274n76

9:7, 192
9:18, 191, 192
9:22, 191
12:13, 271n18
Nehemiah 8, 51

New Testament
Mark 1:40–45, 279n30
Matthew 8:1–4, 279n30
Luke 5:12–16, 279n30

Jewish Writings
Babylonian Talmud
Berakhot
31b, 276n14
40b, 270n33
Shabbat 66b, 195, 196, 265n3, 265n4(c.1)
Yoma 83b, 278n22
Rosh Hashanah 31a, 95, 265n7(c.1)
Ta'anit 23a, 278n24
Megillah 13b, 274n63
Mo'ed Katan 25b, 161, 272n23
Yevamot 87b, 266n21
Nedarim 30b, 266n20
Kiddushin 39b, 268n29
Bava Metzi'a 49b, 278n22
Bava' Batra' 123a, 274n63
Sanhedrin 29b, 278n22
Makkot 23b, 265n6(c.1)
Avodah Zarah
17b, 278n22
25a, 210
Niddah 67b, 274n71
Commentaries
Rabbeinu Ḥananel on BT Shabbat 66b, 265n4
Jubilees 32:33, 273n61
Maimonides
Guide for the Perplexed
1:59, 266n22
139, 266n22
Midrash
Vayosha' 8:4, 95
Lamentations Rabbah 24, 170
Shir Hashirim Rabbah 5:11, 278n15
Mishnah
Berakhot 9:2, 267n20
Shabbat
6, 196
66, 196
Yoma 8:9, 203
Sukkah 5:4, 95
Ta'anit 4:8, 274n68
Sotah 9:11–15, 13
Pirkei Avot
1:2, 135
1:18, 135
6:11, 265n6(c.1)
'Ohalot 1:8, 266n16
Shulchan Arukh
Oraḥ Ḥayyim
670:2, 269n19
Yoreh De'ah 193:3, 274n71

Other works by Wendy I. Zierler

Building a City: Writings on Agnon's Buczacz in Memory of Alan L. Mintz, coedited with Sheila E. Jelen and Jeffrey Saks (Indiana University Press, 2023)

These Truths We Hold: Judaism in an Age of Truthiness, coedited with Joshua Garroway (HUC Press, 2022)

Movies and Midrash: Popular Film and Jewish Religious Conversation (SUNY Press, 2017)

"To Tread on New Ground": Selected Hebrew Writings of Hava Shapiro 1878–1943, coedited with Carole B. Balin (Wayne State University Press, 2014)

Behikansi Atah (*The Collected Writings of Hava Shapiro*, Hebrew), coedited with Carole B. Balin (Resling Press, 2008)

And Rachel Stole the Idols: The Emergence of Modern Hebrew Women's Writing (Wayne State University Press, 2004)

www.ingramcontent.com/pod-product-compliance
Lightning Source LLC
Chambersburg PA
CBHW030004240426
43672CB00007B/818